ENGLISH FICTION AND THE EVOLUTION OF LANGUAGE, 1850–1914

Victorian science changed language from a tool into a natural phenomenon, evolving independently of its speakers. Will Abberley explores how science and fiction interacted in imagining different stories of language evolution. Popular narratives of language progress clashed with others of decay and degeneration. Furthermore, the blurring of language evolution with biological evolution encouraged Victorians to reimagine language as a mixture of social convention and primordial instinct. Abberley argues that fiction by authors such as Charles Kingsley, Thomas Hardy and H. G. Wells not only reflected these intellectual currents, but also helped to shape them. Genres from utopia to historical romance supplied narrative models for generating thought experiments in the possible pasts and futures of language. Equally, fiction that explored the instinctive roots of language intervened in debates about language standardization and scientific objectivity. These textual readings offer new perspectives on twenty-first-century discussions about language evolution and the language of science.

WILL ABBERLEY is a research fellow for the Faculty of English Language and Literature, University of Oxford, exploring concepts of natural mimicry and deception in Victorian literature and the life sciences.

CAMBRIDGE STUDIES IN NINETEENTH-CENTURY
LITERATURE AND CULTURE

General editor
Gillian Beer, *University of Cambridge*

Editorial board
Isobel Armstrong, *Birkbeck, University of London*
Kate Flint, *University of Southern California*
Catherine Gallagher, *University of California, Berkeley*
D. A. Miller, *University of California, Berkeley*
J. Hillis Miller, *University of California, Irvine*
Daniel Pick, *Birkbeck, University of London*
Mary Poovey, *New York University*
Sally Shuttleworth, *University of Oxford*
Herbert Tucker, *University of Virginia*

Nineteenth-century British literature and culture have been rich fields for interdisciplinary studies. Since the turn of the twentieth century, scholars and critics have tracked the intersections and tensions between Victorian literature and the visual arts, politics, social organization, economic life, technical innovations, scientific thought – in short, culture in its broadest sense. In recent years, theoretical challenges and historiographical shifts have unsettled the assumptions of previous scholarly synthesis and called into question the terms of older debates. Whereas the tendency in much past literary critical interpretation was to use the metaphor of culture as 'background', feminist, Foucauldian, and other analyses have employed more dynamic models that raise questions of power and of circulation. Such developments have reanimated the field. This series aims to accommodate and promote the most interesting work being undertaken on the frontiers of the field of nineteenth-century literary studies: work which intersects fruitfully with other fields of study such as history, or literary theory, or the history of science. Comparative as well as interdisciplinary approaches are welcomed.

A complete list of titles published will be found at the end of the book.

ENGLISH FICTION AND THE EVOLUTION OF LANGUAGE, 1850–1914

WILL ABBERLEY

CAMBRIDGE
UNIVERSITY PRESS

University Printing House, Cambridge CB2 8BS, United Kingdom

Cambridge University Press is part of the University of Cambridge.

It furthers the University's mission by disseminating knowledge in the pursuit of education, learning and research at the highest international levels of excellence.

www.cambridge.org
Information on this title: www.cambridge.org/9781107101166

© Will Abberley 2015

This publication is in copyright. Subject to statutory exception and to the provisions of relevant collective licensing agreements, no reproduction of any part may take place without the written permission of Cambridge University Press.

First published 2015

Printed in the United Kingdom by Clays, St Ives plc

A catalogue record for this publication is available from the British Library

Library of Congress Cataloguing in Publication data
Abberley, Will, 1984–
English fiction and the evolution of language, 1850–1914 / Will Abberley.
pages cm. – (Cambridge Studies in Nineteenth-century Literature and Culture)
Includes bibliographical references and index.
ISBN 978-1-107-10116-6 (Hardback)
1. English language–Social aspects–History–19th century. 2. English language–Social aspects–History–20th century. 3. English fiction–History–19th century.
4. English fiction–History–20th century. 5. Language and literature–History–19th century. I. Title.
PE1085.A63 2015
823'.809–dc23 2014046689

ISBN 978-1-107-10116-6 Hardback

Cambridge University Press has no responsibility for the persistence or accuracy of URLs for external or third-party internet websites referred to in this publication, and does not guarantee that any content on such websites is, or will remain, accurate or appropriate.

Contents

Acknowledgements	*page* vi
Introduction: language under a microscope	1
1 The future of language in prophetic fiction	22
2 Primitive language in imperial, prehistoric and scientific romances	56
3 Organic orality and the historical romance	91
4 Instinctive signs: nature and culture in dialogue	128
Conclusion: widening the lens	164
Notes	176
Bibliography	205
Index	226

Acknowledgements

I would like to thank Angelique Richardson of the University of Exeter for her endless, invaluable advice and encouragement during the development of this project. I am also grateful to Exeter's Regenia Gagnier, who challenged and made me refine my arguments. I am thankful to Philipp Erchinger for many interesting conversations that have pushed this study in new directions. Another person deserving of thanks is Sharon Ruston of Lancaster University, whose excellent series of AHRC-funded workshops entitled Theories and Methods: Literature, Science and Medicine inspired new avenues of thought during my research. I have benefited greatly from engaging with the British Association for Victorian Studies, Thomas Hardy Society, Thomas Hardy Association and British Society for Literature and Science, and I would like to thank the committees of these institutions for their work.

I am very grateful to Peter Faulkner for his untiring help with my research into William Morris. I have lost count of the number of stimulating chats we have had over tea, and of the books he has lent me. I thank Isobel Armstrong and James Moore for giving me their time and advice. I am also thankful to Ruth Livesey and her colleagues at the *Journal of Victorian Culture* for rigorous constructive criticism of my work on Morris. I owe a great deal to David Amigoni and Jason Hall for their incisive analyses of my research, which helped me to put this book on a firmer foundation. I am grateful to Virginia Richter for pointing me towards recent examples of paleoanthropological fiction. Further, I am grateful to the staff of the British Library, Bodleian and Beinecke libraries, and the Rare Books and Manuscripts Library at the University of Illinois for their assistance.

I must thank my brother Joe and his wife Karah for putting me up numerous times during research trips. I am eternally grateful to my mother, Tessa Abberley, who has always nurtured my interest in literature and helped me to believe in myself. I wish the same to my father, John

Abberley, sadly no longer with us, whom I will always remember traipsing through the Staffordshire Moorlands loudly quoting Tennyson and Omar Khayyám to bemused ramblers. My final thanks go to Deni, for supporting me throughout this project, and teaching me to laugh and love in a foreign language.

Introduction: language under a microscope

> Under the microscope of the etymologist every word almost discloses traces of its first metaphorical conception
>
> Friedrich Max Müller[1]

> Astonished at the performances of the English plough, the Hindoos paint it, set it up, and worship it; thus turning a tool into an idol: linguists do the same with language
>
> Herbert Spencer[2]

> Language is a vast conglomerate of human fossils. It consists for the most part of fossil forms, fossil beliefs, fossil conceptions, fossil ideas ... [W]e can only express the highest conceptions of modern science in terms invented for us by barbaric predecessors – believers in fetishes, in shamans, in spirits, and in puerile talismans of the most silly description
>
> Grant Allen[3]

What might it mean to place language under a microscope? The popular Victorian philologist Friedrich Max Müller had a clear idea when he addressed a public audience at London's Royal Institution in 1863. Languages, he explained,

> supply materials capable of scientific treatment. We can collect them, we can classify them, we can reduce them to their constituent elements, and deduce from them some of the laws that determine their origin, govern their growth, necessitate their decay; we can treat them, in fact, in exactly the same spirit in which the geologist treats his stones and petrifactions ... or the botanist the flowers of the field. (*Lectures on the Science of Language*, II, p. 1)

The microscope image was not new. The eighteenth-century scholar John Horne Tooke had compared etymology to 'a microscope ... useful to discover the minuter parts of language which would otherwise escape our sight'.[4] However, by Müller's time, the microscope had acquired new associations. It no longer magnified a static world but revealed constant processes of change, from rock formations to developing embryos. Whereas Horne Tooke had viewed speech as an artificial tool, controlled by humans, Müller imagined it as a force of nature, transforming independently over millennia. Through such rhetoric, Müller reified language as an object apart from its users.[5] He presented his work, tracing word forms through history, as a material 'science' that reflected objective truths about humanity. Müller's 'science of language' promised to raise humans to a higher, almost God's eye view of themselves, as he mused

> Man had studied every part of nature ... every nerve and fibre of his own body ... [H]e had meditated on the nature of his soul, on the laws of his mind ... and yet language, without the aid of which not even the first step in this glorious career could have been made, remained unnoticed. Like a veil that hung too close over the eye of the human mind, it was hardly perceived. (1, p. 27)

Müller's microscope promised to take his audience beyond language, to observe it from a higher mental altitude where it would cease to shape them. Studying language as a natural evolution through deep time raised the possibility, in his optimistic view, of transcending sociohistorical perspectives. Language was not simply an object under the microscope, however, but also the tool that observed it. Philologists could not objectify language without also using it, constructing stories of its development.

This study argues that Victorian and Edwardian scientific visions of the evolution of language emerged symbiotically with popular fiction about the subject. Models of linguistic development ranged beyond empirical testability, delving into unrecorded pasts and unknown futures. Imaginative and speculative fiction, particularly, acted as a testing ground for such theories, conjuring visions of primordial and future speech. Fiction genres also helped to form some of these theories, supplying narrative frameworks to represent linguistic change. Utopian, imperial and historical romances, for example, solidified and elaborated concepts of linguistic advancement, primitiveness and decay. Yet, while fiction popularized and brought to life theories of language evolution, the form also destabilized them, exposing the contradictions in placing language under a microscope. Through its rootedness in social particulars, fiction highlighted the contextuality of meaning and the impossibility of detaching language from its users. Further, as researchers increasingly conceived of language as a collection of evolved capacities, some fiction in the realist tradition explored the inseparability of language from the instinctive body. Through these foci, the study offers new readings of seminal and less well-known Victorian and Edwardian texts.

The idea that language was a natural object, evolving through deep time independently of its speakers, derived from the new field of comparative philology. The discovery of ancestral links between Latin, Greek and Sanskrit in the late eighteenth century had encouraged continental scholars such as Franz Bopp and Jacob Grimm to trace the diversification of languages through history. As in geology and embryology, they formulated 'laws' and stages of growth, as though speech was a form of organic life.[6] Following these developments, Victorian language studies constituted an uncertain, amorphous form of knowledge, hovering between physical and historical science (what we now call the humanities). They overlapped with physiology and psychology, anthropology and sociology, concerning the physical production of speech and the somatic processes behind it, both for individuals and communities. Müller's microscope promised to discover the atoms of the human mind, embedded in the metaphorical 'roots' of words. Somewhat differently, towards the end of the century material investigations of the speech organs and brain placed the production of language under a microscope as never before. By analyzing the mechanisms and acquirement of speech, researchers sought the origins and development of consciousness. In 1893 the American phoneticist E. P. Evans compared the role of the phonograph in philology to that of the microscope in bacteriology.[7] The instinctive, infinitesimal parts of vocalization seemed to carry traces of the past, requiring only microscopic analysis to reveal their secrets.

This study builds on the work of Linda Dowling and Christine Ferguson, who have both explored language studies as sources of anxiety in Victorian literature. For Dowling, philology eroded old certainties about the meanings of words and humans' control over them; for Ferguson, evolutionary theories raised the mortifying possibility of speech originating in animal vocalizations.[8] I look beyond these concerns to consider how visions of language evolution developed in dialogue with emerging models of scientific objectivity. Lorraine Daston notes that, for late-Victorian scientists, language was 'at once the essence and the nemesis of scientific objectivity: on the one hand language is what makes public knowledge possible; on the other, it was the distorting lens wedged between mind and nature'.[9] Could language ever be rendered 'scientific', and was this even desirable? While some hailed the imagined objectification of language as progressive, others lamented it as a deadening mechanization of the national spirit. Efforts in philology to control language by objectifying and dissecting it paralleled attempts in other disciplines to control the physical universe through a fixed nomenclature. Philologists often imagined their scholarly discourse as existing 'outside' of the language they described, although they constructed it from the same verbal resources.[10] Such logic mirrored the ideal of literary realism, in George Levine's words, 'to use language to get beyond language, to discover some nonverbal truth out there'.[11] This work, then, is concerned with imaginary evolutions of language in both philology and fiction. By depicting past, future and alternative language, scholars and authors sought to elevate their discourse above the autonomous processes of language change. If fixed laws could be found to predict such change, then humans might retain some control over and mental independence from the language they spoke.

The search for objective language was bound up with the rise of Standard English. The ideal of a deregionalized, unchanging English privileged the discourse of philologists as above the evolution they described. Equally, the Victorian novel might depict many varieties of speech, but it typically subordinated them under Standard English narration.[12] Yet theories and fictions of language evolution also compromised the goal of objectifying language, suggesting that humans had no extra-linguistic base from which to view it. If language evolved irrespective of human intentions, then logic might be imagined as being no longer universal but only as the perspective of one's speech community.[13] Further, conceiving language as an aggregate of instinctive and learned behaviours collapsed the boundary between object and observer, absorbing speakers into autonomous organic and sociological processes. Near the end of the century the novelist and science popularizer Grant Allen summed up the philological consensus that, 'The growth or spread of a language is a thing as much beyond our deliberate human control as the rise or fall of the barometer'.[14] Conversely, authors and scholars who bemoaned Standard English for mechanizing the organic national spirit also, paradoxically, needed it to fabricate an imaginary historic unity between speakers. One of this study's aims, then, is to complicate debates about the history of Standard English. Language standardization was central not only to reifying a nation of speakers, as Tony Crowley argued, but also to privileging scientific truth.[15] Recent scholars have increasingly traced the history of scientific writing as a genre of self-effacement, presenting its 'facts' as above the contingencies of language.[16] This study intervenes in the debate from a literary perspective, arguing that fiction both helped to build the imaginary edifice of objective, scientific language and exposed the cracks in its foundations.

While Ferguson's study focuses on a handful of authors and novels, I take a wider view of fiction in the period, exploring the relationships between philological theory and literary genre. Thought experiments were intrinsic to studies of language evolution, which extrapolated ancestral links between tongues through lexical resemblances. Similarly to how Darwin imagined extinct species beyond the fossil record, philologists imagined extinct languages beyond written records.[17] In 1868 the German scholar August Schleicher published an attempted reconstruction of the Proto-Indo-European language. 'Avis Akvāsas Ka' ('The Sheep and the Horses') was a short fable in hypothetical speech produced through philological comparisons.[18] This reflected a shift in science away from catastrophist explanations of natural phenomena (through causes no longer in operation, such as divine creation) towards uniformitarian ones (through constant, observable processes). Recorded changes in language over time might, then, be used to hypothesize older forms of language, in similar fashion to how the geologist Charles Lyell had hypothesized ancient rock formations. Theories of language evolution thus opened new imaginative frontiers and merged with forms of fictional speculation to envisage past and future speech.

Much fiction of the period existed in dialogue with speculative philology, experimenting with linguistic possibilities that the field made newly imaginable. Fiction could be conceived as a form of 'experiment', as Émile Zola claimed, describing his tales as scientific predictions of the behaviour of humans placed in imaginary scenarios.[19] The fantastical romances which concern much of this study might seem generically opposed to such realist techniques. However, they arguably deploy Zola's experimental method on a larger scale, imagining language evolution via the theoretical models of linguistic science. The exotic, unfamiliar settings of romances, from William Morris's *News from Nowhere* (1890) to H. G. Wells's *The First Men in the Moon* (1901), offered imaginative spaces for thought experiments in linguistic possibility. These experiments involved reviving and fabricating archaic speech, reconstructing the evolutionary past of language, and predicting future development. Fiction more 'realist' in its setting also experimented with evolutionary language theory by exploring the instinctive bases of speech. Novelists such as Thomas Hardy and Wells in his social comedies destabilized conventions of reported speech, depicting instinctive communication in parallel to words. Nonetheless, they still wrote Standard English, often third-person, narrations, even as their ideas about language undermined the notion of an objective, scientific idiom. Their attachment to narrative objectivity contrasted with some

'New Woman' authors of the time such as George Egerton, who experimented with impressionist narration.[20] This difference might be understood within wider gendered discourses of science, which typically opposed masculine intellectual abstraction to embodied female instinct. Yet this binary was countered by alternative models of verbal masculinity as bodily and instinctive, against imitative, conventional femininity.[21] Such ambivalence engaged with debates about the nature of the linguistic past and whether this past was something to reconnect with or escape from.

The cultural traffic between philology and fiction was two-way, with certain fiction genres supplying narrative frameworks for theories of language change. I will trace these evolutionary narratives as rival discourses that pervaded anglophone culture and shaped ideas about language and scientific objectivity. Utopian and imperial romance, for example, helped to frame a discourse which I will call 'language progressivism'. By contrast, historical romance combined with other philological theory to produce a tendency which I call 'language vitalism'. The epigraph quotations from Müller and Spencer exemplify these opposing discourses. Meaning was conceived by language vitalism as an organic essence derived from a primordial epoch of creation. Progressivism saw meaning as an artificial production, something forged by humans as they gained control over chaotic nature. For different reasons, progressivism and vitalism both valued the linguistic past and sought vestiges of it in the supposedly ancient oral cultures of Britain and abroad. Such studies were early examples of what James Clifford calls 'salvage ethnography', which presented its transcription of oral cultures as a chapter in their inevitable extinction.[22] For vitalism, this imagined linguistic past represented a source of spiritual and semantic renewal. For progressivism, it offered a point of orientation as language advanced in the opposite direction. While progressives hailed the imagined objectification of language, vitalists presented it as a kind of semantic decay, rendering speech and thought mechanical.[23] Both envisioned different forms of Jürgen Habermas's 'ideal speech situation' in which discourse could be elevated above ambiguity, misunderstanding and vested interests.[24] Both postulated a perfect correspondence with 'truth' in their idealized languages of the past and future, but struggled to explain how either could be realized outside of cultural perspectives. In either case, the vision of humanity united under a *lingua franca* clashed with the aim to particularize speech, reflecting the soul of a given people, community or individual. Yet, their urge to direct contemporary language towards their respective ideals was derailed by the autonomous processes of change revealed by philology. Whether one located the ideal speech in preindustrial, pseudo-Edenic nature or the evolution of social structures, both views undermined individual control over discourse. Both also often treated language as a passive reflection of thought rather than an active agent which shaped thought. Towards the turn of the century new ideas of language and thought as unstable catalysts of each other undermined both progressive and vitalist narratives.

These two discourses were amorphous and overlapping, with philological and imaginative writers often combining elements from both to suit different agendas. Patriots such as R. C. Trench and Charles Kingsley tried to present modern Standard English as the fulfilment of an organic destiny traceable through history. Likewise, Spencer and several utopians portrayed the progressive mechanization of language as part of a monistic evolution that collapsed oppositions between nature and society. Further, Victorian progress could be imagined as a spiral as well as a straight line, involving the recovery of past strands of development.[25] This muddling of apparently contradictory models of language only increased in the latter decades of the century as the mirage of unitary scientific knowledge dispersed. 'Up to about 1850', William James wrote in 1904, 'almost everyone believed that sciences expressed truths that were exact copies of a definite code of non-human realities'. Now, 'There are so many geometries, so many logics, so many physical and chemical hypotheses, so many classifications, each one of them good for so much and yet not good for everything'.[26] As the physical world fragmented into a plurality of explanations, so language followed suit with the specialization of technical vocabularies and no *lingua franca* to unite them. Linguists also increasingly treated meaning as contextual rather than historical.[27] Instead of searching for one, totalizing explanation of language, some writers began to imagine it as a plurality of systems working in concert. In this way, the fictions of Samuel Butler, Hardy and Wells explore language as a site of dialogue between natural instincts and social convention rather than purely one or the other. The once apparently united science of language was dissolving into multiple objects under many different lenses.

Ideas about language evolution pervaded Victorian and Edwardian literary culture, and this study is necessarily partial in its selection of material. While its arguments might be extended to poetry, I have limited my discussion to fiction.[28] This focus clarifies the emphasis on narrative, tracing competing stories of linguistic change. Continuous prose enabled writers to flesh out these stories in living detail. It also allowed them to mimic the imagined objectivity of science. The novel had emerged in parallel with empiricism, bound up with epistemologies of observation and testimony.[29] The methodical description of prose fiction enabled authors to depict imaginary evolutions of language like anthropologists relating their observations. It enabled them to quote and cite philologists, or play the philologist themselves, listing imaginary grammars and vocabularies. Among authors, Kingsley, Grant Allen, Hardy, Butler, Wells and Jack London command attention due to their interests in philology and biology. Equally, William Morris, R. M. Ballantyne, J. F. Hodgetts and Paul du Chaillu warrant discussion for their interest in an imagined organic linguistic past. Certain genres stand out as literary parallels to the language theory, not only reflecting the latter but also helping to shape it. While language progressivism often appears symbiotic with utopia, language vitalism developed in tandem with historical romance and its later offshoots, such as invasion and fantasy fiction. Similarly, anthropological descriptions of 'primitive' language paralleled imperial and prehistoric romance, which described 'primitive' speech from a supposedly higher altitude. This study is also concerned with realism, as far as the genre can be defined, since efforts to represent reality in fiction depended on language acting as a neutral tool, reflecting extra-linguistic facts.[30] Hardy's, Butler's and Wells's visions of language as an extension of animal instincts had the potential to destabilize this epistemology. Similarly, as such visions undermined the objectivity of the scientific observer, so they also threatened the objectivity of the realist narrator.

Language progress

Language progressivism grew in tandem with ideals of scientific objectivity, so it is with this discourse that the study begins. The first two chapters plot progressivism's emergence through visions of the linguistic future and past. I deal first with the future since these visions represented the ideal conditions to which language studies aspired. Scholars and scientists reasoned that language developed through speakers becoming increasingly mentally independent of it. Comparative philologists organized grammatical change into epochs paralleling the evolution of consciousness. Wilhelm von Humboldt wrote in 1836 that language reflected 'the growth of man's mental powers into ever new and often more elevated forms'.[31] Most anglophone readers first encountered the new philology through anthropologists and sociologists importing its data into wider discussions of social progress.[32] Similarly to such theories of social evolution, language progress became associated with the growth of sympathy and altruism as well as intellect. Utopian fiction both popularized these ideals and helped to shape them by figuring the perfect future society as one without verbal waste, misunderstanding or disagreement. Language progressivism came to revolve around three goals: the mechanization of meaning, detachment from the sensory body, and the merging of speakers into a united 'mind'. If there was one figure whose life's work crystallized these goals (and their contradictions), it was the philosopher Herbert Spencer.

Spencer rose from somewhat obscure origins to become one of the most famous and regularly cited philosophers in the anglophone world.[33] Partly self-educated, he came from a family of religious non-conformists in Derby and worked first as a civil engineer while writing for provincial journals. Steeped from his early years in the radical evolutionary theories of Erasmus Darwin and Jean-Baptiste Lamarck, Spencer formulated a theory of universal development in biology, psychology and society in the 1850s and spent the rest of his career elaborating it. All development, he claimed, consisted of the twin processes of integration and differentiation. The structures of organisms and societies evolved increasingly specialized parts while laying evermore intricate connections between these parts. Spencer's parallel interests in evolution and engineering influenced him to conceive of language as a progressive mechanization, marked by efficiency and precision. The seeds of this idea are visible in notes which he made in his early twenties on ideas for an artificial language. In his *Autobiography* (1904) he recalled, 'The primary aim was that of obtaining the greatest brevity, and, consequently, a structure mainly, or almost wholly, monosyllabic was proposed'.[34] He later described language as 'a tool', valued according to the efficiency with which it conveyed ideas, since 'whatever force is absorbed by the machine is deducted from the result'.[35] Like the railways that Spencer had helped to design, he conceptualized language as a technology undergoing continuous improvement.

Spencer was not a lone voice on the subject of language reform. The Victorian period witnessed frequent proposals for reforms of written English and even the creation of new artificial languages, such as Volapük and Esperanto. Nor were such proposals new. René Descartes, Gottfried Wilhelm Leibniz and John Wilkins had all discussed designing a 'philosophical language' to arrange phenomena into consistent, logical taxonomies.[36] Such ideas influenced the later construction of systematic nomenclatures in botany and chemistry.[37] Efforts to fix scientific notations continued to merge with utopian schemes for perfecting language in the nineteenth century. The polymath William Whewell looked forward to a notation that would unite the sciences, overcoming their different conceptual foundations. He dreamed of an algebraic system mapping on to the world, as though the latter were a divine tongue, awaiting translation. With such a language, humans might become something like gods themselves, as Whewell wrote:

> To trace order and law in that which has been observed, may be considered as interpreting what nature has written down for us, and will commonly prove that we understand her alphabet. But to predict what has not been observed, is to attempt ourselves to use the legislative phrases of nature; and when she responds plainly and precisely to that which we thus utter, we cannot but suppose that we have in a great measure made ourselves masters of the meaning and structure of her language.[38]

Ultimate knowledge of the universe seemed a matter of finding the right symbols to reveal it. As Chapter 1 will show, utopian fiction frequently described the mechanization of language through spiritual images. Tales such as John Macnie's *The Diothas* (1883) linked language reform with discovery of the divine meaning of the universe.

Such notions relied on the assumption, inherited from John Locke, that language was a tool that was consciously crafted to express thought.[39] Yet, by the mid nineteenth century comparative philology had revealed a history of language change separate from human intentions. As the American philologist G. P. Marsh reflected in 1860, 'So truly as language is what man has made it, just so truly man is what language has made him'.[40] Speakers' discourse was shaped by the sociohistorical perspectives of their language. Michel Foucault argued that such anxieties about the autonomy of language spurred efforts 'to neutralize, and as it were polish, scientific language', rendering it 'the exact reflection, the perfect double, the unmisted mirror of a non-verbal knowledge'.[41] The English mathematician George Boole pursued this aim by proposing in the 1850s a system of 'symbolic logic', which expressed all logical propositions as algebraic equations.[42] Controlling language seemed akin to reconstructing it, replacing arbitrary formations with conscious design.

Progressive language mechanization involved contradictions which became more obvious when utopian fiction imagined it in concrete detail. Its twin goals of verbal precision and efficiency involved conflicting models of semantics, treating meaning as something both accumulated over time and assembled in the present. Visions of language becoming increasingly controlled also raised the question of who would control it. Linguistic utopias often predicted the centralization of control over language in tandem with the centralization of power, creating an authoritarian technocracy. Such visions show how ideas of language mechanization engaged with debates about political authority, identifying democracy with chaos. Yet they also often linked language mechanization with individualism, rendering meaning private property. The liberal ideal of the autonomous individual contradicted that of a unified, collective mind.

The ideal of objective language emerged in tandem with an increasing distrust of the human body as a source of knowledge. Psychologists of the mid-Victorian era such as Spencer, Alexander Bain and G. H. Lewes explored consciousness as an unstable network of sensations and habitual associations.[43] Simultaneously, modern science contradicted the apparent evidence of humans' bodily senses, revealing phenomena across scales of space and time that had been previously unimaginable. The antiquity of the earth and the intangibility of electromagnetism and microscopic cell division highlighted the limits of the body as a route to truths about the universe. 'The psychical life', Spencer wrote in 1855, became increasingly 'distinguished from the physical life', as organisms grew in complexity.[44] Hence, orthography developed from hieroglyphs and picture-writing the same as words and thoughts developed from chaotic sensation noises. Progressives conceived the elevation of language above personal and parochial perspectives as a moral as well as a mental evolution. Matthew Arnold presented efforts 'to set a standard' in language usage as part of a general process of restraining humanity's base, egoistic urges. Among animals, he wrote, 'man alone has an impulse leading him to set up some other law to control the bent of his nature'.[45] Progressives also identified linguistic evolution with the advancement of social sympathy and cooperation.[46] Spencer claimed that the 'language of ideas' evolved in tandem with a 'language of emotions' in ever finer shades of tone, rhythm and pitch, 'ultimately enabl[ing] men vividly and completely to impress on each other all the emotions which they experience from moment to moment'.[47] Spencer's model of progress thus fluctuated between refining the body and abstracting from it. Such inconsistency stemmed from efforts to avoid the epistemological relativism implied by his materialist psychology. If all conceptions derived from sensory experience, then how could thought and speech escape bodily subjectivity? Sensations and ideas were defined by their relations with each other in an enclosed system.[48] Meaning was thus a mass of unstable associations that varied depending on group and individual perspectives. Instead of translating nature or the human soul, language might, rather, invent them. In envisioning progressive theory, utopias frequently resorted to spiritualism and telepathy to escape its contradictions. Dreams of direct thought transference enabled them to hold in abeyance the conflicting goals of individual autonomy and collective unity, of dominating the universe and merging harmoniously with it.

Prophetic fiction could challenge ideas of progressive language mechanization and disembodiment as well as promote them. Wells's early scientific romances explore the incompatibility of strictly regulated language and individuality. Tales such as *When the Sleeper Wakes* (1899) associate the fixing of language by a central authority with mass manipulation, reducing people to drones. Wells's training in post-Darwinian science led him to doubt transcendent purpose in nature and meaning in language. He demonstrated this scepticism most fully in his fictions of extraterrestrial intelligence *The War of the Worlds* (1898) and *The First Men in the Moon*. Both tales complicate the ideal of perfect communication, depicting beings whose close communion with each other renders them incapable of sympathizing with outsiders. While the young Wells challenged the discourse of language progress, however, he also illustrated its adaptability and pervasiveness. As his interest grew in the creation of a world state, so Wells succumbed to the contradictory ideas that he had earlier attacked, dreaming of a rational, global *lingua franca*.

Language progressivism also tended towards the disembodiment of language as evolutionary theory linked the body with an instinctive, bestial heritage. Robert Chambers's scandalous *Vestiges of the Natural History of Creation* (1844) argued that speech had evolved from animal vocalizations. He reached this conclusion through comparisons of human and animal bodies, emphasizing 'the glaring fact that, in our teeth, hands, and other features . . . we do not differ more from the simiadae than the bats do from the lemurs'.[49] Chapter 2 thus explores how oppositions between primitive and civilized language revolved around speakers' imagined dependence on or freedom from the instinctive, imitative body. 'All language consists, at the beginning,' Spencer wrote in 1854, 'of symbols which are as like to the things symbolized as it is practicable to make them.' Primitive communicators gesticulated, 'mimicking the actions or peculiarities of the things referred to' with vocalizations 'imitating the sounds the objects make'.[50] Such speech only partially differentiated being from representation; the bushman described his hunt by re-enacting it in gestures and onomatopoeia. Primitive speech apparently consisted of ahistorical, bodily urges and imitative echoes, voiced without reflection. Anthropology seemed to demonstrate the increasing objectivity of western language as it discovered in 'lower' tongues its own evolutionary past. By categorizing 'primitive' language and limiting its potential meanings, westerners strove to elevate their own discourse to a panoramic meta-language. The language of anthropology might serve as a Casaubon-like key to all mythologies, transcending bodily and societal perspectives.

This view was contradicted, however, by another model of primitive language as alienated from the empirical evidence of the body, blinkered by superstitious custom. Christopher Herbert argues that anthropologists of the late Victorian era such as E. B. Tylor reconceived 'savage' society 'from a void of institutional control where desire is rampant to a spectacle of controls exerted systematically upon the smallest details of daily life'.[51] The older Spencer similarly characterized 'savage' society by 'ceremonial regulation', and 'a complicated and often most inconvenient set of customs'.[52] Savage speech constantly redrew the world in response to subjective sensations, yet it was also an unchanging fossil, stubbornly repeating ancestral forms and ideas. This tension is discernible in fictions of the primitive linguistic past by Henry Rider Haggard. Tales such as *Allan Quatermain* (1887) represent Africans as mentally imprisoned by the urges and sensations of the body. Yet they are also embedded in complex networks of tradition, slavishly echoing the voice of the tribe.

Victorians often characterized language as primitive through the ability of Europeans to translate its meanings. Its imagined translatability justified its subordinate position, merely replicating earlier stages of European language. This discourse of primitive translatability can be traced in Grant Allen's ethnographic romances, such as 'The Reverend John Creedy' (1883) and *The Great Taboo* (1890). However, primitive speech too easily understood also threatened to erase the distinction between the civilized and the primitive. Allen's tales thus equivocate on the capacity of European speakers to comprehend primitive speech, also seeking to distance them from it. Equally problematic was the fact of colonized natives learning European languages and thereby transgressing the boundaries between the primitive and the civilized. Allen's fiction both engages with such transgressions and illustrates how anthropologists sought to neutralize them, presenting language learning as primitive imitation.

One way of maintaining the image of primitive speech as instinctive and ahistorical was to construct hypothetical primordial speakers from before any traditions had formed. In the latter decades of the century, prehistoric fiction emerged in dialogue with palaeontology. Evolutionary paradigms of development emboldened authors to imagine the linguistic past before records had begun. Tales such as Wells's 'A Story of the Stone Age' (1897) and Stanley Waterloo's *The Story of Ab* (1897) depict the linguistic past as a series of stepping stones from instinctive and imitative sounds to consciously manipulated symbols. Such tales struggled to define the primitive origins of language evolution, however, since every period in ancestral history was preceded by earlier communicative activity. Further, the more detail in which these authors imagined the linguistic past the less neatly it fed into the present. Instead, their fictions sometimes suggested alternative lines of development with no equivalent in 'civilized' language.

The more that science and fiction attempted to define primitive language, the more it besieged the supposedly objective language of civilization. Tylor's separation of language and 'culture' from heredity rendered civilization and science a thin crust that barely covered humanity's primitive instincts. Simultaneously, the mechanisms of natural selection gave no guarantee of inevitable progress. The progressive model of advancing precision and institutionalized control over language produced the inverse image of language degeneration as a breakdown in such control. In 1874 the Oxford philologist A. H. Sayce wrote: 'The savage has the delight of a child in uttering new sounds, and exhibiting his power and inventiveness in this manner, with none of the restraints by which civilization confines the invention of slang to the schoolboy and the mob.'[53] This view influenced Wells's and Jack London's visions of language degeneration in their scientific and apocalyptic romances such as *The Island of Dr Moreau* (1896) and *The Scarlet Plague* (1912). These tales associate regression to savage and bestial states with the loosening of prescriptive authorities over language, reducing speech to meaningless jabber and primordial instinct.

Language vitalism

Chapter 3 explores a counter-discourse that mourned the imagined modern objectification of language, revering the oral past as a vital heritage to be recovered. Language vitalism grew out of theological and romantic narratives of degeneration from an original state of nature. It assumed that language signified through a living inner essence that directed its growth through history. Jean-Jacques Rousseau and Johann Gottfried Herder had venerated ancient, oral speech as the living essence of a language now weakened by artificial writing.[54] Comparative philology sought to access this organic orality through the history of nations. 'Nations and languages against dynasties and treaties', Müller declared, would 'remodel ... the map of Europe' in the coming age (1, p. 13). In contrast to modern class divisions, Müller imagined a past when speakers were united with each other and their natural environment. The genre of the historical novel interacted with these ideas to produce ideal visions of an organic ancestral speech. However, the efforts of philologists to discover this past and of authors to revive it conflicted with the industrial print culture in which they lived. The illusion of an organic, historically and geographically coherent nation of speakers was dependent on modern, standardized writing and the centralized state. The career of the philologist Max Müller provides a good entry point for outlining such language vitalism and the tensions it tried to contain.

Müller was a great popularizer of comparative philology whose lectures were attended by such famous Victorians as John Stuart Mill and Alfred Tennyson.[55] The young Müller studied languages at Leipzig before coming to England to work on ancient Sanskrit manuscripts gathered by the East India Company. He went on to hold several professorial posts at Oxford, producing a critical edition of the ancient Vedic scripts the *Rig Veda*. A devout Christian, he exemplified a generation of scholars who strove to reconcile religious tradition with modern biblical criticism and scientific knowledge. Müller's mentor Chevalier Bunsen conceived of the world's religions as different symbolic imaginings of the same universal truths, revealed in progressively evolving forms.[56] Müller extended these arguments, tracing kindred concepts between Christian and Hindu scriptures. Language and thought were inseparable, he argued, deriving their power from eternal Kantian mental archetypes or 'roots'. Müller suggested that all words could be traced back to these primordial 'phonetic types', forged by a creative instinct inspired through God (1, p. 429). Müller's model of a lost 'mythopoeic' period in language when each word rang with its semantic origin framed modern language as corrupt. Words were ambiguous and misleading because language evolution was characterized by 'decay' and amnesia. Instead of creating words through divine inspiration, latter-day humans cannibalized the words of their ancestors, reducing their meanings to mere convention. Müller commented:

> Man loses his instincts as he ceases to want them ... Thus the creative faculty which gave to each conception, as it thrilled for the first time through the brain, a phonetic expression, became extinct when its object was fulfilled ... the first settlement of the radical elements of language was preceded by a period of unrestrained growth – the spring of speech – to be followed by many an autumn. (1, pp. 429–30)

Müller's idea of modern language as a kind of fall from Eden paralleled popular views of industrial capitalism as a fall from an idyllic rural past. Similarly to how commentators such as Thomas Carlyle revered ancient society, Müller revered ancient orality. For Müller, the vital essence of language existed in spoken dialect, and the fading of that essence matched the transition from oral to literary society. He stressed: 'Language exists in man, it lives in being spoken, it dies with each word that is pronounced, and is no longer heard'. Print, mass literacy and urbanization extracted language from the ancestral landscapes and communities in which it lived. 'Remove a language from its native soil,' Müller commented, 'tear it away from the dialects which are its feeders, and you arrest at once its natural growth. There will still be the progress of phonetic corruption, but no longer the restoring influence of dialectic regeneration' (1, pp. 51, 66). Alienated from the soil and folk that made it, literary language shrivelled into such verbal corpses as Latin.

Müller's arguments were heard by a British audience that regarded comparative philology chiefly as a means of discovering and consolidating national identity.[57] In 1855 the theologian-philologist Richard Chenevix Trench seized upon the current Crimean War as a reason for the Englishman 'to esteem and prize most that which he has in common with his fellow countrymen'. His audience must know the history of their language, he stated, 'to be ourselves guardians of its purity, and not corrupters of it'.[58] It was on this principle that Trench initiated work on what would become the *Oxford English Dictionary*, seeking a comprehensive history of English. His colleague Frederick Furnivall founded the Early English Text Society in 1864 with the aim of publishing medieval texts, thus helping volunteers to find quotations for the dictionary.[59] Subsuming language history into a national narrative downplayed comparative philology's tendency to destabilize distinctions between nations. Philologists since Herder had assumed that each language contained a unique, living essence that reflected the character and memories of a community. Thus Trench called language 'the embodiment, the incarnation ... of the feelings, thoughts and experiences of a nation'.[60] Müller opposed the equation of languages with racial types, stressing the ultimate unity of the human family. Yet his emphasis on 'native soil' and his rhetoric of 'stock', 'roots' and 'genius' could be easily co-opted in support of nationalist and racialist philology.[61]

The greater problem which comparative philology posed for nationalists lay in its privileging of speech over writing. Beneath the standardized languages of nation states, it discovered common origins that stretched across continents. Müller observed that before 'the bit and bridle of literature were thrown over their necks', speech communities diverged into infinite dialects (1, p. 60). The further back in history that scholars searched for their nation's linguistic origins, the more fragmented and heterogeneous they became. Müller stated:

> As there were families, clans, confederacies, and tribes, before there was a nation; so there were dialects before there was a language. The grammarian who postulates an historical reality for the one primitive type of Teutonic speech, is no better than the historian who believes in a *Francus*, the grandson of Hector, and the supposed ancestor of all the Franks, or in a *Brutus*, the mythical father of all the Britons. (1, pp. 198–99)

Chapter 3 explores how the historical fiction of Müller's close friend Charles Kingsley and his Scottish contemporary R. M. Ballantyne grappled with this problem. They presented their novels such as *Westward Ho!* (1855) and *Norsemen in the West* (1872) as transcriptions of speech that were distanced from the calculation and artifice of modern literary culture. Much like Arnold in his contemporaneous criticism of Celtic tales, they sought to salvage some of the imagined spirit of oral tradition in modern, artificial literature. Antagonistic truth-values collided in these narratives, however, as they vacillated between scholarly historical evidence and spontaneous organic inspiration. Their desire for authentic oral communities also conflicted with their efforts to trace a united national heritage that was only possible in writing.

Some authors and commentators sought to resolve this contradiction by racializing language. While philology traced the precursors of English, scholars increasingly sought England's racial heritage in Old Norse literature. New translations of these texts provided source material for the emerging genre of Viking fiction. Examples of this genre by Paul du Chaillu and James Frederick Hodgetts sought to revive or discover traces of ancient Norse vocabulary in modern English. The desire for a true ancestral language tangled such authors in a search for impossible purity, while British imperialism was uprooting English from its mythical native soil and speakers. Anxieties about racial-linguistic dilution and contamination also refracted the genre of invasion fiction which surged in popularity from the 1870s onwards. Fears of foreign languages invading England along with foreign armies can be seen in the genre from George Chesney's *The Battle of Dorking* (1871) to Saki's *When William Came* (1913). Such fiction externalized in a foreign invader anxieties about internal pressures in England that seemed to be destroying its organic speech heritage. Reverence for an organic, oral past was not, however, inherently nationalistic. William Morris's late fiction combined such reverence with socialist internationalism, presenting the supposed artifice and decay of modern language as effects of industrial capitalism. Writing in a fantasy archaic English, Morris avoided racialist purism by emphasizing an original unity of tongues. This universalism existed in tension, though, with Morris's emphasis on folk speech rooted in local landscapes and ancestral experience.

Whilst language studies evolved towards the end of the century, language vitalism suffered growing criticism. Scholars led by the Yale Sanskritist William Dwight Whitney challenged Müller's claim that words derived from ancient 'roots' and 'died' when these were forgotten. Meaning was 'arbitrary and conventional', Whitney argued, changing through majority usage with no origin required.[62] This rendered meaning a matter of individual mental associations rather than a general *Sprachgeist*.[63] Whitney described language as constantly fragmenting into specialized dialects, reflecting the activities of different groups. The vocabulary of physicists departed from mainstream speech in the same way as sailors' slang, expressing the associations of their speakers.[64] Thomas Hardy's fiction engages with these debates, reworking language vitalism into nostalgia for an oral diversity before the imposition of Standard English. Instead of carrying a mystical power, regional dialect in novels such as *Under the Greenwood Tree* (1872) and *Tess of the d'Urbervilles* (1891) mirrors the communal experiences of its speakers. Standard English appears in these visions as a destroyer of communal identity, absorbing speakers into a more remote national one.

Instinctive signs: nature and culture in dialogue

Language progressivism and vitalism both reified language as a single object evolving over time, either as a technology or a force of nature. Towards the end of the century, however, developments in philology and other disciplines split language evolution into separate phenomena. In Germany, 'Neogrammarian' philologists such as Hermann Osthoff and Karl Brugmann narrowed their focus to sound shifts that occurred in language, irrespective of meaning. The view that meaning was contextual and not transcendent shifted the study of semantic change towards the psychology of individual speakers and the social institutions which regulated their lives. Simultaneously, Darwin and his supporters examined speech as a sociobiological capacity built upon instinctive signs systems such as mating songs and emotional expressions. Chapter 4 considers fiction which engaged with this view of language as a dialogue between biology and culture. Hardy's, Wells's and Butler's narratives explored how bodily instinct and social convention conflicted and coalesced in speech, producing ambiguous, multilayered interactions between people. The fragmentation of language paralleled the fragmentation of a human subject that was no longer sovereign over his or her discourse but was a confluence of sociological and biological processes.

Early theories of social psychology in the period redefined language as a mould that shaped people's mental habits and associations. Ideas and discourse which seemed the property of individuals might turn out to be expressions of what the German philosophers Heymann Steinthal and Moritz Lazarus called *Völksgeist*. Völksgeist was not simply homogeneous, though, but generated diverse mental and social tendencies.[65] G. H. Lewes knew of Lazarus's and Steinthal's work and echoed it in his description of 'the Social Organism' as a 'fund' of past experiences which language had solidified 'in opinion, precept and law, in prejudice and superstition'. Hence, Lewes wrote, 'our opinions are made up of shadowy associations, imperfect memories, echoes of other men's voices, mingling with the reactions of our own sensibility'.[66] Language and ideas thus vacillated between individual experience and communal convention. Speakers could never claim thoughts or meanings as wholly their own because they were embedded in endless networks of influence and appropriation. Simultaneously, Darwin's theories about human evolution suggested a biological element in language. Speech had evolved, Darwin argued, from the natural and sexual selection of instinctive gestures, expressions and vocalizations. Thus, 'when vivid emotions are felt and expressed by the orator or even in common speech, musical cadences and rhythm are instinctively used'. The 'sensations and ideas' which such cadences excited 'appear from their vagueness, yet depth, like mental reversions to the emotions and thoughts of a long-past age'.[67] Unlike Spencer, who viewed language as a linear progression from instinct to convention, Darwin imagined the two working together. Speech, he claimed, was a hybrid, 'half-art and half-instinct'.[68] Whilst, for Spencer, sympathy evolved through the disembodiment of language, Darwin located sympathy in the body's instinctive emotional signals. He wrote: 'Our cries of pain, fear, surprise, anger, together with their appropriate actions, and the murmur of a mother to her beloved child are more expressive than any words'.[69] Civilization was, perhaps, not threatened by the body and its instincts, but built upon them.

Darwin developed his theory of instinctive emotional signs through reading research by figures such as the physiologist Charles Bell and the educator of deaf children William Scott. Both men argued for a 'natural language' of emotions which formed the basis of human bonds, revealed respectively through expressions and manual sign language. 'Every distinct emotion has its appropriate expression', Scott had written, 'and thus a language altogether independent of words exists, displayed by the countenance or action of man ... It is by natural signs that the orator chiefly gives force and energy to his language; and in proportion as his oratory is deficient in the use of these natural signs, it is the less expressive and effective'.[70] Darwin cited Bell and Scott in his work, and similarly argued that instinctive and artificial signs complemented and merged with each other.[71] He noted that expressions which seemed to originate in innate reflex acquired new meanings through repetition in particular contexts. Conversely, Darwin theorized, bodily signals once merely conventional had grown innate through many generations of repetition and Lamarckian use-inheritance: 'Actions, which were at first voluntary, soon became habitual, and at last hereditary'.[72] These arguments further undermined the concept of language as a single object evolving in a coherent direction. Speech was not the embodiment or progressive rise of reason, as Müller and Spencer respectively claimed, but a muddle of instinct and convention, which might convey different messages simultaneously. 'The impassioned orator, bard, or musician,' Darwin wrote, 'when with his varied tones and cadences he excites the strongest emotions in his hearers, little suspects that he uses the same means by which his half-human ancestors long ago aroused each other's ardent passions, during their courtship and rivalry.'[73]

Butler's *The Way of all Flesh* (1903) explores this intersection of nature and nurture in language to depict how children are controlled by, and might escape, the voices of their parents. The novel conceives of heredity and social custom as parallel phonographs, recording and repeating mental-verbal habits through successive generations. Hardy's fiction explores the concept of instinctive signs from the different perspective of sympathy and sexual attraction. His tales frequently depict an instinctive language of emotions shadowing the conventional speech between characters. In tales such as *The Hand of Ethelberta* (1876) he also associates instinctive signs with sympathy between people, which the etiquette of civilization suppresses. Finally, Chapter 4 considers Wells's interest in the creative potential of instinctive babble, viewing it as an antidote to dogma and unthinking verbal habit. His social comedies such as *Tono-Bungay* (1909) and *Kipps* (1905) suggest that obsessions with social correctness and exact knowledge threaten to automatize language and thought. Opposing this automatism, his writing sometimes sought to recapture the primordial instability of language, twisting sounds and meanings out of shape. Such ideas prefigured modernist experiments in later decades. However, Wells ultimately withdrew from the implications of his ideas about language, confining most of his verbal play to personal writings.

The speculative overlap between fiction and language studies enabled Victorians and Edwardians to engage with issues to which twenty-first-century science and linguistics have recently returned. Shifts towards structural linguistics and anthropology from the late nineteenth century onwards would construct 'culture' as an edifice separate from its foundations in 'nature'. These changes rendered orthodox the assumption that the 'nature' of language (if it had one) was fixed and unchanging. Its possible evolution from prehuman communication, and the continuing role of instinct in semantics, became marginalized as idle speculation.[74] Yet the questions raised by fictions of philology remain as compelling as ever. Are words wholly arbitrary? Is there an instinctive component in the production and reception of signs? Is language fundamentally different from animal communication or an anthropocentric construct? This study aims to intervene in such discussions by exploring the literary contexts that framed comparable debates in the past. In the twenty-first century, as in the nineteenth, the stories we construct of the evolution of language determine our relationship with (or estrangement from) the rest of the organic world. Bruno Latour writes: 'For purely anthropocentric – that is, political – reasons, naturalists have built their collective to make sure that subjects and objects, culture and nature remain utterly distinct, with only the former having any sort of agency.'[75] Conversely, conceiving language as a mingling of nature and culture diminishes humans' symbolic agency, absorbing them into a play of signs and interpretation that may pervade many levels of life. This study also intervenes in contemporary debates over the roles of evolutionary and cognitive psychology in literary criticism. Scholars who would study language and literature as products of evolution must recognize that they are not simply windows on to human biology but cultural edifices, the biological foundations of which remain uncertain and speculative. In this sense, we still have much to learn from Victorian efforts in science and fiction to place language under a microscope.

CHAPTER 1

The future of language in prophetic fiction

In 1887 the Polish linguist and creator of Esperanto Ludwig Lazarus Zamenhof published a primer to his artificial language, which stated: 'The reader will doubtless take up this little work with an incredulous smile, supposing that he is about to peruse the impracticable schemes of some good citizen of Utopia'.[1] His comment highlights the reciprocity between fiction and linguistics in visions of the future of language at the time. The immense historical changes charted by philology fuelled speculation about future metamorphoses, and practical efforts to realize them, such as Zamenhof's Esperanto.[2] Zamenhof's hope that his artificial speech would precipitate a new epoch of international sympathy and cooperation reflected widely held beliefs that language and society progressed in tandem. This chapter explores how utopian and prophetic fiction both responded to and framed the discourse of language progressivism. Artificial languages epitomized the goal of objectifying language, reducing it to the passive tool of an independent human intellect. Prophetic fiction similarly invented languages, imagining future forms of perfect communication, although rarely in all of their structural details. These activities can be understood as parallel examples of the progressive desire to rise above the sociohistorical context of one's present language. Objective knowledge consisted of mentally escaping one's inherited language to gain a transhistorical view of linguistic evolution. Industrialization and urbanization in the late nineteenth-century West saw an upsurge in prophetic writing, reflecting what Matthew Beaumont calls 'a culture of expectancy'. Amidst rapid socio-economic transformation, the fictional imaginary future offered a means 'to understand the transitional epoch in which it [was] produced'.[3] The Hegelian model of history depicted humans progressing towards comprehension of their destiny so that predicting progress could be the first step to fulfilling it. In 1881 Tylor wrote: 'Acquainted with events and their consequences far and wide over the world, we are able to direct our own course with more confidence toward improvement. In a word, mankind is passing from the age of unconscious to that of conscious progress.'[4] By inventing languages, either as practical systems for communication or imaginative visions of the future, Victorians and Edwardians seemed to demonstrate the progress of their times and bring the dream of objective language closer to realization.

Visions of language progress were contradictory, however, torn as they were between incompatible models of how words signified meanings. They vacillated between the conflicting ideals of semantic precision and efficiency, between autonomous individual expression and rigid conformity. These competing aims were mirrored in fictional portrayals of language progressing to both liberate individual speakers and regiment them under prescriptive authorities. The goal of controlling language faltered under growing uncertainty in psychology that any autonomous ego pre-existed language.[5] The progressive idea of the human mind controlling verbal meaning hovered uncertainly between individual speakers and the speech community in which they were mere nodes. Towards the end of the century scholars and scientists increasingly challenged the foundational assumptions of language progress. Its reassuring rhetoric of language growing to unite people around objective truth crumbled before new ideas that prefigured the linguistic revolutions of the twentieth century. One author who engaged directly with these problems in his predictive fiction was the young Wells. Several of his early scientific romances depict communication forms which seem to accomplish progressive goals (such as telepathy), only for such supposed progress to produce new breakdowns in sympathy and understanding. Wells's recognition that meaning depended on context and subjective associations problematized the very notion of language progress. However, Wells also exemplifies the durability of progressivism, linked as it was to wider hopes for humanity's future. As he committed himself to the ideal of a world state (which would depend on a 'scientific' *lingua franca*), so Wells ignored the logical inconsistencies in language progress which he had previously exposed.

Mechanizing language

Language progressivism revolved around rescuing Locke's old idea of language as a tool of autonomous minds. The gradual diversification of languages revealed by comparative philology suggested that speech evolved independently of human intentions. Progressives thus conceived of language as *developing* into a tool rather than being eternally so, gaining stability and precision with the advancement of society. The rise of print and Standard English seemed to demonstrate this process, as the anthropologist James Cowles Prichard had commented in 1813: 'The permanency of languages is ... more constant in proportion to the advancement of society. Among civilised nations who have arrived at the knowledge of letters ... writers regulate their style, and the idiom becomes fixed'.[6] Such mechanization of language could be imagined as part of the progressive rise of human control over nature. The mid-century theorist of social evolution Henry Buckle presented civilization as a transition from 'nature modifying man' to 'man modifying nature'.[7] Georg Hegel had claimed that self-consciousness emerged through labour: the worker developed it as he acted upon external objects, differentiating them from himself.[8] Similarly, progressives argued, by objectifying language, humans could abstract themselves from the sociohistorical subjectivities revealed by philology. Instead of being bound by context, meaning might be conceived of as mental substance, its conveyance a matter of precision and efficiency. In 1894 the philologist Otto Jespersen looked forward to an 'ideal language' of the future from which 'irregularity and ambiguity would be banished; sound and sense would be in perfect harmony; any number of delicate shades of meaning could be expressed ... [and] the human spirit would have found a garment combining freedom and gracefulness, fitting it closely and yet allowing full play to any movement'.[9] Language could also be idealized as linking humans with the wider universe, revealing the cosmic elements through the fixing of definitions (what Whewell called the 'language' of nature). However, the goals of verbal mechanization, efficiency and precision relied on incompatible theories of semantics. Visions of such progress vacillated between the accumulation of meanings through time and their destruction in line with new knowledge. This contradiction, which theorists often finessed through abstract discussion, emerged more starkly in fictive imaginings of future language mechanization.

The ideal of verbal mechanization, illustrated in the Introduction above through the example of Herbert Spencer, grew in response to new communication technologies. Through the nineteenth century anglophone society became mediated by writing as never before through the Penny Post, telegrams, memoranda and popular print for newly literature mass audiences.[10] The capacity of writing to record past statements and discussions led commentators to characterize it by semantic accumulation. Single words, Whewell wrote, now signified 'the results of deep and laborious trains of research ... without being in any way impeded or perplexed by the length and weight of the chain of past connexions which we drag along with us'.[11] Horne Tooke had earlier claimed that language developed through abbreviation, condensing words into aggregates to convey complex ideas.[12] Early in the nineteenth century, Charles Babbage's calculating engines had appeared to industrialize this process, reducing the mental processes of arithmetic to algebraic notation. As Babbage wrote with John Herschel, mechanistic symbols promised 'to condense pages into lines and volumes into pages'.[13] The growth of encyclopaedias and dictionaries also seemed to show the growing semantic density of words, collating their historical uses, such as in the *Oxford English Dictionary* project.[14] One of the *OED*'s pioneers, R. C. Trench, described the modern word as 'a concentrated poem', while A. H. Sayce later termed it 'a crystallized sentence, a kind of shorthand note, in which a proposition has been summed up'.[15] Simultaneously, in letters, memoranda and telegrams, styles of 'Commercial English' emerged, stripping words and syntax to a minimum. Telegraphic code-books even compressed sentences into one-word acronyms. Isaac Pitman's phonographic shorthand, first presented in 1837, reduced writing to minimal loops and curves, inviting predictions that it would replace the current orthography.[16] Spencer argued that the process of verbal compression could be observed in terms such as 'good bye', which concentrated the old phrase 'God be with you'.[17] The abbreviations of the present looked set to become the ordinary words of the future.

Parallel to efficiency was the notion that language advanced through increasing exactness. Spencer wrote that language gained 'precision' by 'multiplication of words', which enabled it to 'express directly and perfectly' what would otherwise require misleading, indirect metaphors.[18] At the same time, the rise of Standard English seemed to show humans gaining control over the natural forces of language change, imposing uniformity across regions. Grammatical guides and pronouncing dictionaries grew in popularity through the century, reflecting 'the myth of a perfectible, invariant standard of spoken English, one prescribed for all speakers without exception'.[19] Spencer associated such verbal uniformity with scientific objectivity, assuming that symbols gained fixity as they rose above parochial perspectives. He wrote: 'Each tongue acquires further accuracy through processes which fix the meaning of each word. By and by dictionaries give definitions, and eventually among the most cultivated indefiniteness is not tolerated'.[20] From the mid century onwards, verbal uniformity emerged as a logical correlative to objective knowledge, as news and scientific texts related their 'facts' in increasingly impersonal, passive and conventional styles.[21] At the same time, new technologies seemed to point towards further uniformity in the future. Pitman claimed that, unlike traditional letters, his shorthand captured every possible vocal sound, thus fixing speech on the page. Similarly, later, the phonograph and kymograph promised to regulate speech by analyzing it into reproducible sound waves. Sayce hailed these developments as restraints upon the 'linguistic anarchy' of nature, building a language for which 'means will be found for making the [aural and written] symbols uniform and constant'.[22] Not only could writing visualize the sounds of speech, it might also one day reproduce them, forming a closed circuit of unchanging phonemes and graphemes.

The ideals of verbal precision and efficiency involved antagonistic models of semantics. Efficiency relied on Locke's assumption that words retained their older, individual meanings as speakers compounded them into new aggregates. However, if users were constantly redefining words in response to new knowledge, then progress consisted as much of forgetting old meanings as accumulating them. As Spencer wrote, 'with the advance of language, words which were originally alike in their meanings acquire unlike meanings' because 'there necessarily arises a habit of associating one rather than the other with particular acts, or objects'.[23] If words signified, as Spencer suggested, through habitual associations then what truth-value could they claim beyond convention? They named not essential objects but a grid of shifting, arbitrary divisions. Herbert notes that Spencer's associationist psychology questioned the existence of objects in isolation, recognizing only networks of relations. Spencer wrote, 'every thought involves a whole system of thoughts and ceases to exist if severed from its various correlatives'.[24] Without a natural set of boundaries between sensible objects, words had no basis outside of these seemingly enclosed systems of relations. As Herbert comments, associationism provided the model of synchronic relativity which Ferdinand de Saussure would import into semantics. The more progressives idealized verbal precision and, thus, convention, the more they undermined semantic accumulation, which demanded natural, extra-linguistic conceptions. David Amigoni notes Spencer's recognition in *First Principles* (1862) 'that within every religious and scientific concept was an element of fiction-making, and a space of representation not fully controllable by its writer'.[25] The spherical earth, for example, was not a fact verifiable by the senses but a 'symbolic conception', imagined through reference to sensible, round objects. While Whewell presented nature as a 'language' that scientists were striving to translate, Spencer suggested instead that they invented it: 'we are led to suppose we have truly conceived a great variety of things which we have conceived only in this fictitious way; and further to confound with these certain things which cannot be conceived in any way'.[26] Spencer avoided the vortex of relativism, however, through faith in a 'non-relative', objective reality beyond present knowledge.[27] The belief that conventional language would progress teleologically towards such transcendental truth enabled progressives to ignore its semantic relativism.

The logic of verbal mechanization, and its contradictions, can be seen in Edward Bulwer-Lytton's vision of a superior language in his subterrestrial romance *The Coming Race* (1871). A Tory peer in the House of Lords, Bulwer-Lytton combined his interests in mesmerism and evolution in the novella with Swiftian satire on western democracy. The tale depicts an American discovering an underground super-race named the Vril-ya destined to replace humans. The narrator describes their society as 'an aristocratic republic' united around scientific and literary authorities, unlike the divided classes of the upper world. Vrillians remember the democracy of their ancestors as 'one of the crude and ignorant experiments' of barbarism.[28] Bulwer-Lytton presents future progress as the consolidation of elite authority, demonstrated in Vrillian language which is tightly controlled by 'scholars and grammarians' (p. 86). This vision opposes the democratization of language norms through mass print and popular politics. As such, it chimes with Arnold's view that 'knowledge and truth' depended on 'the highly-instructed few, and not the scantily-instructed many'.[29] He defined 'culture' as 'the best which has been thought and said', which did not come from the masses but must be prescribed to them.[30] Conversely, J. S. Mill had complained that modern language-users 'find their resources continually narrowed by illiterate writers, who seize and twist from its purpose some form of speech which once served to convey briefly and compactly an unambiguous meaning'.[31] By contrast, Vrillian words are united in their meanings, while also preserving their historical significance. In this way, Vrillian language exhibits the contradiction between diachronic accumulation and synchronic precision. The narrator suggests that the two have been achieved harmoniously: while 'preserving so many of the roots in the aboriginal form', Vrillian language has yet 'attained to such a union of simplicity and compass ... the gradual work of countless ages and many varieties of mind'. He continues: 'Though now very compressed in sound, it gains in clearness by that compression. By a single letter, according to its position, they contrive to express all that with civilised nations in our upper world it takes the waste, sometimes of syllables, sometimes of sentences, to express' (pp. 84–86). The narrator's comments prompt the question of how Vril-ya speech can both archive past knowledge and describe the world objectively.

It seems to rise above sociohistorical perspectives while simultaneously recording and repeating them.

Bulwer-Lytton solves this problem by switching from language progressivism to vitalism. The Vril-ya's unified scientific knowledge does not simply fix conventional meanings for words, but returns them to their primordial origins. Bulwer-Lytton dedicated his tale to Max Müller and the description of Vril-ya language is underpinned by the philologist's concept of original, mental-verbal 'roots'. 'It is surprising', the narrator comments, as words became inflected,

> to see how much more boldly the original roots of the language project from the surface that conceals them. In the old fragments and proverbs of the preceding stage the monosyllables which compose those roots vanish amidst words of enormous length ... But when the inflectional form of language became so far advanced as to have its scholars and grammarians, they seem to have united in extirpating all such polysynthetical or polysyllabic monsters, as devouring invaders of the aboriginal forms. Words beyond three syllables became proscribed as barbarous, and in proportion as the language grew thus simplified it increased in strength, in dignity, and in sweetness. (pp. 85–86)

The compounded elements of Vril-ya words are not concrete but abstract: the 'root' sounds which Müller claimed signified eternal, abstract ideas. Hence, 'An (which I will translate man), Ana (men); the letter *s* is with them a letter implying multitude, ... Sana means mankind; Ansa, a multitude of men ... Gl ... at the commencement of a word infers an assemblage or union of things ... as Oon, a house; Gloon, a town (i.e., an assemblage of houses)' (pp. 86–87). The Vril-ya have analyzed and named the atomic parts and mechanisms of the universe only to rediscover things previously felt by intuition. The phoneme *zoo* prefixes

> words that signify something that attracts, pleases, touches the heart – as Zummer, lover; Zutze, love; Zuzulia, delight. This indrawn sound of *Z* seems indeed naturally appropriate to fondness. Thus, even in our language, mothers say to their babies, in defiance of grammar, 'Zoo darling'; and I have heard a learned professor at Boston call his wife (he had been only married a month) 'Zoo little pet'. (p. 93)

Vril-ya words are 'compressed' into single letters, but, instead of being arbitrary notations, these letters are rediscoveries of natural sound symbols. Such word roots guide science to reveal objective truths which humans had always dimly conceived. Hence, Bulwer-Lytton suggests that Victorian ideas of 'mesmeric clairvoyance' prefigure the universal energetic agencies that Vril-ya science proves empirically (p. 48). Yet, the narrator can only master 'the rudiments of their language' because his own lacks equivalent words for Vrillian knowledge (p. 49). When they define 'vril', the 'unity of energetic agencies' through which they control nature, he confesses: 'I understood very little, for there is no word in any language I know which is an exact synonym for vril. I should call it electricity, except that it comprehends in its manifold branches other forces of nature, to which, in our scientific nomenclature, differing names are assigned, such as magnetism, galvanism, &c' (p. 47). These difficulties contradict the notion that future science is adumbrated in the linguistic past. Bulwer-Lytton's equivocation between semantic models highlights a paradox in language progress. It sought to escape the past yet also needed to connect with it in order to present meaning as purposive evolution rather than synchronic convention, unguided by any transcendental authority.

Language progressives often imagined such transcendental authority as a fundamental force behind all physical phenomena. Victorians from Michael Faraday to John Tyndall viewed the conservation of energy as potentially the key to this agency, while Spencer presented 'persistence of force' as the power behind evolution.[32] Bulwer-Lytton frames the mysterious power of 'vril' by quoting Faraday's claim 'that the various forms under which the forces of matter are made manifest, have one common origin; or, in other words, are so directly related and mutually dependent that they are convertible, as it were into one another' (p. 47). Language and thought could be imagined as forms of such convertible energy, weaving into the fabric of the universe. One Vrillian tells the narrator:

> no form of matter is motionless and inert: every particle is constantly in motion and constantly acted upon by agencies ... the current launched by my hand and guided by my will does but render quicker and more potent the action which is eternally at work upon every particle of matter, however inert and stubborn it may seem. If a heap of metal be not capable of originating a thought of its own, yet, through its internal susceptibility to movement, it obtains the power to receive the thought of the intellectual agent at work on it. (p. 132)

Like Spencer's 'non-relative' existence beyond present knowledge, the idea of a universal energetic agency enabled the possibility of symbols not only mapping but also affecting reality. The goals of describing and controlling the world might converge, with language shaping as well as reflecting it. When science finishes decoding the universe, its symbols will cease to be arbitrary, their meanings or 'thoughts' acting directly upon matter.

John Macnie's utopia *The Diothas* (1883) similarly predicts future science closing the gap between being and representation. As in *The Coming Race*, it reveals the anti-democratic impulse behind the search for semantic authority through science. Macnie was a Scottish linguist and mathematician who obtained a master's degree from Yale in 1874 before becoming Professor of Modern Languages at North Dakota. His time at Yale coincided with the rise to prominence of its most famous philologist, William Dwight Whitney, who argued that language was conventional. Meanings changed, he claimed, through shifts in majority habit, functioning like a democracy.[33] Macnie's utopia rejects such synchronic semantics, however, along with the democratic ideology it implied. Arthur Lipow notes that American positivism emerged in opposition to mass democracy, requiring elites to direct the rational organization of society.[34] *The Diothas* reflects this tradition, depicting a future in which a strict technocracy replaces the old 'extremes of democracy and lawlessness' ruled by populist 'charlatans'.[35] Equally, it avoids the semantic relativism theorized by Whitney through uniform language set by scientific authority.

Macnie published other books on geometry and algebra, and his utopia reflects his belief in the hidden mathematical unity of nature, which future language would reveal. Journeying centuries hence through hypnosis, the narrator finds a people who have deciphered nature's signs. His guide explains: 'Chemistry long ago ceased to be an experimental art. It is now a strictly deductive science, in which, by the proper manipulation of symbols and formulas, interesting or important discoveries may be made without the necessity of handling a re-agent or an instrument' (p. 85). As humans evolve towards Lamarckian harmony with their environment, so language evolves to absorb its referents. In this way, Macnie's chemists are able to grow beef-steaks from maize crops by altering their algebraic formulations. The guide continues: 'our experts are able, not only to imitate any definite compound known to exist in nature, but even to invent others'. Control over nature is reduced to framing consistent symbols and definitions. Personal and class perspectives vanish as science abstracts language from bodily subjectivity: 'Most great questions have been so thoroughly discussed, if not settled ... that oratory, as implying an appeal to the emotions, is practically a thing of the past' (pp. 103–04). Discussions now concern 'establishing a theorem in exact science'. Speech has reached the exactitude previously only found in geometry and algebra, with the guide declaring, 'all sciences worthy of the name are now but branches of mixed mathematics' (p. 119). This echoed a wider belief among mathematicians that algebra might unite humans, thus overcoming the subjectivity of language. George Boole had described mathematics as 'universal reasoning expressed in symbolic forms'.[36] The transcendental authority for symbolic meaning that Bulwer-Lytton found in the conservation of energy, Macnie imagined in algebraic equations.

Again, the idea of symbols gaining control over nature vacillates between diachronic and synchronic models of semantics. Macnie's future speech is both an accumulation of meanings through time and a notation for the latest knowledge. The narrator's guide explains: 'The present universal language is based upon the Anglian of your day much as that was based upon Saxon', with an 'enormous increase of the vocabulary by the adoption of a great variety of synonyms from many languages'. The 'dozen different words signifying a dwelling' have expanded to 'more than a hundred; each, when appropriately employed, conveying a different shade of meaning' (p. 118). Macnie suggests that linguistic precision depends on convention: synonyms from other languages must lose their etymological meanings to mark new distinctions. Such conventionality is undercut, though, by the trope of efficiency. Writing is now so compressed that 'a complete file of the *London Times* for a year' can be 'concentrated into the space of a sheet of foolscap' (p. 61). Ubiquitous phonographs have precipitated 'an enormous curtailment in the length of speeches', rendering them a dense code of cross-references. Every utterance signposts an archive of past discourse so that 'though a trope is not an argument, it may be efficiently employed to illustrate an argument, or even be used as an elegant substitute for one' (pp. 102–03). Equally, in speech, 'the words of most frequent use in the language had been reduced to monosyllables ... no words of more than three syllables were tolerated' (p. 187). The nineteenth-century place names recalled by the narrator have been superseded by shorter contractions, such as 'Uespa' for 'West Point', causing one woman to tease him: 'How lavish of breath you must have been in those old times!' (p. 303). Phonetic decay becomes subsumed into the progressive refinement of ideas. Signs cannot be wholly conventional because this would relativize their meanings and render arbitrary their connection with the external world. For language to become a transparent window upon nature, it must merge with nature, exhibiting the same purposive growth. By this logic, Macnie's future speakers cannot suppress all bodily, emotional expression with social conventions. They refine Spencer's 'language of emotions' to a minimal notation so that, when an estranged couple reunite, the narrator 'read in their eyes what was to me a revelation of how much of a long repressed feeling can be expressed in one look, – trust, joy, love, beyond the power of words' (p. 48). Married couples routinely spend their first year apart, communicating via telephone 'the delicate shading of thought possible to the living voice alone, and the mental stimulus arising from the present collision of thought with thought ... the reciprocal interaction of two minds' (p. 158). The abstractions of mathematics thus blur in Macnie's ideal speech with the emotional, sensory body, albeit spiritualized by technology. In order to progress towards correspondence with nature, language must both forget and reconnect with its past, both abstract from the body and re-enter it from the immaterial position of 'mind'.

Meetings of minds

The contradictions in progressivism led to speculation on communication transcending the body through telepathy or spiritualism. Such disembodiment cohered with the aims of scientific objectivity. Victorian scientific truth, George Levine comments, became characterized by 'the radical distrust of the corporeal, the contingent, the personal. Salvation – religious, aesthetic, or epistemological – depends on the capacity of the self to get outside of itself'.[37] Freed from the subjective, bodily frame of reference, telepathy and spiritualism promised unlimited sympathy between minds and access to the noumenal universe. Yet visions of this ideal were torn between privileging the individual and dissolving it in a wider whole. The single mind gained control over its expression; yet, to enter direct communion with other minds, it had to relinquish this autonomy for a common mental currency.[38] Equally, disembodied individuals controlled the universe, bending its symbols to their intentions; yet, they also lost agency, becoming utterances of a higher, cosmic power. Late nineteenth-century utopias of telepathic or spirit communication exemplified these tensions. They imagined individual minds attaining sovereignty over discourse only to lose it, merging in communal consciousness or the infinite mind of God.

Models of language progressing from local subjectivity and ambiguity to universal objectivity and precision persistently involved disembodiment. Anthropologists from Tylor and L. H. Morgan to George Romanes argued that language evolved from gesture to speech with the abstraction of ideas.[39] This process had reached its furthest extent, they claimed, in philosophy that had no referents in material sensation. 'Gestures, in being more or less always ideographic, are much more closely chained to sensuous perceptions', Romanes wrote; 'No sign talker, with any amount of time at his disposal, could translate into the language of gesture a page of

The future of language in prophetic fiction

Kant'.[40] Tylor agreed: 'By eliminating from speech all effects of gesture, of expression of face, and of emotional tone, we go far towards reducing it towards the system of conventional, articulate sounds which the grammarian and comparative philologist habitually consider as language'.[41] Yet, even in writing, language remained moored to the subjective experiences of the body, framing abstractions from 'material metaphor'. In matters of language, Tylor complained, 'we have gone too little beyond the savage state, but are still as it were hacking with the stone celts and twirling laborious friction-fire'.[42] Christine Ferguson notes that Tylor's view paralleled spiritualist urges, with both seeking the abstraction of language and consciousness from material bases.[43] Yet, the materialization of mind in psychology would seem to remove any transcendental authority from human ideas, rendering them mere aggregate sensations. How, then, could ideas be meaningful without reference to bodily sensations?

The answer depended upon how one defined sensation. Roger Luckhurst observes: 'The method and mode of communication in the nervous system was unknown at the time ... In the higher reaches of the central nervous system the nerves disappeared off the scale of the Victorian microscope, becoming vanishing points'.[44] Like electricity, sensory signals seemed to jump between gaps in the physical nerves, suggesting that consciousness might extend beyond the body. Scientists such as Helmholtz had studied the nervous system in parallel to electric circuits, describing them through analogies with each other. If the wired social body mirrored nervous communication with the individual body, then perhaps some continuity existed between the two.[45] Charles Bray wrote in 1866: 'We have no difficulty in conceiving of electricity as existing freely throughout space; but thought or mind, and electricity, are the same force in different forms ... Mind is in connection with all other mind'.[46] Older ideas of animal magnetism thus gave way to notions of 'thought-atmosphere', 'psychic force' or ether. In 1882 the Society for Psychical Research coined the word *telepathy*, denoting the transmission of mental impressions without the aid of known sense organs. Henry Drummond later described this as 'theoretically the next stage in the Evolution of Language'. He built his conclusion upon the model of progressive mental-symbolic disembodiment, stating: 'When a speaker soars into a very lofty region, or allows his mind to grapple intensely and absorbingly with an exalted theme, he becomes more and more motionless, and only resumes the gesture-language when he descends to commoner levels'. Telepathy, he claimed, was foreshadowed by the telegraph and telephone. As they advanced communication 'from the icy physical barriers of space, to a nearness closer than breathing', so humans must evolve further 'in the direction of what one can only call spirituality ... If Evolution reveals anything ... it is that Man is a spiritual being and that the direction of his long career is towards an ever larger, richer, and more exalted life'.[47] Drummond's prediction, delivered in 1894, drew on a body of thought which prophetic fiction had long been exploring. Evolution towards direct thought transference promised to unite speakers with both each other and the wider cosmos.

One of the first utopias with telepathy at its centre was Edward Bellamy's 'To Whom this May Come', published a year after his famous *Looking Backward* (1888). *The Coming Race* had suggested that by 'animal magnetism' 'the thoughts of one brain [might] be transmitted to another, and knowledge be thus rapidly interchanged' (p. 22). However, Bellamy's tale presents such communication as a biological rather than a technological evolution. It depicts a race of mind-readers whose hereditary ability produces a united, harmonious society. Bellamy was the son of a Baptist minister, who absorbed Auguste Comte's concept of a religion of humanity as a replacement for his wavering faith in God. The transcendentalism of R. W. Emerson enabled him to relocate divinity in human beings. As a young man in 1874, he had written of the 'tendency of the human soul to a more perfect realization of its solidarity with the universe'.[48] Paradoxically, this self-consciousness coincided with a progressive dissolution of self into wider circles of being. He commented: 'the cardinal motive of human life ... is a tendency and a striving to absorb or be absorbed in or united with other lives and all life ... As individuals we are indeed limited to a narrow spot in today, but as universalists we inherit all time and space'.[49] Similarly, Bellamy's story struggles to balance his ideal of absolute sympathy with individuality, and the privileged status of humans with their merging into the wider universe.

Bellamy's tale describes telepathy as a spiritual apotheosis. Unlike 'the laborious impotence of language', it enables people to bridge the 'gulf fixed between soul and soul'.[50] Mind-readers cannot lie or misconstrue each other because 'it is always one another's real and inmost thought that they read' (p. 398). They exchange their mental states directly instead of through material analogies: 'It is by the mind, not the eye, that these people know one another ... The absolute openness of their minds and hearts to one another makes their happiness far more dependent on the moral and mental qualities of their companions than upon their physical' (p. 408). Such perfect communication relies on Locke's view of thoughts as the property of a sovereign, inner self. Language, for Bellamy, is unreliable not because it cannot express thoughts, but because it does so linearly rather than, as they are held in the mind, simultaneously. Among the mind-readers, the narrator explains, 'pictures of the total mental state were communicated, instead of the imperfect descriptions of single thoughts which words at best could give' (p. 400–01). Again, semantic progress is imagined as accumulation and efficiency, searching for a comprehensive symbol that will condense many simultaneous thoughts into one. Yet, materialist psychology was challenging the assumption of a stable mind that preceded sensory and symbolic experience. As T. H. Huxley wrote in 1874, Descartes's claim that animals were machines could be equally applied to humans, whose bodies constantly acted without conscious reflection.[51] Further, words did not simply name phenomena but created them. Spencer had argued that perceptions which 'appear as one' were really successions of mental states compounded 'by constant association'.[52] Hence, the apprehension of an object, which seemed unitary through habit, actually involved the rapid, successive apprehension of distance, form, colour and movement. The apparently sovereign mind combining ideas simultaneously was an illusion produced by infinitesimal, successive mental states. Language thus named clusters of thoughts rather than individual ones, compounded arbitrarily and differing with the associations of individuals. Denser symbolic compounds would not offer a closer reflection of the mind but only a more elaborate fiction of it.

Bellamy's tale attempts to rescue Locke's autonomous mind by presenting it as emerging in tandem with telepathy. The more the mind-readers comprehend each other the more they comprehend themselves. However, this reproduces the Cartesian division between mechanical body and sovereign mind since there must be a deeper, 'inner' mind to transmit thoughts and 'read' those of others:

> Of all they see in the minds of others, that which concerns them most is the reflection of themselves, the photographs of their own characters ... [Man] is compelled to distinguish between this mental and moral self which has been made objective to him, and can be contemplated by him as impartially as if it were another's, from the inner ego which still remains subjective, unseen, and indefinable. In this inner ego the mind-readers recognize the essential identity and being, the noumenal self, the core of the soul, and the true hiding of its eternal life, to which the mind as well as the body is but the garment of a day. (pp. 410–11)

Bellamy glosses over the disintegration of an autonomous self with what psychologists call 'the homunculus fallacy', explaining cognition by positing a self-conscious agent behind it.[53] His telepathy penetrates the psyche only to bury it in a deeper 'inner ego'. The thoughts of the mind-reader become the external signs of this inner ego, which transmits and apprehends them as 'mental pictures' (p. 403). Minds abstract from bodies only to replicate the old duality, with a kind of mental body protecting their individuality: 'like the touch of shoulder to shoulder, like the clasping of hands, is the contact of their minds and their sensation of sympathy' (p. 402). Bellamy's mind-readers suggest both that the atoms of consciousness are knowable and nameable and that these atoms will reveal a stable, united identity. As one mind-reader comments to the narrator: 'It is you they understood, not your words' (p. 393). By focusing on the gaps between minds, the tale downplays the conceptual disintegration of the individual mind.

On a wider scale, telepathy and spiritualism promised both objective knowledge of the natural universe and mystical union with it. Similarly as such ideas protected individual souls by merging them in a collective, so they privileged humanity by merging it with the cosmos. This paradox is revealed in Byron A. Brooks's utopia *Earth Revisited* (1893), in which the contemporary narrator dies and reincarnates a century later. The New York author was a committed spiritualist and inventor of typewriters, printers and telegraph devices. Brooks's novel combined this knowledge of communication technology with his faith, imagining 'souls' transmitting messages beyond body and grave. By treating consciousness as convertible energy, telepathy offered to connect humans directly with the 'language' of nature. Charles Babbage had earlier imagined the conservation of energy immortalizing human speech, writing: 'Every atom, impressed with good and with ill, retains at once the motions which philosophers and sages have imparted to it ... The air itself is one vast library, on whose pages are forever written all that man has ever said or woman whispered'.[54] Spiritualists seized upon such images of endless energy transference to charge the cosmos with anthropocentric significance. In 1893 the American Samuel Weil claimed: 'There is a spiritual, as well as a physical evolution ... The whole universe, though apparently unmoral, has a sublime moral purpose and destiny. Nature is a tremendous workshop for the ultimate perfection of man'.[55] Instead of thoughts being mere temporary energy forms, the physical universe becomes an archive and inventory of human consciousness.[56]

Earth Revisited imagines this anthropocentric telos through the invention of 'harmonic telegraphs'. These machines convert thoughts into music that is transmittable across the globe as electric pulses. The narrator's guide Dr Merivale explains, 'you know that sound and speech, light, heat and electricity are all other forms of force known to us, are but pulsations of the all-pervading ether that fills the universe'. Thoughts and feelings are 'things' floating between bodies, as the narrator muses: 'Light, heat, sound, life and love itself, were but the pulses of the all-pervading spirit of the universe'.[57] Brooks conflates the imagined endurance of speech through the cosmos with the survival of thoughts and feelings beyond the body. The narrator pines for the long-dead sweetheart of his former life, and receives 'thought-messages' from her. These are manifested as both physical letters which seem to appear out of nowhere and, at another time, 'a small square of light' projecting 'in glowing letters, "Teresa lives. You shall see her"' (pp. 169, 203). Psychical life, while separable from the body, retains a presence and agency in the monistic universe, however elusive to nineteenth-century knowledge. As the narrator reflects, 'Matter cannot cease to be. Much less can the soul. The immortality of the atom is the guarantee of the immortality of the soul' (p. 315). The deceased Dr Merivale is quoted speaking to his daughter from beyond the grave, claiming to 'have demonstrated that the mind, the pure thought of man, can extend itself through the invisible ether which is the substance of the universe and impinge itself upon other minds' (p. 276). The mind is imagined escaping the body and its temporal logic, enabling communication across past and present. As in Bellamy's tale, so Brooks relies on traditional spiritual vocabulary to smooth over the tension between synchronic and diachronic semantics. In his vision, words are not arbitrary clusters of associations but vessels of eternal spirit. Material space and time must bend to the immortal human psyche, which remains necessarily mysterious, as Merivale comments: 'Nothing can be more mysterious than that I can talk to you; that the vibrations of the viewless air made by my lips can convey my thought to your mind, and that thus two souls can converse together in magnetic sympathy' (p. 201). The mystery derives from the assumption that coherent, autonomous selves precede speech rather than emerging through it.

Brooks's privileging of the human psyche enables him to present western science as progressing towards universal, extra-linguistic truth. His utopia illustrates this assumed universality through its future society communicating with extraterrestrials and animals. The possibility of signalling to other planets became a popular talking point in the 1880s and 1890s, with various theories advanced for finding a common language.[58] In 1892 Francis Galton proposed communicating with Mars via reflected solar rays, conveying the universal concepts of mathematics.[59] *Earth Revisited* imagines such signalling in practice, with Martians reciprocating. 'Truth is the same in all worlds', Merivale explains, so that the 'immense equilateral triangle' built on America's western plains was answered on Mars by the same figure, 'and, enclosing it, an immense circle of light – the symbol of all truth and perfection ... We are preparing to flood the desert of Sahara, leaving an immense circular island' (pp. 95–96). The assumption that sign-making develops in tandem with western values is also demonstrated in the utopia's speaking animals. The narrator meets a dog who understands English and replies in Morse code-like barks. This event might seem to resonate with the late-Victorian anxieties noted by Ferguson about the barriers disintegrating between animal and human communication.[60] Yet Brooks protects the privilege of human speech by depicting it as the telos of evolution. While Darwin described language as random mutations and adaptations, Brooks regards it, and its categories, as predestined. The dog has developed western standards of politeness and sympathy in tandem with his speech capacity. His human interpreter tells the narrator: 'He says you don't seem to recognize him. But he is delighted to see you again, apparently in health' (p. 79). The dog's owner hails the prospect of humans discovering 'the hidden thoughts and experiences and reasonings of the brutes, which have hitherto been as unknown to us as the depths of ocean or the composition of the stars' (p. 81). Yet, the discovery only reveals the same values and concepts of humans, or rather westerners, assumed to be the destiny of all evolution.

The anthropocentric (and western-centric) teleology on which language progressivism relied emerges most starkly in John Jacob Astor's scientific romance *A Journey in Other Worlds* (1894). Born into the rich New York Astor family, the author patented inventions including a pneumatic road improver and a 'vibratory disintegrator', which produced gas from peat moss.[61] Astor was a friend of the newspaper editor and spiritualist W. T. Stead, who may have informed his thinking, and perished alongside him on the *Titanic* in 1912. Astor's interest in spiritualism emerges in his tale of explorers who travel to Jupiter and Saturn, only to meet the spirits of dead humans. In Astor's vision, disembodied spirits represent a higher stage of life, which advances through increasing control over nature. The novel depicts human cultivation of nature, like Astor's own inventions, as an evolutionary destiny. Arriving on Jupiter, the first thought of Astor's voyagers is to regulate it, introducing crops and species from Earth. As one remarks, 'It would be an awful shame if we allowed it to lie unimproved'. Human life and, by extension, western civilization, are presented as inevitable stages in the universal progress; one explorer gauges Jupiter's arrested development on the basis that 'we certainly have seen no men, or anything like them, not even so much as a monkey'.[62] Later, on Saturn, the travellers meet the spirit of a deceased man, who explains that they form part of a wider, endless progression, which 'depends largely on your command of the forces of nature'. He predicts that humans will one day induce earthquakes and raise new continents, since 'God made man in his own image; does it not stand to reason that he will allow him to continue to become more and more like himself?' (pp. 155–56). Astor's super-evolved spirits present human consciousness as an emerging power, rather than product, of the universe.

This autonomy is contradictory, however, since it only emerges through the preset plan of a creator. Human discourse becomes immortal by embodying the expression of a higher being. The explorers are able to summon the spirits by prayer, their speech and thoughts penetrating the subtler levels of existence on which the spirits dwell. They then converse in English with a spirit, who apprehends their thought and speech as different manifestations of the same energy, stating: 'I see the vibrations of the grey matter of your brain as plainly as the movements of your lips; in fact, I see the thoughts in the embryonic state taking shape' (p. 159). The physical universe becomes a medium of 'souls', manifesting signals as the movements of a telegraph receiver register electromagnetic pulses. Astor's confident vision of total human mastery over nature, including death, again exposes the tension between the individual and the collective in language progress. The spirit's ability to foresee the speech and embryonic thoughts of the explorers undermines their self-mastery. Their progress towards disembodied, higher life is driven not by personal agency but by what Spencer called the 'Unknown Cause', a mysterious force that catalyzed evolution in all organisms.[63] As before, Astor preserves individual agency within this model through the incompatible logic of an immortal soul. Disembodied souls, the spirit claims, 'circulate' infinitely through the universe after being 'moulded' and 'stamp[ed]' on the 'mint' of Earth (p. 195). Unlike other organisms, humans acquire an unchanging essence, manifested in their consciousness. Yet, contradictorily, this essence is not fixed, as the spirit explains that disembodied souls continue to evolve and are only beginning to learn how to contact the embodied. Astor's coupling of perfect, telepathic communication with immortality is undermined by the evolutionary dynamic through which they emerge. His future humans are both produced by the universe's processes and, yet, independent of them; both constantly changing and coalescing, yet, eternal, individual souls. The deeper that predictive fictions probed the logic of language progress, the more they exposed its contradictions.

Questioning progress

One author who explored rather than avoided these contradictions was the young H. G. Wells. Influenced by Darwin, the former science teacher challenged ideas of teleological progress through his early scientific romances.[64] His reading in psychology and sociology influenced him to see language as a network of unstable associations, beyond individual control. Far from making language their tool, modern speakers seemed, to him, drones of mass suggestion. This view was as much political as scientific. The socialist-sympathizing Wells rejected Spencer's coupling of free-market economics with the growth of individuality. As his tale *The First Men in the Moon* implied, individual autonomy and collective unity in relation to language were not complementary but opposing tendencies. Further, with scientific nomenclature fragmenting into specialist vocabularies, Wells questioned the ideal of a united, comprehensive language, associating the search for it with dogmatism. However, Wells the utopian social-planner retained belief in some kind of language progress, regarding a global, scientific language as requisite for a peaceful world state. In later writings, he would repress his radical ideas about language, aligning with the authoritarian visions of earlier utopian authors.

Wells's close reading of Darwin made him sceptical of metaphysics and teleology and open to new arguments that rendered meaning wholly contextual. Darwin's view of nature as a self-regulating system paralleled the growing tendency among philologists to regard language as self-regulating. Whitney claimed that individual speakers made changes to language which spread or disappeared with majority usage, undirected by any external authority. Similarly, Darwin argued that species evolved from individual mutations, which spread when favoured by environmental pressures, without any overriding plan. Wells's tutor and friend Edwin R. Lankester observed that previously essential organs shriveled as they ceased to advantage the species. He extended this point to language change, noting that standards altered in line with the 'decay or diversion of literary taste'.[65] Darwin concurred with this view in *The Descent of Man* (1871), suggesting that language change was often as random as biological mutation. Many words appeared or changed meaning, he wrote, through 'mere novelty . . . for there is in the mind of man a love for slight changes in all things'.[66] Both words and species could only be understood, then, through their position in wider contexts. Hence, Darwin compared vestigial organs to written silent letters; ancestral traces became 'useless' in the current natural or spoken environment.[67] While language had, perhaps, progressed as a capacity, its meanings did not develop according to some transcendent plan but depended on context.[68] The philosopher G. F. Stout wrote in 1891 that 'the signification of words varies according to the context in which they appear', rendering the idea of a 'usual meaning' for a term a 'fiction'.[69] These comments were published in *Mind*, a journal which Wells read frequently and would later write for himself. Such ideas about the contextuality of thought and verbal meaning influenced new views of the language of science as necessarily tentative and pragmatic. In 1907 the psychologist and close friend of Wells, William James would describe the naming of things 'less as a solution, then, than as a program for more work, and more particularly as an indication of the ways in which existing realities may be changed'.[70] As scientific disciplines polarized into different, incompatible logics, so words appeared increasingly relative, signifying only within specific uses and contexts.

The influence of these ideas on Wells can be seen as early as 1891 in his first published article 'The Rediscovery of the Unique'. He suggests here that primordial humans might have been better suited for scientific investigation than modern westerners because they were not bound by dogmatic classifications. Rather than grouping phenomena under artificial common nouns, their speech of concrete substantives recognized that 'all being is unique'.[71] Wells concluded: 'Science is a match that man has just got alight. He thought he was in a room ... and that his light would be reflected from and display walls inscribed with wonderful secrets and pillars carved with philosophical systems wrought into harmony'. Yet, now that the match was alight, he 'see[s] his hands lit and just a glimpse of himself and the patch he stands on visible, and around him, in place of all that human comfort and beauty he anticipated – darkness still'.[72] Language obstructed induction with assumptions of underlying order, as Karl Pearson similarly wrote: 'men of science are coming to recognise that mechanism is not at the bottom of phenomena, but is only the conceptual shorthand by aid of which they can briefly describe and resume phenomena. That all science is description and not explanation'.[73] In this light, the goals of linguistic precision and unity appeared dangerously dogmatic. Pearson worried about the necessary 'obscurity' of language in physics, which often caused physicists to become 'entangled in the meshes of such pseudo-sciences as natural theology and spiritualism'.[74] The young Wells equally criticized psychical researchers for their 'over-hasty' belief, mistaking words such as *spirit* for transcendent realities.[75] His concern about words shaping facts instead of vice versa also emerged in his early journalism on science teaching. In an 1894 article he criticized the past 'elaborate system of lecturing, note dictating, "model answer" grinding ... and a mechanical copying out from the text-book'. Courses should instead, he argued, 'develop a clear and interrogative habit of mind' through practical experiment, rather than rote-teaching theory.[76] Intellectual freedom consisted of disturbing settled linguistic systems, not conforming to them.

The idea that language mechanization encroached upon individual mental autonomy haunted several of Wells's early prophetic fictions. His tale 'A Story of the Days to Come' (1897) depicts lovers from different social classes, Elizabeth and Denton, eloping together. This defiance of convention paralleled the life of Wells; he had escaped the life of a draper to become a teacher and writer, and divorced his cousin-wife to live with his middle-class former pupil. However, such non-conformity is more difficult to imagine in Wells's future, with mass crèches and hypnotism indoctrinating people as to their place in society. Chapter 4 explores how Wells repeatedly used the phonograph as an image of verbal and mental conformity, and such machines are ubiquitous in his future world. Regulating speech and behaviour through constant suggestion, they minimize disorderly individualism. Citizens mechanically quote mantras, such as 'violence is no remedy', from the 'Modern Man's Book of Moral Maxims'.[77] The psychologist Edmund Gurney had suggested that language might circumvent thought by suggestion, eliciting effects beneath conscious volition. Gurney described hypnosis as '*conscious* reflex action', by which hypnotists established nervous associations, stimulating subjects to automatic 'words or movements' on cue and without thought.[78] In this way, Elizabeth's father pays a hypnotist to wipe his daughter's memory of her relationship with Denton. When Denton accosts her in the street, she speaks 'almost as one who repeats a lesson. "No, I do not know him. I know – I do not know him"' (p. 191). Such verbal suggestion also occurs through advertisements bombarding pedestrians with abbreviated messages. Far from advancing knowledge, these shortened phrases are merely a trick of the market hawker. On the street, projected text advertising a hat shop declares: '"ets r chip t'de", or simply "ets". And in spite of all these efforts ... so trained became one's eyes and ears to ignore all sorts of advertisement, that many a citizen had passed that place thousands of times and was still unaware of the existence of the Suzannah Hat Syndicate' (p. 242). Consumerism erases individual expression and imagination. Dreams become standardized commodities which people 'order' from hypnotists, while Elizabeth's father frowns on Denton's archaic tendency to write poems. The couple's rebellion involves their invention of 'a little language of broken English that was, they fancied, their private possession'

(p. 183). This extends to their child, whom they nickname 'Dings' while attempting to raise her themselves, before poverty forces them to leave her in the state crèche.[79] The erosion of mental-linguistic autonomy is illustrated most pathetically by Elizabeth's other, middle-class suitor, Bindon. Facing death, he resolves to record his voice for posterity, only to realize that he has nothing to say. The narration verbalizes his thoughts: 'Might one not try a sonnet? A penetrating voice to echo down the ages, sensuous, sinister, and sad ... In the course of half an hour he spoilt three phonographic coils, got a headache' and abandoned the plan (p. 318). Wells's mechanization of language renders people products instead of masters of discourse, robbed of an individual voice.

Wells's political concerns emerge more starkly in *When the Sleeper Wakes* (1899), in which verbal mechanization brings 'aristocratic tyranny'.[80] The Victorian protagonist Graham is transported two centuries hence to a world where revolution has just overthrown the old order. Yet, the rebel leader Ostrog has no interest in empowering the masses, regarding them as mere tools of suggestion. He explains: 'The day of democracy is past ... The common man now is a helpless unit. In these days we have this great machine of the city, and an organisation complex beyond his understanding ... The Crowd is a huge foolish beast ... It can still be tamed and driven' (pp. 235, 237). In 1894 Wells had reviewed Benjamin Kidd's *Social Evolution*, which argued that societal progress reduced the intelligence of the masses as they acquired fixed roles.[81] For the majority, Kidd wrote, 'simple-minded and single-minded devotion' to one's duties were becoming more important than intellectual inquiry.[82] Wells's future education system extends this process, drilling people's verbal-mental habits through intensive hypnosis:

> Instead of years of study candidates had substituted a few weeks of trances, and during the trances expert coaches had simply to repeat all the points necessary for adequate answering ... all operations conducted under finite rules, of a quasi-mechanical sort that is, were now systematically relieved from the wanderings of imagination and emotion, and brought to an unexampled pitch of accuracy. Little children of the labouring classes, so soon as they were of sufficient age to be hypnotised, were thus converted into beautifully punctual and trustworthy machine minders, and released forthwith from the long, long thoughts of youth. (pp. 215–16)

With most children raised by machines, people become correspondingly mechanical, their actions and thoughts circumscribed by rigid verbal routines. Needing only to perform simple, repetitive tasks, the underclass speaks a tongue akin to the images of 'primitive' language explored in the next chapter. Among factory hands, Graham hears 'scraps like Pigeon English, like "nigger" dialect, blurred and mangled distortions ... with the drifting corpses of English words therein' (p. 133). The same process has occurred in 'A Story of the Days to Come', in which the underground machine-workers fight and snarl at each other in barely intelligible 'dialect'. An equivalent 'dialect, a code of thought' narrows the sympathies and ideas of the upper world, preventing them from challenging the status quo: 'a language of "culture", which aimed by a sedulous search after fresh distinction to widen perpetually the space between itself and "vulgarity"' (pp. 265–66). Rigid class boundaries render people incapable of imagining or verbalizing anything outside of their social perspective. Wells's societies of the future divide and rule through verbal parochialism, narrowing mental interests and sympathies.

Verbal integration also limits individual agency, with mass media homogenizing speech and ideas. Ostrog's elite control the masses by instilling habitual, barely conscious verbal associations. Phonographic speakers or 'babble machines' in every street and home dispense non-stop propaganda slogans which the population echoes. When rebels refuse to disarm after the revolution, Ostrog tells Graham: 'We are setting the Babble Machines to work with counter suggestions in the cause of law and order' (p. 234). Ostrog seems to reference Gustave Le Bon's influential work *The Crowd: A Study of the Popular Mind* (1896), mocking Graham's democratic ideals: 'The Crowd as Ruler! Even in your days that creed had been tried and condemned' (p. 235). Wells would cite Le Bon in his later non-fiction, and his tale coheres with the French sociologist's arguments about mass media manipulating populations.[83] Le Bon claimed that language addressed to the masses used words associatively, evoking vague mental 'images' and emotions: 'the word is merely as it were the button of an electric bell that calls them up'.[84] The masses of Wells's tale seem subject to such verbal automatism. As a troop of African police put down a rebellion in Paris, 'all the mechanisms were discoursing upon that topic, and the repetition of the people made the huge hive buzz with such phrases as "Lynched policemen", "Women burnt alive", "Fuzzy Wuzzy"' (p. 253). Again, the shortening of utterances renders meanings less precise, as sound bites evoke vague associations (such as racial stereotypes) rather than conveying compacted information. Broadcasting Graham's voice and image to the world, Ostrog instructs him to 'say something': 'Not what you used to call a Speech, but what our people call a Word – just one sentence, six or seven words ... If I might suggest – "I have awakened and my heart is with you"' (p. 148). Abstracted from particular contexts, words lose their semantic precision, devolving into emotional triggers. Wells's tale critiques language progressivism by presenting its processes as reducing mental-linguistic autonomy. Yet, it also questions the possibility of total, centralized control over language and thought, since meaning is contextual. This renders Ostrog's power less secure than he imagines. He mocks Graham's democratic ideals, observing that the babble machines 'taught' the people their revolutionary song during a palace coup. However, Graham wonders, 'can you teach them to forget it?' (p. 283). The workers demand further political reform, and continue to sing the song even as the machines instruct them not to. Meaning slips from Ostrog's control as the rebels appropriate his song and invest it with new significations. They similarly listen to the babble machines for information on the coming strike against them, ignoring the calls to stop rebelling. The semantic instability of language which enables elites to manipulate the population might also be the basis of resistance to such authorities. The narrative leaves this question open, ending with Graham's death in aerial combat, the fate of the revolution uncertain.

Wells's scepticism of language's progress found its most radical expression in his fictions of extraterrestrial telepathy. These tales critique the goals of objective representation and communication between minds as dogmatic and destructive of individuality, imagination and sympathy. In 1896, when Galton expanded his ideas about communicating with extraterrestrials into an article in the *Fortnightly Review*, Wells voiced a different opinion on the subject. 'No phase of anthropomorphism is more naïve than the supposition of men on Mars', he wrote. 'The place of such a conception in the world of thought is with the anthropomorphic cosmogonies and religions invented by the childish conceit of primitive man.'[85] Wells would illustrate this point two years later in *The War of the Worlds*, in which Martians seek to exterminate humanity. Although the invaders are mentally united by telepathy, they have no sympathy for or interest in communicating with humans. The novel refers to a 'great light' observed on Mars in 1894, but the narrator speculates that rather than being a sign to planet Earth, it was 'the casting of the huge gun, in the vast pit sunk into their planet, from which their shots were fired at us'.[86] When the authorities signal to the landed visitors with flags, 'the Martians took as much notice of such advances as we should of the lowing of a cow' (p. 60). Collective consciousness folds their sympathy into an exclusive, closed system, rendering them less communicative with outsiders than the apparently primitive humans. The narrator remarks of the beings whose brains have expanded while their bodies shrivelled: 'Without the body the brain would, of course, become a mere selfish intelligence, without any of the emotional substratum of the human being' (p. 211). The Martian collective recapitulates the egotism of supposedly 'lower' life, becoming one body with no remorse for life outside of it. Darwin had presented sympathy as an instinctive inheritance rather than a product of civilization, positing common emotional expressions between humans and animals (see Chapter 4). Wells similarly suggests that mind is built upon physical sensation and instinct so that, disembodied, it loses the ability to engage with other life forms.[87] Equally, human language is incapable of comprehending the Martians when fixed by dogma. This problem is demonstrated through a curate who shelters with the narrator from the invaders, and who struggles to reconcile them with his scriptural perspective. '"What does it mean?" he said. "What do these things mean? . . . Why are these things permitted? What sins have we done? . . . What are these Martians?"' The narrator's responding question ('What are we?') highlights the arrogance of humanity in positioning itself and its categories at the centre of the universe (p. 112). The curate assumes that all things must have a human significance, the whole cosmos being utterances of God. His anthropocentricity blinds him to the randomness of nature, which develops without transcendental plan. The more fixed and internally consistent a communication system becomes, the less able it is to engage with chaotic reality or the perspectives of outsiders.

Wells extended his critique of utopian language progressivism in *The First Men in the Moon*, in which two lunar explorers encounter an underground civilization of antlike creatures. Captured by these 'Selenites', as the explorers calls them, the eccentric Dr Cavor reasons: 'The problem is communication . . . Of course they are minds and we are minds; there must be something in common. Who knows how far we may not get to an understanding?'[88] Wells's narrative subsequently challenges Cavor's assumption that thought and truth are universal rather than perspectival. Like the Martians, the Selenites seem to have perfected communication, conversing together without ambiguity. Yet, again, this fixed system of signs and concepts renders them unable to sympathize or empathize with outsiders. Further, their collective consciousness exposes the contradiction of progressive individual autonomy within a wider integration. Cavor's first attempts to communicate with the Selenites fail because he accosts individuals, assuming that they are 'minds' rather than one, collective mind. Different classes in the colony perform different mental operations, communicating together in mechanized codes. Calfherds on the moon's surface speak and think in a 'dialect' of 'accomplished mooncalf technique', while the mathematician's 'voice becomes a mere stridulation for the stating of formula; he seems deaf to all but properly enunciated problems' (p. 305). Some Selenites are all muscle with scarcely any mental activity, relaying sensations and following nervous commands from the 'Grand Lunar' at the centre of the network. Even this, however, is only a 'gigantic ganglion' with no individual psyche; other Selenites must discharge the various operations of cognition, 'wabbling jellies of knowledge' 'carried from place to place in a sort of sedan tub' (pp. 306–07). Whereas anthropocentric utopias imagined telepathy developing with the greater individuation of minds, Wells's Selenites suggest the opposite. Their collective identity relies on the obliteration of individual thought, agency and expression. Cavor remarks: 'every citizen knows his place. He is born to that place, and the elaborate discipline of training and education and surgery he undergoes fits him at last so completely to it that he has neither ideas nor organs for any purpose beyond it' (p. 304). The Selenites' disregard for individual life is evidenced by their passivity after Cavor and his companion initially kill some of them. They only cut off Cavor's communication with planet Earth, and possibly kill him, after learning the unthinkable – that human nations wage war on each other, and thus threaten the Selenite collective. The future of communication represented by the Selenites does not enhance individual identity but rather destroys it, along with the western values it reflects.

Wells's tale satirizes the teleology of language progressing towards universal truth through the parallel development of humans and Selenites. Rather than converging, their world-views are mutually incomprehensible, and Wells equivocates over their relative superiority. The Selenites regard humans as living in 'social savagery', storing their knowledge in books rather than in the distended heads of a class born to memorize. Cavor comments of the moon-dwellers, 'in intelligence, morality, and social wisdom are they colossally greater than men' (p. 291). This superiority seems to be demonstrated by the Selenites gradually learning broken English and western numerals, while Cavor fails to master their symbols. However, the humans innovate technology to travel to the moon while the Selenites remain static. Wells seems to have partly built his Selenites upon Galton's speculations about communicating with extraterrestrials. The Selenites somewhat resemble the race of 'highly developed ants' whom Galton imagined signalling the principles of arithmetic and geometry to planet Earth. Galton's ants signal numerals up to 8 rather than using a decimal system, reflecting the senders' '6 limbs and 2 antennae'.[89] Yet, Galton assumes that the universal truth of mathematics will bridge such vast biocultural differences. Cavor mentions a 'paper by the late Professor

Galton' on signals that could convey 'those broad truths that must underlie all conceivable mental existences' (p, 146). Although, initially, the Selenites ignore Cavor's attempts to trace equilateral triangles with his finger, they later speak broken English through a joint effort. The further communication advances, however, the more incompatible human and Selenite perspectives appear. The moon-dwellers learn concrete nouns and verbs easily enough, Cavor states, but 'when it came to abstract nouns, to prepositions, and the sort of hackneyed figures of speech, by means of which so much is expressed on earth, it was like diving in cork-jackets' (p. 300). Selenite understanding depends on analogies with their own anthill-like society, rendering Cavor's descriptions of terrestrial life opaque. Cavor reports of his conversations with the Grand Lunar:

> For a long time I had great difficulty in making him understand the nature of a house. To him and his attendant Selenites it seemed, no doubt, the most whimsical thing in the world that men should build houses when they might descend into excavations, and an additional complication was introduced by the attempt I made to explain that men had originally begun their homes in caves, and that they were now taking their railways and many establishments beneath the surface ... There was also a considerable tangle due to an equally unwise attempt on my part to explain about mines ... I told him of lions and tigers, and here it seemed as though we had come to a deadlock. For, save in their waters, there are no creatures in the moon not absolutely domestic and subject to his will ... [T]he idea of anything strong and large existing 'outside' in the night is very difficult for them. (pp. 329–32)

The idea that meaning is context-bound would later lead linguists such as Edward Sapir to argue for linguistic relativity. 'No two languages are ever sufficiently similar to be considered as representing the same social reality', Sapir wrote in 1929: 'The worlds in which different societies live are distinct worlds, not merely the same world with different labels attached'.[90] Wells's alien communications prefigure this notion to an extent, suggesting that language develops towards the expression of not universal truths but only particular social perspectives. However, as I will show, Wells ultimately balked at these ideas because they threatened his goal of a world state. Having released the genie of linguistic relativism in his early fiction, the Edwardian Wells would struggle to bottle it up again.

World peace and a global *lingua franca*

The ideals of scientific objectivity and a global *lingua franca* became mutually validating in the late nineteenth century. 'How great a help it would be,' wrote the English physiologist Michael Foster in 1894, 'if there were only an international tribunal before whom every new name had to go, and who would, as it were, stamp the coin of science before it was allowed to pass into circulation'.[91] A single, international speech promised to prove the universality of scientific truth, while the empirical facts of science promised to raise language above sociogeographic perspectives. Lorraine Daston notes that botanists such as Alphonse de Candolle strove to decompound and name their objects of study along internationally agreed lines, like a 'global map pieced together by a community of far-flung observers'.[92] Such work coincided with efforts to construct a logical, denationalized *lingua franca*. In 1879 the German priest Johann Schleyer combined vocabulary and grammar from many languages to invent Volapük, followed a decade later by Zamenhof's Esperanto, then Idiom Neutral, Ido and many more.[93] The Austrian physicist and artificial language proponent Richard Lorenz wrote in 1910 that scientists had set the template for these systems. Developing uniform specialist vocabularies between their countries, he stated, they had become 'accustomed to think in this language apart from their nationality'.[94] Other commentators envisaged the building of a global, scientific communication system through an expanded form of English. English's mongrel heritage, importing words from diverse sources, seemed to serve as a model for future development, pooling the world's knowledge into one gigantic vocabulary.[95] The ideal of linguistic unity glossed over the intensifying divergence of the sciences into specialist technical dialects, preserving faith in monolithic truth. While Wells was suspicious of efforts to fix language, he also rejected parochialism, seeking truth in the synthesis of diverse perspectives. His hopes for a rational, scientific future were thus bound up with the need for a common medium of intercourse and a global state. This commitment led much of his Edwardian writing to succumb to the teleology and contradictions of progressivism that he had previously exposed. Wells's inconsistency illustrates the ideological stakes of language progress, which sought a more peaceful world through the ascent of science. Whilst nationalist militarism grew across Europe, Wells imagined linguistic unification as the prerequisite to a rational, peaceful future. And while he dreamed of linguistic unity on the macro level, he struggled to reconcile this with his other ideal of individual verbal-mental freedom. Wells's desire for both verbal fixity and flexibility encapsulated the conflicted goals of language progressivism, seeking stability, yet change; authoritarianism, yet individualism.

The tension between prescriptive authority and individual autonomy inevitably haunted projects in the period to build a new global language. Zamenhof dreamed of Esperanto producing mental and emotional synthesis across the world, predicting that, 'Books being the same for everyone, education, ideals, convictions, aims, would be the same too'.[96] How, though, could such homogeneity be achieved without the forceful imposition of one language or social perspective upon other speech communities? No sooner did Schleyer and Zamenhof begin to win supporters than factions appeared demanding changes to the languages.[97] Zamenhof commented that, with knowledge currently divided across many tongues, 'we are often obliged, even in speaking our own language, to borrow words and expressions from foreigners, or to express our thoughts inexactly'. With a single language 'the prime motor of civilisation ... would grow richer, and reach a higher degree of perfection than is found in any of those now existing'.[98] Yet, even if speakers retained their native tongues, translating their expressions into an international language required common, a priori concepts from outside of social contexts. Otherwise, as several commentators noted, the new world language would gradually fragment into separate dialects, adapted to the experiences of different communities.[99] As Wells gradually convinced himself, the future world language would need to be controlled by a central authority to prevent it dividing again into isolated variants, reflecting local perspectives.

Wells's interest in a world language grew through the Edwardian period along with his belief in a future world state. Mixing with socialist reformers such as Beatrice and Sidney Webb and G. B. Shaw, he came to imagine the future as a process of rationalization, overcoming dogmas such as nationalism.[100] In 1897 he began corresponding with the philosopher of language Victoria, Lady Welby, who argued that the maturation of science and civilization were entwined with the rationalization of language.[101] This idea was reflected in his book *Anticipations* (1901), which predicted a future world state mediated by one language. He echoed Zamenhof's rhetoric of universal access to the world's knowledge, writing that, as scientists cooperated in a global community, people 'will escape from the wreckage of their too small and swamped and foundering social systems, only up the ladders of what one may call the aggregating tongues'.[102] In every region where multiple languages are spoken, 'Almost inevitably with travel, with transport communications, with every condition of human convenience insisting upon it, formally or informally a bi-lingual compromise will come into operation'.[103] Wells imagined a common language as an amalgamation of national perspectives in *A Modern Utopia* (1905). He distinguished his vision from previous 'static' utopias which had claimed to depict the end of development. Unlike the rigid, repressive futures that had formed his earlier dystopias, his ideal society would be 'kinetic', continuing to involve 'friction, conflicts and waste, but the waste will be enormously less than in our world'.[104] A global speech would not be brought about by one tongue defeating others, but by the 'wedding and survival of several in a common offspring'. Different ways of segmenting reality across tongues would be 'superposed and then welded together through bilingual and trilingual compromises' (p. 22). Wells's imagery allows for *parole* to react upon the universal *langue*, with individuals and groups all adding and adjusting bricks in the overall edifice.

Wells argued that framing eternal linguistic rules ran contrary to science, assuming that 'the whole intellectual basis of mankind is established, that the rules of logic, the systems of counting and measurement, the general categories and schemes of resemblance and difference, are established for the human mind for ever' (p. 20). Yet inductive science undermined a priori concepts, showing that 'there is no being, but a universal becoming of individualities ... What folly, then, to dream of mapping out our minds in however general terms, of providing for the endless mysteries of the future a terminology and an idiom!' Thus, Wells's future world language in *A Modern Utopia* has no single designer or group of designers and will never be finalized. 'All mankind will' possess 'a common resonance of thought, but the language they will speak will still be a living tongue, an animated system of imperfections, which every individual man will infinitesimally modify' (pp. 21–22). People will unite as language-makers rather than be united under a language predesigned by elites. Wells's vision of verbal autonomy within unity remains at a high altitude, saving him the trouble of explaining how all individuals could equally influence a scientific technocracy. As the rise of Standard English showed, processes such as urbanization and state centralization inevitably privileged some speakers over others. Further, how could speakers contribute equally to the language if they were not innately equal, as Wells implied through his tentative support of eugenics?[105]

Wells was still avoiding these questions in his 1913 novel *The World Set Free*, which imagines leaders forming a world state after the destruction of atomic warfare. Although figuring English as the base of the future *lingua franca*, Wells is careful to denationalize it, rendering Modern English as akin to Anglo-Saxon before its mixture with Norman French:

> The language was shorn of a number of grammatical peculiarities, the distinctive forms for the subjunctive mood for example and most of its irregular plurals were abolished; its spelling was systematised and adapted to

the vowel sounds in use upon the continent of Europe, and a process of incorporating foreign nouns and verbs commenced that speedily reached enormous proportions. Within ten years from the establishment of the World Republic the New English Dictionary had swelled to include a vocabulary of 250,000 words, and a man of 1900 would have found considerable difficulty in reading an ordinary newspaper.[106]

Wells plays down the Anglocentrism of his vision: English does not simply absorb other tongues but is restructured by them. Here he strays into the logic of verbal efficiency, suggesting that no past meanings will be lost in the aggregation. While Edwardian speakers would struggle to read future English, 'on the other hand, the men of the new time could still appreciate the Older English literature'. This claim seems bizarre, given the great lexical and grammatical changes envisaged. Wells imagines the 'scientific' restructuring of language offering an objective view-from-nowhere in which meanings are no longer bound by context. Or, rather, all possible contexts are paradoxically compressed into a composite language. Again, semantic accumulation implies the tightening of prescriptive authority, with language acting as a vast archive of the past. Against the rhetoric of democratic autonomy, Wells ends *A Modern Utopia* with the narrator hoping to dissolve into 'a synthetic wider being, the great State, mankind, in which we all move and go, like blood corpuscles, like nerve cells, it may be at times like brain cells, in the body of a man' (p. 372). Similarly, *The World Set Free* avoids problems of semantic relativism by treating speech and thought as the behaviour of vast Spencerian networks rather than individuals. As one of the organizers of the world government King Egbert declares, 'Science . . . is the mind of the race', imposing an imaginary unity upon diverse theories and methods (p. 162). The narrator explains the prior carnage of world war through the discrepancy that 'the political structure of the world at that time was everywhere extraordinarily behind the collective intelligence' (pp. 76–77). As in the utopias discussed above, Wells buries problems of semantic instability by presenting language as the internal communication of a single 'mind'.

In spite of his individualist ideals, Wells sometimes implies in his Edwardian writing that scientific, global speech will require the sacrifice of individual expression. In *The World Set Free*, a vaguely described 'World Council' sets the rules of global speech, which spreads in tandem with standardized education and urbanization, wiping out rural communities and dialect. The narrator states: 'That shy, unstimulated life of the lonely hovel . . . that hoarding, half-inanimate existence away from books, thought or social participation and in constant contact with cattle, pigs, poultry and their excrement is passing away out of human experience' (pp. 216–17). Instead of combining sociohistorical perspectives, Wells's world language replaces them with that of a scientific elite. His linguistic prescriptivism comes into sharper focus in his treatise on social evolution *Mankind in the Making* (1903), in which he offers instructions on the treatment of infants. Children should not be confused by different tongues, he proclaims, or mothers succumbing to their instinctive 'feelings' and babbling 'baby talk'. Rather, the child 'requires to be surrounded by people speaking one language, and speaking it with a uniform accent'.[107] This strict regimentation of infant speech and experience echoes the mass conditioning which Wells had previously warned of in his dystopias. Such homogenization is necessary, Wells explains, to stabilize meaning in language. While the advancement of science procures 'a perpetual necessity for new words, words to express new ideas and new relationships', these should only be framed by experts in their fields. 'The neologisms of the street and the saloon' are detrimental to such progress, perpetuating obsolete concepts and muddling word definitions.[108] Wells imagined countering such unregulated verbal invention with 'an English Language Society'. Words and their uses, he states, would be governed by a 'non-hereditary aristocracy' imposing 'a common scientific and, in its higher stages at least, a common educational organization'.[109] Wells's authoritarian impulse would ultimately lead him to the vision in *The Shape of Things to Come* (1932) of a global 'Language Bureau' fixing the uses of words.[110] He also campaigned in the 1930s for the creation of a 'World Brain' or global encyclopaedia 'to hold men's minds together in something like a common interpretation of reality'.[111] Global cooperation seemed only achievable through homogenization of speech and thought around a central authority.

Wells illustrated his belief in the necessity of a single, centrally controlled language in his novel of impending global conflict *The War in the Air* (1908). The tale presents linguistic nationalism as a driving force behind war and imperialism. Instead of combining their language and knowledge for the common good, military powers seek to force their national speech on others. Thus, while France and Britain consolidate their empires, 'the German alliance still struggled to achieve its dream of imperial expansion, and its imposition of the German language on a forcibly united Europe'.[112] In contrast to the scientists who were striving to pool their knowledge in one language and community, the tale depicts governments and individuals divided by distrust, selfishness and misunderstanding. The novel's pointless world war is shortly preceded by an engineer developing a new flying machine and selling it to the highest-bidding government. Different languages, and the national perspectives they encode, prevent states from empathizing and sympathizing with each other, escalating the conflicts. This process is played out in miniature when Wells's cockney anti-hero Bert Smallways is marooned with two German soldiers, and their inability to communicate precipitates a 'war' between them. Having reluctantly killed one, Bert wishes to befriend the other who has fled, but is prevented by the language barrier: 'If I knew some German, I'd 'oller. It's jest not knowing German does it. You can't explain' (p. 226). Yet mere mechanical language-learning is still insufficient to overcome narrow-minded nationalism, as Wells demonstrates through the mixed-heritage German commander Lieutenant Kurt. Half English and schooled in England, he speaks with the colloquialisms of its privileged class, exclaiming 'ra-ther!' and promising to give America 'what for' (pp. 85–86). Upon hearing of the sinking of Germany's prize warship, he vacillates between linguistic identities: '"Barbarossa disabled and sinking!" he cried. "Gott im himmel! Der alte Barbarossa! Aber welch ein braver Krieger!" ... For a time he was wholly German. Then he became English again. "Think of it, Smallways!"' (p. 111). While intellectually capable of switching between tongues, Kurt's emotions cling to an essential nationhood, asserting that he is 'German nonetheless' without explaining how. Esperanto makes a brief appearance on bilingual advertisements when Bert crash-lands in an American town. His problems communicating even in American English, though, suggest that no two nations can share a 'common' language while remaining grounded in nationalist perspectives. This is highlighted by his attempt to buy food in a local 'shop' for English shillings: '"He calls A store A shop," said the proprietor, "and he wants A meal for A shilling. May I ask you, sir, what part of America you hail from?"' (p. 235). The autonomy of nation states causes languages to diverge, reflecting different practices and world-views. The only solution discernible in Wells's Edwardian fiction is a scientific elite directing speech and thought into a single channel. While the World Council controls language in *The World Set Free*, psychologists prepare to regiment the population's cognition. As the leader Karenin states: 'Psychologists are learning how to mould minds, to reduce and remove bad complexes of thought and motive, to relieve pressures and broaden ideas' (pp. 279–80). The hypnotism and mass suggestion that Wells once feared become triumphs of social integration. Unlike his dystopias, which imagined the effects of such techniques upon individuals, Wells's state-building visions remain at a distance, avoiding the logical contradictions that his earlier fiction had exposed.

Wells's work illustrates the amorphousness of language progressivism as a discourse, serving equally socialist and capitalist, imperialist and internationalist agendas. It also illustrates the yearning which progressivism expressed for a transcendental authority that would reveal universal truth outside of sociohistorical perspectives. In contrast to Wells's earlier mockery of spiritualist anthropocentrism, *The World Set Free* ends with the ageing Karenin facing death without fear of oblivion. 'For indeed is it Karenin who has been sitting here talking', he asks a friend; 'is it not rather a common mind, Fowler, that has played about between us?' (p. 283). The following war years would see Wells attempting to resurrect monotheism in *God the Invisible King* (1917). His temporary conversion to the idea of 'a personal and intimate God' put a religious name to the ultimate truth which he had previously imagined as the end of progress.[113] Wells's dream of a united, scientific language assumed that such truth could one day be represented. This faith in science as the ultimate aggregator of thought contradicted prevailing trends. As the Introduction above has outlined, investigators increasingly used pragmatic technical vocabularies for specific problems with no fixed semantic centre. Wells had bemoaned this tendency in 1894, warning that researchers were isolating themselves by writing 'in the dialect of their science'.[114] Such anxiety about linguistic disunity stemmed from the fear that no coherent, external authority existed to render language objective. The notion that language evolved independently of speakers' intentions contained the seed of semantic relativism, confining meaning to context. However, the utopian desire for a transcendent purpose amidst the rapid changes of modernity caused writers from Bellamy to Wells to ignore such implications. As world war loomed, so Wells clung to the hope that science and civilization were more than arbitrary signs for relative concepts. Language progressivism kept semantic and epistemological relativism at bay by interpreting their symptoms, such as ambiguity, as transitions in a wider teleology. As the next chapter explores, this teleology depended on contrasting classifications of primitive language to demonstrate the operations of progress. The future could only be predictable through opposing images of the past.

CHAPTER 2

Primitive language in imperial, prehistoric and scientific romances

In the mid nineteenth century humanity's past expanded massively. The excavation of human tools and remains beneath long-extinct species reduced millennia of civilization to a brief epilogue, preceded by many forgotten chapters of history.[1] This past expanded still further in the wake of Darwin's arguments for the transmutation of species. These revelations stretched the history of language far beyond written records and complicated its imagined origins. As Sayce commented in 1874, 'our sole wonder must be, not at the diversity of languages, but at the paucity of the wrecks of ancient speech that still remain spread over the face of the earth. The modern races of mankind are but the selected residuum of the infinitely varied species that have passed away: the same surely will hold good of language'.[2] Lacking direct source material, linguists and creative writers generated narratives of the primitive linguistic past by inverting models of language progress. Primitive language and civilized, progressive language were defined in binary opposition to each other. If civilized language was precise, efficient and objective, then primitive language could be imagined as vague, tautologous and subjective, chained to the instinctive body and societal custom. The figure of the primitive speaker thus acted as a surrogate for anxieties about the roles of context and instinct in communication, which undermined the ideal of objective discourse. It is, therefore, unsurprising that the white, middle-class, male writers discussed here typically represented the primitive speaker as other (be it non-European, female, working-class or extinct subspecies). Others have explored how the imperial romance genre interacted with anthropological writing to produce images of humanity's primitive past.[3] This chapter similarly argues that visions of primitive language grew in tandem with forms of romance fiction, which offered speculative spaces to elaborate and test these visions. This dynamic can be traced through Haggard and Allen's tales of interactions between different races, and in early examples of the prehistoric romance. However, the more that science and fiction attempted to define primitive speech, the more they eroded the boundaries between it and supposedly civilized language. Wells and London's evolutionary romances highlight this issue, revealing the 'primitive' foundations on which western language was built.

Body language

In 1864 the British explorer William Winwood Reade wrote of the difficulties due to their language of converting Africans to Christianity:

> The African dialects are minute, but always physical. They have few words to express the commonest qualities or emotions ... Mere reason is cold and unintelligible to the savage. He must be terrified and awed before his languid nature can be excited to enthusiasm. The fire and the sword are tangible weapons of faith; words appear to him mere shadows.[4]

Winwood Reade's words vividly exemplify the popular Victorian construction of primitive speech as inseparable from the body, enslaved to its urges and sensations. Such views reversed the logic of progressive verbal disembodiment to imagine humanity's nonage, when symbols were not yet distinct from the bodies transmitting them. Embodied, primitive speech enabled writers to transfer on to an exotic other anxieties about the arbitrariness of classification, springing as it did from bodily senses and associations. Yet, paradoxically, primitive speech was also imagined as alienated from the body. Some writers suggested that it obstructed empirical induction with dogmatic superstition and taboos, which overrode evidence of the senses. In this way, primitive speech transposed on to the raced or gendered other anxieties about the influence of society upon individual thought and expression, which undermined speaker autonomy. Thus while one tendency located primitive speech in the individual, subjective body, another defined it as the suppression of individual perspectives by a rigid social body. This conflict is illustrated in the imperial romances of H. R. Haggard.

Nineteenth-century progressives constructed primitive speech as unconscious and automatic, like a bodily reflex. As they envisioned language advancing towards a Cartesian division of thought from body, so they portrayed it beginning in instinctive automatism. Romanes remarked: 'the advent of self-consciousness enables a mind, not only to *know*, but to *know that it knows*; not only to *receive* knowledge, but also to *conceive* it'. Linguistic advancement enabled 'the human mind ... to stand outside of itself, and thus to constitute its own ideas the subject-matter of its own thought'.[5] Huxley similarly argued that science involved recognizing the arbitrariness and anthropomorphism of language, which distorted as much as it revealed. He wrote: 'the philosopher who is worthy of the name knows that his personified hypotheses, such as law, and force, and ether, and the like, are merely useful symbols, while the ignorant and the careless take them for adequate expressions of reality'. In primitive speech, by contrast, representation remained undifferentiated from being. It used signs without comprehending the nature of signification, misleading its speakers into 'intellectual shadow-worship'.[6] Comte characterized the lowest stage in human development as fetishism, the worship of physical objects as supernatural beings. As Peter Melville Logan notes, in the fetish, 'object and god, signifier and signified, are one and the same ... [R]ather than a representation of meaning, the fetish is meaning itself'.[7]

The characterization of primitive speech as unconscious and undifferentiated from the body emerged in theories of the origins of words. Spencer wrote: 'The lowest form of language is the exclamation, by which an entire idea is vaguely conveyed through a single sound; as among the lower animals'.[8] Certain emotions seemed to instinctively express themselves in certain sounds and gestures. Thus Tylor speculated that expressions of malice grew from the gritted teeth of the snarl in 'vocalized gesture-signs'.[9] Tylor, F. W. Farrar and Hensleigh Wedgwood also traced word origins to onomatopoeia, suggesting that speech began in imitative sounds.[10] In contrast to the conventional speech of civilization, Tylor claimed, such utterances were 'self-expressive', indicating gender through the hardness or softness of their sounds and size through their length.[11] Primitive language might be imagined as thoughtless echoing, rooted in the sensations of the physical body. The anthropologist John Lubbock described 'savage' vocabulary as 'rich ... for everything, in fact, which they can see and handle. Yet they are entirely deficient in words for abstract ideas; they have no expressions for colour, tone, sex, genus, spirit ... man, body, place, time ... nor such a verb as "to be"'.[12] By ignoring the different contextual associations of native words, anthropologists were able to present them as merely failures to grasp the higher truths of western abstraction. Nineteenth-century missionaries typically compiled native dictionaries by searching for equivalents to European terms rather than considering meaning in context.[13] Thus Sayce claimed that Cherokee language had many verbs for washing different objects but none for washing in general.[14] If primitive speech was not wanting in generalizations, then it lacked distinctions. The first terms, Sayce claimed, had been 'sentence-words', which were yet to distinguish things from their properties. Hence, 'the

Tasmanians, when they wanted to denote what we mean by "tall" ... had to say "long legs"'.[15] Unlike self-scrutinizing science, primitive language was unconscious of itself, discharging its metaphors and designations like reflexes. Speakers remained buried in their bodies, understanding signs only as subjective sensations or associations.

The publication of Tylor's *Primitive Culture* in 1871 also emphasized a contradictory view of primitive speech, which was characterized by rigid social convention. This model framed savages as alienated from the evidence of their senses by superstitious belief in the categories of their language. The idea of progress as speakers gaining sovereignty over language figured primitive speakers as conversely produced by their language. Tylor wrote: 'The savage is firmly, obstinately conservative. No man appeals with more unhesitating confidence to the great precedent-makers of the past; the wisdom of his ancestors can control against the most obvious evidence of his own opinions and actions'.[16] Linguistic primitiveness, perhaps, resided not in the isolation of the individual speaker but in her embedding in an inflexible structure of conventions and traditions. Individuals, and even whole communities, were not 'originators' of their customs, he wrote, 'but the transmitters and modifiers of the results of long past ages'. The 'early tyranny of speech over the human mind' prevents his savage from apprehending the relations of things clearly.[17] Walter Bagehot similarly claimed that 'savages ... do not improve' their social state because of a cemented 'cake of custom' which conformity to tradition prevented them from breaking.[18] While western science recognized metaphors as adaptable fictions, primitive society lacked such nominalism, unable as it was to scrutinize words apart from things. Tylor claimed: 'Analogies which are but fancy to us were to men of past ages reality. They could see the flame licking its yet undevoured prey with tongues of fire ... what we call poetry was to them real life'.[19] Through the 1870s Spencer also described the primitive mind as enslaved to verbal convention while the civilized consciously reshaped it. Primitive words, he wrote, 'grow up unawares ... by metaphor which some observable likeness suggests. Among civilised people, however, who have learnt that words are symbolic, new words are frequently chosen to symbolise new ideas'. Hence, tribal chiefs forbade the utterance of their names, 'conceiving that a man's name is part of his individuality, and that possession of his name gives power over him'.[20] Primitive speech fluctuated between the individual, the sensory body and the dogmatic conventions of society.

Haggard's African romances embody this tension. His savage speakers are isolated bodies, enslaved to urges and sensations, yet they are also slaves of ancestral custom. The 'ethnographic' romance genre emerged in the 1870s and 1880s in response to colonialism and evolutionary and racial theories that justified it.[21] Bradley Deane describes the 'lost world' narrative, which Haggard helped to pioneer, as 'the perverse offspring of the imperial romance and the utopian novel, energizing the political fantasies of the present not with a dream of what might be, but of what has been'.[22] Haggard's tales drew on his experiences in Africa as a colonial administrator and on anthropological theory, for which he received instruction from his friend and collaborator, Andrew Lang. Lang had been mentored at Oxford by Tylor, and his *Custom and Myth* (1884) described 'the rude beginnings of human language' as vocal and gestural mimicry and musical expressions of emotion. Over time, he suggested, the 'numina' of savage speech developed into the self-conscious 'nomina' of civilization.[23]

Haggard's tales illustrate these ideas, depicting Africans as frozen in the childhood of thought, even as they romanticize Zulu heroism.[24] They often associate the speech of the Zulu warrior Umslopogaas with unconscious bodily urges. In *Allan Quatermain*, when the eponymous Englishman is reunited with his Zulu comrade, Quatermain's quiet 'how do you do' contrasts with his friend's loud, uncontrolled exclamations: 'Koos! Baba! (father) . . . clever one! watchful one! brave one! quick one! . . . Koos! Baba!' The short, repetitious bursts follow each other without order, like expulsions of pent-up energy rather than conscious constructions. Quatermain emphasizes this point by interrupting Umslopogaas's torrent of speech with the comment: 'Has all thy noisy talk been stopped up since last I saw thee that it breaks out thus, and sweeps us away?'[25] Unlike his Europeans, Haggard's Africans are susceptible to the hypnotizing sensations of speech, its tones rousing their emotions instinctively. Quatermain states: 'I had let him run on thus because I saw that his enthusiasm was producing a marked effect upon the minds' of other natives, whom Quatermain wishes to recruit for his adventure. Even Umslopogaas is hypnotized by his own voice, working himself into a violent rage, which causes Quatermain to interrupt again: '"Be silent", I said, for I saw that he was getting the blood fever on him' (p. 24). Unable to fully separate being from representation, the primitive speaker embodies his tales and becomes lost in them. As Umslopogaas later admits: 'I am rough, I know it, and when my blood is warm I know not what to do' (p. 191). Haggard also depicts the savage story-teller embodying his tale in the novel of tribal warfare *Nada the Lily* (1892). While the story is mostly narrated by an old African witch doctor, it is enclosed by a white editor who meets him and transcribes his words. The explorer states of the old man: 'he acted rather than told his story. Was the death of a warrior in question, he stabbed with his stick, showing how the blow fell and where; did the story grow sorrowful, he groaned, or even wept ... This man, ancient and withered, seemed to live again in the far past'.[26] To use Saussure's terminology, primitive signification cannot occur through speech's more arbitrary symbols, but must be 'motivated' by icons of gestural resemblance.[27] Whereas westerners can detach utterances from bodies, reporting others' words from a distance, primitive stories are inextricable from the bodies that lived them.

Allan Quatermain further opposes embodied African speech to European abstraction through the naming practices of Umslopogaas. In contrast to Quatermain's technical nomenclature, he names weapons according to their effects on his sensorium: 'a double four-bore belonging to Sir Henry – was the Thunderer; another, my 500 Express, which had a peculiarly sharp report, was "the little one who spoke like a whip"; the Winchester repeaters were "the women, who talked so fast that you could not tell one word from another"' (p. 43). While Quatermain's language is weighted with knowledge of the guns' mechanics, grouping them according to their components, Umslopogaas distinguishes only the sounds which strike his senses. His acts of naming recall Tylor's description of primitive speech as imitation and unconscious metaphor. Umslopogaas not only names his axe, but also 'seemed to look upon [it] as an intimate friend, and to which he would at times talk by the hour, going over all his old adventures with it ... he would consult "Inkosi-kaas" if in any dilemma'. Unlike Europeans, who gender objects by mere convention (or rarely at all, in the case of English) Haggard's Zulu imagines his axe as a 'woman', explaining that it 'was very evidently feminine, because of her womanly habit of prying very deep into things' (pp. 43–44). Rather than being the tools of his autonomous mind, metaphors shape the primitive speaker's ideas and perceptions. He seems, rather, the tool of his metaphors, unable to think outside of them. In an underground cavern, Umslopogaas personifies echoes of the explorers' voices as invisible observers: 'They can copy what one says, but they don't seem to be able to talk on their own account, and they dare not show their faces'. When Quatermain explains that Umslopogaas hears merely an echo, the Zulu replies: 'I know an echo when I hear one. There was one lived opposite my kraal in Zululand, and the Intombis [maidens] used to talk with it. But if what we hear is a full-grown echo, mine at home can only have been a baby' (p. 108). Primitive speech reduces all phenomena to anthropomorphic agents; rooted in the sensory body, it cannot help but self-project.

The image of the savage body naming the world according to its solipsistic sensations clashes in Haggard's tales with that of rigid conformity to tribal tradition. Lang wrote in 1882, chastising philologists who claimed to describe 'primitive' language: 'the most backward races of which history and experience tell us anything have already complicated rules, stereotyped customs, developed language ... Thus they are far from being "primitive"'.[28] Savages represented not so much the primordial individual human as an early – fossilized – stage of society. Haggard's breakthrough novel, *King Solomon's Mines*, reflects this concept through Quatermain discovering the antique Kukuana people, whom centuries of despotic rule have frozen in time. They speak 'an old-fashioned form of the Zulu tongue, bearing about the same relationship to it that the English of Chaucer does to the English of the nineteenth century'.[29] This linguistic stasis mirrors their societal stasis, ruled for many centuries by the seemingly immortal witch-woman Gagool. One tribe member tells the explorers how she replaced the former king with one loyal to her by interpreting a famine and birthmark upon the latter man as supernatural signs. Under this manipulation, 'the people being mad with hunger, and altogether bereft of reason and knowledge of the truth, cried out, "The king! The king!"' Instead of voicing individual sensations and associations, the Kukuanas are an undifferentiated mass with one voice. They cry in unison as the new king seizes the throne: '*Twala is king*! Now we know that Twala is king!' (p. 111). This lack of individuation is more explicit when the explorers meet Twala before crowds of his people. 'Eight thousand voices rang out the royal salute', repeating the words of Gagool: '"*It is the king,*" boomed out eight thousand throats, in answer. "*Be humble, people, it is the king*"' (p. 127). The king is as much embedded in the complex system of superstitious restraints as are his subjects, explaining that a woman must be sacrificed to bring prosperity: '"It is our custom, and the figures who sit in stone yonder" (and he pointed towards the three distant peaks) "must have their due".' He quotes by heart the nation's dogma, illustrating their bondage to verbal convention: 'Thus runs the prophecy of my people: "If the king offer not a sacrifice of a fair girl, on the day of the dance of maidens, to the Old Ones who sit and watch on the mountains, then shall he fall, and his house"' (p. 161). Savage customs are perpetuated by maxims handed down by tradition. In this culture of mental-verbal rigidity, the explorers can only win the Kukuana's support by exploiting their superstition, claiming to put out the sun during an eclipse. Haggard highlights the role of society in primitive speech and thought through the deposed prince Ignosi participating in this deception.

His exile from Kukuanaland and exposure to other societies enables him to think outside of its dogmas. He thus tells the explorers, 'I am of the Zulu people, yet not of them' (p. 47). He helps the explorers to perform miracles before the Kukuana, presenting a rifle as a 'magic tube' that kills 'with a noise' (pp. 104–05). Before the explorers install him as the new king at the end of the tale, he promises to abolish witch-hunts. Primitiveness might arise less from subjective, bodily perceptions than from the rigid interpretive conventions that regulate them.

In contrast to the progressive ideal of tongues and perspectives integrating, primitive speech could be imagined as purist, confined by narrow tradition.[30] An anonymous *Cornhill* article on 'Primitive Language' in 1863 claimed that 'what creates and enriches language is intercourse with others – commercial intercourse more than any other', rendering isolated tribes relics of tradition.[31] Haggard uses such social isolation in *King Solomon's Mines* to avoid positioning Ignosi on an equal level with his white comrades. On becoming king of Kukuanaland, he vows to fight outsiders who come seeking its jewels. This rejection of commercial exchange coincides with his resurgent superstition, naming the area's mountains after his companions, which 'shall be "*hlonipa*" even as the names of dead kings, and he who speaks them shall die' (p. 269). Returned to his native society, Ignosi seems to lose the perspective that he previously held over it, believing in the dogmas that he once exploited. Haggard's Zulus are usually monolingual, unlike his Europeans, who move freely between languages. Umslopogaas in *Allan Quatermain* is a repository of his people's ancient customs and world-view, ossified in Zulu language. When the adventurers discover a lost race of white Africans, all but Umslopogaas quickly master their speech. The narrator states, 'he did not wish to learn that "woman's talk"', and brandished his axe when approached by prospective teachers (p. 159). When flyting with enemies before battle, he exhaustively lists his ancestors, highlighting his conformity to tradition: 'I, Umslopogaas, of the tribe of the Maquilisini, of the people of Amazulu, a captain of the regiment of the Nkomabakosi: I, Umslopogaas, the son of Indabazimbi, the son of Arpi the son of Mosilikaatze, I of the royal blood of T'Chaka' (p. 230). The past Zulu social structure in which these names and titles were meaningful has been swept away by white rule. Haggard wrote in his preface to *Nada the Lily* that, while earlier in the century 'the Zulus were still a nation; now that nation has been destroyed, and the chief aim of its white rulers is to root out the warlike spirit for which it was remarkable, and to replace it by a spirit of peaceful progress'.[32] As the last survivor of his race, Umslopogaas exemplifies the 'discourse of extinction' that Patrick Brantlinger has traced through Victorian representations of natives who refused to adapt to western rule. Brantlinger argues that Victorians often represented indigenous peoples as doomed to extinction by their own primitive customs, thus normalizing colonial violence and oppression.[33] In *Allan Quatermain,* Umslopogaas's death in battle seems inevitable, since, in an era of capitalism, he is unable to deviate from warrior tradition, declaring: 'Man is born to kill. He who kills not when his blood is hot is a woman, and no man. The people who kill not are slaves'; 'Better is it to slay a man in fair fight than to suck out his heart's blood in buying and selling and usury after your white fashion' (p. 47). Haggard's archaic English emphasizes the Zulu's mental fossilization. He is unwilling and unable to change. Associating Zulu honour with Elizabethan speech chimes with the nostalgic tendency of many writers in the period for past speech, which is imagined as truer and more natural than modern language (see Chapter 3). However, Haggard's romantic Zulus are unable to move between stages of social and mental development like whites are. While the latter descend in battle to 'the savage portions of our nature', as Allan writes, the pure savage cannot think or act beyond this (p. 13). This idea of savagery as mere, unchanging 'nature' conflicts, however, with the importance of custom and tradition suggested elsewhere by Haggard. Primitive speech thus appears, contradictorily, as both natural and social, emanating from the individual body and repressing it.

Unspeakable savagery

Translating supposedly primitive speech was problematic, since it subordinated native to western language, yet suggested equivalence between them. Progressivism framed primitive words and concepts as understandable to the colonizer, since they merely replicated earlier stages of his own language. In 1908 the anthropologist J. G. Frazer declared: 'The savage is a human document, a record of man's efforts to raise himself above the level of the beast'.[34] Yet, colonialism also required an insurmountable gulf between primitive and civilized. 'Hard as it is for a Papuan to compass a modern abstraction,' wrote the philologist R. G. Latham in 1862, 'it is nearly as hard for a German or an Englishman to understand these rudimentary abstracts of our nonage' used by primitive speakers. 'The simple fact of his being able to write at all,' Latham continued, 'removes him from that state of mind in which alone they approach distinctness.'[35] Grasping the meaning of primitive signs was like attempting to recall the wild imaginings of infancy. Tylor claimed that westerners could only access the 'mythic idealism' in which savage signs signified through the hallucinations of narcotics, fasting and dreams.[36] Many writers also associated civilization with the moral repression of bodily urges, rendering primitive feelings untranslatable. Joss Marsh describes the Victorian period as 'a golden age of euphemism' marked by a belief in the progressive expunging of vulgarity from print. It was the era of bowdlerized Shakespeare, when trousers became 'indescribables', whores 'fallen women' and madhouses 'asylums'.[37] Brantlinger notes, 'one form of exaggeration that occurs in many missionary texts involves the trope of unspeakability'.[38] Such rhetoric presented western moral superiority through its lack of equivalent terms for practices such as cannibalism or sexual promiscuity. Yet, refusing to verbalize such things was comparable with the superstitious taboos of primitive language. Representations of primitive language, then, wavered between the describable and indescribable, between objective description and moral censorship.

These tensions permeate Grant Allen's 1890 novel of an English couple shipwrecked among Polynesian cannibals *The Great Taboo*. Allen was a prolific science writer and ardent follower of Darwin, Spencer and Frazer. This background, together with years spent teaching in Jamaica, fed his interests in race and mental and linguistic evolution.[39] He published many articles on etymology and corresponded with Sayce, whose ideas matched Allen's descriptions of 'primitive speech' as grammatically and intellectually simple.[40] In an article of 1894 on this subject, Allen cites as an example 'negro English' in which 'tenses and persons are frequently lost. "Him gwine town" ... "Him eat"'.[41] Western language proves its superiority by analyzing and classifying its inferiors. Allen's novel reflects this notion through the English castaways Felix and Muriel translating the islanders' speech and, thus, gaining control over them. An accomplished linguist, Felix is able to speak the islanders' dialect, recognizing it as an offshoot of Fijian. This categorization of their verbal morphology precedes categorization of their minds. Unravelling the logic of their 'Great Taboo' enables Felix to kill the chief Tu-Kila-Kila and usurp his status as a god. The tribe's mental-linguistic stasis is demonstrated by the fact that a seventeenth-century English sailor previously decoded their customs and became chief. Reciting his tale to a parrot famed for its longevity, he bequeaths the tribe's secrets to the Victorian castaways. The Boupari tribe is incapable of apprehending itself from such an abstract perspective. When Felix asks one to define the word 'Korong', designating a superstition, the man can only reply: 'Why, Korong is Korong ... You are "Korong" yourself'. The narrator comments that the islander was 'so rigidly bound by his own narrow and insular set of ideas, that he couldn't understand the difficulty Felix felt in throwing himself into them'.[42] Felix's communication problems suggest that meaning is dependent upon social perspectives, thus rupturing the primitive–civilized binary. Perhaps Boupari meanings can only be understood in context. Allen the journalist wrote that 'Savages always depend greatly on context and the pointing finger to bring out their words', framing civilization as conversely above contexts and perspectives.[43] Allen maintains this distinction through Felix guessing the nature of 'Korong' by comparing Boupari customs with classical myths. After they pour water over his and Muriel's heads, he recalls reading that 'it was a custom connected with Greek sacrifices ... If the victim shook its head and knocked off the drops, that was a sign that it was fit for the sacrifice, and that the god accepted it' (pp. 64–65). All the significations of Boupari customs are contained within European history and need only be matched to the corresponding words for translation. The Bouparis' ritual of sacrificing strangers to renew their crops is, as Allen admits in his preface, adapted from Frazer's *The Golden Bough* (1890), 'whose main contention I have endeavoured incidentally to popularize in my present story' (p. v). Boupari language and customs are relics of the West's past rather than independent sign systems functioning on their own terms.

Allen's representation of Boupari language as decipherable to westerners clashes with his efforts to differentiate savagery from civilization. Maintaining a distance between the two necessitates some loss of meaning in translation. Hence, when Tu-Kila-Kila is bitten by the island's tabooed parrot, the narrator warns: 'one must be a savage one's self, and superstitions at that, fully to understand the awful significance of this deadly occurrence'. This caveat does not prevent the following explanation, however: 'To draw blood from a god and, above all, to let that blood fall upon the dust of the ground, is the very worst luck' (p. 167). The rhetoric of unspeakable savagery recurs through the narrative. Before the shipwreck, Felix speculates to Muriel that 'some unspeakable and unthinkable heathen orgy' is occurring on the nearby island (p. 6). A subsequent scene of human sacrifice confirms this, only for the narrator to cut it short: 'the rest, a European hand shrinks from revealing. The orgy was too horrible even for description' (p. 24). Later, in a rage at his wife, Tu-Kila-Kila 'flung her away from him to the other side of the hut with a fierce and untranslatable native imprecation' (p. 176). Allen's narrator balances the two priorities of decipherability and difference: while civilized language can classify Boupari ideas and practices, it does so at a distance through general, abstract categories. Although some specific Boupari words are untranslatable, their functions can still be grouped under 'superstitions' or 'imprecations'. When one Boupari observes that Felix (the supposed god of water) fell from the sky yesterday, 'Felix wrung his hands in positive despair. It was clear indeed that to the minds of the natives there was no distinguishing personally between himself and Muriel and the rain or the cyclone' (p. 112). Westerners can classify primitive thought processes but not empathize with them.

Tylorian classification destabilized the primitive–civilized binary, however, revealing superstitious survivals in western language. Tylor's theory of survivals allowed for pockets of primitiveness to endure within wider structures of advancement. 'Even the modern civilized world has but half learnt this lesson,' he wrote, 'and an unprejudiced survey may lead us to judge how many of our ideas and customs exist rather by being old than by being good.'[44] Allen similarly suggested that primitive vocalizations continued to underlie civilized speech, such as when a diner exclaims, 'Wah, wah, wah, wah!' to prevent sugar being put in his tea. The continuing use of such instinctive noise, he wrote, showed that 'there never is a moment when human speech does not refresh and renew itself from these primitive sources'.[45] In *The British Barbarians* (1896), Allen would satirize Victorian conventions of respectability through a time traveller from the future examining such 'taboos'. Similar barbs at religion, monarchy and sexual repression appear in *The Great Taboo*. The narrator states that Tu-Kila-Kila 'accepted his own superiority as implicitly as our European nobles and rulers accept theirs' (p. 23). The Bouparis' ritual signs mirror those of European Christianity, reflecting kindred superstitions. During ceremonies, the Bouparis make 'a rapid movement on their breasts with their fingers which reminded Muriel at once of the sign of the cross in Catholic countries' (p. 46). Allen also satirizes English prudery, with Muriel's aunt fretting, after the couple's return, that they lived together for so long without being married. The narrator remarks: 'Taboos, after all, are much the same in England as in Boupari' (p. 280). Such point-scoring maintains the idea of civilization as a progressive clearing away of old superstitions by self-aware, scientific reason. Yet, language is not always a reliable test of this progress, as Allen suggests through the Frenchman Peyron, who is also stranded upon the island. Like the Bouparis, he is monolingual, and naively divides the world 'into Paris and the Provinces' (p. 181). His delight at being able to converse in French with Felix and Muriel suggests that civilized language can be fetishized – worshipping sound regardless of sense. He effuses: 'figure to yourself the joy and surprise with which ... I hear again the sound, the beautiful sound of that charming French language. My emotion, believe me, was too profound for words' (p. 181). Conversely, he interprets the English sailor's record, repeated by the parrot, as an extinct primitive language: 'It is a much more guttural and unpleasant tongue than any of the soft dialects now spoken in Polynesia. It belonged, I am convinced, to that yet earlier and more savage race which the Polynesians must have displaced' (p. 185). The later discovery that this primeval babble is English highlights the danger of treating speech as intrinsically civilized or primitive.

The primitive–civilized binary was further threatened by so-called savages learning European speech. Did language reflect the fixed nature of its speakers or merely the structure of their society? Buckle and Tylor argued the latter, suggesting that a primitive speaker transplanted into civilization would absorb its speech and ideas.[46] Allen's narrative broaches this issue through the young Boupari girl Mali learning English as a servant in Queensland before returning to the tribe. While Muriel is unable to speak Boupari, Mali converses with her in English, potentially upsetting the balance of western superiority. Allen probed this problem more directly in his earlier tale 'The Reverend John Creedy' (1883), depicting an Oxford-educated African who becomes a missionary. Allen's time teaching in Jamaica heightened his awareness of the unreliability of language as a test of race. In one essay he recalled instructing a class that through learning a man's name, such as John Smith, they might gauge his Anglo-Saxon heritage, only for one student so-named to laugh, 'for *this* John Smith was a pure-blooded negro'.[47] Allen's tale extends this disjunction between language and race, depicting an African whose 'voice was of the ordinary Oxford type, open, pleasant, and refined, with a certain easy-going air of natural gentility, hardly marred by just the faintest tinge of the thick negro blur in the broad vowels'.[48] Creedy also proves himself an able orator, speaking to his English audience 'fervently, eloquently, and with much power of manner about the necessity for a Gold Coast Mission ... John Creedy had been noted as one of the readiest and most fluent talkers at the Oxford Union debates' (p. 15). The gulf between primitive and civilized language might consist only in the loose network of social influences in which speakers lived.

Some commentators avoided this implication through the Lockean division of language into external sounds and internal sense. The anthropologist James Hunt claimed that African language learning merely testified to their memory, which was 'one of the lowest mental powers'.[49] Spencer similarly denigrated language learning as an inferior knowledge to science. While scientific knowledge encouraged the mind to challenge fixed views of reality, language learning caused pupils 'to accept without inquiry whatever is established'.[50] An unaccomplished monoglot, Spencer even tried to present his failure in languages as a sign of intellectual strength. His *Autobiography* claimed that, rejecting 'everything purely dogmatic', he naturally resisted the 'rote-learning' of grammars.[51] Ferguson notes that this dismissal of language learning as mere imitation, 'put non-whites in an archetypal damned-if-you-do, damned-if-you-don't position', so that both speaking and not speaking western language were signs of primitiveness.[52] However, the idea of primitive imitation, in which words only signified through contextual association, raised the troubling possibility that all meaning functioned in this way. Progressives guarded against such possibilities by racializing meaning, suggesting that speakers were physically predisposed towards certain ideas. Sayce wrote: 'As words are carried down the stream of time they change in both outward form and inward meaning, and this change is in harmony with the physiological and psychological peculiarities of the particular people that use them'.[53] Primitive and civilized ideas could be imagined as somehow embedded in the hereditary brain.

The Great Taboo uses this strategy to separate native from acquired European speech. The Bouparis imitate European language as sound without meaning. Felix's guard repeats verbatim the French song of Peyron, only to then describe it as mere 'chatter, chatter, chatter, like the parrots in a tree; tirra, tirra, tirra; tarra, tarra, tarra; la, la, la; lo, lo, lo'. The guard's speech 'with a very good Parisian accent' is sound without sense, produced by 'that wonderful power of accurate mimicry which is so strong in all natural human beings' (p. 92). Mali's broken English is not mere sound imitation, but it fails to bridge the mental gulf between savagery and civilization. Her inability to correctly conjugate verbs and modify nouns in the language mirrors her inability to grasp its mental hinterland, which contradicts Boupari superstition. Returned to Boupari from Queensland, she has reverted to the old superstitions, telling Muriel: 'no god in Queensland ... Methodist god in sky, him only god that live in Queensland. But no use worship Methodist god over here in Boupari ... All god here make out of man. Live in man. Korong! What for you say a man can't be a god! You god yourself!' (p. 62). Learning the language of civilization has failed to give Mali any higher perspective over her native one. Her English words signify only through the conventional associations of her former life as a servant. The narrator comments, 'it never for a moment occurred to her simple mind to doubt the omnipotence of

Tu-Kila-Kila in his island realm any more than she had doubted the omnipotence of the white man and his local religion in their proper place (as she thought it) in Queensland' (p. 153). Although using the English term *god*, the mental conception she attaches to it is rooted in Boupari superstition. While primitive speakers can learn the habitual uses of English, its logical abstractions lie beyond them.

'The Reverend John Creedy' is more conflicted on the matter of primitive imitation and hereditary semantics. Upon returning as a missionary to his African homeland, Creedy reverts to its savage practices. Allen indicates the hereditary component in such primitiveness through Creedy's seemingly half-organic memory of Fantee language. Creedy 'noticed rather uneasily that every phrase and word, down to the very heathen charms and prayers of his infancy, came back to him now with startling vividness and without an effort' (pp. 20–21). He later tears up his vestments to join a native dance as a 'reeling, shrieking black savage', showing that 'instinct had gained the day over civilisation' (p. 24). These events seem to confirm the racial determinism bluntly expressed by the uncle of Creedy's fiancé Ethel: 'a nigger's a nigger anywhere, but he's a sight less of a nigger in England than out yonder in Africa. Take him to England, and you make a gentleman of him: send him home again, and the nigger comes out at once in spite of you' (pp. 11–12). However, Creedy's language destabilizes this simple division between true racial essence and acquired social manners. English speech and the civilized ideas it encodes compete in Creedy, with his hereditary primitiveness, collapsing the boundaries between nature and nurture. Horrified at the sight of him dancing semi-naked, Ethel collapses and sickens. Yet, Creedy is able to fool his dying wife with soothing English words into thinking that his reversion was a mere dream: 'For civilization with John Creedy was really at bottom far more than a mere veneer; though the savage instinct might break out with him now and again, such outbursts no more affected his adult and acquired nature than a single bump supper or wine party at college affects the nature of many a gentle-minded English lad' (pp. 27–28). His vow at the end of the tale never to speak English again is thus as much an act of suppression as resignation to his 'true' nature. The narrator comments, 'The truest John Creedy of all was the gentle, tender, English clergyman' (p. 29). This blurring of boundaries between native and acquired tongue is reinforced when the disgraced Creedy deceives missionaries into thinking him an ordinary native, but then accidentally speaks to them in English. The narrator's explanation that 'he forgot himself for a moment' suggests that Creedy's Englishness, for all his reversion, has taken root in his unconscious psyche (pp. 26–27). It is not his performance of civilized whiteness which falters but that of his 'natural' Fantee identity. Creedy's decision to 'go to my own people' at the end is followed by the claim that travellers may now see him 'among a crowd of dilapidated negroes who lie basking in the soft dust' (p. 30). The vagueness of Allen's final image, losing Creedy in a crowd, betrays the impossibility of presenting him as simply another heathen savage. Creedy may not be able to fully sustain his civilized self in heathen Africa but, like Clem returning to Wessex in Hardy's *Return of the Native* (1878), he can no longer be fully at home there either. In both his language switching and self-imposed silence, 'acquired nature' undermines the idea of a primitive essence fixed in biology.

Allen wrote a preface to the tale, claiming that it illustrated 'the intensely impressionable African mind', capable of 'fall[ing] from the pinnacle of civilization to the nethermost abysses of savagery'.[54] However, Creedy also suggests the anxiety that the language and values of civilization might be equally fragile among westerners, mere grafts upon primitive instinct. Allen attempts to explain the success of Creedy's sermon to an English audience, including his future wife Ethel, by way of primitive emotional triggers in his oratory. The narrator comments: 'Perhaps there was really nothing very original or striking in what he said, but his way of saying it was impressive and vigorous. The negro, like many other lower races, has the faculty of speech largely developed' (p. 15). However, the ones shown to be impressionable here are not Africans but Englishwomen. Creedy's sermon rouses Ethel and her aunt's instincts so that '[they] forgot his black hands, stretched out open-palmed towards the people, and felt only their hearts stirred within them by the eloquence and enthusiasm of that appealing gesture' (p. 15). Yet grouping Creedy and the women together as equally primitive threatens Allen's racial boundaries, which forbid miscegenation. Ethel recoils instinctively when Creedy proposes to her: 'John Creedy saw the shadow on her face, the unintentional dilatation of her delicate nostrils, the faint puckering at the corner of her lips, and knew with a negro's quick instinct of face-reading what it all meant.' This revulsion contradicts her earlier attraction to him, though, which was also instinctive, sparked by his rousing oratory. Allen now suggests that Ethel's attraction is mediated by intellect, stating that her vicar and his wife 'had argued themselves out of those wholesome race instincts ... and they were eager to argue Ethel out of them too' (p. 17). The tale contradicts itself in opposing primitive instinct to civilized culture, suggesting that white civilization relies as much upon instinct as intellect. Ethel's uncle, who opposes miscegenation, appeals to her instinctive revulsion, stating: 'our instincts wasn't put in our hearts for nothing. They're meant to be a guide and a light to us in these dark questions' (p. 17). Allen's concept of linear development from primitive instinct to scientific rationality breaks down, with instinct underlying civilization no less than savagery. In its contradictions, Allen's tale highlights the fear that primitive signs are all too speakable for Europeans.

Lost origin or missing link?

One means of protecting civilized speech from equivalence with the primitive was to hypothesize forms of primordial speech before tradition or convention could emerge. Researchers such as Darwin, Hippolyte Taine and R. L. Garner inferred the nature of early speech through observation of infants and animals. Avoiding the problem of sociolinguistic tradition, proto-speech could be imagined as mainly or wholly instinctive. Alongside this anthropological theory, the new genre of prehistoric fiction sought to give a voice to the archaeological records. As Darwin had imagined hypothetical species to fill the gaps in the fossil record, so such fiction imagined hypothetical speech forms between animal and modern, human communication. Depicting primitive speech as half way between bodily automatism and conscious symbolism framed modern language as contrastingly controlled and self-aware. By locating instinct in the primordial past, writers could downplay its continuing influence. Introducing an early example of the genre *The Pre-Historic World* (1876), Élie Berthet wrote: 'We have striven to reconstruct, to revive, this unknown world ... we shall be glad to have been the literary pioneer who first penetrated regions so long unknown'.[55] Yet, the further back writers traced the history of speech, the more its origins fragmented, undermining the sense of linear progress. Victorian debates about language origins mirrored earlier geological ones, divided between catastrophism and uniformitarianism.[56] The claim that language had appeared suddenly, fully formed, clashed with ideas of gradual evolution from animal communication. Tracing an instinctive heritage in speech threatened to expose unstable, primitive foundations, undermining the objectivity of modern discourse.

Reconstructions of verbal prehistory rested on a Lamarckian teleology in which the development of the individual speaker recapitulated that of the language faculty. Schleicher described primitive words as 'the cells of speech, not yet containing any particular organs for the functions of nouns, verbs etc., and in which these functions (the grammatical relations) are no more separated yet than respiration or digestion are in the one-celled organisms'.[57] Romanes wrote that words traced back to their oldest states presented 'so generalized a type as to include, each within itself, all the functions that afterwards severally devolve upon different parts of speech. Like those animalcules which are at the same time but single cells and entire organisms, these are at the same time single words and independent sentences'.[58] Late-Victorian psychology typically approached the mind of the child as an index of the evolutionary past.[59] Thus in 1877 Darwin tracked the verbal development of his young son, beginning in purely 'instinctive cries'. Yet, Darwin noted, 'After a time the sound differs according to the cause, such as hunger or pain'. The boy spontaneously invented 'words of a general nature', such as '*Mum*', meaning food, 'in a demonstrative manner or as a verb, implying "Give me food"'.[60] In the same year, Taine argued that the infant's verbal instinct was so inventive 'several vocabularies may succeed one another in its mind ... Many meanings may be given in succession to the same word'.[61] Such examples appeared to substantiate progressive theory, revealing primordial, instinctive voices untamed by social tradition. Positioning instinctive signs in a prehistoric epoch protected modern language as the tool of self-conscious minds abstracted from biological automatism.

Such a teleology is discernible in Wells's tale 'A Story of the Stone Age'. In an article of the same year, 1897, Wells argued that the transition from individual to society hinged upon 'habit, the trick of imitation'.[62] His tale applies this theory to speech, as habitual, group associations replace individual, instinctive vocalizations. Palaeolithic children are introduced frolicking in the water: '"Boloo!" they cried. "Baayah. Boloo!" ... Stark-naked vivid little gipsies active as monkeys and as full of chatter, though a little wanting in words'.[63] Yet, through group interaction, these sounds assume a regularity, mediating communal experience. This is illustrated in a moment of affection between the man Ugh-lomi and his lover Eudena after he defends them from a bear attack:

> He looked at her steadfastly for a moment, and then suddenly he laughed.
>
> 'Waugh!' he said exultantly.
>
> 'Waugh!' said she – a simple but expressive conversation. (pp. 99–100)

Wells further shows the transition from instinct to convention by an old woman who unites the tribe under her hypnotic orations; although she 'had more words than any in the tribe ... Sometimes she screamed and moaned incoherently, and sometimes the shape of her guttural cries was the mere phantom of thoughts' (p. 134). Translating her utterances, the narrator comments: 'Her cries were strange sounds, flitting to and fro on the borderland of speech, but this was the sense they carried' (p. 131). Wells's friend Edward Clodd had earlier described primitive man's conceptions as 'a tangle of confusion, contradiction, and bewilderment ... he dimly noted the differences, which, in the long run, lead the mind to comparisons, and thereby lay the foundation of knowledge – of the relation between things which we will call cause and effect'.[64] These relations remain untangled among Wells's primitive speakers, who designate both fire and sunlight as 'Brother Fire', and who cannot differentiate things from their names. As the embers of their fire fade, Ugh-lomi and Eudena call desperately for 'Brother Fire' as though the word will reignite them (p. 96). The narrator's reported or, rather, approximated speech lends clarity to the speakers' intentions which the original utterances lack. When Eudena wishes to warn Ugh-lomi of their approaching enemies, the habitual associations of their speech lack the intricacy to convey this abstraction. She can only express the idea by performing it in her immediately present body:

> She cried: 'Ugh-lomi, the tribe comes!' Ugh-lomi sat staring in stupid astonishment at her ... She sought among her feeble store of words to explain ... She ... caught up the new club with the lion's teeth, and put it into Ugh-lomi's hand, and ran three yards and picked up the first axe.
>
> 'Ah!' said Ugh-lomi, waving the new club, and suddenly he perceived the occasion. (pp. 155–6)

Wells's translation of this primordial speech both distances it from and positions it in a teleological path towards modern English. The incoherent noises and ideas of his cave people will gradually stabilize and accumulate, replacing superstition with science.

Wells's teleology is complicated, however, by Darwinian natural selection, which, as the last chapter has outlined, pluralized development, undercutting notions of progress. Organisms adapted to environments with no overriding plan or definite, individual origins. Where was 'the borderland of speech' in which Wells's tale imagined the genesis of humanity? Patrick Parrinder argues that 'A Story of the Stone Age' reflects uncertainties in the 1890s about the heritage of humans and their Neanderthal cousins, using the terms 'Stone Age' and 'Palaeolithic' interchangeably.[65] Doing so avoided relativizing modern humans as one subspecies among many, suggesting a linear evolution, ending in modern civilization. Wells's teacher Huxley hailed speech as the great barrier between humans and other animals, having seemingly sprung into being fully formed.[66]

However, Darwin challenged such catastrophism, arguing that vocal signals and thought had catalyzed each other into increasingly elaborate forms. 'As monkeys certainly understand much that is said to them by man,' wrote Darwin, 'and as in a state of nature they utter signal-cries of danger to their fellows, it does not appear altogether incredible, that some unusually wise ape-like animal should have thought of imitating the growl of a beast of prey, so as to indicate to his fellow monkeys the nature of the expected danger.' For Darwin, there was no single genesis when thought and symbolism suddenly appeared. Animals were not simply instinctive, he claimed, but capable of some reasoning.[67] Lubbock extended this point, arguing that animals learned conventional signs besides their instinctive ones. He recounted teaching a dog to fetch paper cards to express its wants, such as '"bone", "water", "pet me"', showing its capacity to associate ideas.[68] Conversely, in human communication, Romanes stated, instinct and convention shaded into each other 'by gradations', becoming indistinguishable.[69] These arguments threatened the narrative of linear, mental-verbal progress, compromising the language of science and civilization with enduring instincts.

Wells's tale engages with these problems obliquely through the incongruous presence of speaking animals. Departing from the realistic reconstruction of Stone Age society from anthropological sources, Wells's beasts converse with each other like figures in a fairy-tale. As Wells translates the nascent speech of humans, he translates the impulses and associations behind animal noises. When a grizzly bear chases the humans, 'he made a continuous growling grumble. "Men in my very lair! Fighting and blood. At the very mouth of my lair. Men, men, men. Fighting and blood"' (p. 69). Later, after a scuffle with Ugh-lomi, the bear struggles to comprehend the man's axe, musing: 'He has a sort of claw – a long claw that he seemed to have first on one paw and then on the other. Just one claw' (p. 104). He also attempts to classify humans as a cross between 'monkey and young pig', although their fire, 'the red thing that jumps' remains beyond him (p. 90). Verbalizing these mental processes, Wells collapses the division between mute, instinctive beasts and thinking, symbolic humans. As with humans, so animals' ideas are shaped to an extent by habit. Even C. L. Morgan, who doubted much supposed animal cognition, admitted that instinct and habit were often blurred. For example, did birds feign wounds out of sheer organic impulse or imitation of the flock?[70] Wells suggests the influence of incipient habit and tradition upon the bear through his interactions with a younger mate. He is, the narrator states, 'a bear of experience' who builds classifications from a long life of impressions (p. 104). He shares some of this experience with his mate, telling her of the simian-swines he encountered. The bear seems thus to ventriloquize the intermediate verbal-mental forms between apes and humans that Wells left out of his tale. The male tells the female of a 'bright thing' among the humans 'like that glare that comes in the sky in daytime – only it jumps about' (p. 105). While the humans' term for heat and light, 'brother fire', lacks the precision of modern English, the bear's conceptions are even vaguer. Primordial speech blurs into a continuum between human and animal communication. Wells's ideas on this matter share common ground with the American naturalist Richard Garner, who claimed to have isolated a vocabulary of simian proto-words by observing monkeys.[71] He recorded their vocalizations on a phonograph, concluding that the sounds had distinct meanings, such as warning of threats. In translating nature, Wells's omniscient narrator, like Garner, suggests that all life might be understood as layers upon layers of sign systems. In his *Text-Book of Biology* (1893), Wells mused that 'Zoology is, indeed, a philosophy and a literature to those who can read its symbols'.[72] Similarly, in his tale, instinct becomes another tongue, which the narrator translates. When Ugh-lomi mounts a wild horse, '"Hold tight", said Mother Instinct, and he did' (p. 117). Instead of revealing an origin of language, evolution dissolves it into infinite systems of nature.

The American journalist Stanley Waterloo similarly vacillated between linguistic catastrophism and uniformitarianism in *The Story of Ab* (1897). Waterloo's cavemen straddle the border between humans and apes, their speech developing in step with their bodies. His preface to the tale posits that 'the mysterious gap' of 'Paleolithic from Neolithic man never really existed. No convulsion of nature, no new race of human beings is needed to explain ... the relatively swift changes from one form of primitive life to another more advanced'. The development of tools and social organization merely reflected ongoing 'growth, experiment, adaptation, discovery'.[73] The mother of the hero Ab exemplifies this intermediacy, with strips of hair covering her shoulders and back, while 'her thumb was nearly as long as her fingers' (p. 13). Waterloo's depiction of the language of these proto-people wavers, though, between singular, human origins and missing links with animal communication. One of the first utterances in the narrative evokes Darwin's claims of speech emerging from song as Ab's mother emits 'a strange call, a quavering minor wail ... The call was answered instantly and the answering cry was repeated as she called again, the sound of the reply approaching near and nearer all the time'. As Ab's father comes, the exchange becomes 'a conversation, an odd, clucking, penetrating speech in the shortest of sentences' (p. 17). Yet, even as speech descends into instinctive noise, the anthropologist-narrator seeks definite, describable origins for words. Hence, 'The name of Ab's father was One-Ear, the sequence of an incident occurring when he was very young, an accidental and too intimate acquaintance with a species of wildcat ... The name of Ab's mother was Red-Spot, and she had been so called because of a not unsightly but conspicuous birthmark' (p. 29). Waterloo suggests that some primitive words emerged through conventional associations gradually ascribed to instinctive sounds. While such words were not consciously created, modern civilization could deduce their origins. For example, Ab's name

> was merely a convenient adaptation by his parents of a childish expression of his own, a labial attempt to say something. His mother had mimicked his babyish prattlings, the father had laughed over the mimicry, and, almost unconsciously, they referred to their baby afterward as 'Ab' until it grew into a name which should be his for life. There was no formal early naming of a child in those days; the name eventually made itself, and that was all there was to it. (p. 30)

The narrator suggests that some such primitive associations might even survive in modern speech. Ab's friend Oak receives his name from the tree on which his parents hang his cradle, prompting the narrator to comment: '"Rock-a-by-baby upon the tree-top" was often a reality in the time of the cave men' (p. 31). Seeking to rationalize the origins of words, Waterloo resists the looming sense, in language, of subjective meaning built upon immediate sensations. As in Wells, the omniscient narrator embodies a fantasy of objective, scientific language above perspectives. Yet, tracing word origins on this small scale only distracts from the wider lack of origins for language as a capacity. The narrator-anthropologist is unable to completely historicize and, thus, control his language as it merges into an infinity of precursors.

Jack London's novella *Before Adam* (1906–07) seeks still remoter origins of speech and finds them correspondingly more elusive. London was an avid reader of Darwin and Spencer, and his fiction often struggled to accommodate their different views.[74] Spencer's teleological evolution tending towards univocal perfection collides in London's work with Darwin's sense of random mutation and adaptation. The Spencerian view emerges in London's tale when it opposes primitive noise and confusion to civilized discrimination and abstraction. The narrator locates his tale in 'the Mid-Pleistocene' when 'man, as we to-day know him, did not exist. It was in the period of his becoming'.[75] The narrative problematizes this teleology, however, revealing multiple strands of ancestry in which ideas and sympathy do not advance in tandem. Darwin had argued that the moral senses were products of animal instinct instead of civilization, mediated by gestures, expressions and vocal sounds. Such arguments undermined the binary between primitive and civilized speech, linking ethical advancement back to primordial instinct. Although London's tale does not abandon the idea of language progressing technically, it challenges simplistic primitive–civilized binaries. London suggests that civilization might even depend on some instinctive signs.

London's narrator is a modern American who, through a freak of heredity, relives the life of his prehuman ancestor 'Big-Tooth' in his dreams. This conceit structures London's opposition between primitive and civilized language, as the modern speaker builds a coherent narrative from the confused conceptions of his ancestor. Big-Tooth and his fellows are incapable of such narration, as the narrator comments: 'if my mother knew my father's end, she never told me. For that matter I doubt if she had a vocabulary adequate to convey such information' (p. 37). While the modern speaker is 'both actor and spectator', thinking that he thinks and knowing that he knows, as Romanes put it, the primitive is embodied action without reflection. The narrator remarks: 'It is I, the modern, who look back across the centuries and weigh and analyze the emotions and motives of Big-Tooth, my other self. He did not bother to weigh and analyze. He was simplicity itself. He just lived events' (pp. 129). This lack of self-knowledge is highlighted by the absence of personal names among Big-Tooth's kind: 'we bore no names in those days; were not known by any name. For the sake of convenience I have myself given names to the various Folk I was more closely in contact with' (pp. 4)–41). Such interventions by the narrator frame modern western language as a teleological development from his ancestor's grunts. London probably knew of Garner, since the latter's theory of simian speech was widely popularized in American print, and both authors published pieces months apart in the *Windsor Magazine* in 1904.[76] Garner claimed to distinguish eight or nine 'monophones' used by monkeys to express vague conceptions, further differentiated by vocal tones.[77] London's proto-hominids communicate at a stage beyond this, with 'a vocabulary of thirty or forty sounds', also modified by tones. Of Big-Tooth's utterances, the narrator comments: 'I call them SOUNDS, rather than WORDS, because sounds they were primarily. They had no fixed values, to be altered by adjectives and adverbs. These latter were tools of speech not yet invented ... We had no conjugation. One judged the tense by the context' (pp. 37–38). London stresses the teleology of speech development by depicting communication among Big-Tooth and his companions as repeated false starts, failing to reach the abstraction of his descendants. They cannot pass on knowledge or vicarious experiences to each other by speech alone, relying on gestural 'pantomime'. Hence, when Big-Tooth leaves the trees to join a horde of cave-dwellers, one 'gave me to understand that in that direction was some horrible danger, but just what the horrible danger was his paucity of language would not permit him to say' (pp. 73–74). Big-Tooth must himself encounter the aggressive 'Fire People' dwelling in this area before he can understand. When a violent 'atavism' among their band, Red-Eye, kills one member and steals his mate, the socialist-sympathizing London suggests that their collective outrage prefigures later human cooperation. Yet, they fail to unite against Red-Eye 'because we lacked a vocabulary. We were vaguely thinking thoughts for which there were no thought-symbols ... We tried to freight sound with the vague thoughts that flitted like shadows through our consciousness' (pp. 169–70). As in Waterloo's tale, London frames such vocalizations as both the seeds of later, civilized, speech and as fundamentally remote from it. He links primitive and civilized speech along a continuum, but also keeps them separate to protect the latter's privileged position.

Such teleology is complicated, however, by the presence of multiple proto-hominid races, of which Big-Tooth's are not the most technically advanced. The aforementioned Fire People appear closer to modern humans, walking upright and clothing themselves in animal skins, while Big-Tooth's 'Folk' are naked and bent forward. The Fire People have developed archery and catamarans, and plan military campaigns through their more copious and abstracted speech. The narrator states that they 'had speech that enabled them more effectively to reason, and in addition they understood cooperation' (p. 185). The Fire People demonstrate these abilities when they attack the Folk's caves with fire and arrows, a 'wizened old hunter directing it all. They obeyed him, and went here and there at his commands. Some of them went into the forest and returned with loads of dry wood, leaves, and grass' (p. 207). Schleicher had speculated 'that not all organisms that found themselves on the way to becoming human have attained to the evolution of language ... [b]ut succumbed to retrogression and ... gradual extinction'.[78] London's Folk exemplify this idea, dying out along with their nascent speech. Yet, London's narrative also challenges such linear progression, locating germinal values of civilization among the gentler Folk. With all their intelligence and verbal abstraction, the Fire

People are not morally superior, as the narrator comments, they were 'carnivorous, with claws and fangs a hundred feet long, the most terrible of all the hunting animals that ranged the primeval world' (p. 185). The narrator admits that his ancestor's band lacked the Fire People's practical 'steadfastness of purpose', yet 'in the realm of the emotions, we were capable of long-cherished purpose' (p. 89). When the Fire People hunt Big-Tooth and his friend Lop-Ear, the latter stays with his traumatized companion, despite his fear. The narrator interprets this act 'as a foreshadowing of the altruism and comradeship that have helped make man the mightiest of the animals ... I see visions of Damon and Pythias, of lifesaving crews and Red Cross nurses, of martyrs and leaders of forlorn hopes, of Father Damien, and of the Christ himself ... whose strength may trace back to the elemental loins of Lop-Ear and Big-Tooth' (pp. 85–87). The Folk's 'sociable and gregarious' impulses prefigure modern human communities, while their collective, rhythmic chattering represents 'art nascent' (p. 171). London further questions univocal progress by qualifying his description of the violent Red-Eye as 'an atavism'; for 'the males of the lower animals do not maltreat and murder their mates ... Red-Eye, in spite of his tremendous atavistic tendencies, foreshadowed the coming of man, for it is the males of the human species only that murder their mates' (p. 167). The narrator suggests that Big-Tooth bequeathed his 'racial memories' by mating with a lone female, possibly descended from the Fire People, although the vicissitudes of heredity remain unknown. Instead of all prehumans advancing teleologically towards modern humans, London implies that *Homo sapiens* might be hybrids of diverse evolutionary tangents. This possibility undermines the primitive–civilized binary, revealing the roles of supposedly primitive instincts in modern civilization. As London indicates by locating the narrative in a modern speaker's heredity, primitive language might be inescapable, its primordial significations transmitted in the blood.

The primitive within

The more that fiction in the period tried to define primitive speech, the more it threatened to contaminate civilized language. If the latter was a hereditary characteristic, as Spencer and Sayce implied, then civilized speakers were as much products of nature as primitive speakers were. Alternatively, if civilized language was produced by social convention and tradition, as Tylor argued, then beneath this veneer of acquired habit remained primordial instincts and unconscious bodily signs. Wells and

London were both intensely interested in the endurance of instinctive communication, but also worried about its potential to undermine civilization. Against the instinctive sympathy suggested in *Before Adam* was the fear of degenerate violence and anarchy. Ideas of societal and biological progress produced inverse concepts of degeneration when the imagined demands of progress were not met.[79] Utopian ideals of rational state-building and scientific authority existed in opposition to fears of fragmentation and disorder without central, controlling authorities. Huxley claimed that humankind's 'ethical' evolution had emerged not in harmony with but in opposition to the 'cosmic' forces of nature.[80] Without the strict maintenance of artificial conventions and traditions, humans might regress to their primitive instincts. Yet, equally, by protecting humans from the struggle for survival, such artificial life could also degrade the bodies and minds on which civilization was built. These ideas inflected theories of linguistic and aesthetic degeneration, in which 'decadent' experiment became identified with atavism. The influence of such theories is discernible in several of Wells's and London's fictions of the 1890s and 1900s. They imagined degeneration as the breakdown of central authority over language, shattering speech into private idiolects and instinctive noise. Yet, both authors also viewed individual, instinctive speech as a means of resistance to mindless social convention. Their dark visions of primitive instincts overwhelming civilized speech clashed with more ambivalent attitudes to instinctive communication as potentially valuable to society.

Similarly as late-Victorian utopias often idealized central authority over language, many commentators identified verbal degeneration with the breakdown of such authority. The criminologist Cesare Lombroso defined degenerative language in 1889 as 'a tendency to puns and plays upon words ... a tendency to speak for one's self, and substitute epigram for logic, an extreme predilection for the rhythm and assonances of verse in prose writing, even an exaggerated degree of originality'.[81] Daston argues that discourses of objectivity from the mid nineteenth century onwards divided science and art into 'incommensurable ways of knowing'. Scientists and authors such as Hermann von Helmholtz and Charles Baudelaire opposed the conscious, scientific manipulation of symbols to the instinctive 'tact' of the poet.[82] Lombroso exemplified this opposition, diagnosing poetic language as a symptom of hereditary insanity while himself writing in an idiom that 'sought to purge itself of extravagant metaphor, to produce a pure medium of description ... freed from the partiality and subjectivity of its own past'.[83] Symbolist poets such as Paul Verlaine and Stéphane Mallarmé had experimented with the evocative potential of words apart from their conventional meanings. They sought to trigger indirect associations, as Mallarmé famously quipped: 'We do not write poems with ideas, but with words'.[84] The reactionary critic Max Nordau identified such unravelling of lexical categories with degeneration, writing that the symbolist utterance 'sinks into a meaningless vocal sound, intended only to awaken diverse agreeable emotions through association of ideas'.[85] Regenia Gagnier argues for a widespread perception during the period of literary 'degeneration' as 'the sacrifice of whole to the development of the part'.[86] In this vein, Havelock Ellis wrote in 1889, quoting Paul Bourget: 'A style of decadence is one in which the unity of the book is decomposed to give place to the independence of the page, in which the page is decomposed to give place to the independence of the phrase, and the phrase to give place to the independence of the word'.[87] Without conforming to a larger structure of relations, the rogue word or phrase lost semantic clarity, floating vaguely through indefinite associations. Simultaneously, the growth of popular print triggered fears of the unregulated speech of the masses eroding the fine distinctions of English. The journalist Charles Mackay warned in 1888 that '"slang" that was formerly confined to tramps, beggars, gipsies, and thieves' had now 'invaded the educated and semi-educated classes' through popular print.[88] Wells and London are interesting authors to consider in this regard, since both came from humble origins and wrote for popular audiences. Their fiction often sided with the elitists and reactionaries, however, fearing the degenerative anarchy of unregulated speech.

Wells expressed such fear of anarchy in 'Morals and Civilisation', writing that, since civilization was merely 'a fabric of ideas and habits', the loss of these would return humanity to primitive violence and disorder. He imagined 'the suddenly barbaric people wandering out into the streets, in their night-gear, their evening dress … esurient and pugnacious, turning their attention to such recondite weapons as a modern city affords – all for the loss of a few ideas and a subtle trick of thinking'.[89] Wells had earlier written that humans carried in their bodies 'the rapid physical concentration, the intense self-forgetfulness of the anger burst, the urgency of sexual passion in the healthy male, the love of killing'. Instead of effacing these instincts, convention had only diverted them into less destructive channels, so that 'what we call Morality becomes the padding of suggested emotional habits necessary to keep the round Palaeolithic savage in the square hole of the civilised state. And Sin is the conflict of the two factors'.[90] Language shaped mental suggestions that underpinned civilization. As Chapter 2 has illustrated, Wells's utopianism was

Primitive language in three romance settings 83

technocratic and authoritarian, relying as it did on scientific authority to mould minds and speech into harmony. Conversely, less verbal regulation would allow the resurgence of primitive instincts, with speech degenerating into unconscious noise.

Wells realized this vision in *The Time Machine*, in which a Victorian scientist travels into the future, discovering a shrunken, childlike population with only rudimentary speech. The time traveller states:

> Either I missed some subtle point or their language was excessively simple – almost exclusively composed of concrete substantives and verbs. There seemed to be few, if any, abstract terms, or little use of figurative language. Their sentences were usually simple and of two words, and I failed to convey or understand any but the simplest propositions.[91]

With machines providing for their needs, the Eloi's speech has degraded into aimless play. They coo meaninglessly to each other, passing their days in 'a melodious whirl of laughter and laughing speech' (p. 58). Wells makes explicit the link between art for art's sake and language degeneration, suggesting that, when not used as practical tools, words lose their meanings. The narrator comments: 'This has ever been the fate of energy in security; it takes to art and to eroticism, and then comes languor and decay' (p. 76). When speech lacks a unifying purpose, used merely as a toy to evoke sensations, it ceases to connect speakers with each other or their predecessors. The narrator states: 'all the traditions, the complex organizations, the nations, languages, literatures, aspirations, even the mere memory of Man as I knew him, had been swept out of existence' (p. 145). The tale links this degeneration with the loss of writing, which had once fixed meanings and usage. Only the 'decaying vestiges of books' are now to be found, a 'sombre wilderness of rotting paper', the uses of which humanity has long forgotten (p. 161). Without authorities controlling word usage, society's accumulation of knowledge and ideas falls away, returning humans to raw instinct.

This fear of language disintegrating without prescriptive authority also shapes Wells's *The Island of Dr Moreau* (1896). The eponymous Moreau is a scientist who vivisects animals to resemble humans and then trains them to talk. Shipwrecked on Moreau's island, the narrator Prendick at first fails to realize that the doctor's creations are not human and holds some conversations with them. By whip and torture, Moreau has forced them to repeat a parody of the Ten Commandments: 'Not to go on all-fours; that is the law. Are we not men?'[92] This system of verbal rituals collapses when the animals revert to their primal instincts, killing Moreau and resuming their primal grunts and barks. Moral and mental categories and institutions disintegrate along with word definitions. Without fixed forms and meanings, speech becomes instinctive noise. Prendick observes: 'Imagine language, once clear-cut and exact, softening and guttering, losing shape and import, becoming mere lumps of sound again' (p. 230). The novel repeatedly depicts the beast-folk's speech as shapeless and blurred, with Prendrick observing during a saying of the Law: 'The speaker's words came thick and sloppy, and though I could hear them distinctly I could not distinguish what he said. He seemed to me to be reciting some complicated gibberish' (p. 74). Wells indicates the importance of linguistic authority in controlling primitive vocal instinct by Moreau's law against 'jabbering', branding the bodies of creatures that succumb to it. The novel ends on a Swiftian note, with Prendick returning to England, only to be horrified at the atavism of its people. On London's streets 'prowling women would mew after me; furtive, craving men glance jealously at me', while, in church, 'it seemed that the preacher gibbered "Big Thinks", even as the Ape-man had done' (p. 247). Shunning humans, Prendick limits his life to books and chemistry experiments, concluding that it will be 'in the vast and eternal laws of matter ... that whatever is more than animal within us must find its solace and its hope' (p. 248). Wells implies that, without some authority maintaining abstract, conventional rules, civilized speech threatens to degenerate into instinctive noise.

Yet the tale also challenges linguistic authoritarianism. As Chapter 1 above showed, Wells worried about specialized technical dialects ossifying into dogma. 'The man trained solely in science falls easily into a superstitious attitude', Wells wrote; 'he is overdone with classification. He believes in the possibility of exact knowledge everywhere. What is not exact, he declares is not knowledge'.[93] Moreau exemplifies the cruelties that science may talk itself into when alienated from the common stream of speech, becoming as unsympathetic as Wells's Martians or Morlocks.[94] 'To this day I have never troubled about the ethics of the matter,' Moreau tells an appalled Prendick. 'The study of Nature makes a man at last as remorseless as Nature.' He reduces Prendick's moral objections to his experiments as mere primitive instinct, arising from personal experience of pain. Moreau declares, 'This store which men and women set on pleasure and pain, Prendick, is the mark of the beast upon them ... You cannot imagine the strange, colourless delight of these intellectual desires! The thing before you is no longer an animal, a fellow-creature, but a problem! Sympathetic pain, – all I know of it I remember as a thing I used to suffer from years ago' (pp. 136–37). In terms of morals and sympathy, Moreau's speech is no more advanced than the noises of the creatures that later kill him.

Further, Wells's early scientific romances sometimes suggest that instinctive signs might be instrumental to the progress of sympathy and even some forms of knowledge. The time traveller's ability to communicate and sympathize with the Eloi depends on their common vocabulary of instinctive gesture and expression. Apparently marooned in the future world and endangered by the Morlocks, he retains his spirits and sanity by cuddling, playing and dancing with the Eloi Weena. Prendick avoids being killed by the beast-folk through his ability to read their instinctive signs, anticipating the breakdown of their engrafted society. His instincts seem to realize the truth about the beast-folk before his conscious mind, detecting malevolent beasts while their conventional speech and appearance denote humanity. The vision of a hairy, strange-faced servant 'struck down through all my adult thoughts and feelings, and for a moment the forgotten horrors of childhood came back to my mind. Then the effect passed as it had come. An uncouth black figure of a man, a figure of no particular import, hung over the taffrail against the starlight' (p. 36). When he looks upon three others in the group, 'there was something in their faces – I knew not what – that gave me a queer spasm of disgust. I looked steadily at them, and the impression did not pass, though I failed to see what had occasioned it' (p. 47). Instinct is not simply chaos but a form of knowledge and a sign system in parallel to conventional speech with unique uses. Humans are only able to control nature by persisting as part of it, as is illustrated by Prendick's confrontation with one of the beast-folk who chases him through the forest. His instinctive fear enables him to recognize and exploit the same instinct in his pursuer: 'Setting my teeth hard, I walked straight towards him. I was anxious not to show the fear that seemed chilling my backbone ... I advanced a step or two, looking steadfastly into his eyes ... He turned again, and vanished into the dusk' (pp. 77–78). The human ascendancy comes of a combination of instinctive and conventional signs, instead of one obliterating the other. The narrative confirms Moreau's claim that sympathy springs from bodily instinct rather than reason. While Prendick grieves for the howling victims of Moreau's vivisection, 'Yet had I known such pain was in the next room, and had it been dumb, I believe – I have thought since – I could have stood it well enough. It is when suffering finds a voice and sets our nerves quivering that this pity comes troubling us' (p. 68). Instinctive vocal signs of emotion do not destroy but rather sustain sympathetic society. As Chapter 4 explores further, language sometimes appeared for the young Wells a site of collaboration between instinct and convention.

The linguistic edifice of civilization is similarly threatened by destabilizing primitive instinct in several of Jack London's tales. Yet London also presents primitive instinct as a dynamic force in language, enabling a Nietzschean individualism that resists mass conformity. London's life and intellectual influences shaped conflicts in his writing between supporting traditional cultural authorities and rejecting them. He lived as a seaman, tramp and gold prospector before becoming a writer through a difficult process of self-education. Although mainly an autodidact, London briefly studied English at the University of California, Berkeley, dropping out after six months due to financial difficulties. The biographer John Perry notes that, although he criticized the university as dry and passionless, London planned to return one day to attain his diploma.[95] His often autobiographical novel *Martin Eden* (1908) endorses linguistic authority, even while challenging the privileged social classes associated with it. The rough sailor protagonist Eden seeks to improve his language, with the middle-class English undergraduate Ruth instructing him to study 'grammar'. London depicts Eden's discovery of abstract knowledge and stable expression in books as an awakening, so that, when he reads poetry criticism, 'as the grammar had shown him the tie-ribs of language, so that book showed him the tie-ribs of poetry... beneath the beauty he loved finding the why and wherefore of that beauty'.[96] London believed in physiological foundations for verbal meaning, and he advocated Spencer's 'Philosophy of Style' throughout his career.[97] Spencer described language as a conversion of energy, transmitting ideas between minds with increasing precision. Eden develops the same view before reading Spencer, deciding that 'the great writers and master-poets ... knew how to express what they thought, and felt, and saw ... had discovered the trick of expression, of making words obedient servitors'. He idealizes Spencerian system building 'reducing everything to unity, elaborating ultimate realities, and presenting ... a universe so concrete of realization that it was like the model of a ship such as sailors make and put into glass bottles'.[98] London's visions of primitive language from around the same time reflect his faith in rigidly controlled Standard English as a prerequisite to knowledge and reason. In contrast to such acquired, conventional language, instinct fragments expression and the self into automatic processes without intelligence or volition.

London characterized primitive speech by a lack of prescriptive authority in his post-apocalyptic tale *The Scarlet Plague*. After a pandemic annihilates most of humanity, an ex-professor of English, Smith, impotently watches his language degenerate through successive generations of survivors. Without literacy or regulatory institutions, words lose their meanings as survivors return to a superstitious, hunter-gatherer existence. Much of the narrative concerns Smith's futile attempts to pass on his knowledge to his grandchildren, whose speech has withered to 'monosyllables and short, jerky sentences that was more a gibberish than a language'.[99] Hearing them, Smith muses to himself: 'Strange it is to hear the vestiges and remnants of the complicated Aryan speech falling from the lips of a filthy little skin-clad savage' (p. 177). To render this speech intelligible, the omniscient narrator claims to report it in partial translation: 'The boy did not exactly utter these words, but something that remotely resembled them and that was more guttural and explosive and economical of qualifying phrases' (p. 22). Like the roads and buildings of California's cities, English has crumbled into isolated monosyllables without the literary infrastructure to support abstract ideas. Deprived of education and writing, the narrator explains, English has 'gone through a bath of corrupt usage'. Once distinct words and concepts have merged into each other so that speakers can no longer imagine any difference between them. Smith's grandson reprimands him for over-complicating the colour scheme with words like 'scarlet' and describing crab as a 'toothsome delicacy': 'Crab is crab, ain't it?', 'Scarlet ain't anything but red is red' (pp. 22, 35). The abstract, scientific ideas of civilization depend on a stable, authoritative centre directing language use. Without this control, language loses its complex categories of expression, which have been built up by generations of science and culture. Deprived of the abstraction of writing, the 'savages' understand words only through reference to the body. They replace abstract terms with concrete nouns and verbs, turning scavengers into 'food-getters', and the scarlet plague into 'red death' (p. 53). Like the survivors' numeracy, which has shrunk to the number of fingers on their hands, so their nomenclature is unable to retain nouns that do not equate to familiar physical actions.

London's apocalyptic vision reflected his fear of primitive speech resurging among the barely educated working class from which he had risen. *The Scarlet Plague* presents the working class as degenerate savages, exemplified in the 'perfect brute' that dominates the band of survivors and sets a trend for the society that follows. 'In the midst of our civilization, down in our slums and labor ghettos', Smith laments, 'we had bred a race of barbarians, of savages; and now, in the time of our calamity, they turned upon us like the wild beasts they were and destroyed us. And they destroyed themselves as well' (pp. 105–06). While sympathetic to the poor, London's socialism sometimes veered toward Wellsian authoritarianism, suggesting that their thought and language must be directed by elites. In this vein, Smith hoards books in a cave and prophesies, 'Some day men will read again; and then, if no accident has befallen my cave, they will know that Professor James Howard Smith once lived and saved for them the knowledge of the ancients' (pp. 175–76). Language and society are teleological developments which can only develop towards the current western scientific and literary institutions. London suggests this through Smith not only classifying his descendants' current state but also predicting future regression. Cassandra-like, he states: 'You are true savages. Already has begun the custom of wearing human teeth. In another generation you will be perforating your noses and ears and wearing ornaments of bone and shell. I know' (p. 39). Similarly, in his novel of socialist revolution *The Iron Heel*, London depicts the mental and verbal degradation of the working class as resulting not from direct repression but rather from neglect. Capitalism fails to develop them emotionally and intellectually, as the narrator Avis states: 'Common school education, so far as they were concerned, had ceased. They lived like beasts in great squalid labor-ghettos, festering in misery and degradation ... In all truth, there in the labor-ghettos is the roaring abysmal beast the oligarchs fear so dreadfully – but it is the beast of their own making'.[100] Avis presents the speech of this degraded folk as instinctive noise, requiring regulation by higher authorities. She knows that the current revolution is doomed (although a future one will succeed) upon hearing the bestial shouts of the 'mob' confronting the army. This 'awful river... surged past my vision in concrete waves of wrath, snarling and growling, carnivorous ... dim ferocious intelligences with all the godlike blotted from their features and all the fiendlike stamped in, apes, and tigers' (p. 265). In London's contradictory vision, primitive speech is both a reversion to primordial nature and a product of artificial society.

Alongside London's belief in the need for institutional authority over language ran a conflicting reverence for the primitive body as a source of mental-verbal individualism. London was strongly influenced by Nietzsche, claiming in 1914 that he had 'been more stimulated by Nietzsche than any other writer in the world'.[101] Jonathan Berliner argues that in 'his recurrent praise of primordial supermen, London presents nature as a brutal force but crucially one that could be harnessed for socialistic purposes'.[102] Nietzsche argued that society created metaphorical 'intuitions' which overrode natural instincts. The coming

Übermensch would rediscover these instincts, speaking in 'forbidden metaphors and unheard-of combinations of concepts ... demolishing and deriding the old conceptual barriers', breaking through artificial dogmas.[103] *The Iron Heel* describes its socialist hero Ernest Everhard as 'a Superman, a blond beast such as Nietzsche has described', who shatters the logic of capitalism and Christianity with powerful oratory (p. 5). Whilst well read in history and science, Everhard is also a creature of the body, with bulging muscles and instinctive passion behind his convictions. Ernest's future wife, Avis, writes of one of his speeches: 'It was not so much what he said as how he said it. I roused at the first sound of his voice. It was as bold as his eyes. It was a clarion-call that thrilled me. And the whole table was aroused, shaken alive from monotony and drowsiness' (p. 6). Ernest's closeness to the body renders him a stubborn materialist, dismissing the language of 'metaphysics' as sophistry. Like Reade and Lubbock's savages, words are to him mere shadows, as he tells one conservative rival, 'You've got to put it in my hand ... The wise heads have puzzled so sorely over truth because they went up into the air after it' (p. 13). Such an apparently primitive perspective enables Ernest to break through the worship of words which maintain the status quo. Contradicting her images of the masses as a primitive rabble, Avis elsewhere describes them as 'phrase slaves' blinded by vague abstractions. 'The utterance of a single-word', she states, 'could negative the generalisations of a lifetime of serious research and thought ... Vast populations grew frenzied over such phrases as "an honest dollar" and "a full dinner pail"' (p. 62). Conversely, as in *Before Adam*, instinctive feeling and vocalization form the basis of solidarity, as Everhard says of his conversion to socialism, 'I was in touch with great souls who exalted flesh and spirit over dollars and cents, and to whom the thin wail of the starved slum child meant more than all the pomp and circumstance of commercial expansion and world empire' (p. 61). London's imagined future revolution appears both to elevate language to the utopian level of pure intellect and to return it to instinctive signs of sympathy.

London's short story 'When the World was Young' (1910) similarly complicates primitive speech, associating it with ideals of rugged masculinity diluted by artificial modernity. The tale depicts a modern, educated American, James Ward, reverting to the behaviour of an ancient, Teutonic ancestor. He roams the forests by night, fighting beasts, and bursts into instinctive song, seemingly inherited. 'By some quirk of atavism,' the narrator states, 'a certain portion of that early self's language had come down to him as a racial memory.'[104] Such vocalizations are involuntary, illustrating biological processes overwhelming the individual self and its expression. They 'always irresistibly rushed to his lips when he was engaged in fierce struggling or fighting' (p. 84). Such outbreaks threaten Ward's ability to function within conventional, modern society, filling him with the urge to violently 'paw and maul' his genteel fiancée at dinner parties (p. 90). Yet, such instinctive speech also encodes values of bravery and self-sacrifice. During one reversion, Ward defends his new wife and dogs against a bear attacking their property. The cries of his hounds trigger Ward's instincts, first drawing him to the bear and, second, sending him berserk upon it: 'the human brute went mad. A foaming rage flecked the lips that parted with a wild inarticulate cry' (p. 94). Yet, after slaying the bear, he sees his horrified wife and 'felt something snap in his brain' so that 'the early Teuton in him died' (p. 95). London suggests that civilization emasculates men, with the fully 'modern' Ward fearing the dark outside, hiding behind locked doors and burglar alarms. This anxiety contrasts with Ward's earlier state when his primitive self chased away a terrified would-be burglar. Against the model of primitive speech as chaotic noise, London presents Ward's instinctive vocalizations as extremely stable, enduring through 'thrice a thousand years' (p. 93). A philologist at Ward's university classifies his songs as 'early German, or early Teuton, of a date that must far precede anything that had ever been discovered and handed down by the scholars' (p. 84). As in Bulwer-Lytton's *The Coming Race*, London exchanges language progressivism for vitalism, lamenting the loss of natural, Indo-European values and identity. Modern, industrialized life shrivels speakers into effete creatures of convention, divorced from the feelings they once voiced instinctively. London's representation of primitive speech as a source of natural manliness and sympathy resonates with a wider tendency in the period to revere ancient speech as organic and, thus, of a higher truth-value than modern literature. The next chapter will explore this counter-tendency in which fiction and philology opposed a natural, living verbal past to a dead, mechanized modernity. The perfect communication and semantic stability that progressives hoped for in the future, vitalists imagined in the lost past. Instead of threatening to destroy meaning, primitive instinct might form its natural source.

CHAPTER 3

Organic orality and the historical romance

The Victorian philologist J. W. Donaldson wrote in 1839 that, for ancient speakers, poetry 'streamed freely from the breast ... replete with the richest and most significant compounds'. By contrast, centuries of writing and science had reduced modern English to 'barren elegances of logical prose'.[1] Donaldson's words reflected a view of language evolution that would persist through the century and define itself in opposition to ideals of objective, scientific language. Unlike progressives such as Spencer who hailed modernity's supposed mechanization of language, some philologists and creative writers mourned this process for destroying the living essence of language. Conceiving of language as a kind of organism, vitalist philology contrasted the imagined artifice and deadness of modern language with nostalgic visions of past purity and vigour. Language vitalism grew from romantic and biblical traditions which idealized a past golden age before modern degradation. In response to the social instability of industrial capitalism, many Victorians looked to history for models of a supposedly more natural order.[2] Equally, as science undermined traditional narratives of creation, vitalist philology offered a substitute for Eden through the origins of nations.[3] It imagined a mystical power in language that was rooted in human instincts and nurtured by the supposedly more natural society of the past. In 1860 the philologist F. W. Farrar waxed nostalgic for the linguistic vitality of England's ancestors, lamenting: 'our very civilization has robbed us of this happy and audacious power. Nature spoke more to them than to us'.[4] Vitalist philology strove to compensate for this decline by rediscovering the ancient etymologies of words before they had 'decayed', in Müller's phrase. At around the mid century the dialect-poet William Barnes referred to the philologist of 'that increasing class who wish to purify our tongue, and enrich it from its own resources'.[5] In contrast to the progressive idols of efficiency and precision, vitalist philology fetishized verbal purity, imagining meaning as a kind of racial inheritance.

Historical fiction promised ways of reconnecting with this organic verbal past. Katie Trumpener notes that many early Scottish, Irish and Welsh nationalists identified their struggle specifically with orality, conceiving their 'new national literary history under the sign of the bard'. This reverence of oral folk culture influenced much historical fiction to locate its imagined national origins in embodied speech.[6] Yet historical fiction also exposed the contradictions in language vitalism. Charles Kingsley and R. M. Ballantyne's historical romances locate the living essence of English in oral society before the inauthentic substitutions of writing. Kingsley and Ballantyne downplay their tales' textuality, presenting them as transcripts of speech. Such poses clashed, however, with the documentary historical methods on which their genre was based. Efforts to bring prose into an organic relation with the past often involved racializing language. Paul du Chaillu and J. F. Hodgetts's historical fiction fetishized archaic words as expressions of Teutonic blood. Yet, such exclusivity contradicted the logic of racial-linguistic intermixture used to justify British imperial unity. Problems of authentic language origins are similarly refracted through invasion fiction of the late-Victorian and Edwardian period. Such narratives are torn between the desire for a united national voice and the anxiety that such a voice would be inorganic and susceptible to counterfeiting. Language vitalism was not, however, always politically conservative or nationalist. William Morris's prose romances combined reverence for ancient language with socialism and internationalism. Morris's vision of self-defining speech communities existed in tension, though, with socialism's need for delocalized language. Similarly, Thomas Hardy's fiction mourns the vanishing of rural dialect that placed speakers close to nature. Yet Hardy complicates this attitude with readings of Darwin and Mill which undermined ideas of pastoral stasis, pure origins and 'natural' society.

Printing voices

Language vitalism in Victorian historical fiction was characterized by negotiations of the gap between speech and writing.[7] Comparative philology modelled speech as the life of language, and writing as mere dead records of it. Literate society might therefore be imagined as alienated from orality and the natural values it encoded. Brantlinger has argued that Walter Scott's vision of oral Highland society depicted 'the spread of English, of literacy, and even the popularity of his own novels, as evidence of the death of chivalry and the advent of a kind of universal mediocrity'.[8]

Kingsley and Ballantyne were both heavily influenced by Scott. Kingsley opened his Conquest-era novel *Hereward the Wake* (1865) by comparing England's past to the Highlands 'embalmed forever in the pages of Walter Scott'.[9] Ballantyne came from a family of Edinburgh publishers who had been closely involved with Scott's career. The authors' historical fiction similarly idealized oral society as heroic through its closeness to nature and truth. Presenting their writing as a kind of speech, Kingsley and Ballantyne distinguished it from artificial modernity, aiming to partially restore the organic oral past. However, both were also committed patriots, supporting British union and empire, which were only possible through writing. The organic orality they revered could only be reconciled with national culture by, perversely, behaving like writing. Eric Hobsbawm observes that print produced the 'optical illusion' of an 'eternal', homogeneous national tongue.[10] Rather than evolving across borders or splitting within them, ancestral English needed to appear standardized in order to reflect the undivided national mind.

The reverend and professor Kingsley was exposed to provincial dialect through his childhood in Devon and Northampton, and counted Müller and Barnes among his friends. In an 1848 lecture series, with which Kingsley collaborated, his colleague A. B. Strettell described words as not 'arbitrary' but 'living powers', embodying thought.[11] Writing and artificial city life detached words from the organic logos that coined them, producing, Strettell lamented, 'those hollow conventionalities of expression which we so often meet with in daily life'.[12] These influences would seem to set Kingsley against the perceived artifice of Standard English. However, as a member of the Christian Socialists, Kingsley sought a common language to unite England's classes. The narrator of his social-problem novel *Alton Locke* (1850) complains of priests' rarefied language: 'If he would only have talked English! if clergymen would only 'preach in English'! and then they wonder that their sermons have no effect!'[13] In the collaborative lecture series Kingsley claimed that the thoughts and speech of all countrymen 'pass through the same course of intellectual growth, through which the whole English nation has passed'. Each speaker is 'a microcosm' of the national tongue, drawing on the same hinterland of etymologies.[14] Yet this common heritage could only exist through alienating, disembodied writing.

This contradictory urge towards oral communities, yet also delocalized nationalism, shapes Kingsley's Elizabethan adventure *Westward Ho!* (1855). The tale of the Spanish Armada's defeat presents the speech of its heroes as natural and true in contrast to mechanical writing. The narrator questions whether the rote learning of a nineteenth-century 'national school' is superior to the natural virtue of his naval hero Amyas Leigh. Amyas's 'broad Devonshire accent' mirrors his 'savage' physical skills in outdoor practicalities. Victorian school pupils might mock his ignorance, the narrator concedes, but he is their superior in 'manhood, virtue and godliness'.[15] Incapable of lying, Amyas exemplifies Müller's concept of the logos in which speech and thought were one (1, p. 427). Associating alienating writing with Catholicism, Kingsley frames the Reformation as a restoration of organic orality (ignoring its focus on Scripture). Amyas's Anglican faith flows naturally from him 'not even knowing whether he is good or not, but just doing the right thing without thinking about it, as simply as a little child, because the Spirit of God is with him' (p. 48). Conversely, his Catholic cousin Eustace joins the Jesuits and interrogates his soul, 'according to certain approved methods and rules, which he has got by heart'. This mechanical faith causes Eustace to smuggle encrypted 'bulls, dispensations, secret correspondences, seditious tracts' around England (p. 55). He attempts to lure the heroes into a trap by leaving a 'dirty note' warning of Irish spies. Ironically, despite being written by a Devonian, the note arouses suspicion through its deviation from West Country dialect. Of the lines, 'By deer park end to-night ... Grip and hold hym tight', the squire comments: 'We say "to" and not "by" ... [a]nd "man", instead of "him"' (p. 88). Kingsley's reference to dialect highlights how rarely it appears elsewhere in the novel. Speech is mostly reported in Standard English, giving English a unitary existence across space and time.[16] The narrator imagines a timeless 'plain English', which reflects universal common sense, cutting through sophistry. Eustace, the narrator explains, is removed to the Continent to be 'trained as a seminary priest; in plain English, to be taught the science of villainy, on the motive of superstition'. Yet the rational, empiricist 'plain English' spoken by Amyas is at odds with his folk culture. While Amyas sees through the superstitions of Catholic doctrine, the narrator informs us that 'he devoutly believed in fairies ... and held that they changed babies, and made the mushroom rings on the downs to dance in' (p. 7). Amyas never speaks of such beliefs, though, and Kingsley identifies them with earlier times before the formation of the national spirit of 'plain English'. Among the few characters that use Devon dialect is the fortune-teller Lucy, positioning it in the preliterate, pagan past: 'I'm most mazed to see ye ... you hain't made up your mind ... Ben there's a way to 't, a sure way' (pp. 71–72). Kingsley neutralizes the potential challenge that dialect poses to national unity by placing it in a perpetual retrospect.[17]

The contradiction in Kingsley's vision between organic orality and national writing comes into sharpest focus when Amyas meets Edmund Spenser. Watching for Spanish ships off the coast, the poet tries to justify to Walter Raleigh his propensity for 'imitating the classical metres'. This debate is arrested, though, when he hears Amyas sing a song learnt from his mother. It is a pure natural outpouring, as Amyas remarks, 'Cocks crow all night long at Christmas, Captain Raleigh, and so do I' (p. 165). Kingsley's narration centres the conflict in the scene between artificial, foreign hexameters and instinctive English rhyme. Thanks to Amyas's example, the narrator assures us, 'the matter was finally settled, and the English tongue left to go the road on which Heaven had started it' (p. 162). The scene reflects popular criticism of the use of hexameters in Victorian poetry. Lord Saintsbury would later attack the practice as an artificial imposition upon English from a dead language. Conversely, Saintsbury argued that the ballad quatrain, which Spenser hears Amyas singing, resonated naturally with an English 'inner ear'.[18] The more obvious opposition which Kingsley's narrator avoids discussing, however, is between Amyas's oral recital and Spenser's disembodied writing. Kingsley downplays this opposition by placing quotations from Spenser's writing in his character's mouth, as though they were oral compositions. His rhetoric also diverts attention away from the diverse branches of English: the journey from past to present is a single 'road'. Patriotism demanded that the oral varieties of the past be standardized in the national writing of the present.

Hereward the Wake, Kingsley's tale of resistance to the Norman Conquest, is fraught by the same tension between speech and writing. Like Amyas, the hero Hereward seldom separates thought from speech, exploding with spontaneous, alliterative war chants during battle. He is also a poor dissembler, impulsively voicing his war-cry 'A Wake! A Wake!' (p. 310) when enemies are near, giving away his position. When he proposes to resist William of Normandy it is through face-to-face speeches, to which his supporters respond with one voice: 'we are free men!' (p. 180). Conversely, writing is associated with skullduggery. Hereward flees England after being outlawed for robbing a monk. Instead of confronting him directly, the Anglo-Saxon regime (corrupted by Catholicism) hatches his exile through a series of letters. His outlawing is circulated via 'a parchment, with an outlandish Norman seal hanging to it' (p. 32). The subsequent Norman regime with its Domesday Book and feudal laws contrasts with the nostalgic vision of self-governing oral communities. Kingsley glosses over this problem, though, by presenting Hereward's eventual capitulation to King William as oral and embodied. Hereward fights William's administration while it remains faceless but, upon their meeting, he 'put his hands between William's hands, and swore to be his man' (p. 340). This fantasized reconciliation of Norman king with indigenous English downplays the administrative serfdom which William introduced, and its more distant relations mediated by writing. As in *Westward Ho!*, Kingsley ignores the destruction of speech varieties, charting the progress of one language and nation through history. Far from dying in the eleventh century, Hereward's spirit of freedom lived on in 'Bold Outlaws' like Robin Hood. For centuries afterwards, they 'talked and sung of Hereward, and all his doughty deeds, over the hearth in lone farm-houses', keeping alive 'the spirit of Freedom' that would 'mould them into a great nation' (p. 370). Kingsley's rhetoric of continuity suggests that Victorian literature might be restored to this line of organic inheritance.

Seeking to present himself as heir to the oral past rather than destroyer of it, Kingsley frames his texts as transcripts of speech.[19] In the 1848 lectures, Kingsley commented: 'the art of writing English is, I should say, the art of speaking English'.[20] Instead of mourning the death of poetic orality in prose, Kingsley celebrates prose as potentially 'the highest poetry'. Coupled with 'richness and vigour' of spirit, it is 'a free and ever-shifting flow of every imaginable rhythm and metre, determined by no arbitrary rules, but only by the spiritual intent of the subject'. While 'the majority' of prose is hollow conventionality and imitation, the privileged voice is purified through it.[21] The opening to *Westward Ho!* merges prose conceptually with speech, warning that 'if now and then I shall seem to warm into a style somewhat too stilted and pompous, let me be excused for my subject's sake, fit rather to have been sung than said, and to have proclaimed to all true English hearts, not as a novel but as an epic' (p. 2). The acknowledgement of formal differences between novel and epic hides the greater disjunction between recital and text. The tale presents itself as not a calculated, industrial product, but as an outpouring from the soul. Kingsley always wrote rapidly, as Müller recalled after his friend's death: 'He was, in one sense of the word, a careless writer ... He did it with a concentrated energy of will which broke through all difficulties ... but the perfection and classical finish are wanting in most of his works'.[22] The publisher Charles Kegan Paul remembered how Kingsley 'would work himself into a white heat over his book, till, too excited to write more, he would calm himself down by a pipe, pacing his grass-plot in thought, and in long strides'.[23] These anecdotes frame Kingsley's writing habits as bodily exertion and outpouring rather than mental abstraction. *Westward*

Ho! further emphasizes its pseudo-orality with barbs at modern publishing culture. The narrator observes: 'story-telling, in those old times, when books (and authors also, lucky for the public) were rarer than now, was a common amusement' (p. 216). In a similarly critical allusion to coverage of the British military in Crimea, we are told:

> Battles (as soldiers know, and newspaper editors do not) are usually fought, not as they ought to be fought, but as they can be fought; and while the literary man is laying down the law at his desk as to how many troops should be moved here, and what rivers should be crossed there ... the wretched man who has to do the work finds the matter settled for him by pestilence, want of shoes, empty stomachs, bad roads, heavy rains, hot suns, and a thousand other stern warriors who never show on paper. (p. 168)

Kingsley's antagonism to modern print culture and authorship presents his voice, by contrast, as embedded in the action. The speaker withdraws from the persona of a 'literary man' sitting 'at his desk' and seems, momentarily, to inhabit the soldier trudging through the battlefield.[24]

The pseudo-orality of Kingsley's narration is undercut by a scholarly register stressing the tale's historical accuracy. Kingsley would become a Cambridge professor of History in 1860, and was well acquainted with the analysis of primary documents pioneered by historians such as Edward Gibbon. This methodical, evidence-based 'truth' diverged from the natural 'truth' imagined to flow spontaneously from the human voice. Amyas's meeting with Spenser in *Westward Ho!* is introduced with a historian's distanced attention to dates, context and attribution: 'the commonweal of poetry and letters, in that same critical year 1580, was in far greater danger from those same hexameters than the common woe of Ireland (as Raleigh called it) was from the Spaniards' (p. 161). Similarly, in *Hereward the Wake* the narrating voice sometimes shifts from the rhetoric of oral tradition to documentary evidence, reproducing family genealogies and citing contemporary chronicles. Abstract comparisons and empirical facts replace local anecdote and organic inspiration: 'The campaigns of Hannibal and Caesar succeeded by the same tactics as those of Frederic and Wellington; and so, as far as we can judge, did those of ... William of Normandy' (p. 206). Both narratives draw attention to themselves as textual constructs rather than inspired speech to prove their historical authenticity. Megan Perigoe Stitt argues that Victorian historical fiction separated 'the concept of language as history ... from the narrator's ability to select and footnote and explain *with* language. As long as dialects keep their strangeness, they are objects of study – and language (in the voice of the narrator's present) retains its ability to talk about itself'.²⁵ Similarly, Kingsley's authorial voices place the characters' voices at a remove from the reader through imaginary acts of translation. The epigraph to *Westward Ho!* states that their words and deeds have been 'rendered into modern English' (p. iii). Similarly, in *Hereward*, parentheses inform the reader of movements between spoken Anglo-Saxon, Danish, Latin and Cornish. While these tropes render the tales more historically plausible, they also alienate their tellers from the auratic oral culture of old.

Tensions between organic, oral 'truth' and written, evidential 'truth' similarly permeate Ballantyne's novels of Viking ancestry *Erling the Bold* (1869) and *Norsemen in the West* (1872). Ballantyne's novels resemble Scott's *Waverley* series, associating orality with natural independence and chivalry. In *Erling*, Viking speech resists the encroaching centralization of power by the tyrant Harald Haarfager. At Viking councils, Harald's sophistry is unable to sway his countrymen, whose oral culture 'accustomed [them] to think and reason closely'. They had, the narrator remarks, 'the laws of the land "by heart", in the most literal sense of those words, – for there were no books to consult and no precedents to cite in those days; and his hearers weighed with jealous care each word he said'.²⁶ Unlike the mass of written legislation and precedents of Westminster and the judiciary, Viking law is written on, and grown from, its subjects' hearts. *Norsemen* also celebrates the natural truthfulness of oral Vikings as they discover America. Viking deeds always match their words, as the sea-king Karlsefin counsels a youngster: 'how contemptible it is to threaten and not perform'.²⁷ Crewman Hake later demonstrates this advice when he claims that his arrows never miss their target. As Karlsefin challenges him to prove it, 'The words had scarcely left his lips when an arrow stood quivering in the knot referred to' (p. 141). Against such idealized speech, the Vikings foresee the untruthfulness of writing when recording their adventures in verse. Biarne is glad that they lack the Romans' writing, for with oral records, he claims, 'the measure and the rhyme would chain men to the words, and so to the truth' (p. 69). Biarne's comment points to the potential unreliability of Ballantyne's writing, based as it is on a trail of transcriptions and translations of ancient sagas.

Ballantyne plays down this problem by privileging certain readers with a kind of inner ear that enables them to detect the mysterious ring of truth in documents. Further, such scholars are able to read between the lines of the text, connecting imaginatively with the oral history that preceded it. Ballantyne's narrator states that despite 'man's well-known tendency to invent and exaggerate, it still remains likely that all the truth would be retained, although surrounded more or less with fiction ... Men with penetrating minds and retentive memories, who are trained to such work, are swift to detect the chaff amongst the wheat' (p. 217). Readers such as Ballantyne are heirs to the Viking skalds through their 'penetrating minds and retentive memories', echoing the Vikings who 'think and reason closely', remembering laws by heart. Researching the written facts deeply enough will enable the privileged sage to break through them and accurately reimagine the preceding oral culture. Allen Frantzen argues that Victorian Anglo-Saxon studies blurred the distinction between documented 'beginnings' and mythical 'origins'.[28] For historians such as J. R. Green in *A Short History of the English People* (1874), *Beowulf* and *The Anglo-Saxon Chronicle* were only points of departure for mythologizing 'the fatherland of the English Race' in the forests of Germany.[29] Ballantyne similarly treats documents as stepping stones to imagined ancestral experience. In a key battle scene of *Erling*, the narrative protests its fidelity to original manuscripts, yet, also claims to transcend them: 'There were scalds in both fleets at that fight, these afterwards wrote a poem descriptive of it, part of which we now quote'. The long passage, detailing the battle, is followed by the narrator explaining: 'In this poem the scald gives only an outline of the great fight. Let us follow more closely the action of those in whom we are peculiarly interested' (pp. 367–69). Ballantyne reverses the logic of past verse, grounded in subjective particulars, giving way to the broad generalizations of prose history. Instead, it is the ancient manuscript which reduces the tale to 'an outline' and the modern novelist who restores the even older subjectivity of oral story-telling. *Norsemen* suggests that the imaginative author might revive the skaldic aura by combining scholarship with personal, embodied experience. 'Minor details', the preface states, have been drawn from the author's 'own knowledge and personal experience of life in the wildernesses of America' (iv). Ballantyne's time working with trackers in Canada for the Hudson's Bay Company positions him in the oral tradition, restoring first-person testimony to the tale. In order to reach mythical origins instead of mere evidential beginnings, Ballantyne's writing must reconnect with embodied speech.

Ballantyne also frames himself as heir to the skaldic past through his ancient speech imitating modern writing. In *Norsemen* the warrior Thorward tells his love-struck friend, 'although the course of your courtship runs smooth, there is an old proverb – descended from Odin himself, I believe – which assures us that true love never did so run' (p. 46). The remark positions Shakespeare's literary genius as skaldic genius, inherited through generations of speakers. Equally, after the boy Olaf ventures into the forest and is captured by natives, his self-remonstrations seem to anticipate the King James Bible: 'If I had loved father better, perhaps I would have obeyed him better'. The narrator comments, 'it would almost seem as if Olaf had heard of such a word as this – "If ye love me, keep my commandments!"' (p. 287). By imagining an unchanging linguistic spirit, Ballantyne charts a teleological path from oral Old Norse to literary English. Equally, he traces his novel's verisimilitude to the inheritance of Nordic skald-craft. The Vikings' poem records are composed by the whole community, babbling with different voices and styles. After they land in America, Karlsefin recites their voyage as poetry. However, his companion Biarne objects to the omission of an episode where a whale swam near the ship, and speaks a page-worth of verse describing it. 'Hence it appears in this chronicle,' notes the narrator, 'and forms an interesting instance of the way in which men, for the sake of humorous effect, mingle little pieces of fiction with veritable history' (p. 63). In framing such narrative techniques as oral inheritance, Ballantyne narrows the gap between historical writing and oral prehistory. As Vikings were instinctively disposed to Christianity, so the Victorian sage-author instinctively recognizes the living truths behind the manuscripts. Where, though, were these instincts to be located? As historical fiction struggled to close the gap between oral past and literary present, language easily became conflated with race.

Language nostalgia and race

Ballantyne's *Erling* closes with the comment: 'there is perhaps more of Norse blood in your veins than you wot of, reader ... for much of what is good and true in our laws and social customs, much manly and vigorous in the British Constitution ... dwelt in the breasts of the rugged old Sea-kings of Norway!' (p. 437). Racial theory offered to organicize language as a substitute for orality, locating the living power of words in the blood. From the 1850s onwards, physical anthropology increasingly divided humans into fixed races with inherited characteristics.[30] The speech of the past was, perhaps, not lost, then, but lying dormant in its speakers' descendants. 'Where is the Englishman,' demanded Joseph Bosworth's *Compendius Anglo-Saxon and English Dictionary* (1848), 'that does not feel his heart beat with conscious pride and independence when he considers his *Freedom*? ... How tame is the Romanised *Liberty*, in comparison ... This is the true, heartfelt *Freedom* and we derived it from our Anglo-Saxon forefathers'.[31] Such racialized philology framed word meanings as instinctively felt rather than socially acquired. Carlyle had described language as a vast genealogy of forgotten 'Hero-Poets': 'For every word we have, there was such a man and poet. The coldest word was once a glowing new metaphor ... Our English Speech is speakable because there were Hero-Poets of our blood and lineage'.[32] The Teutonic nature of this originating race was popularized in the second half of the century by new translations of ancient Anglo-Saxon and Norse texts such as *Beowulf*, the *Heimskringla* and *Burnt Njal*.[33] Meanwhile, increasing immigration into Britain could be easily conceived as racial-linguistic invasion and contamination.[34] The historian E. A. Freeman traced England's social divisions to its loss of authentic racial identity through influxes of foreign elements. His *History of the Norman Conquest* (1867–73) lamented how many 'true, ancient, and vigorous Teutonic words ... have perished from our classical speech, and now come among us as strangers'.[35] Forced to speak through structures of thought and feeling alien to its racial spirit, the English voice had lost much of its power. The Viking fiction of James Frederick Hodgetts and Paul du Chaillu strove to revive this organic voice through etymology. Excavating ancient words and meanings promised to trigger racial impulses, reuniting speakers with their natural heritage. However, this strategy was as likely to collapse the myth of a united nation as it was to reinforce it, revealing mongrel origins. Equally, Victorian imperialism clashed with the rhetoric of pure, racial-linguistic essences, threatening to uproot English from its mythical native soil and speakers.

The idea of organicizing modern English by separating 'native' elements from foreign impositions was put into practice by the Viking fiction of James Frederick Hodgetts. His 1885 novel *The Champion of Odin* mourns English alienation from the ancestral speech while discussing the strictness of 'Northern honour':

> It is a strange circumstance, but one illustrating the intimate connection between thought and language, that as the keen sense of the all-important sanctity of this abstract sentiment died out, so the word for it became extinct, and we have been forced to borrow (or steal) one from the very race which we have least cause to love, the Romans! Our own word *ar* or *aer* is dead, and we use *honour*![36]

By planting such words in his texts, however, Hodgetts challenged the 'death' of organic English word roots. Perhaps, if classical learning could be replaced by ancient Norse, English would recover its 'living powers', lying dormant in the national bloodstream. Hodgetts's preface is explicit in this aim, encouraging schoolboys to excavate their heritage: 'English boys, as a rule, are too open and straightforward to feel any pleasure in the stories of the deities of Olympus ... They will find the myths of their own race far less objectionable ... and they have besides the advantage of appealing directly to their own Teutonic impulses' (p. iv). Hodgetts was a literature professor, and his ideas of connecting writing with readers' racial predispositions cohered with justifications of English as a discipline. The Icelandic translator George Dasent had argued that the 'monstrous mosaic' of modern English could only be purified through universities teaching the national tongue through its Teutonic parents.[37] Writing in the 1880s when English studies had become more established, Hodgetts suggests that education will reawaken the Old Norse lying dormant in English blood. He peppers his novel with Norse words as though to nudge English back towards its organic roots. The narrator explains that the Viking king lived in a '"Burg", or tower, as we now say, using a debased Norman word instead of our own dear English, though that still lives in such names as Edinburgh' (p. 35). The hero Orm describes his enemies as 'nithings', which a footnote translates as 'a person of contempt' (p. 3). Further translations and contextual hints introduce the reader to more Norse words, which subsequently enter the text's lexis: 'a small sword, or dirk', 'a death-song, or "drapa"', 'sagas and qvidas, or legends and lays, were sung' (pp. 46, 70, 336). Hodgetts's Norse vocabulary mirrors the Icelandic and Scandinavian phrasebooks which became popular in England as late-Victorian tourists journeyed northwards in search of their roots.[38] Perhaps the unity and vigour of the Viking past could live again in English speech reconnected with words of those times.

Paul du Chaillu's novel *Ivar the Viking* (1893) suggests a similar restoration of the organic national voice through etymology. The French-American author and anthropologist had argued persistently that English origins were Scandinavian rather than Anglo-Saxon. His novel, aimed at popularizing this view, quotes William Gladstone in its preface. 'When I have been in Norway, or Denmark, or among Scandinavians,' the former Prime Minister writes, 'I have felt something like a cry of nature from within, asserting (credibly or otherwise) my nearness to them ... [T]his, I have learned, is a very common experience with British travellers'.[39] The English speaker's authentic Nordic vocabulary has been replaced by Latinate word roots, so that his unity with Scandinavians can only be expressed through an instinctive 'cry of nature'. Like Hodgetts, du Chaillu attempts to revive forgotten Norse words through his narration. The Viking women live in '"skemmas", or bowers', while the warrior Hjorvard wields a '"sax", or single-edged sword' and wears '"brynja", or chain-armour' (p. 7). Du Chaillu also traces fragments of Norse words in modern English, reuniting them with the original experiences and environments that coined them. Ship-captains are referred to as 'styrmen', meaning 'to steer their own ships' (p. 50). Among Vikings, 'all the numerous buildings formed a vast quadrangle, enclosing a large plot of grass called "tun", or town' (p. 3), while '"drekis" or dragon ships ... derived their names from the fact that their prows and sterns were ornamented with the head or tail of one or more dragons' (p. 9). The organic truthfulness which du Chaillu strives to restore in language is reflected in the 'name fastening' ritual which his hero Ivar undergoes as a child. His father declares: 'Ivar shall the boy be named after his grandfather ... he will ... be called his father's son, for he will wage war from early age, and wander far and wide' (p. 26). Unlike modern England, in which the names of ancient families could be bought, Vikings embodied the lineage of their names. Freeman traced the loss of authentic names to Norman feudalism when serfs were named according to their barons rather than ancestral tribes. 'A man who bears a surname formed from an English name,' he states, 'may be set down without doubt as being of Old-English descent. But when a man bears a surname formed from a Norman name, the name itself proves nothing.'[40] Hodgetts and du Chaillu's Viking fictions strive to compensate for this lost identity by awakening racial memories through fragments of the old speech.

The wish to purify an exclusive stock of ancient word roots conflicted with the popular image of English as an absorbent, heterogeneous conglomerate. Carlyle's Hero-Poets were as much Norman as Anglo-Saxon. Jacob Grimm had predicted that English would become a world language by uniting Teutonic and Romance speech.[41] Citing Grimm's prediction, Trench described English as a Teutonic 'base' with a Latinate 'superstructure'. Rather than being diluted by foreign forms, Trench argued, English had 'imported' them as passive material.[42] Hodgetts repeated this rhetoric in an 1885 lecture. The Normans might have conquered England militarily, he stated, but, linguistically, 'instead of our becoming Norman, the Normans became English'.[43] The image of the seafaring Viking or emigrating Teuton naturalized British imperialism as an urge inherited in the blood and perhaps also in speech. Hodgetts's *Champion* notes 'the Viking boast, that the sun never sets in the land of his birth. Strange that we, descendants of those very Vikings, should boast in the same way, but with a somewhat different sense, that the sun never sets on the English flag' (pp. 1–2). Yet this colonizing impulse led to a mixture of races and tongues, which undermined the model of pure roots. Hodgetts's King Alfred triumphs through his ability to shift between tongues. 'Disguised as a skald, or minstrel, and knowing the dialect perfectly', he sings lays of Odin to Viking leaders and gathers the information needed to retake the throne (p. 360). Alfred's plural voices imply that racial-linguistic purism will be unsustainable in future national and imperial networks of relations. Equally, du Chaillu's Viking heroes (and embryonic Englishmen) are schooled in foreign tongues, 'for it was absolutely necessary for Vikings to understand the language of the countries with which they traded or upon which they made war, for, as we have said, their commercial or warlike expeditions extended far and wide' (p. 43). Racial-linguistic purism collides with pragmatic movement between tongues and identities. Instead of springing from a single source, English appears a heterogeneous patchwork, adding and shedding materials contingently.

Hybrid origins feature even more prominently among the racially and linguistically mixed American colonists of Ballantyne's *Norsemen* (1872). Norwegians, Icelanders, Scots and even a Turk are among the crew. While Scottish bondsmen awe the ship with songs of their homeland, the mercenary Tyrker punctuates the text with Turkish exclamations. Language and national character appear even more fluid through the Viking Krake, whose time spent as a prisoner in Ireland has caused him to absorb the national accent and character. In this way, Krake reflects the 'hauntings of Celtism' which Arnold diagnosed in the English spirit.[44] While the national blood and character were mainly Teutonic, he argued, elements of the aboriginal Celt had persisted, such as in English awkwardness and humour. Speaking with an ineradicable 'twang', Krake blithely sings Irish songs of victory against the Danes (p. 82). His claim that he 'became an Irishman' is borne out in his stereotypical wit and communicativeness (p. 87). Ballantyne echoes the popular idea of Irish primitiveness through Krake's ability to communicate in gestures with Native Americans: 'Krake proved himself to be the most eloquent speaker in sign-language ... consisting not only of signs which might indeed be described, but of sounds – guttural and otherwise – which could not be spelt' (p. 349).[45] The figure of Krake suggests a more diverse racial-linguistic heritage than Freeman's Anglo-Saxonism. Yet, as Ballantyne makes clear, this Celtic blarney is not inherited but acquired through social contact, eroding the linkage between language and race. The link is further eroded by representations of the Vikings' relations with Greenland savages or 'Skraelingers'. After initial skirmishes, they begin to trade with each other. Like the pidgin English associated with non-Europeans, Skraelinger speech is represented as a distortion of Norse. Asked by the Viking Leif if he will go fishing tomorrow, one replies: 'Kite right, kite right, smorrow, yis, to-morrow'. Leif laughs at this: 'You'll speak Norse like a Norseman if you live long enough' (p. 204). In spite of Ballantyne's attempts to differentiate Skraelinger Norse from the Norse that preceded English, the encounter problematizes linguistic heritage. By presenting Vikings as embryonic British colonizers, Ballantyne risks contaminating his pure roots of Nordic heritage. The more the Vikings absorb outsiders into their linguistic dominion, the less reliable their language becomes as a record of exclusive ancestry.

This historical heterogeneity of English lent a note of despair to efforts to excavate pure racial-linguistic heritage. Freeman lamented that pure English was irrecoverable since it had grown for nearly a thousand years in defiled forms. 'So strong a hold have the intruders taken on our soil,' he complained, 'that we cannot even tell the tale of their coming without their help.'[46] Equally, Hodgetts and du Chaillu can only render Norse words meaningful for English readers by surrounding them with explanatory words from the modern lexis. The latent organic 'impulses' which Hodgetts projected into English minds are triggered not by the old words themselves but by the contextual scaffolding which he erects around them. Supposedly revived words like *skemma* or *nithing* only signify as synonyms for modern words (*bower* and *coward*). Hodgetts's novel in particular suggests the anxiety that modern English cannot reunite with its Nordic origins through repeated caveats regarding translation. Before battle, the heroes hear priestesses 'singing a song of which we attempt to give a translation, but it is very weak when compared with the original' (p. 63). Later, as the warriors set sail, 'they sang a rough wild strain, the words of which it is very difficult to render into modern English. The following is as near an approach as we have been able to make' (p. 104). Hodgetts's narrator apologizes for the inadequacy of modern English to bear the heroic weight of the Norse sagas, even as he imitates their alliterative form: 'No words of ours, in our debased modern tongue, are strong enough to describe the storm of applause sounding from the shields struck by the mighty swords' (p. 112). In Chapter 1 above it was shown how utopian fiction implied the superiority of future languages through its inability to translate them. These examples show historical fiction using the same technique to idealize the mythical origins of language. Semantic ambiguity and deferral seemed diseases of the present, caused by speakers' estrangement from their organic 'roots'. Divorced from these origins and crossed with foreign strains, English was left rootless and mechanical, signifying only through convention. This idea set the template for anxieties about future impositions of foreign tongues – a natural companion to fears of military invasion towards the turn of the century.

'Es ist verboten': language invasions

Victorian invasion fiction, beginning in 1871 with George Chesney's *The Battle of Dorking*, drew on fears of England being overrun by continental powers (notably a unified Germany).[47] As historical fictions had revered past purity, invasion narratives envisioned further contaminations of English. This trope was bedeviled by the same contradictions as the mythical organic national speech in historical romance. Where and when was the pure essence of English to be found? The organic national tongue depicted in invasion fiction is often as much threatened by its own pluralism as by external invaders. Philology might seem to obstruct the dynamic of (typically) German invaders imposing alien speech upon England, since the two tongues had been traced to common 'Teutonic' origins. Yet the data of philology could be fitted to different geopolitical agendas, drawing boundaries as well as connections. The philologist George Stephens emphasized English's 'Nordic' roots over Teutonic ones, lobbying Westminster in 1864 to support England's Danish cousins in their war against Prussia.[48] Stephens similarly conceptualized English studies as a war against alien aggressors who strove to annex Anglo-Saxon as a dialect of German. 'Our people and our language,' he warned, 'are being rapidly transferred to a race with whom we have no particular connection, and whose qualities are not such as to make any amalgamation desirable ... let us guard it from the hands of the invaders!'[49] Following the Franco-Prussian War and subsequent German unification, Germanophobia continued to equate military with linguistic conquest. The conflict differed to previous wars, being followed by a long period of occupation in which Prussian soldiers were billeted among the French population. In *The Germans in France* (1874), *Times* correspondent Henry Edwards described how the soldiers had marked these territories with their language. A number of German words, he notes, 'will long be remembered in the provinces occupied during the war'.[50] While written messages in German were distributed among bewildered French peasants, its words infiltrated French speech. One speaker is quoted: 'Soldat Prussienn nix capout!' meaning 'the Prussian soldier has not yet been done for!' German is also inscribed in graffiti on buildings near Paris: 'Nach Paris', 'Capout', 'Napoleon Capout' and 'Das ist gewiss Napoleon!', the latter referring to the popular German military song the 'Kutschke Lied'.[51] Such imposition of alien language and associations would be a recurrent trope of invasion fiction.

Lieutenant Colonel Chesney wrote *The Battle of Dorking* to agitate for the reorganization of Britain's defences. In a letter to John Blackwood, whose magazine later published the tale, Chesney suggested achieving this end by 'describing a successful invasion of England, and the collapse of our power and commerce in consequence'.[52] He found a vivid means of portraying such disempowerment through the imposition of the German language, as had occurred in occupied France. After being routed on the battlefield, the narrator awakes in a deceased friend's house to find it occupied by Germans. Chesney associates their foreign speech with plunder and desecration, as they devour the dead man's larder: '"Sind wackere Soldaten, diese Englischen Freiwilligen," said a broad-shouldered brute, stuffing a great hunch of beef into his mouth with a silver fork, an implement I should think he must have been using for the first time in his life'.[53] The narrator also speaks German after being taken prisoner, but his words are reported in English, thus separating him from the invaders. The one example of a German attempting English is mangled by German syntax: '"Auf dem Wege, Spitzbube!" cried the brute, lifting his rifle as if to knock me down. "Must one prisoners who fire at us let shoot"' (p. 90). The English language is similarly broken in the speech of the defeated natives. After the battle which has widowed her, the wife of the narrator's friend 'explained in broken sentences how matters stood' (p. 88). Even more voiceless are two English privates whom a German guard tries to execute on a whim. The narrator saves them by appealing to a commanding officer in German while the pair 'cast an imploring glance at me ... utterly unable to make themselves understood' (p. 90). The subjugation of English to a provincial dialect is indicated by the narrator's implied audience, which is not England as a whole but merely 'my grandchildren' (p. 17) who are preparing to emigrate.

Fears of German hegemony grew stronger in succeeding decades as the new state expanded its navy. Saki's *When William Came* (1913) reflected this anxiety through an invasion of the English tongue in parallel to that of the country. Returning from abroad, the Englishman Murrey Yeovil finds London 'a bilingual city, even as Warsaw'.[54] A series of laws in the expanding German empire had imposed the German language upon public signage and administration in Polish, Danish and Alsatian areas.[55] Saki's tale expands this practice to England, turning Victoria Street into 'Viktoria Strasse'. When Yeovil requests a cab journey to 'Twenty-eight, Berkshire Street', the driver corrects him: 'Berkschirestrasse, acht-und-zwanzig' (p. 30). England's changing patterns of speech index the invasion of German bodies. This is confirmed by a bilingual policeman in a park who informs Yeovil that walking on the grass 'ist verboten'. His speech registers London's changing demographics, as the officer explains: 'About as many foreigners as English use the parks nowadays; in fact, on a fine Sunday afternoon, you'll find three foreigners to every two English' (pp. 73–74). A later scene suggests London transforming into an outpost of Germany through the conversations of statesman Herr von Kwarl. He dines in the Brandenburg café 'at the lower end of what most of its patrons called the Regentstrasse' (p. 91). The sheer number of incoming German speakers is imagined erasing the indigenous language and its marks upon the landscape. It is owing to 'the steady influx of Germans since the war,' von Kwarl notes, that 'whole districts are changing the complexion of their inhabitants, and in some streets you might almost fancy yourself in a German town' (p. 101). The twin dilution of language and blood is demonstrated through English social climbers marrying into the newly dominant German aristocracy. To Yeovil's disgust, the newly-wed socialite Mrs Mentieth-Mendlesohnn is now 'wont to describe herself' as 'one of the Mendlesohnns of Invergordon' (p. 148). The etymologies and family names in which historical fiction located English identity are to be suppressed, and foreign names and words implanted. Von Kwarl explains that the invaders must 'coax' England's youth 'to forget' their separate history so that 'Anglo-Saxon may blend with German ... under the sceptre of the Hohenzollerns' (pp. 106–07). Saki implies in the final scene, though, that English voices will not so much blend with German ones as be silenced by them. When crowds at an official parade begin to sing and whistle subversively, 'uniformed police and plainclothes detectives sprang into evidence on all sides; whatever happened there must be no disloyal demonstration. The whistlers and mockers were pointedly invited to keep silence, and one or two addresses were taken' (pp. 320–21). The English have been devoiced.

Nonetheless, Saki's vision of German replacing English is as much a critique of modern urban and print culture as it is a warning of future invasion. Artificial city life empties words of meaning and speakers of independent thought. Cut off from its rural roots, speech becomes 'shrill, mechanical repartee' (p. 127) uttered by 'parrot men and women that fluttered and chattered through London drawing-rooms and theatre foyers' (p. 223). Murrey Yeovil's name frames him as an outside observer of this process, connoting ancient heraldry and rural England. At his wife Cecily's dinner parties, Yeovil notices 'an incessant undercurrent of jangling laughter, an unending give-and-take of meaningless mirthless jest and catchword ... a noisy, empty interchange of chaff and laughter' (p. 126). Yeovil's friend Dr Holham explains that most Londoners are happy 'saying nothing worth saying, but ... saying it over and over again ... echoing the same catchwords' (p. 60). Words become dead fossils, exchanged mechanically. Canon Mousepace, a clergyman at Cecily's parties, is described as hewing platitudes from the 'inexhaustible quarry' of 'the dictionary of the English language' (p. 236). Mousepace opines of a pianist that such talent brings 'responsibility'. He fails to define such responsibility, though, and the German-appearing milieu in which he moves betrays the hollowness of his words. Embarrassingly, his platitude is later repeated by another reveller, the narrator remarking: 'The quarry of the English language was of course a public property, but it was disconcerting to have one's own particular barrow-load of sentence-building material carried off before one's eyes' (p. 245). Mechanized print turns speakers into parasites upon the authentic past and audiences into passive consumers. This passivity is illustrated through the exorbitant taxes and curbs on freedom, which Londoners impotently read of in newspapers. Although abandoning plans to resist the invasion, Yeovil still appears to reject the artificial culture which enabled it by moving to the country. Even this pastoral idyll is an imitation, though, the estate having been sold off by its hereditary owners. Purchased through a parasitic middle-man who keeps its details on a stylograph, the property is one of many vacated and on the market, mainly to rich Germans. Saki's foreign invaders thus merely accelerate a long-running socio-economic estrangement of people from the land. When a local doctor regales Yeovil with tales of the village, his story-telling, or perhaps Yeovil's reception of it, seems denationalized by print culture. Listening, Yeovil's mind runs intertextually into the culture of the invading nation: 'It was a little like Hans Andersen, he decided, and a little like the *Reminiscences of an Irish R. M.*, and perhaps just a little like some of the more probable adventures of Baron Munchausen' (p. 300). For all the doctor's apparent authenticity, 'a living unwritten chronicle of the East Wessex hunt' (p. 299), his auratic story-telling cannot be separated from the international flow of textual influence. Saki's depiction of invaders devoicing the nation clashes with the underlying anxiety that the nation has no authentic voice to lose.

Language standardization also provoked anxiety that English identity could be counterfeited by foreigners. Edwards noted how Prussians had seized French newspapers and printers to publish propaganda urging natives to capitulate.[56] With growing immigration into Britain, popular anxieties arose that immigrants could secretly aid invasions. Walter Wood's novel *The Enemy in Our Midst* (1906) imagined such an invasion from within. London's German immigrants, Wood's narrator explained, 'spoke the language of the people as understandably as they spoke it themselves', enabling them to infiltrate the establishment.[57] In this atmosphere, the emerging genre of spy fiction looked to decentralized forms of speech, such as dialect, technical language and code, to defend it against infiltration.[58] This dynamic is exemplified in Erskine Childers's *The Riddle of the Sands*, in which two Englishmen unravel a German conspiracy to invade England while yachting in the Baltic. The tale begins with the narrator Carruthers receiving an invitation to join his friend Davies for duck-shooting in the region – the first of many coded messages in their adventure. A self-confessed 'duffer at sailing', Carruthers learns nautical vocabulary in parallel to his gradual discovery of the conspiracy.[59] When Davies narrates his voyage thus far in sailing terminology, Carruthers confesses, 'this was Greek to me' (p. 73). Equally, the maps and charts which guide them appear at first to Carruthers like obscure ciphers. Their code of directions and measurements must be unravelled along with the 'riddle' of the North Sea sandbanks where the invasion is being prepared. The sands appear on the chart as 'dotted patches ... becoming unintelligible ... a confusion of winding and intersecting lines and bald spaces' (p. 88). Davies's log-book is equally obscure, 'a mass of short entries with cryptic abbreviations' and a page torn out (p. 48). This obscurity proves its worth, however, when Germans later ransack the vessel and its log-book. Authorial footnotes regularly refer the reader to diagrams of the maps and charts which drive Davies and Carruthers's discussions. By sharing this frame of reference, the reader is shown the importance of context to their nautical exchanges, which bars malicious outsiders from understanding them. Yet, this fragmentation into specialized dialects also aids the invasion's conspirators. When Carruthers eavesdrops on one of their meetings, he finds that 'Immersed in a subject with which they were all familiar, they were elusive, elliptic and persistently technical. Many of the words I did catch were unknown to me. The rest were, for the most part, either letters of the alphabet or statistical figures' (p. 289). The standardized language of print is defended from imitation by signs rooted in technical and personal contexts.

Childers's strategies for defending the national voice also threaten to tear it apart and permeate its boundaries with those other nations. Carruthers mimics German identity in order to eavesdrop on the conspirators, responding to the hails of other ships 'as gruffly and gutturally as I could' (p. 282). Like the imagined German spy in England, he speaks 'like a native' (p. 6). Yet, the narrative also posits an innate national vocality, which outsiders can never entirely counterfeit nor natives suppress. It is this mystical racial recognition (Saintsbury's 'inner ear') which pricks the heroes' suspicion of the English traitor Herr Dollmann. While Dollmann speaks perfect German, Davies recognizes him as a fellow countryman through mysterious intuition. 'It was something in his looks and manner,' Davies later explains; 'the way he talked – I mean about cruising and the sea, especially ... I felt we understood one another, in a way that two foreigners wouldn't' (p. 80). A similar inkling drives Carruthers to perceive the same in Dollmann's daughter, as he recounts: 'By her voice, when she spoke, I knew that she must have talked German habitually from childhood; diction and accent were faultless, at least to my English ear; but the native constitutional ring was wanting' (pp. 192–93). Beneath the profusion of codes and private languages, Childers suggests a natural, native voice which spans the country and sticks ineradicably to the tongues of its emigrants. This notion of a single national voice was valuable to invasion fiction because it enabled authors to present their texts as expressions of it. Chesney's *Battle of Dorking* appears as the transcribed speech of an everyman figure addressing his descendants: 'You ask me to tell you, my grandchildren, something about my own share in the great events that happened fifty years ago.' Simultaneously, this homely, embodied voice blurs with the nation as a whole, shifting between first-person singular and plural: 'For us in England it came too late ... We English have only ourselves to blame' (p. 17). The anonymity of the text's author in its initial publication enhanced this sense of a national voice.[60] Childers similarly speaks for the nation through the 'editor' to Carruthers's narration. His epilogue shifts into the first-person plural: 'nothing short of a successful invasion could finally compel us to make peace. Our hearts are stout' (p. 335). These invocations of a monologic national voice with one will foreshadow the mass conscription and persecution of conscientious objectors in the Great War to follow. Modern war, which mobilizes the whole nation, seems to necessitate the suppression of language variation and dialogue.

The idea that language variety might defend Britain against invaders is explored most fully in P. G. Wodehouse's parody of the genre. *The Swoop!, or How Clarence Saved England* (1909) imagines simultaneous invasions by nine countries, producing a babble of languages on the island. Germans and Turks are unable to converse with the Chinese, whose plans are equally derailed by the Welsh language. The Eastern invaders wander for a week in the countryside 'having lost their way near Llanfairpwlgwnngogogoch, and having been unable to understand the voluble directions given to them by the various shepherds they encountered'.[61] British linguistic disunity becomes an asset, disorienting the invaders as to whom or where they are invading. Similarly, the invaders are defeated not by British armies marching to one voice but by the secret handshakes, passwords and slang of a group of boy scouts. The 14-year-old Clarence Chugwater and his friends turn the invaders against each other by fabricating snubs and insults between them in a newspaper. Upon hatching this plan, the scouts burst into a private, pseudo-savage chant, 'Een gonyama-gonyama! ... Invooboo! Yah bo! Yah bo! Invooboo!' The narrator ironically describes this as 'The voice of Young England – of Young England alert and at its post!' (p. 37), highlighting the instability of a national voice. Clarence embodies the everyman voice of invasion fiction *ad absurdum*, sighing for 'my England' while his family chatter about cricket tournaments (p. 11). Upon arresting the German leader Prince Otto, he declares 'I am England!' only for the Prince to puncture his bombast on a point of grammar:

> 'England, thou art free! ... Let the nations learn from this that it is when apparently crushed that the Briton is to more than ever be feared.'
>
> 'Thad's bad grabbar,' said the Prince critically.
>
> 'It isn't,' said Clarence with warmth.
>
> 'It is, I tell you. Id's a splid idfididive.' (p. 62)

The Prince's jibe (incapacitated by a blocked nose) illustrates the babble of voices inherent to the novel form, which undermines a monologic national voice. Yet, the same dialogism also precipitates the invaders' downfall: German and Russian generals deliver lectures in England's music-halls, only for the opposing armies to heckle them off stage. Wodehouse similarly mocks the genre's authorial poses, prefacing his tale with a short note from 'The Bomb-Proof Shelter, London, W'. Parodying the sanctimony of professional scaremongers, he claims that the story 'has been written and published purely from a feeling of patriotism and duty. Mr. Alston Rivers' sensitive soul will be jarred to its foundations if it is a financial success. So will mine. But in a time of national danger we feel that the risk must be taken' (p. 5). Such satire undermines the idea of a single national voice. The babble of voices points to how England might defend itself not so much from foreign invaders as from its own coercive jingoism. Yet, the lack of bloodshed and comical routing of the invaders leaves this point unpronounced. Wodehouse's carnivalesque dialogues unfold in a world in which war has no serious consequences. While mocking monologic voices which call the nation to arms, *The Swoop!* foresees none of the seismic horrors which they would soon beget.

Morris: progressive language nostalgia

Thus far, fictional engagements with the imagined organic roots of language seem to have tended towards racial exclusion and xenophobia. However, Victorian interest in national origins could also be fitted to liberal and leftist politics.[62] William Morris's fiction combined nostalgia for organic language with international socialism. The London polymath was influenced by John Ruskin's admiration for preindustrial crafts and Gothic architecture, in which he imagined work and art united. Morris's letters suggest equal enthusiasm for language of the past. In 1885 he wrote to a friend:

> You see things have very much changed since the early days of language: once everybody who could express himself at all did so beautifully, was a poet for that occasion, because all language was beautiful. But now language is utterly degraded in our daily lives, and poets have to make a new tongue each for himself: before he can even begin his story he must elevate his means of expression from the daily jabber to which centuries of degradation have reduced it.[63]

Morris read Trench's philological works at Oxford and later corresponded with Farrar and Müller.[64] His idealization of past language closely resembles the latter two's vision of a primordial 'mythopoeic' period of speech. 'Language,' wrote Farrar, 'though not the result of convention, tends to become conventional in the process of time, but this very tendency is often a mark of decay and ruin.' 'Words, of which the composition was originally clear', have their meanings 'worn away like the image and superscription of a coin', becoming 'mechanical (i.e. unmeaning of itself) by corruption'.[65] Instead of coining words to reflect their self-defined world, people now echoed the fixed terms and ideas of convention. Yet, what seemed inevitable for Farrar was only a product of capitalism for the socialist Morris and, therefore, potentially reversible. The challenge lay in reconciling organic, local language with socialist internationalism. His fiction also struggles to answer how humanity might regain organic language while retaining the history, unity and class consciousness enabled by writing.

Morris echoed his notion that a poet must 'make a new tongue' in his tale of the medieval peasants' revolt *A Dream of John Ball* (1886–87). The Victorian narrator, who time-travels to this epoch through a dream, hears a rousing speech by the rebel leader, and comments: 'while John Ball had been speaking to me I felt strangely, as though I had more things to say than the words I knew could make clear: as if I wanted to get from other people a new set of words'.[66] Such new words turn out to be old ones excavated from Teutonic roots. The peasants' natural urges for community and equality seem embedded in their Teutonic vocabulary and syntax. Tales are 'foregathered' rather than collected; John Ball calls the feudal lord 'foeman' instead of enemy (pp. 35, 16). He also positions verbs near the ends of alliterative sentences, evoking Anglo-Saxon verse: 'woe worth the while! too oft he sayeth sooth' (p. 36). Like social cooperation, poetic creation is instinctive in Teutonic speech. The narrator appears among the peasants as a minstrel, telling the Icelandic saga of Sigurd, of which Morris had earlier written a version in archaic English. 'As I told it,' he reports, 'the words seemed to thicken and grow, so that I knew not the sound of my own voice, and they ran almost into rhyme and measure as I told it' (pp. 16–17). Equally, in Morris's utopia *News from Nowhere* (1890), Teutonic language seems to revive in parallel to organic, socialist society. Morris's vision transforms London into a garden city free of industrial labour, restoring harmony between humans and nature. Anglo-Saxon words have sprung back into speech along with the crafts which industrial capitalism suppressed.[67] The antiquarian Hammond tells the Victorian narrator 'Guest' that older native terms have replaced Latin 'long-tailed words'.[68] The Anglo-Saxon 'mote', for example, serves for administration (pp. 199, 37). This reversion to older speech mirrors the return of oral society, as Hammond mentions '[the] meeting of the neighbours, or mote, as we call it, according to the ancient tongue of the times before bureaucracy' (p. 121). While people have forgotten most nineteenth-century books, they treasure the folk-tales collected by Jacob Grimm, the imaginative roots of the Teutonic race. Morris's socialist future lies in restoring the linguistic past.

This concern with Teutonic origins would seem to sit awkwardly with Morris's internationalism. After co-founding the Socialist League in 1884, Morris wrote: 'For us neither geographical boundaries, political history, race, nor creed makes rivals or enemies; for us there are no nations, but only varied masses of workers and friends'.[69] Gagnier observes that Morris conceived of 'a nativist love of the land' and 'socialist internationalism' as enablers, rather than contradictions, of each other.[70] Yet, the tradition of romantic philology, growing in tandem with ideas of nationalism, threatened to undermine such 'situated cosmopolitanism'. Herder had emphasized local particularity against cultural universals, writing that word meanings 'are so specifically national, so much in conformity with the manner of thinking and seeing of the people, of the inventor' that the foreigner was unable to 'strike them right'.[71] Instead of generating alternative labels for a common reality, languages represented the sociohistorical subjectivities of their speakers. International communication and cooperation thus demanded a common language or, at least, common values above local perspectives.

One model which might have influenced Morris's efforts to resolve this conflict was, perhaps surprisingly, that of the establishment figurehead Matthew Arnold. Arnold's lectures on Celtic literature stressed the hybridity of England's national origins. Modern cosmopolitan English, he claimed, could be enriched by translations of ancient Celtic literature. Arnold contended that such translations could appeal to the latent Celtic spirit in the English character, and proposed an inclusive view of cultural inheritance. 'We may have the good of our German part,' he wrote, 'the good of our Latin part, the good of our Celtic part; and instead of one part clashing with the other, we may bring it in to continue and perfect the other.'[72] For Arnold, the supposed endurance of the Celtic 'spirit' despite the destruction of the Celtic languages by English testified to the detachability of language from race. Although Morris was less sanguine about the decline of the Celtic languages, he similarly viewed English as a potential vehicle for hybrid, heterogeneous identities. Writing to the Welsh politician Henry Richard in 1882, he stated that, despite his upbringing in London, 'I think I may claim to be considered one of the Cymry', since his grandparents on both sides had come from Wales. 'I am I assure you very proud of my nation,' he continued, 'and its lovely ancient literature as far as I know it by translation, since unfortunately I only know a few words of the difficult but beautiful language of my forefathers.'[73] Morris suggests that translation offers means of transcending the perspective of one's native language, absorbing the viewpoints and experiences of others. However, as with Arnold, the potential detachability of language from race remains unclear. Although Morris approaches Welsh as a foreign language due to his upbringing, he implies that his ancestry renders him naturally attuned to its resonances. In this way, his celebration of Welsh literature does not so much transcend national-linguistic perspectivism as rescue it. Its translation promises to finally bring English language and race into true alignment by acknowledging their composite character.[74] Such translation seems less about opening oneself to the other than rediscovering forgotten aspects of oneself. It is hard to imagine how groups such as Jews could find a place in Morris's national-linguistic inheritance.

Nevertheless, the racial-linguistic past could become more inclusive depending on how far back one chose to trace it. Morris's solution to the problem of languages creating different perspectives mirrored that of Müller, who maintained that all languages must descend from common 'roots'. Anna Vaninskaya argues that Morris's evocations of a Gothic past 'were indebted' to Müller's comparative mythology.[75] Equally, his faith that natural ideas (leading to socialism) underlay all speech was enabled by Müller's philosophy of language origins. Unlike physical anthropology, which often linked languages to racial types, Müller's philology presented speech as proof of a united human nature. 'Our body is our uniform,' he wrote. 'It matters very little whether it is black or white. Language, on the contrary, is the very embodiment of our true self.'[76] Similarly, for Morris, the roots of organic language lay not in racial exclusion but in universal human nature, unstifled by industrial modernity. In 1886 he wrote that the 'Germanic tribes' of old 'had an elevated literature founded on the ideas of the dignity of life which naturally spring from the consciousness of belonging to a corporation of freemen'. His contrasting view that the Romans were 'commercial and individualistic' derived not from the natural essence of their language but from the social state that had distorted it.[77] Latin is not innately corrupting in *News from Nowhere*, as the boatman Dick demonstrates, responding to the unfamiliar term 'education': 'I know enough Latin to know that the word must come from *educere*, to lead out' (p. 43). The mechanical 'boy-farms' that 'education' signifies for the narrator are produced by artificial Victorian society rather than some natural essence in the word. Instead of privileging one line of ethno-linguistic descent, Morris traces all lines to a common set of ideas. Müllerian philology provided a model to reach the universal through the particular. While words were shaped over time by particular environments, tracing their journeys backwards always led to metaphors for the same 'root' abstractions.

This faith that communal ideas naturally underlay all human speech enabled Morris to reject hegemonic centres of culture and embrace localism. He seized upon Marx's prediction that government would wither away after the revolution, imagining the future as a return to localized, transparent etymologies. In an 1888 letter, Morris hoped for an end to cultural homogenization. Communities after his revolution 'would grow together or dissolve as convenience of place, climate, language, &c. dictated'.[78] Languages might speciate and hybridize through the peaceful migration of speakers, as indicated by the Nowhereian commingling of tongues. Many children, Guest is told,

> can talk French, which is the nearest language talked on the other side of the water; and they soon get to know German also, which is talked by a huge number of communes and colleges on the mainland. These are the

principal languages we speak in these islands, along with English or Welsh, or Irish, which is another form of Welsh ... and besides our guests from over sea often bring their children with them, and the little ones get together, and rub their speech into one another. (p. 45)

Tongues cannot conflict with each other because they are kindred, grown from the same roots. This invalidates both British colonization of Ireland and Irish nationalism. Irish 'is another form of Welsh' in the same way English is another form of German. Philology seems to point the way to one nation of humans, naturally predisposed (in Morris's interpretation) to a federation of socialistic communes.

Morris's notion of universal, socialist inclinations hidden in the roots of language attempted to reign in the fragmenting definitions of socialism in the 1890s.[79] He wrote *News from Nowhere* during quarrels among factions of his Socialist League, which would culminate in him leaving the organization.[80] These conflicts are refracted through its dream of a common, socialist language. Although Nowhereian society accommodates different political opinions, it is far more united than Victorian socialism.[81] The narrative opens with the narrator, Guest, witnessing a shambolic debate 'up at the League' in which 'there were six persons present, and consequently six sections of the party were represented' (p. 7). By contrast, the Nowhereians' knowledge of word origins harmonizes their feelings, obviating institutions to enforce them. Unlike the unstable values of capitalism, Nowhereian nomenclature breaks things down into objective material properties.[82] An old man punctures the puffery of expensive clothes, explaining that the bourgeoisie of the past wore 'breeches made of worsted velvet, that stuff that used to be called plush some years ago' (p. 59). Buildings are named to reflect the labour inside them, as Dick explains: 'we don't call them factories now, but Banded-workshops; that is, places where people collect who want to work together' (p. 66). Renaming things and unpacking their definitions challenges the petrified fictions of capitalism. One Nowhereian lists 'our units of management, a commune, or a ward, or a parish (for we have all three names, indicating little real distinction between them now, though time was there was a good deal)' (p. 121). Rooted in undivided material nature, their speech sees through capitalism's nonce distinctions and nonce concepts.[83] The notion of 'idleness', used in the nineteenth century to justify wage slavery, is to the Nowhereians an outlandish fairy-tale, nicknamed 'Blue devils' and 'mulleygrubs' (pp. 58–59). In a society which has restored the natural pleasure of work, the concept is ridiculous and thus matched to nonsense words.

Reuniting words with their etymologies enables the Nowhereians to rediscover the communal cooperation which Morris imagined as human nature. In 1887 Morris predicted 'the happy days when society shall be what its name means'; *society* deriving from the Latin *socius*, meaning comrade.[84] Morris's fellow socialists had begun to address each other as comrade in the 1880s, but the Nowhereians have dropped even this word with its military connotations.[85] Instead, they are all 'neighbours', derived from the Anglo-Saxon *nēah* (nigh) and *būr* (dweller). In the absence of artificial hierarchies and nations, others are defined by physical proximity. As Dick comments, French is not the tongue of a separate people but 'the nearest language talked on the other side of the water'. Morris's etymological unmaking of English reveals humanity as naturally of one mind, divided only by distance.

Morris denationalized English further in his last romances, forging an idiom which seemed to reunite and, yet, purify archaic threads of Indo-European speech. In a fantasy world resembling medieval Europe, Morris replaces French and Latin imports with old Germanic words and syntax. Hence, *The Water of the Wondrous Isles* (1897) begins: 'Whilom, as tells the tale, was a walled cheaping-town hight Utterhay, which was builded in a bight of the land'. Morris also coins compounds from Teutonic roots: people seek not *accommodation* but 'houseroom', and are not *famished* but 'hunger-weary'.[86] Marcus Waithe argues that Morris evolved this renewed English through translating the Icelandic sagas. He sought to open English to the 'strangeness' of ancient Icelandic, Waithe suggests, challenging narrow nationalist culture with a 'pluralistic utopianism'.[87] Nor is this fantasy English exclusively Teutonic; it admits Latinate words, provided they are of sufficient antiquity, such as *bestia* in the term 'way-beast' for an ass.[88] Indeed, characters in one tale refer to their *lingua franca* as 'Latin', as though it preceded the division of Romance tongues from Germanic.[89] Morris's monoglot worlds imagine an inclusive, cosmopolitan inheritance, collapsing the binary between native and alien.

Attempting to revive such Adamic speech in print entangled Morris's late fiction in contradictions. Romantic philology located the life of language in orality, while writing caused its decay, alienating words from speakers. Müller described speech diverging into different dialects like 'parallel streams' while 'artificial' literary idioms resembled 'stagnant lakes' or 'the frozen surface of a river' (1, pp. 51, 64–65). How, then, could 'natural' speech have the global homogeneity only possible in writing? This contradiction is discernible in the ignorant–learned, creative–moribund speech of the Nowhereians. All their creativity seems diverted into the visual arts, their language trawled from the past.[90] While the narrator vaguely mentions poems and story-telling, these are typically repetitions of old folk-tales. Clara complains that poets seldom write of the modern life around them, reaching either for mythology or history (pp. 140–42). Hammond turns her comment into a barb at the realist novel, but it nonetheless highlights the artistic stasis of Nowhere. Literary creation is unseen by Guest, except for vague references to 'telling stories', which might, again, be old tales recycled (p. 187). As for narrative, so for language. As standardized print recedes, speech ought to morph rapidly into a plethora of dialects. Nowhereians blithely report that 'the plague of book-making' is waning, read little and communicate mostly verbally (p. 30). The little language change in evidence, though, is destructive, with the loss of Victorian words and meanings. Morris stressed the necessity of such forgetting in 1887, envisaging 'a day when ... the words poor and rich, though they will still be found in our dictionaries, will have lost their old meaning; which will have to be explained by great men of the analytical kind'.[91] A Nowhereian girl illustrates this ideal, gaily singing the Chartist 'Song of the Shirt', 'unconscious of' the 'real meaning' of its 'terrible words of threatening and lamentation' (p. 92). Such a return to static, pastoral ignorance is difficult to reconcile with Marx's model of revolution as a dialectical heightening of consciousness. Class consciousness did not originate in a prehistoric state of nature but developed through the contradictions of capitalism. R. Jayne Hildebrand interprets the Nowhereians' unreflectiveness as a rejection of capitalist individualism, acting communally through habit rather than conscious thought. Against atomized models of 'Economic Man', Morris's utopian community remembers collectively as a social aggregate.[92] Yet, the idea that Nowhereians act through unreflective habit places them close to Victorians who parrot the conventional usage of words rather than seeking out their etymologies. If Nowhereians have forgotten capitalism and returned to a pastoral past, then what is to prevent history repeating itself? Morris's incoherent answer seems to be that they have not forgotten. Characters like Dick, who seldom read, nonetheless frequently reference books in order to challenge Victorian values. The boatman alludes to Dickens and Shakespeare, calling his dustman friend 'Boffin' and pointing out a house mentioned in *Richard III*. He also refers to an 'old Jewish proverb-book', 'silly old novels' and 'idiotic old books about political economy' to prove the absurdity of capitalism (pp. 31, 69, 27). Perhaps the Nowhereians know so much Victorian writing because their 'epoch of rest' creates little new language or narrative.

Despite Morris's rhetoric of tongues emerging and dissolving freely, Nowhereian reported speech exhibits no such variation. Barring a few Anglo-Saxonisms, every character speaks Standard English. Morris abolishes class distinctions and centres of linguistic authority only to universalize the voice of the upper class. Upon initially meeting Dick, Guest notes, 'He seemed to be like some specially manly and refined young gentleman, playing waterman for a spree' (p. 14). Dick's refined speech reflects his apparent good breeding, as when he is asking: 'Shall I put you ashore at once or would you like to go down to Putney before Breakfast?' The discourse of his friend Bob is even more etiquette-laden: 'Guest, we don't know what to call you: is there any indiscretion in asking you your name?' (p. 25). Dowling argues for a repressed 'ideal of aristocratic sensibility' in Morris's aesthetics, and his utopia's lack of dialectal variety, at least, exemplifies this.[93] Guest associates the bad old days with cockney speech, admonishing a man nostalgic for the nineteenth century: 'What you mean is that you de-cockneyized the place' (p. 209). Morris's essays often portray cockney as degenerate, blaming mechanical toil for causing the poor 'to talk coarsely and ungrammatically, to think unconsecutively and illogically, to be uneducated, unrefined, bigoted, ignorant and dishonest'.[94] Equally, despite the rhetoric of languages 'rub[bing] into each other', the unchanging tongues of Morris's utopia remain wholly separate. Maidens sing Welsh songs alongside the English, but there is no intermixture between them. National borders have fallen, yet languages remain balkanized, chained to their standardized centres. Such standardization is necessary for establishing a common set of truths and values under which to live. Morris implies as much in his letter to Bainton, conceding that his communes would retain the shadow of a government to hold delegations with each other:

> but the delegates would not pretend to represent any one or anything but the business with which they are delegated. e.g. we are a shoe making community chiefly ... are we making too ... many shoes? ... Absolute facts and information would be the main business of public assemblies ... gradually all public business would be so much simplified that it would come to little more than a correspondence: 'Such are the facts with us, compare them with the facts with you, you know how to act'.[95]

Ironically, the freer and more natural Morris imagines language becoming, the more static and monologic is the result. Morris only regained his organic paradise by freezing language into fossils of its former life – the very image which Müller used to describe decayed Victorian language.

Hardy's dialogic nostalgia

The contradictions in language vitalism stemmed from it glossing over the tendency of speech to mutate and diversify, fixating upon pure origins or a single line of descent. Thomas Hardy's fiction stands out against this trend, lamenting the disappearance of regional dialects while, simultaneously, stressing laws of random change. Hardy's fiction-writing career coincided with debates in language theory that undermined old vitalist assumptions. From the 1870s onwards, Whitney challenged Müller's doctrine of natural word 'roots', arguing that meaning was conventional. Hardy's fiction mirrors this conflict over language. He was influenced by Barnes's vitalist nostalgia for vanishing rural dialect, having grown up in Dorset and been mentored by the older dialect-poet. Yet Hardy's reading of Mill and Darwin also made him sympathetic to conventionalist arguments. The language nostalgia which emerges in Hardy's later fiction is not so much for one, fixed state as for dialogue between variants. In a conversation recorded by William Archer, Hardy attacked notions of 'English as a dead language – a thing crystallized at an arbitrarily selected stage of its existence, and bidden to forget that it has a past and deny that it has a future. Purism, whether in grammar or in vocabulary, almost always means ignorance'.[96] His fiction challenges prescriptive standardization less for defiling or deviating from the 'pure' roots of English than for its intolerance of variation, forcing speakers into static, narrow-minded monologism.

Hardy sometimes presented dialect as pure and natural when challenging popular assumptions that it was inferior to Standard English. In an 1881 letter to the *Spectator*, he expressed 'regret that, in order to be understood, writers should be obliged thus slightingly to treat varieties of English which are intrinsically as genuine, grammatical and worthy of the royal title'.[97] Dialect's genuineness hinged on its longevity, placing it closer to the 'roots' from which natural meaning apparently stemmed. Barnes described Dorset dialect as 'purer ... than the dialect which is chosen as the national speech; purer, inasmuch as it retains many words of Saxon origin, for which the English substitutes others'.[98] Hardy's second published novel, *Under the Greenwood Tree*, similarly legitimizes dialect through its longevity in the wedding that closes the narrative. Educated bride Fancy Day 'strictly charged her father and the tranter to carefully avoid saying "thee" and "thou" in their conversation, on the plea that those ancient words sounded so very humiliating to persons of decent taste'.[99] Hardy replaced 'decent' with 'newer' in subsequent editions, enhancing the opposition between time-honoured dialect and the fashionable whims of Standard English.[100] The tranter's wife Mrs Dewy scorns her relatives' dialectal talk of 'taties', boasting of how her family ate 'taters' or 'very often "pertatoes" outright' (I, p. 119). When she is alone with her husband, however, we find Mrs Dewy 'leaving off the adorned tones ... and returning to the natural marriage voice' (I, p. 124). Further, the words in which Reuben Dewy remembers proposing to her are among his more dialectal: '"Ann," said I ... "Woot hae me?"' (II, p. 21). While people imitate the bourgeois national language among society, dialect remains entwined with the raw urges of nature. This link between dialect and nature is further confirmed in the denouement when, in spite of her prejudices, Fancy weds the dialect-speaking Dick over the cosmopolitan vicar Maybold. Like the songs which Dick and his choir sing in harmony with the seasons, dialect appears timeless and natural.

Hardy continued to question the naturalness of the spread of Standard English through later fiction. In *Tess of the d'Urbervilles* (1891) the narrator refers to 'the labourers – or "workfolk", as they used to call themselves immemorially till the other word was introduced from without'. Standard English represents cultural hegemony enforced through material economics as England's industrial centres expand. The same passage mocks 'the process, humorously designated by statisticians as "the tendency of the rural population towards the large towns" ... really the tendency of water to flow uphill when forced by machinery'.[101] National education and centralized government promote Standard English over natural, ancient dialects. Hardy also uses this technique to challenge Standard English in *The Trumpet-Major* (1884), peeling back its impositions to reveal the native names they have supplanted. Overcombe resident Anne ventures to the coast and 'gazed from the cliff at Portland Bill, or Beal, as it was in those days more correctly called'.[102] Hardy similarly splits the narrative across linguistic epochs in 'The Melancholy Hussar of the German Legion' (1890), with the late-Victorian narrator offering dialectal place names in parallel to their standardized replacements. Of the soldiers' plan to desert their regiment, we are told: 'Christoph was to go ahead of them to the harbour where the boat lay, row it round the Nothe – or Look-out as it was called in those days'.[103] The expansion of national government, naming the land after a fort, has effaced the folk name that described the land's timeless function in the community: for looking out to sea. In 'The Distracted Preacher', Hardy associates dialect with traditions of liquor smuggling. In contrast, he associates Standard English with centralized government, which was seeking to eliminate such practices in the 1830s.

The young, non-native minister Stockdale is introduced to the smugglers' dialect by his landlady Lizzy Newbury. She defines 'this dark' as 'what we call the time between moon and moon', and explains the use of a boat-towed 'creeper – that's a grapnel' to find whiskey barrels hidden in the sea. Lizzy argues that villagers have practised such smuggling 'for generations': 'My father did it, and so did my grandfather'.[104] Like the Wessex dialect, smuggling for Hardy is not a deviation from English culture but a folk heritage preceding the modern state. Hardy suggests the ancient naturalness of smuggling by merging the offending barrels with the landscape, buried under trees to escape the detection of excisemen. Stockdale's Standard English, though, prioritizes the king's government over the local community. Ancient local language and the values it encoded are suppressed by recent national ones, as the tale's denouement highlights with Lizzy's marriage to Stockdale. Repenting her smuggling, she helps him to write a tract against the practice, which he prints in 'many hundreds of copies'.[105] These examples show Hardy using the model of pastoral stasis to question the naturalness of Standard English and centralized administration. Depicting them as recent impositions frames the supplanted local language and customs as correspondingly timeless and organic.

The example of smuggling dialect, however, exposes the precariousness of this opposition, which Hardy would explore more in later works. Smuggling dialect did not precede the culture of customs and excise but developed in parallel to it. Lizzy and her co-conspirators refer to the whiskey tubs as 'things' and talk of 'burn[ing] off' their vessels to conceal their activities from authorities. Instead of representing static folk culture which modernity corrupted, Hardy's smugglers' dialect suggests parallel streams of language adapting in response to their environments. Darwin's model of nature replaced pastoral stasis with endless variation and adaptation with no clear origins or purpose. Hardy's reading of Darwin is discernible in his above-mentioned letter to the *Spectator* defending his use of dialect. Standard English is 'the all-prevailing competitor' which triumphs in 'the struggle for existence' through urbanization. Its advantages are a matter of chance, having grown in an area which would become the capital, while other dialects' 'only fault was that they happened not to be central'.[106] Hardy presents Standard English and provincial dialect as sibling variants, advantaged or crippled by material conditions, not by any inherent qualities. His fiction illustrates this point when switches between Standard English narration and dialectal speech of the past reveal forgotten, short-lived linguistic fads. In 'A Tradition of Eighteen Hundred and Four' (1882), a long-dead speaker, Old Selby, is recalled telling of life during the Napoleonic wars. Selby refers to Napoleon as 'that great Corsican tyrant (as we used to call him)', marking the fading of the Napoleonic wars in popular memory and the slogans they coined.[107] The nickname chimes with hyperbolic journalese, muddying the opposition between pastoral orality and fragmented print culture. Similarly, in 'A Changed Man' (1900) a group of Napoleonic-era Hussars are observed singing the popular contemporary ditty, '"The girl I left behind me" (which was formerly always the tune for such times, though it is now nearly disused)'.[108] Forgotten buzzwords and phrases are dredged up from even more recent times in 'The Fiddler of the Reels' (1893) when an old man remembers the Great Exhibition of 1851. He explains:

> None of the younger generation can realize the sense of novelty it produced in us who were then in our prime. A noun substantive went so far as to become an adjective in honour of the occasion. It was 'exhibition' hat, 'exhibition' razor-strop, 'exhibition' watch; nay, even 'exhibition' weather, 'exhibition' spirits, sweethearts, babies, wives – for the time.[109]

The linkage of novel experiences with transitory verbal fashions evokes Darwin's comment that language sometimes developed through 'mere novelty and fashion' without any greater purpose. Hardy also shows the divergence of dialects in action through the idiolects of characters like Japeth Johns in 'Interlopers at the Knap' (1884).[110] The milkman, who has a supporting role in his friend Darton's thwarted marriage, speaks in a 'well-known style', which marks him off from other dialectal speakers.[111] He combines Standard English vocabulary with non-standard syntax, declaring: 'I shouldn't call Sally Hall simple. Primary, because no Sally is'; 'this don't become you'; 'I was going to speak practical' (pp. 118, 133). His pronunciation also deviates from both standardized and dialect speech, as Hardy indicates by marking his words with misspellings, unlike those of other characters ('Quite the contrairy, ma'am'; 'the natyves': pp. 127, 118). Like Wells's Mr Polly (see Chapter 4 below) he twists words into surprising new shapes, dismissing Darton's proposed bride as 'a red-herring doll-oll-oll' (p. 133). Such speech shows the constant change revealed by philology, which seemed to occur independently of society – rural or industrial.

Hardy also often undermines pastoral language stasis by depicting speech as social behaviour rather than natural growth. He was heavily influenced by the writings of Mill, whose *Logic* (1843) conceptualized language as a grid of mental associations that was standardized through custom. This was underpinned from the 1858 edition onwards by a quotation attributed to the philosopher Alexander Bain: 'the language in which we grow up teaches us all the common philosophy of the age. It directs us to observe and know things which we should have overlooked; it supplies us with classifications ready made'.[112] Language as social activity did not, however, rule out nostalgia for the language of past societies. Hardy's characters often code-switch between speech variants, suggesting nostalgia for times before one form dominated. In an 1898 review of *Wessex Poems*, Archer complained: 'Mr Hardy seems to lose all sense of local and historical perspective in language, seeing all the words in the dictionary on one plane ... equally available and appropriate for any and every literary response'. Hardy subsequently replied: 'Your happy phrase, "seeing all the words in the dictionary on one plane" ... touches, curiously enough, what I had thought over'.[113] Whitney described language as a democratic institution in which standards emerged through majority usage. Hardy's reading of Mill, however, warned him of the potential tyranny of institutions and majorities. 'Social tyranny,' warned *On Liberty* (1859), was 'more formidable than many kinds of political oppression, since, though not usually upheld by such extreme penalties, it leaves fewer means of escape, penetrating much more deeply into the details of life, and enslaving the soul itself'.[114] Mill had also warned in *Logic* of narrow, scientific word definitions erasing the 'ancient experience ... thoughts and observations of former ages' of which language was 'the conservator' and 'keeper-alive'. 'In every age a certain portion of' linguistic distinctions 'fall asleep' as 'the human mind, in different generations, occupies itself with different things'.[115] Future generations may be enlightened by past word meanings in ways contemporary knowledge cannot imagine, but only if this history has been preserved.

These ideas are manifested in Hardy's portrayal of modern intolerance of linguistic diversity, often identified with a narrowing of knowledge and sympathy. In a foreword to an edition of Barnes's poems, Hardy lamented that many a dialect word suppressed by Standard English 'dies; and ... leaves no synonym'.[116] His 1887 novel *The Woodlanders* shows such change rendering the younger generation strangers to their native environment. After being educated in the town, Grace Melbury lacks the words to distinguish the subtleties of her rural home. This is in contrast to the woodsman Giles, whose dialect and life in the forest enable him to 'read its hieroglyphs as ordinary writing'.[117] Hardy registers the narrowing of Grace's vocabulary through her return in Giles's gig.[118] On the way, he notes a pile of apples, designated 'bitter-sweets', only for Grace to glance at the fruit of another orchard, distinguished by Giles as 'John-apple trees' (p. 49). Grace admits to having 'forgotten' the difference: in urban-centred

Standard English, one apple or orchard is much like another. Language standardization also narrows sympathy, as Grace's later husband, the middle-class Fitzpiers, demonstrates. He tells Grace: 'I feel as if I belonged to a different species from the people who are working in that yard' (p. 226). Even the Standard-English-speaking Grace fails to enter Fitzpiers's sphere of sympathy, as he courts her while indulging his desires with another village woman in a secluded meadow. The Standard-English-speaking Alec d'Urberville is equally lacking in sympathy in his implied rape of Tess. When the wealthy heir later becomes a Christian preacher, his guilt remains self-centred, commanding his former victim to 'swear that you will never tempt me – by your charms or ways' (p. 356). Her love Angel Clare, although seemingly a free-thinker, is also mentally hemmed in by dogma. The educated clergyman's son cannot comprehend his wife's plural identities, so that, upon her confession of her past 'trouble', he concludes: 'the woman I have been loving is not you' (p. 260). Having been to national school, Tess 'spoke two languages: the dialect at home, more or less; ordinary English abroad and to persons of quality' (p. 18). It is perhaps this duality of voices which enables her to recognize the contradictions and plural selves in others, forgiving Angel's past fornication and distrusting the absoluteness of Alec's conversion. Angel, who speaks only Standard English, is unable to extend the same broad-mindedness to Tess. The division of speech into the correct and the deviant dovetails with dogmatic moral binaries which categorize people as saved or damned, true or false. Language standardization enforces mental and moral stasis, forcing the complex plurality of experience and identity into rigid grooves.

In view of Hardy's sympathy for rural dialect, it is initially puzzling that more of it does not appear in his fiction. Barnes's poetry required extensive glossaries to explain its dialect words and was even published in 'common English' translations. Conversely, Hardy's fiction often waters down the dialect of rustic characters. Norman Page commented that Hardy's fiction gives more impressions of dialect than examples of it.[119] Wessex speech is usually marked by archaic syntax, non-standard pronunciations and occasional dialect words. Some short tales such as 'A Tradition' consist mostly of rustic speech, with Standard English narrations only introducing and contextualizing their dialectal story-tellers. Nevertheless, only a few words usually require a glossary (in Selby's case, 'mid', 'afore', 'climmed'). His other language, when modified at all, is marked by only minor clippings and phonetic spelling to indicate pronunciation ('Proossians', 'a-making', 'afeard', 'sperrits'). At other times, characters' speech becomes standardized mid-way through the tale, their first dialectal utterances having established non-standard linguistic identity and thus served their purpose. At the beginning of 'The Withered Arm' (1888), Rhoda Brook drops articles and conjugates verbs differently from the narrator: 'down in barton', 'if you do see her', 'her hands be white'.[120] Yet, in her exchanges with Gertrude Lodge, her speech loses these features. The middle-class Gertrude's long, poly-clausal sentences enable Hardy to indicate Rhoda's non-standard speech through her contrasting monosyllabic brevity, without dialectal differences: 'Did he charge much?', 'And what did you see?'[121] Critics have suggested various reasons for this watering down of dialect. The publishing industry was London-centric and the ancient rural community that Barnes had addressed was rapidly vanishing.[122] Hardy's wish to avoid caricatures of rural speech also caused him to downplay dialectal difference.[123] Further, scholarship on dialect in the period, such as that of the English Dialect Society, was steeped in a zeitgeist of inevitable extinction. The society disbanded in 1896 upon completing its dictionary, to which Hardy had contributed, assuming that no further dialects would emerge.[124] Hardy seemed to agree with this view in his 1908 preface to Barnes's poetry, lamenting that, 'since his death, education in the west of England as elsewhere has gone on with its silent and inevitable effacements, reducing the speech of this country to uniformity, and obliterating every year many a fine local word'.[125] However, as his mention of education makes clear, Hardy sees nothing natural in linguistic uniformity. The homogeneity of Standard English is produced by social dogma and coercion. At the heart of Hardy's ideas about language are variation and, yet, also interconnectedness. Hardy's mixture of dialects and registers opposes linguistic 'purism', provincial or standardized, nostalgic not for pastoral purity but dialogic cacophony. As English seemed to become increasingly homogenized, so Hardy's fiction would look to a larger opposition between communication systems invented by society and those inherited through biology. The next chapter will consider how for Hardy the conventional signs of grammar and vocabulary are only one medium alongside natural signs, transmitted and decoded instinctively – and potentially in conflict with the language of civilization. The model of language as a kind of organism alive with independent life enabled philologists and authors to privilege their descriptions of it as a neutral meta-discourse. Even though language vitalists mourned the rise of supposedly objective, scientific language as a deadening influence, their insights relied on this self-conscious detachment. Yet, as with the primitive origins of speech, the imagined vital roots of language fragmented the more that Victorians tried to isolate and magnify them.

CHAPTER 4

Instinctive signs: nature and culture in dialogue

Progressivism and vitalism both reified language as a single, unitary entity that was, in its ideal form, either wholly natural or wholly artificial. Conversely, this chapter considers fiction of the *fin de siècle* which explored speech as a pluralist dialogue between instinct and convention. Darwin viewed language as 'half-art and half-instinct', splitting it into multiple, potentially conflicting systems. In his work, speech conventions codified in dictionaries and grammars represented only the upper crust of communication. Beneath it, in the physical voice and body, lay primordial emotional triggers, operating separately from conscious language and thought.[1] At the same time, the social psychology of Spencer, Lewes and others reconceptualized thought and speech as the collective activities of a 'social organism'. These developments compromised speakers' control over their discourse, absorbing it into wider sociological and biological imperatives. Speakers appeared less autonomous, unitary agents bending language to their will than passive conduits of the (often opposing) messages of custom and instinct. The fiction of Butler, Hardy and Wells explored this tension by depicting interactions between their characters as multilayered and conflicted. While words on paper conveyed one meaning, the tone, expression and gestures of the body speaking them might suggest others. A constant question looming over these imaginative explorations was where in communication instinct ended and convention began. The two often merged together, as significant habits become hereditary in Butler's fiction while for Hardy instinctive signs and urges attach to new, conventional triggers. Approaching speech as a contingent, half-conscious adaptation enabled authors to experiment with it, as in symbolist poetry, which aimed to stimulate 'primordial ideas' through indirect associations.[2] Wells was interested in the potential of instinctive babble to unsettle language, enabling novel trains of thought and expression. However, steeped in realist tradition and ideals of objective language, Wells was ambivalent about unleashing such unconscious instincts in his writing.

His father's voice: hereditary speech and the phonograph in Butler's *The Way of All Flesh*

Butler's interest in evolution and inheritance made him question individual agency and identity, imagining language as a bio-social process that produced speakers instead of vice versa. In an 1895 lecture, Butler urged his audience to imagine a group of people 'phonographed ... so that their minutest shades of intonation are preserved', and the record replayed 'say a hundred years hence. Are those people dead or alive? Dead to themselves they are, but while they live so powerfully and so livingly in us, which is the greater paradox – to say that they are alive or that they are dead?'[3] In Butler's Lamarckian view of heredity, ancestral experience structured individual behaviour with no clear distinction between biology and society.[4] The phonograph offered an image for such genetic recording; its tiny impressions seemed to visualize heredity's transcriptions in the blood. Yet social convention also channelled people's thoughts and utterances into rigid, predefined grooves. A central question for Butler, then, was how individuals might escape the mental-linguistic grooves carved by their predecessors. Butler's writing career was shaped by a series of rebellions: against his family upbringing, organized religion, and, finally, Darwinian orthodoxy. His semi-autobiographical novel *The Way of All Flesh* (1903) repeatedly describes thoughts and speech as 'grooves' which people fall into and struggle to escape.[5] In lieu of individual agency in speech, Butler emphasized the dynamic interplay between custom and heredity, each stimulating and repressing threads of inheritance in the other. Gillian Beer argues that Butler found an escape from the 'claustrophobic' implications of his theory of heredity by emphasizing potential future transformations.[6] For language, however, such change might derive as much from excavating latent potentialities in one's socio-biological heritage as from new experiences.

Butler's vision of language as an inheritance grew from his Lamarckian belief that the habits of organisms became instincts for their offspring. This idea was crystallized by the radical writer George Drysdale in his treatise *The Elements of Social Science* (1855), of which Butler would own a copy:

> We call each human being a distinct individual, because he has been produced by an act of generation, and lives independently. But in truth we are not distinct individuals. Each of us is formed of a part of his two parents, a part which is indeed separated from them, but which once was included in their individuality. Hence we are merely a part of our parents, largely developed, and existing independently; and therefore, a man who

has given birth to children, does not wholly die at death, but a part of him survives in his offspring. In this way, man is in a manner immortal on this earth.[7]

Extending this line of thought, Butler speculated in a notebook, 'perhaps reading and writing will indeed one day come by nature ... [Words] are parvenu people as compared with thought and action'.[8] Butler read Spencer, Bain and Lewes, who materialized thought as a development of bodily sensations and emotions. 'Words are organised thoughts, as living forms are organised actions', his notebook states. 'How a thought can find embodiment in words is nearly, though perhaps not quite, as mysterious as how an action can find embodiment in form.'[9] While words might not yet be transmitted through heredity, then, the 'ideas' they signalled could be, blending into instinct. In an 1890 lecture, Butler claimed that some ideas must be instinctive because language was unable to define them. The concept of 'thought', for example, was so entrenched in heredity that conventional words could not describe it. 'Definitions', he stated, 'are useful as mental fluxes, and as helping us to fuse new ideas with our older ones', but 'we know too well what thought is, to be able to know that we know it ... Whoever does not know this without words will not learn it for all the words and definitions that are laid before him'.[10] Thought is indefinable, because its semantic roots lie beneath conscious language in heredity. Speech is only superficially volitional; it is structured by a vast aggregate of mental habits, many of them automatic. As Butler states, 'thought, for the most part, flies along over the heads of words, working its own mysterious way in paths that are beyond our ken ... that central government ... which we alone dub with the name of "we" or "us"'.[11] The conventional use of words cannot be separated from the organic development of ideas, which words by no means master. Butler's belief that heredity was organicized memory filled individual thoughts and utterances with ancestral echoes.

Butler wrote *Flesh* between 1873 and 1884, but withheld publishing it until his death due to its obvious parallels with his own family. The novel follows several generations of the Pontifex family, particularly Ernest, who struggles to escape the influence of his relations. Like Butler, Ernest has a father in the clergy (Theobald) who expects his son to pursue the same career. Theobald, in turn, lives in the shadow of his more successful, domineering father, similarly as Thomas Butler was overshadowed by his bishop father. Like Butler, Ernest renounces Christianity, later becoming a writer on radical ideas. Communication in the novel is haunted by ancestral voices and signs, both from the primordial past and still living individuals. Darwin had argued that facial expressions derived from animal communication, and Butler suggested the same: 'Eyes are verbs, and glasses of wine are good nouns enough as between those who understand one another ... for the most part it is in what we read between the lines that the profounder meaning of any letter is conveyed'. There were, he continued, 'words unwritten and untranslatable into any nouns that are nevertheless felt as above, about and underneath the gross material symbols that lie scrawled upon the paper'.[12] Such instinctive signification abounds among the characters in Butler's novel. The narrator Overton recalls how 'my sisters eyed me to silence' whenever he disagreed with his father (p. 5). The young Theobald reluctantly enters the clergy because he 'feared the dark scowl which would come over his father's face upon the slightest opposition' (p. 31). Physical violence also seems an instinctive language of the primitive family unit. Successive generations of Pontifex patriarchs beat their offspring when words fail to control them. Butler also presents violence as a sub-language among the lower class, evoking the imagined embodiment of primitive speech described in Chapter 2 above. Ernest's words cannot prevent his servant-wife Ellen's bouts of alcoholism; a hereditary affliction. She only regains some stability after eloping with a butcher who regularly 'blacked her eye, and she liked him all the better for it' (p. 352). Theobald ceases to beat Ernest as he grows older, but instinctive aggression continues to warp their conversations. Overton states, 'As long as communication was confined to the merest commonplace all went well, but if these were departed from ever such a little he invariably felt that his father's instincts showed themselves in immediate opposition to his own. When he was attacked his father laid whatever stress was possible on everything which his opponents said' (p. 413). Ernest feels unable to escape this family instinct, later deciding to live apart from his own children. Hereditary feelings, and signs triggering them, lurk beneath the surface of language, operating in spite of conscious wishes.

Evolution equally rendered the voice a site of unconscious emotional triggers. Butler's notebook describes how he reviewed his writing by reciting it to a listener, revealing new layers of meaning: 'I feel weak places at once when I read aloud where I thought, as long as I read to myself only, that the passage was all right'.[13] The unconscious signs of speech seemed to enhance sympathy between speakers. In his lecture on language, Butler remarked: 'The language is not in the words but in the heart-to-heartness of the thing ... [s]o it is not by the words that I am too presumptuously venturing to speak to-night that your opinions will be formed or modified.

They will be formed or modified, if either, by something that you will feel, but which I have not spoken'.¹⁴ In *Flesh* such non-verbal impulses effect Ernest's temporary conversion to evangelism. When he hears a Simeonite speak with 'impressive' voice the Lord's Prayer and a single line from the Bible, 'the text, familiar though it was, went home to the consciences of Ernest and his friends as it had never yet done. If Mr. Hawke had stopped here he would have almost said enough' (p. 222). While mocking the logic of Hawke's speech, the narrator tracks his delivery like music, beginning with 'singular quietness' and building to 'greater warmth', before he 'ended rather abruptly'. These instinctive vocal signs, the narrator states, 'had produced an effect greater than the actual words I have given can convey to the reader; the virtue lay in the man more than in what he said ... their effect was magical' (p. 226). Religious zeal is built on instinctive signs and emotions beyond conscious thought.

Flesh deconstructs the individual speaker, with characters echoing gestures and even phrases of their forebears. In a post-marital tiff with Christina, Theobald's smile 'was succeeded by a scowl which that old Turk, his father, might have envied' (p. 58). He vents his frustration by stamping on the floor of their carriage; later, his father angrily 'stamped as Theobald had done' (p. 75). Parents loom large through their proximity in the evolutionary sequence. 'Offspring should, as a general rule, resemble its own most immediate progenitors,' Butler wrote, 'that is to say, that it should remember best what it has been doing most recently.'¹⁵ When the adult Ernest meets the daughter of Dr Skinner, a pretentious theologian, she seems to have inherited her father's 'voice and manner of speaking'. Her pompous aesthetic statements echo her father's pronouncements on the 'deeper meaning' of biblical passages: 'For me a simple chord of Beethoven is enough. This is happiness' (p. 417). Recalling his meeting with Skinner, Overton highlights the musicality of the man's delivery, lending pseudo-profundity to banal statements. Asked what he wants for supper, Skinner pauses dramatically, before intoning: 'Stay – I may presently take a glass of cold water – and a small piece of bread and butter' (p. 114). Thirty years later, in the presence of Miss Skinner, Ernest's

> Mind's ear seemed to hear Miss Skinner saying, as though it were an epitaph: –
>
> 'Stay:
> I may presently take
> A simple chord of Beethoven,
> Or a small semiquaver
> From one of Mendelssohn's Songs without Words'. (p. 417)

This propensity of children to echo their parents inflects Ernest's struggle to escape Theobald's influence. As a child, Ernest often hides from his father's voice when it is resounding from another room. Returning home after secretly helping the disgraced ex-servant Ellen, he sneaks inside to the sound of Theobald's 'angriest tones'. These make him feel like Jack 'when from the oven in which he was hidden he heard the ogre ask his wife what young children she had got for his supper' (p. 172). Anxious that his actions will be discovered, Ernest 'next day and for many days afterwards ... trembled each time he heard his father's voice calling for him'. Part of Ernest's anxiety at the sound of his father's voice might derive from an anxiety, yet half-conscious, of it persisting inside him as genetic data. Biology seems to equate almost to destiny, with Overton commenting that Theobald and Christina would have to be born again 'of a different line of ancestry for many generations' to lose their mental rigidity (p. 280). Ancestral voices appear inescapable, solidified as they are by generations of habitual actions and suggestions.

Despite his hereditarian beliefs, Butler's notion of 'habit' also emphasized the conventionality of language. Mill, whom *Flesh* references several times (pp. 322, 208), had described language as man-made custom. Words and their uses were shaped by social institutions, such as family and state. Consciousness was conditioned by a 'Social Organism', as G. H. Lewes termed it, a 'fund' of past experiences, which language solidified (see Introduction above). Butler cited Lewes in his work, throwing a different light on his phonograph imagery.[16] Perhaps custom, more than heredity, shaped the unconscious grooves into which language channelled thought. Lewes had described linguistic creativity as the forging of new molecular 'channels' in the brain, while convention moved always in old ones: 'inferior minds think the thoughts of others and write the phrases of others'.[17] Butler presented language convention as limiting thought in his Swiftian satire *Erewhon* (1872), in which scholars in a Lilliput-like society scorn originality: 'A man's business, they hold, is to think as his neighbours do'.[18] They use words ritualistically rather than to convey ideas. One professor reprimands a student 'for want of sufficient vagueness' while another is excluded 'for having written an article on a scientific subject without having made free enough use of the words "carefully," "patiently," and "earnestly"'.[19] Butler's notebook described words as 'scaffolding ... for the building up of imperfect thought'; they 'impede and either kill, or are killed by, perfect thought'.[20] Language ossified when speakers mistook symbolic convention for ultimate truth. Similarly, in *Life and Habit*, Butler wrote:

> The metaphors and *façons de parler* to which even in the plainest speech we are perpetually recurring (as, for example, in this last two lines, 'plain,' 'perpetually,' and 'recurring,' are all words based on metaphor, and hence more or less liable to mislead) often deceive us, as though there were nothing more than what we see and say, and as though words, instead of being, as they are, the creatures of our convenience, had some claim to be the actual ideas themselves concerning which we are conversing.[21]

Words endanger mental freedom when fetishized as ends in themselves or, as Butler would later describe them, 'covenanted symbols'.[22]

In *Flesh*, Ernest perhaps flees less from a hereditary 'voice' than from verbal convention. When, as an adult, he severs contact with his parents, Overton remarks: 'achievement of any kind would be impossible for him unless he was free from those who would be for ever dragging him back into the conventional' (p. 299). Theobald exemplifies rigid verbal convention, his repressed clerical existence turning him into a repository of clichés. His speech runs in automatic grooves, sometimes producing absurdities. He determines to buy a watch 'answering every purpose', which causes Overton to comment: 'Theobald spoke as if watches had half-a-dozen purposes besides time-keeping, but he could hardly open his mouth without using one or other of his tags, and "answering every purpose" was one of them' (p. 180). Similarly, after Ernest goes to Cambridge, 'Theobald said he was "willing to hope" – this was one of his tags – that his son would turn over a new leaf now that he had left school, and for his own part he was "only too ready" – this was another tag – to let bygones be bygones' (p. 199). The strong hold of convention over his personality causes him to echo and mimic the majority. Overton states: 'the reader, if he has passed middle life and has a clerical connection, will probably remember scores and scores of rectors and rectors' wives who differed in no material respect from Theobald and Christina' (p. 73). From this perspective, Theobald, and his father before him, beat their children less from primal aggression than from the social pressure to conform. Butler's narration highlights how linguistic fashion shapes this pressure, noting the popular idea that, 'if their wills were "well broken" in childhood, to use an expression then much in vogue, they would acquire habits of obedience' (p. 22). Verbal conventions structure social norms, legitimizing actions which might otherwise seem unreasonable. Overton charts Theobald's thought process as a young father, which is shaped by the axioms of a 'long course of Puritanism': 'The first signs of self-will must be carefully looked for, and plucked up by the roots at once before they had time to grow. Theobald picked up this numb serpent of a metaphor and cherished it in his bosom' (p. 89). Theobald literally beats his son's speech into the standardized shape, interpreting the infant's mispronunciation as stubborn self-will. 'Don't you think it would be very nice,' he tells Ernest, 'if you were to say "come" like other people, instead of "tum"?' before hitting him when he continues to blur his phonemes (p. 96). Puritan fetishizing of the written word as original truth breeds intolerance of linguistic variety.

Butler's narrative spans across several generations and this enables it to historicize the growth of linguistic conventionality, which is tied to social status, in the Pontifex family. Theobald's father George rejects his family's dialect when he goes into business, advancing himself by echoing the language of respectability. His diary of a European tour reads like an assortment of quotations from fashionable writers. Overton comments: 'I felt as I read it that the author before starting had made up his mind to admire only what he thought it would be creditable in him to admire, to look at nature and art only through the spectacles that had been handed down to him by generation after generation of prigs and impostors. The first glimpse of Mont Blanc threw Mr Pontifex into a conventional ecstasy.' George's contrived effusions rely on John Trumbull's 'The Prophecy of Balaam' (1773), as he recalls '"at distance dimly seen" ... this sublime spectacle' (p. 14).[23] Similarly, two generations later, convention stifles the verbal facility of Ernest's sister Charlotte. She absorbs the vocabularies of Christianity and respectability without interrogating their meanings. Overton states: 'she has fallen under the dominion of the words "hope," "think," "feel," "try," "bright," and "little," and can hardly write a page without introducing all these words and some of them more than once' (p. 415). Butler links linguistic convention with mental stasis most absurdly in Theobald's horror at creeping Tractarian changes to Anglican services. He winces as a new generation of parishioners refer to 'the Creed' instead of 'the Belief' and use the Latin 'Alleluia' instead of the Germanic 'Hallelujah' (pp. 391–92). Theobald submits to most of the changes, though, his habitual conventionality rendering him impotent against majority custom. Ernest is trained to behave similarly so that, as a schoolboy, he, 'caught up, parrot-like, whatever jargon he heard from his elders, which he thought was the correct thing, and aired it in season and out of season, as though it were his own' (p. 150). How, then, might sons escape the voices of their parents, with long-term heredity and short-term convention conspiring to rob them of mental-linguistic agency?

If speakers attain any agency, it is through their experiences reacting upon this heritage. The grooves on early phonographs warped themselves out of shape with each replay, allowing for some individuality in Butler's image.[24] In 1880 he wrote that 'each individual life' added 'a small (but so small, in any one lifetime, as to be hardly appreciable) amount of new experience to the general store of memory'.[25] Conventional symbols accelerated this process, modified by each new generation to describe their different experiences. Butler lectured: 'The thought is not steadily and coherently governed by and moulded in words, nor does it steadily govern them. Words and thought interact upon and help one another, as any other mechanical appliances interact on and help the invention that first hit upon them.'[26] The meanings of words changed according to their uses. Each man 'appropriate[s]' the words of his predecessors, Lewes wrote, 'but he does not simply echo their words, he rethinks them ... He cannot think their thoughts so long as his experiences refuse to be condensed in their symbols'.[27] In acrimonious letters to his father, Butler often echoed the latter's words, altering their meanings. After losing money through bad investments, he quoted his father: '"Pray let no false shame hinder you from making a clean breast of it". I have done nothing which I am ashamed of and have nothing to make a clean breast of'.[28] Ernest does the same in *Flesh*, his inner monologue interjecting as his father refers to 'your Latin and Greek': '"They aren't mine," thought Ernest, "and never have been"' (p. 147). Butler also reworked his parents' words by placing them verbatim in the mouths of Ernest's parents. The wisdom which Butler's parents imagined themselves sharing is transformed into empty clichés. His father's phrase 'making a clean breast of it' appears on Theobald's lips (p. 276). Butler's novel also appropriated a letter which his pregnant mother had written to her children in case she died in labour. Christina's letter to the Pontifex children is almost identical.[29] Both assume that the meanings of their words will remain fixed through time, exhorting 'try to remember, and from time to time read over again the last words [of your mother]' (p. 105). The message which Butler's mother imagined echoing the same truths down the ages becomes, in her son's hands, an indictment of pious delusion. Christina's belief that 'your father' will suffer immense 'sorrow' at her death is contradicted by Theobald's earlier hesitation about marrying her and later 'want of emotion' when she dies (p. 394). According to Butler's friend Henry Festing Jones, Theobald's comment repeated endlessly at Christina's deathbed ('I could not wish it prolonged') echoed Butler's father in the same situation.[30] Words, Butler argued, 'have no more to do with the ideas they serve to convey than money has with the things that it serves to buy'.[31] The words of one's predecessors could serve radically different meanings.

This semantic plasticity of symbols aids Ernest's escape from his parents' influence. Ernest loses his faith not by discarding his father's Bible but by rereading it. His experiences enable him to see contradictions where he once found divine wisdom. 'He made the New Testament his chief study,' states Overton, 'going through it ... as one who wished neither to believe nor disbelieve, but cared only about finding out whether he ought to believe or no' (p. 284). Later, as a radical writer, Ernest argues 'that though it would be inconvenient to change the words of our prayer book and articles, it would not be inconvenient to change in a quiet way the meanings which we put upon those words' (p. 403). Words once interpreted as literal realities might be reconceived as metaphors for the limits of human knowledge. Evolutionary theory was effecting this change to the meanings of 'origin' and 'species', once imagined as definite and eternal.[32] The nexus of adaptation revealed no absolute genesis or categorical boundaries, turning these terms into hypothetical abstractions. As organisms are modified by their actions, so words are modified by their use. Thus single generations can transform the meanings of words, as Overton remarks of the evolutionist Ernest: 'His father and grandfather could probably no more understand his state of mind than they could understand Chinese' (p. 420). Nonetheless, Butler leaves the question of individual agency uncertain. As a writer challenging the institution of marriage, Ernest comments: 'I am bursting with these things, and it is my fate to say them' (pp. 396–97). What appears autonomous speech might form part of a larger development.

Butler's voices of heredity and society are not single but plural. Struggling with the puzzle of heredity and variation, Darwin had written that 'each living creature must be looked at as a microcosm – a little universe, formed of a host of self-propagating organisms, inconceivably minute and as numerous as the stars in heaven'.[33] What seemed like a deviation from heredity could be the return of a latent strain. In a revision to *Life and Habit*, Butler wrote:

> [The individual's] past selves are living in him at this moment with the accumulated life of centuries. 'Do this, this, this, which we too have done, and found our profit in it', cry the souls of his forefathers within him ... 'Withhold', cry some. 'Go on boldly', cry others. 'Me, me, me, revert hitherward, my descendant', shouts one as it were from some high vantage-ground over the heads of the clamorous multitude. 'Nay, but me, me, me', echoes another; and our former selves fight within us and wrangle for our possession.[34]

Heredity is no united chant but an anarchic cacophony. The means of resisting one voice might lie in succumbing to another. When Theobald forces his son into a clerical education, Ernest receives contrary orders from a 'voice' of heredity, commanding: 'obey me, your true self, and things will go tolerably well with you, but only listen to that outward and visible old husk of yours which is called your father, and I will rend you in pieces even unto the third and fourth generation as one who has hated God; for I, Ernest, am the God who made you' (pp. 132–33). This voice causes Ernest to pursue his instinctive interests, such as music, diverting him from his education. As Overton remarks, while he struggled to remember the Classics, 'anyone played him a piece of music and told him where it came from, he never forgot that, though he made no effort to retain it' (p. 196). The instinctive signs of music derail his language education so that Theobald complains, 'Why, when he was translating Livy the other day he slipped out Handel's name in mistake for Hannibal's' (p. 124). Butler suggests that Ernest's musical 'instinct' descends from his great-grandfather, who played the organ, and also emerges in his aunt Alethea. Upon discovering the fortune which Alethea has left to him, Ernest remarks: 'If I were rendering this moment in music ... I should allow myself free use of the augmented sixth', before voicing 'a laugh that had something of a family likeness to his aunt's' (p. 373). Ernest's escape from the groove set by his father involves returning to an older hereditary one.

Equally, conventional language could be imagined as a muddle of competing traditions. Lewes called it 'a shifting mass of truth and error, for ever becoming more and more sifted and organised into permanent structures of germinating fertility or of fossilised barrenness'.[35] Similarly, for Butler, individuals who seem like agents of change often turn out to be units in larger, long-running processes. Overton compares Ernest's apostasy to a moth hatching from its 'cocoon', accelerated by the shock of his imprisonment (p. 284). His experience germinates seeds of doubt already sown by conversations with a free-thinking neighbour and reading *Vestiges of Creation*. This doubt is not simply a unitary, linear development, though, but one of many potentialities previously repressed. Overton comments how *Vestiges* had been 'forgotten before Ernest went up to Cambridge', yet its ideas would re-emerge, modified, in Darwin's *On the Origin of Species* (p. 208). Ernest's recovery of the book from the past counters the assumption of a Darwinian 'revolution' after 1859: all ideas grow from previous forms. Much of Butler's public row with Darwin stemmed from this view that Darwin was only the latest in a line of evolutionists.[36] Similarly, Ernest's escape from the church recapitulates Theobald's failed attempt to do the same when young. Theobald requests not to be ordained, only for his father to coerce him into it. Theobald's religious doubts are feebler than Ernest's partly because of the faith's stronger theoretical position in the early nineteenth century. As Overton recalls, in this time 'there was just a little scare about geology', but literal belief in the Genesis narrative remained strong (p. 52). Ernest's interpretation of Scripture as metaphorical builds on earlier shifts in geology which undermined biblical chronology. Theobald also prefigures his son's later iconoclastic writings against marriage through his own reluctance to marry. The 'voice' of conventional respectability is too strong for him to resist, however, similarly as a voice of heredity causes Ernest to rebel:

> He would drive back to Crampsford; he would complain to Mr and Mrs Allaby; he didn't mean to have married Christina; he hadn't married her; it was all a hideous dream; he would – But a voice kept ringing in his ears which said: 'YOU CAN'T, CAN'T, CAN'T'.
>
> 'CAN'T I?' screamed the unhappy creature to himself.
>
> 'No', said the remorseless voice, 'YOU CAN'T. YOU ARE A MARRIED MAN.' (p. 58)

Slumping back in his wedding carriage, Theobald 'for the first time felt how iniquitous were the marriage laws of England. But he would buy Milton's prose works and read his pamphlet on divorce' (p. 58). Equally, as experience impels Ernest to find new meaning in evolutionary writing, so it gives Theobald a new perspective on old religious texts. Conventional language is an entangled bed of idea-seeds, which sprout or wither in different environment.

For all of Butler's iconoclasm, it is worth noting that he did not seek to destroy words. Indeed, in some cases he defended old words against writers who rejected them as unscientific. While Huxley made a point of removing *God* from his explanations of the universe, Butler remarked in *Luck or Cunning?* (1886): 'What convention or short cut can [better] symbolise for us ... that which cannot be rendered – the idea of an essence omnipresent in all things at all times everywhere[?]' The word only became misleading, Butler suggested, when it had 'been lost sight of as a convention and ... converted into a fetish, and now that its worthlessness as a fetish is being generally felt, its great value as a hieroglyph or convention is in danger of being lost sight of'. To erase *God* from the lexicon was to repeat the mistake of religion, assuming that words could exist 'in actual correspondence with a more or less knowable reality'.[37] Symbols were stepping stones for ideas which preceded and soared beyond the conscious self. Overton suggests in *Flesh* that speakers proceed more often by faith than by definite knowledge. Interrogating the difference between 'external' and 'internal', he claims, 'will knock our whole system over'. To make any progress, the speaker must assume the separation of the two concepts 'when we find this convenient, and unity between the same when we find unity convenient' (p. 311). On this basis, Ernest the evolutionist continues to take the Sacrament annually and believe in 'a something as yet but darkly known which makes right right and wrong wrong' (p. 304). In our current ignorance, Butler suggests, why not call this something God? Words which seem obsolete might signpost traces of an idea in which future generations will see a greater significance, and build upon. It was in this sense that Butler judged Darwin's theories unoriginal. 'Buffon, Erasmus Darwin, and Lamarck believed in natural selection to the full as much as any follower of Mr Charles Darwin can do', he wrote. 'They did not use the actual words, but the idea underlying them is the essence of their system.'[38] The future would bring words for ideas nascent and unspoken in the present. As an unpopular writer, Butler consoled himself with the notion that later generations would find new meanings in his works, writing: 'Homer and Shakespeare speak to us probably far more effectually than they did to the men of their own time, and most likely we have them at their best'.[39] Their embodied lives were but 'embryonic stages', developing to their fullest centuries later in the readings of future audiences. Ernest and Butler's apparent liberation from the voices of their fathers might be better understood as a refashioning. Instead of trusting in symbols as the revealed mind of God, they trust in the unconscious, partly instinctive life of 'thought' which works around language. Language seems not simply analogous to heredity but part of it, collapsing instinct and custom into a monistic network of potentialities.

Speaking of sex in Hardy's fiction

While Butler explored the concept of instinctive signs through parent–child relations, Hardy explored its role in love and sexual attraction. He was influenced by Darwin and Arthur Schopenhauer, who stressed the sexual urge as a fundamental instinct. He also read Charles Fourier's arguments for free love and J. M. McLennan's theory that marriage had originated in the trading of females, undermining its legitimacy.[40] The issue was close to home for Hardy: his passion for his first wife Emma faded over time and seems to have transferred to flirtations and obsessions with other women.[41] In 1892 he spoke of his frustration at pressures on authors to idealize marriage and ignore debates over divorce: 'I do feel very strongly that the position of man and woman in nature ... things which everybody is thinking and nobody saying – might be taken up and treated frankly'.[42] Roger Ebbatson observed that Hardy's fiction 'projects the non-linguistic codes which pertain in sexual matters in animal and human worlds' on to intimate scenes between his characters so that 'spoken language gives place to interpersonal communication derived from biology'.[43] Hence, many of his characters are drawn together by music or dance. At what point, though, did language separate from such instinctive codes, forged by sexual selection? Angelique Richardson argues that nature and culture often exist 'in fertile reciprocity' in Hardy's writings, leaving him 'caught between biology and philosophy, between, in essence, Darwin and Mill, and not always able to accommodate both'.[44] While Mill argued for the conventionality of speech, Darwin posited a natural vocabulary of instinctive signs for emotions and unconscious urges. Richardson notes that for Hardy 'instinct is often related to a greater authenticity of feeling and action, a greater truth value'.[45] Instinctive communication encodes sympathy in his fiction which conventional language suppresses. The path to a more humane society might lie in rediscovering these bio-semiotics rather than stifling them. Yet, as with Butler, Hardy rejected simple dichotomies of nature and culture. Human communication emerges in his vision as multilayered, with plural sign systems pulling speakers in different directions.

The idea of instinctive emotional signs is discernible in Hardy's fiction from his first published novel *Desperate Remedies* (1871). The tale suggests that forms of animal magnetism might mediate instinctive amatory signs. Characters send and receive them at the speed of Helmholtz's nerve signals without conscious deliberation. When Cythera first meets her future husband Springrove, their eyes lock together, the narrator noting: 'a clear penetrating ray of intelligence had shot from each into each, giving birth to one of those unaccountable sensations which carry home to the heart before the hand has been touched or the merest compliment passed, by something stronger than mathematical proof, the conviction, "A tie has begun to unite us"'.[46] When a rowing trip enables the nascent lovers to be alone in close proximity, they avoid returning to shore at once. The narrator states: 'It was the turn of his face to tell a tale now. He looked, "We understand each other – ah, we do, darling!" turned the boat, and pulled back into the Bay once more' (p. 49). Faces also tell 'tales' outside of verbal convention in *Far from the Madding Crowd* (1874), as the narrator states: 'There are accents in the eye which are not on the tongue, and more tales come from pale lips than can enter an ear. It is both the grandeur and the pain of the remoter moods that they avoid the pathway of sound.' The comment refers to a chance encounter between the much pursued Bathsheba and the suitor whom she has just refused by letter, Boldwood. Their stilted conversation is a veneer, Hardy suggests, to the intense feelings communicated by Boldwood's face and Bathsheba's cheeks. It is because these signs constitute an instinctive language of their own, the narrator implies, that 'those who have the power of reproaching in silence may find it a means more effective than words'.[47]

Hardy often suggests an authenticity in instinctive signs, lacking in conventional language, by linking them to wider environmental rhythms.[48] Vocality connects humans to primal nature in *The Return of the Native* when the narrator finds a 'linguistic peculiarity' in the winds blowing through Egdon Heath. Alone there, awaiting her lover, Eustacia Vye exhales unrestrainedly, 'her articulation ... but as another phrase of the same discourse as' the winds. Her vocalization exists outside the social convention of words: 'There was a sense of spasmodic abandonment about [her sigh] as if, in allowing herself to utter the sound, the woman's brain had authorised what it could not regulate'.[49] Hardy emphasizes the opposition between natural impulse and social restraint further when her lover appears: 'a low laugh escaped her – the third utterance which the girl had indulged in tonight' (p. 60). Primordial expressions may only be vocalized in solitude or clandestine relations. Public circles demand the 'regulation' of voice within conventional parameters. Like several of Hardy's lovers, Eustacia becomes infatuated after hearing her future mate's voice.[50] Words form only the semantic surface above the instinctive significations: 'it was not to the words that Eustacia listened; she could not have recalled, a few minutes later, what the words were. It was to the alternating voice ... All emotional things were possible to the speaker of that "good night"' (p. 117). Equally, in Hardy's last published novel *The Well-Beloved* (1897), Pierston's infatuation with Avice, who resembles her mother of the same name, is again mediated by a vocal music separate from words:

> she attracted him by the cadences of her voice; she would suddenly drop it to a rich whisper of roguishness, when ... soul and heart – or what seemed soul and heart – resounded. The charm lay in the intervals, using that word in its musical sense. She would say a few syllables in one note, and end her sentence in a soft modulation upwards, then downwards, then into her own note again ... The subject of her discourse he cared nothing about – it was no more his interest than his concern. He took special pains that in catching her voice he might not comprehend her words.[51]

In 1870 the musicologist Colin Brown had written of a musical notation he designed to represent speech, arguing 'that every sound in the scale has its own peculiar and characteristic mental effect'.[52] Hardy supports this idea of a definite system of emotional vocal signals by developing Pierston's obsession through bathetically mundane conversations. He quizzes Avice on her laundry washing methods, the narrator wryly noting: 'Nature was working her plans for the next generation under the cloak of a dialogue on linen'.[53]

Instinctive signs sometimes also mediate sympathy for Hardy, implying that civilization dulls this faculty rather than creates it. Darwin had traced sympathy to the natural selection of united groups over individual organisms. Spencer linked such sympathy to the development of vocal 'music', predicting an ideal future when this 'language of emotions' would unite humans completely (see Chapter 1). *The Return of the Native* flirts with this ideal during a secret meeting between Eustacia and Clym. As they embrace and kiss, the narrator states: 'They remained long without a single utterance, for no language could reach the level of their condition – words were as the rusty implements of a by-gone barbarous epoch, and only to be occasionally tolerated' (p. 197). The passage evokes Tylor's teleological vision of language giving way to a kind of telepathy. Yet, its context – between two lovers on the primordial heath – is far removed from civilization. The sympathy between Eustacia and Clym might be read as an animal magnetism of sorts, mediating the same primordial signs as those previously transmitted between the couple. Clym and his mother enjoy a similar oneness of feeling when she comes to accept his plans to stay in Egdon. While 'he had despaired of reaching her by argument', he instead does so 'by a magnetism which was as superior to words as words are to yells'. Their sympathy is mediated by biology rather than symbols: 'he was a part of her ... their discourses were as if carried on between the right and left hands of the same body' (p. 191). The fullest communication might consist not of humans repressing their instincts but of submitting to them.

While Hardy was wary of idealizing dialect as natural, his fiction nonetheless often associates its replacement by Standard English with repression of instinctive signs and sympathy. Through standardization, speech became mechanized into rigid rules, coinciding, for Hardy, with the silencing of vocal impulses. This process is shown in Hardy's only novel set in the city, *The Hand of Ethelberta*. Urban sophistication consists of repressing instinctive signs which go unregulated in the country. The narrator states: 'a slight laugh from far down the throat and a slight narrowing of the eye were equivalent as indices of the degree of mirth felt to a Ha-ha-ha! and a shaking of the shoulders among the minor traders of the kingdom; and to a Ho-ho-ho! contorted features, purple face, and stamping foot among the gentlemen in corduroy and fustian who adorn the remoter provinces'.[54] This suppression distances people from each other in the struggle for status. Ethelberta's bourgeois acquaintants politely agree to join her on an outing, yet 'from first to last Ethelberta never discovered from the Belmaines whether her proposal had been an infliction or a charm, so perfectly were they practised in sustaining that complete divorce between thinking and saying which is the hall-mark of high civilization' (p. 227). In this society of appearances, Ethelberta is punished for expressing her feelings transparently. Her protector Lady Petherwin cuts Ethelberta out of her will for not continuing to publically mourn Lady Petherwin's son, who died during his honeymoon with Ethelberta. Ethelberta refuses to fake emotions in the name of respectability, remarking: 'I should have been more virtuous by being more unfeeling. That often happens' (p. 88). The more that social convention represses instinctive, sympathetic signs, the more emotionally atomized people often become in Hardy's fiction. In *A Laodicean* (1881) the genteel bastard William Dare exemplifies this notion to a Machiavellian extreme. He cheats and blackmails his way through life 'with the flawless politeness of a man whose speech has no longer any kinship with his feelings'.[55] His speech is utterly standardized, without a trace of locality, 'in cold level words which had once been English, but which seemed to have lost the accent of nationality'.[56] Somerset notes how Dare uses speech to conceal rather than express himself: 'I never can quite make out what you are, or what your age is'. Dare replies that he is 'a citizen of the world. I owe no country patriotism, and no king or queen obedience'.[57] Dare's most elaborate scheme is to make heiress Paula Power fall in love with his father, securing a rich inheritance for himself. Although a great dissembler, Dare lacks the ability to transmit the instinctive signs of sexual attraction and sympathy, and so must recruit his amorous but guileless father to win Paula's heart.

Instinctive signs might even mediate sympathy beyond species boundaries. Hardy had a lifelong interest in animal welfare, writing in 1910 to the Humanitarian League: 'the most far-reaching consequence of the establishment of the common origin of all species is ethical'.[58] In 1895 he sent the passage of the infamous pig-killing in *Jude the Obscure* (1895) to the editor of the *Animal's Friend*, suggesting that it be reproduced in the journal. He wrote that the passage 'might be made useful in the teaching of mercy in the slaughtering of animals for the meat market – the cruelties involved in that business having been a great grief to me for years'.[59] The scene, in which Jude slaughters a pig, engages with the popular idea that humans and animals shared a common language of vocalized emotions.[60] Considering connections between Darwin and Hardy, Caroline Sumpter notes that Darwin's *Expression* had described pigs vocalizing differently to convey pain or pleasure, as in the human voice.[61] In spite of his learning, Jude does not object with logical, reasoned arguments and cannot explain why the pig's suffering horrifies him. His grief is triggered by the animal's vocalizations. Preparing for the slaughter, Jude's 'cheerfulness was lessened' by the animal's 'voice [which] could be continually heard from a corner of the garden'.[62] As they bind him down, the pig's 'squeak of surprise, rose to repeated cries of rage'. When Jude fetches the sticking-knife, 'the animal's note changed its quality. It was not now rage, but the cry of despair; long-drawn, slow and hopeless'. Bleeding to death, 'the dying animal's cry assumed its third and final tone, the shriek of agony; his glazing eyes riveting themselves on Arabella with the eloquently keen reproach of a creature recognizing at last the treachery of those who had seemed his only friends'.[63] Jude's reaction is not acquired through convention but is an innate vocabulary of sympathy. He is also affected when the distant 'shrill squeak' of a rabbit caught in a trap awakes him at night. He cannot help but 'picture the agonies of the rabbit' and 'could rest no longer till he had put it out of its pain'.[64] Treating communication as apart from biology, humans narrow their sphere of potential sympathy.

We must beware, however, of simple dichotomies between selfish civilization and sympathetic nature in Hardy's view of speech. Asquith argues that 'the language of the intellect is relatively unimportant' to the feelings of Hardy's characters: the music of emotion is the main force.[65] While there is much truth in this argument, intellect and emotion also shade into each other. Hardy presents people as negotiations of nature and culture, rather than in such as way that the latter falsifies the former. Sexual attraction and sympathy are not only animal urges, but also imaginative extensions of these urges, enabled by the mental scaffolding of language. Shortly before Cytherea and Springrove's first kiss in *Desperate Remedies*, one sign system seems to invade the other, reversing the conventional meanings of words in a surge of passion. Having brought his mouth to the 'brink' of Cytherea's, Springrove whispers 'as much to himself as to her', 'May I?' The narrator states:

> Her endeavour was to say No, so denuded of its flesh and sinews that its nature would hardly be recognized, or in other words a No from so near the affirmative frontier as to be affected with the Yes accent. It was thus a

whispered No, drawn out to nearly a quarter of a minute's length, the O making itself audible as a sound like the spring coo of a pigeon on unusually friendly terms with its mate. (pp. 53–54)

Laying aside the disturbing implication, noted by Phillip Mallett, 'that a woman's "No" is merely an erotically charged "Yes"', the passage is ambiguous about how instinctive these instinctive signs really are.[66] While comparing Cytherea's vowel to an instinctive mating sound, the narrator also suggests calculation, stating that she was 'conscious of her success in producing the kind of word she had wished to produce'. Although biology forges such messages, consciousness enables individuals to modify them. Cytherea's cooing is, in Darwin's words, 'half-art and half-instinct'. She is no mere slave of instinct in opposition to masculine intellect. For both her and Springrove, individual agency emerges through interferences in larger, automatic processes. In 1907 Hardy wrote: 'The will of man is ... neither wholly free nor wholly unfree ... [W]henever it happens that all the rest of the Great Will is in equilibrium the minute portion called one person's will is free, just as a performer's fingers are free to go on playing the pianoforte of themselves when he talks or thinks of something else and the head does not rule them'.[67] Hardy's lovers are conduits of the Will to life in their instinctive vocalizations, but their ability to manipulate these signs for premeditated effect renders them partly intentional.

Desperate Remedies undermines the intellectual language–instinctive noise dichotomy through the former reacting upon the latter. The mental abstraction enabled by language links signs, originally instinctive, to complex chains of association. Darwin recognized this issue, writing: 'every true or inherited movement of expression seems to have had some natural and independent origin. But when once acquired, such movements may be voluntarily and consciously employed as a means of communication'.[68] The instinctive signs of attraction that draw Cytherea and Springrove together transmit along imaginative pathways enabled by language. Springrove occupies the position of prospective lover in Cytherea's thoughts before they meet: her brother's reports of him interact with Cytherea's instinctive receptiveness to a mate. In her 'symbol-loving girlhood', the sight of her bare ring finger conjures images of an unseen man (p. 21). Similarly, after their meeting, thought, elaborated by language, channels her sexual instinct into endless interpretations of his words: 'she repeated [them] to herself a hundred times ... toying with them, – looking at them from all points, and investing them with meanings of love and faithfulness ... her reason flirted with her fancy as a kitten will sport with a dove' (p. 36). Instinctive gestures can turn into floating signifiers while neutral movements become charged with emotional associations. In the boat with Springrove 'when his hands came forward to begin the pull, they approached so near to her that her vivid imagination began to thrill her with a fancy that he was going to clasp his arms round her. The sensation grew so strong that she could not run the risk of again meeting his eyes at those critical moments' (p. 46). Humans' capacity to draw indirect associations destabilizes the instinctive sign system. Sexuality changes from a closed circuit of fixed signals and responses to a dynamic structure of interpretation, appropriation and displacement.

Instinctive signs are similarly displaced into conventional meanings in *Tess* when Alec's conversion diverts his signs of sexual desire into religious zeal. Darwin wrote of 'the impassioned orator' moving audiences by vocal patterns instinctively associated with courtship and rivalry' (see Introduction above). Hearing Alec quote the Scripture, Tess notes 'a grim incongruity' between the words and 'this too familiar intonation, [which] less than four years earlier, had brought to her ears expressions of such divergent purpose'. The narrator continues:

> The former curves of sensuousness were now modulated to lines of devotional passion. The lip-shapes that had meant seductiveness were now made to express supplication; the glow on the cheek that yesterday could be translated as riotousness was evangelized to-day into the splendour of pious rhetoric; animalism had become fanaticism; Paganism, Paulinism; the bold rolling eye that had flashed upon her form in the old time with such mastery now beamed with the rude energy of a theolatry that was almost ferocious ... The lineaments, as such, seemed to complain. They had been diverted from their hereditary connotation to signify impressions for which Nature did not intend them. (p. 390)

Asquith concludes from this passage that Alec's conversion is illusory: he is a 'puppet' of the instincts of his 'brutal ancestors ... powerless to divert himself from the destiny laid out by his hereditary endowment' (p. 100). His new faith certainly seems to fall away when he meets Tess alone later and 'the corpses of those old fitful passions which had lain inanimate amid the lines of his face ever since his reformation seemed to wake and come together as in a resurrection' (p. 412). Yet Alec's identity is more complicated than false piety disguising a 'true', unchanging nature as a sexual predator. Although tempted by the voice and gaze of Tess, Alec does not force himself upon her as before, even when his faith falters. He commands her to avert her eyes from him, before fleeing to read over a letter from the parson who helped to convert him. Mental abstraction produced by language enables him to avoid emotional triggers. Further, the dogma of respectability acts upon him as a kind of secondary instinct, channelling sexual passion into abnegation. At a later meeting, when he moves to embrace Tess, she implores him: 'think – be ashamed!' causing him to wander away 'indeterminately' (p. 412). Alec schemes to possess Tess again, but through marriage; a compromise between instinct and social convention. Hardy later wrote: 'I am more than ever convinced that persons are successively various persons, according as each special strand of their characters is brought uppermost by circumstances'.[69] Alec's conversion illustrates this indeterminacy of self, his instinctive signs of emotion altering their meanings under different influences.

While instinctive signs can assume the mechanics of convention, conventional words and gestures attach themselves associatively to instinct. Some characters' utterances escape their conscious intentions, rousing contrary urges. In *Far from the Madding Crowd* the rakish Troy woos Bathsheba with calculated verbal jousting, only for her reaction to trigger the feelings which his words had counterfeited. His showy wit gives way to a simple declaration of love with, the narrator notes, 'an intonation of such exquisite fidelity to nature that it was evidently not all acted now' (pp. 205–06). As the exchange continues, 'a factitious reply had been again upon his lips, but it was again suspended, and he looked at her with an arrested eye. The truth was, that as she now stood – excited, wild, and honest as the day – her alluring beauty bore out so fully the epithets he had bestowed upon it that he was quite startled at his temerity in advancing them as false' (p. 206). Humans are melting pots of potential urges, producing contradictory messages through different bodily media. When Bathsheba commands her suitor turned employee Gabriel to leave, 'a paleness of face invisible to the eye' is 'suggested by the trembling [of her] words'. Striving to repress her feelings, which would typically be conveyed through blushing, she only diverts them to her voice. By contrast, Oak expresses undying love in 'a steady voice, the steadiness of which was spoilt by the palpableness of his great effort to keep it so' (p. 225). The absence of instinctive vocal signs can be as significant as their presence, illustrating Oak's efforts to convert his sexual desire into principled chastity. Similarly, in *Ethelberta* instinctive emotional signs find alternative outlets when characters try to repress them. Ethelberta greets her old flame Christopher with a steady voice, but 'the calmness was artificially done, and the astonishment that did not appear in Ethelberta's tones was expressed by her gaze. Christopher was not in a mood to draw fine distinctions between recognized and unrecognized organs of speech. He replied to the eyes' (p. 105). Conversely, when Christopher later tells her that he 'cannot conscientiously put in a claim upon your attention' due to his precarious finances, 'a second meaning was written in Christopher's look, though he scarcely uttered it' (pp. 196–97). She chooses, though, to respond to his convention-bound words and ignore the expression imploring her to wait for him. Hardy's many selves transmit conflicting messages from the same body.

Perhaps the greatest of these conflicts lay in the mating call function of the voice against the moral restraint it was made to preach in civilized speech. The verbal etiquette of Hardy's characters often breaks down in being uttered as instinctive vocal signs awaken urges which their words aim to repress. Boldwood attempts to propose to Bathsheba with restraint, only for the performance to break away from these intentions, along with their ordered syntax: '"Say the words, dear one, and the subject shall be dismissed; a blissful loving intimacy of six years, and then marriage – O Bathsheba, say them!" he begged in a husky voice, unable to sustain the forms of mere friendship any longer' (p. 442). Bathsheba is quiet for fear of further inflaming not only Boldwood but also herself. Listening to his protestations, 'she strove miserably against this femininity which would insist upon supplying unbidden emotions in stronger and stronger current' (p. 239). Speech similarly short-circuits in *The Trumpet-Major* when John Loveday stammers uncontrollably before Anne Garland, caught between duty and desire. Despite his unspoken love, he tries to recommend his brother Bob, only for his delivery to break up: 'B-B-Bob is a very good fel-' (p. 356). In another exchange, he avoids voicing certain words, so charged are they with instinctive feeling. 'I have been thinking lately,' he tells her, 'that men of the military profession ought not to m—ought to be like St. Paul, I mean' (p. 359). Under an emotional siege, language flees into circumlocutions. By contrast, Anne's other suitor Festus Derriman simplifies the syntax and vocabulary of his proposal and jettisons etiquette with his rising passion. Speaking to Anne's mother after his first approach fails, he implores: '"Ask her to alter her cruel, cruel resolves against me, on the score of my consuming passion for her. In short," continued Festus, dropping his parlour language in his warmth, "I'll tell thee what, Dame Loveday, I want the maid, and I must have her"' (p. 333). Unable to trust themselves to speech, Hardy's reluctant lovers can only resist instinct by curtailing conversations or communicating in writing, which enables the illusion of a unitary, conscious self, separate from instinct.

Yet even the binary of instinctive bodily signs versus mechanical writing proves unstable. Imagination, articulated by language, enables written signs to substitute for instinctive ones, triggering amatory feelings. In 'On the Western Circuit' (1891), the young lawyer Raye begins an epistolary romance with the servant girl Anna, ignorant that her letters are in fact written by her mistress Edith. These letters charm Raye through channels seemingly beyond verbal convention and to a greater extent than his brief meeting with Anne. 'He could not single out any one sentence and say it was at all remarkable or clever,' the narrator states; 'the ensemble of the letter it was which won him.'[70] Edith's writing conceives 'pretty fancies for winning him' while Anna's dictated words leave him cold.[71] The division between bodily passions and scribal intellects collapses when Raye marries Anna, only to realize, too late, that Edith authored the letters. Declaring that 'in soul and spirit I have married you', he shares a bittersweet kiss with Edith.[72] Writing's triumph over the body in stirring romantic feelings is illustrated in the final scene as Raye rereads the letters during his honeymoon journey, ignoring the woman at his side. The imagination invests writing with the frissons of instinct which might, ultimately, become more affecting than the bodily signs for which it substituted.

Hardy extends this idea in 'An Imaginative Woman' (1894). Here the neglected wife Ella falls passionately in love with the poet Robert Trewe, whom she never meets. When she holidays in his room, his etchings on the wall become 'the thoughts and spirit-strivings which had come to him in the dead of night ... [a]nd now her hair was dragging where his arm had lain when he secured the fugitive fancies; she was sleeping on a poet's lips, immersed in the very essence of him, permeated by his spirit as by an ether'.[73] Her imaginings are shaped by instinctive drives, as the narrator comments, 'The personal element in the magnetic attraction ... was so much stronger than the intellectual and abstract that she could not understand it'. Directing her fancy is 'the instinct to specialise a waiting emotion on the first fit thing that came to hand ... being a woman of very living ardours, that required sustenance of some sort, they were beginning to feed on this chancing material' (p. 12). Abstract thought displaces instinctive drives into symbols; Ella invests objects linked to Trewe with emotional significance. His wall scribbles become 'so intense, so sweet, so palpitating, that it seemed as if his very breath, warm and loving, fanned her cheeks from those walls' (p. 17). The love-signs which Ella decodes are entirely imaginary, yet they render her embodied, present husband a mere shadow in her feelings. After Trewe commits suicide, she pines away and dies in childbirth. Hardy ends the tale by toying with the possibility that such fancies might transmute into biological realities. Ella's husband finds a photograph of Trewe and lock of his hair, and, comparing them with her last child, concludes that Trewe is the father. Despite the dramatic irony of the scene, Hardy suggests that the resemblance does not lie wholly in the widower's subjective eye: 'By a known but inexplicable trick of Nature there were undoubtedly strong traces of resemblance to the man Ella had never seen; the dreamy and peculiar expression of the poet's face sat, as the transmitted idea, upon the child's, and the hair was of the same hue' (p. 32). The detail echoes an earlier scene when, deprived of meeting Trewe, Ella 'tried to let off her emotion by unnecessarily kissing the children, till she had a sudden sense of disgust at being reminded how plain-looking they were, like their father' (p. 25). Could Ella's imagined love affair have somehow genetically transmitted the 'idea' of Trewe to her child? Not only might instinctive signs become conventionally symbolic, but conventional symbols might also channel instincts, and even be echoed through racial descent. Symbols blur the boundaries in Hardy's vision between organisms and their behaviour. In the place of natural truth which artificial language had seemed to falsify, Hardy's fiction reconceives language as an endless dialogue with a heritage both cultural and biological. Like their users, signs and meanings are not anchored by ultimate origins or essences but exist in a state of ongoing negotiation and becoming.

Creativity and the babbling instinct in Wells's early fiction

While Hardy explored instinctive signs as the foundation of sympathy, the young Wells sometimes celebrated them even more as fundamental to the imagination. This claim might seem doubtful, given Wells's association of instinctive noise with degeneration in such tales as *The Island of Dr Moreau*. However, in an era when Darwin's work had collapsed common-sense views of nature, progress might be imagined as a battle against dogma and mental-linguistic conformity. In this sense, Wells viewed the babbling instinct which caused humans to coin new words and reshape speech as a potential source of creativity. Wells the social utopian envisioned language directing instincts with increasing precision, so that 'a living thing might be taken in hand and so moulded and modified that at best it would retain scarcely anything of its inherent form and disposition'.[74] Yet, this model also produced the dystopian image of society churning out standardized citizens without individual thought. Sylvia Hardy identifies 'an unresolved conflict between Wells the social reformer, who wanted language to be unitary and universally comprehensible, and Wells the artist, who enjoyed the anarchic and subversive possibilities of linguistic diversity'.[75] I contend that Wells located these 'anarchic and subversive possibilities' in the babbling instinct which scientists were investigating through observations of infants. For Wells, fetishizing words as facts rendered speakers social automatons in the same way pure instinct would render them biological ones. Wells thus sometimes sought to inject the babbling instinct into his early writing, misspelling and mangling the English language as an exercise in mental freedom. However, he ultimately withdrew from the implications of such experiments, which undermined his utopian dream of scientific, objective language.

Like Butler, Wells was drawn to the phonograph as an image of verbal convention. As a young man in 1888, he complained in a letter to a friend of the servants he was living with: 'THEY ARE DAMNED PHONOGRAPHS, BLOODY TALKING DOLLS'. Wells was residing with his mother at the mansion where she worked, and the verbal automatism of her colleagues seemed to him to reflect their unthinking submission to class hierarchy. He remarked: 'They are all dead – purely automatic ... Each of 'em have fifteen remarks to say over & they get through the lot each mealtime. "The days draw out nicely." "The frost continues." "The poor souls without coals must suffer!" & so on'.[76] Wells returns to phonographic imagery in an early article, demanding why social engagements required the 'fetish flow' of endless conversation. Most of 'this social law of gabble,' he continues, 'is akin to responses in church, a prescription, a formula.'[77] Wells proposes that each diner fit a phonograph 'under his chin' to fulfil the mechanical function for him. In a later essay, he writes:

> there is something of the phonograph in all of us, but in the sort of eminent person who makes public speeches about education and reading, and who gives away prizes and opens educational institutions, there seems to be little else but gramophone. These people always say the same things, and say them in the same note. And why should they do that if they are really individuals? ... There must be in these demiurgic profundities a rapid manufacture of innumerable thousands of that particular speech about 'scrappy reading', and that contrast of 'modern' with 'serious' literature, that babbles about in the provinces so incessantly. Gramophones thinly disguised as bishops, gramophones still more thinly disguised as eminent statesmen, gramophones K. C. B. and gramophones F. R. S. have brazened it at us time after time.[78]

Wells's satire on clichéd public speeches taps into the imaginative association of the time, noted by Jonathan Sterne, between sound reproduction and meaningless conventional speech. Demonstrating his phonograph, Edison had quoted the nursery rhyme 'Mary had a Little Lamb' into the machine, producing 'a transmission without a message'.[79] These early articles reveal a different Wells to the later social planner who confidently prophesied a consistent, global language gaining control over nature (see Chapter 1 above). The 'fabric of ideas and habits' which Wells described humans passing on through language could mechanize thought as well as liberate it. What once gave humans agency might later rob them of it as custom became secondary instinct and people echoed each other mechanically.

Wells targeted such echoing in his Edwardian satires, identifying linguistic convention with mental stasis. In *The Food of the Gods* (1904) he highlights the alienation of common language from modern scientific knowledge, which fails to fit with its rigid conceptual categories. Thus, when scientists discover a way of accelerating the growth process in organisms, the wider public is unable to grasp the significance of this event. One provincial doctor diagnoses the rise in gigantism among babies as degeneration, citing 'the most gifted ... philosopher' Max Nordau: 'He discovered that the abnormal is – abnormal, a most valuable discovery, and well worth bearing in mind. I find it of the utmost help in practice. When I come upon anything abnormal, I say at once, This is abnormal.'[80] The doctor's stereotyped view of the world forces him into circles of tautology when he encounters new phenomena that confound his preconceptions. The image of human phonographs is repeated through parish councillors assailing the scientists with legal threats after enormous animals stampede through their villages. 'Clinging phonographically to prearranged statements', they declare: 'We hold you responsible, Mister Bensington, for the injury inflicted upon our parish, Sir. We hold you responsible'.[81] Mentally limited by language, they think only of narrow personal interests. A memorable example of echoing in the tale occurs when a 35-foot boy escapes his captives and stomps into central London. Baffled by the tiny people who divide themselves between slums and mansions, he exclaims: 'What are all you people doing with yourselves? What's it all for?' His questions parallel other giants' attempts to reform this fragmented society, devising vast housing and infrastructural systems. Such plans are thwarted, however, by the small-minded self-interest of local government, businesses and trade unions. Equally, instead of uniting people under a common purpose, the giant-child's question only sparks a mindless 'new catchword. Young men of wit and spirit addressed each other in this manner, "Ullo 'Arry O'Cock. Wot's it all for? Eh? Wot's it all bloomin' well for?"'[82] Verbal convention smothers the imagination, reducing challenges to the status quo to absurd jokes that the populace can only echo.

The phonograph's separation of vocal sound from meaning reverberates through the class privilege associated with certain accents in Wells's social comedies. Wells represents upper-class speech through misspellings, with rivals competing to over-enunciate socially privileged phonemes. Elocution and conversational etiquette had become industries in the nineteenth century as the *nouveau riche* strove to cover their ancestral tracks.[83] Wells lampoons these industries in *Kipps* (1905), the tale of a draper who inherits a fortune. Recruiting a bourgeois tutor, Kipps attempts to sharpen his tongue for high society. Wells implies the superficiality of such refinement by misspelling the speech of the teacher: 'what are you doang hea?' he asks, before instructing Kipps to read 'nace novels', listen to 'Vagner or Vargner' and wait for 'a long taime'.[84] The more precisely that Wells's bourgeoisie imitate the tones of supposed respectability, the more their speech appears thoughtless sound reproduction. This continues in *Tono-Bungay* (1909) when the narrator George describes his upbringing in the provincial village of Bladesover. Residents vie for the most 'emphatic articulation', mimicking the local aristocrat Lady Drew: 'recomm-an-ding', 'great quan-ta-ties', 'extremelay', 'so am tawled'.[85] This echoing extends from phonemes to whole conversations at high tea where, 'day after day the talk was exactly the same':

> 'Sugar, Mrs Mackridge?' my mother used to ask ... The word sugar would stir the mind of Mrs Mackridge.
>
> 'They say,' she would begin, issuing her proclamation – at least half her sentences began 'they say' – 'sugar is fatt-an-ing, nowadays'.
>
> ... 'What won't they say next?' said Miss Fison ... Mrs. Booch would produce a favourite piece from her repertoire.
>
> 'The evenings are drawing out nicely,' she would say, or if the season was decadent, 'How the evenings draw in!' It was an invaluable remark to her; I do not know how she would have got along without it. (pp. 20–21)

These phrases echo the human 'phonographs' against whom Wells raged in his letters. Wells often genders such verbal conventionality as peculiarly feminine, opposing George's intellectual narration to Mrs Booch's repetition of 'a small set of stereotyped remarks that constituted her entire mental range' (p. 19). The same opposition frames George's disastrous marriage, which mirrors Wells's short-lived union with his cousin Isabel. George laments, 'she seemed never to have an idea of her own but always the idea of her class' (p. 198). She demonstrates the potential of Wells's 'acquired factor' to ossify into a kind of secondary instinct. Conventional language and behaviour has given her 'an immense unimaginative inflexibility – as a tailor-bird builds its nest or a beaver makes its dam' (p. 227). Femininity appears characterized by slavish adherence to convention.[86]

Opposing such verbal convention, the young Wells had a long-running interest in experimenting with language. Sylvia Hardy notes that Wells's reading of Darwin and William James gave him a radical scepticism of verbal representation: words were provisional tools for exploring reality rather than reality itself.[87] As Wells argued in 1903, abstractions like number, class and kind were 'merely unavoidable conditions of mental activity – regrettable conditions rather than essential facts. The forceps of our minds are clumsy forceps, and crush the truth a little in taking hold of it'.[88] The seemingly eternal truths of language had been constructed arbitrarily upon instinctive vocalizations. This commingling of instinct with convention emerges in Wells's humorous early journalism. 'The Pleasure of Quarrelling' describes this activity as 'a natural function of the body. In his natural state man is always quarrelling – by instinct. Not to quarrel is indeed one of the vices of our civilisation, one of the reasons why we are neurotic and anæmic'.[89] Another article bemoans the 'decay' of 'swearing' among civilization, its 'bad words' having become 'conventional' and 'orthodox'. Like quarrelling, 'a good flamboyant, ranting swear is Nature's outlet. All primitive men and most animals swear. It is an emotional shunt. Your cat swears at you because she does not want to scratch your face'.[90] Such vocalizations are less about the abstract meanings of words than the physical body conveying its excited state. Further, as 'Of Conversation' suggested, the continuous 'babblement' of speech might represent an instinctive act, mediating friendly relations. As Chapter 2 discussed, evolutionary theory had transformed infant babble into a primal force of linguistic creativity. Taine's account of a child's transition from instinctive 'twittering' to conventional speech involved much spontaneous word creation. 'Originality and invention are so strong in a child', Taine wrote, 'that if it learns our language from us, we learn it from the child ... [I]t is an original genius adapting itself to a form constructed bit by bit by a succession of original geniuses'.[91] Infants' coinages contradicted their parents' fixed demarcations of the world. In applying the same word to different things, they drew striking, unexpected analogies. Hence, Taine's infant applied its onomatopoeic name for a dog 'oua-oua' to a goat whose size and shape resembled the dog named.[92] As Wells argued, the primitive speaker could engage imaginatively with the infinite variety of phenomena, unlimited by preset classifications. The primordial babbling instinct gave human conceptions a plasticity that was essential to social and intellectual growth.

Wells always played with language, drawing on what he would later understand as the babbling instinct to coin and modify words. His early letters resound with a cacophony of nicknames, referring to himself variously as 'Bertie', 'Buss', 'Buzz' and 'Busswhacker'.[93] He subjected his second wife Amy Catherine Robins to a 'string of nicknames', from 'Bits', 'Snitch' and 'It' to the seemingly random 'Jane'.[94] He also enjoyed misspelling words for comic effect, conjuring unexpected associations.[95] His autobiography reproduces doggerel verse written for Amy Catherine, misspelling and inventing words à la Edward Lear. His poem 'The Pobble', for example, evokes a mysterious monster against which Wells is the only protection: 'Me what you fink is simply Fungy / Me what you keep so short of Mungy / Me what you keep so short of Beer / Is your only chance when the Pobble is near'.[96] Wells attempted to justify such verbal play intellectually in an essay of 1897. 'People are scarcely prepared to realize what shades of meaning may be got', he claimed, from treating spelling as 'an art' rather than 'a matter of right and wrong'. Demonstrating, Wells instructs the reader to

> take a pen in hand and sit down and write, 'My very dear wife'. Clean, cold, and correct this is, speaking of orderly affection, settled and stereotyped long ago. In such letters is butcher's meat also 'very dear'. Try now, 'Migh verrie deare Wyfe'. Is it not immediately infinitely more soft and tender? Is there not something exquisitely pleasant in lingering over those redundant letters, leaving each word, as it were, with a reluctant caress? Such spelling is a soft, domestic, lovingly wasteful use of material.[97]

Non-standard spellings access chains of connotation, which cluster around sounds and letters unpredictably. 'Try', Wells continues,

> 'Mye owne sweete dearrest Marrie'. There is the tremble of a tenderness no mere arrangement of trim everyday letters can express in those double *r*'s. 'Sweete' my ladie must be; sweet! Why pump-water and inferior champagne, spirits of nitrous ether and pancreatic juice are 'sweet'. For my own part I always spell so, with lots of *f*'s and *g*'s and such like tailey, twirley, loopey things, when my heart is in the tender vein.[98]

Wells is unclear about where these associations originate. Are they by-products of convention or instinct? Wells's emotions, tied up with the sounds and shapes of his letters, seem to signify not directly through the English lexis but through disruptions of it by some force from without.

Wells's essay engaged with a rising interest among psychologists and linguists in instinctive, unconscious elements of speech. Phoneticists such as Henry Sweet divided speech into atomic sounds, feeding speculation that these sounds might have corresponding atomic meanings.⁹⁹ Sayce suggested that such vague sound-thoughts might have evolved before conventional symbols, so that 'the ideas they convey are so wide and general as to cover an almost infinite series of derived meanings'.¹⁰⁰ In the 1890s the German researcher Karl Otto Erdmann argued that words signified through a mixture of conventional denotation and instinctive connotation. Erdmann formalized this distinction into the 'begrifflicher Inhalt' (intellectual content) and emotional 'Nebensinn' (connotation) which sounds triggered.¹⁰¹ Simultaneously, in the United States, E. W. Scripture analyzed recorded speech slowed down, concluding that the 'intellectual and emotional centres' constituted parallel sign systems. He claimed that 'the singer or speaker must feel what is to be said if he wishes to say it properly'. Emotional expression erupts through the cracks of conventional signs and conscious will. Hence, 'it is a familiar principle with orators and singers that to produce the full vocal effect they must first arouse the emotion itself and then allow it to find its natural expression'.¹⁰² More broadly, Freud would describe unconscious cognition as the external force inflecting Wells's scribbling. Analyzing slips of the tongue in 1901, he wrote: 'Almost invariably I discover ... a disturbing influence [in such slips] of something *outside* of the intended speech ... a single unconscious thought ... [or] a more general psychic motive, which directs itself against the entire speech'.¹⁰³ The elements of speech seemed to be a site of conflict between instinctive drives and conscious will. Such doubling of the voice might be found in writing as well as speech, as Wells's reference to 'tailey, twirley, loopey things' suggests. Several prominent Victorians, including Spencer, considered writing an offshoot of a common primordial 'language' of images.¹⁰⁴ Wells's tender associations with looping letters echo this primal synaesthesia, triggering the emotions with a supposedly arbitrary orthography.

Instinctive babble and vocalization often disrupt conventional discourse in Wells's social fiction, diverting thought into new channels. In *Tono-Bungay*, George's Aunt Susan challenges the image of feminine verbal conventionality through her inventive slang. George relates how she 'applied the epithet "old" to more things than I have ever heard linked to it before or since. "Here's the old news-paper", she used to say to my uncle. "Now don't go and get it in the butter, you silly old Sardine!"' (p. 90). Her 'extensive web of nonsense' provokes hysterical laughing fits in her husband Edward, whose 'slipshod' mouth emits equally 'curious expressions'. If the other residents of Bladesover are gramophones, then Susan and Edward are broken ones incapable of using language without warping it into new shapes. Edward speaks of 'the stog-igschange' and names the spurious tonic that makes him rich from the phrase 'Ton a' bunk, eh?' Yet, George suggests that the phonemes in Edward's coinage appeal to mysterious, hidden associations: 'it was simple and yet in some way arresting. I found myself repeating the word after I had passed; it roused one's attention like the sound of distant guns. "Tono" – what's that? and deep, rich, unhurrying; – "*Bun*–gay!"' (p. 145). When most inspired by his business plans, Edward's verbal ejaculations break into onomatopoeic noises, as he thunders to George: 'Wo-oo-oo-osh! Your science and all that! Wo-oo-oo-osh!' (p. 152). Edward's vocal explosions reflect the anarchic energy of capitalism, which bursts through the torpor of feudalism. He complains that there is 'no development – no growth' in Bladesover, and longs to '*do* something ... I can't stand it ... I must invent something' (pp. 63, 74). Wells's portrait of Edward contradicts liberal models of industrial capitalism as rational; rather, it emanates from instinctive drives which orderly feudalism had stifled. Social progress might not necessarily consist of language becoming ever-more regimented, but could involve rediscovering the chaotic energy of instinct. George's classical education reflects this, as he comments: 'Socrates rhymes with Bates for me, and ... I use those dear old mispronunciations still ... if I met those great gentlemen of the past with their accents carelessly adjusted I did at least meet them alive, as an equal, and in a living tongue' (p. 80). The babbling instinct helps speakers to appropriate ancestral speech, shaping language rather than language shaping them.

It might be objected that Edward's instinct-driven linguistic creativity ultimately breaks with past dogmas only to enforce new ones of commodity value. Edward's advertisements turn Tono-Bungay into a cash-cow through language carefully calibrated to trigger unconscious urges and associations. The texts are punctuated 'with every now and then a convulsive jump of some attractive phrase into capitals'. Hence, '"Many people who are MODERATELY well think they are QUITE well", was one of his early efforts. The jerks in capitals were, "DO NOT NEED DRUGS OR MEDICINE", and "SIMPLY A PROPER REGIMEN TO GET YOU IN TONE"' (p. 168). George's omission of the text in between highlights the sub-linguistic sensations to which such advertising appeals, its capitals mimicking a shout or cry. This transference of instinctive signs into writing is obviously degenerate in Wells's vision, forming part of his critique of capitalism. However, discourse in the novel is not degenerative simply through the incursion of instinctive signs; it degenerates through words ossifying into imagined realities.

Edward's invention of the term *Tono-Bungay* invites the assumption that it must name some extra-linguistic reality. Even Edward is vulnerable to this fallacy, as George observes, 'I never really determined whether my uncle regarded Tono-Bungay as a fraud, or whether he didn't come to believe in it in a kind of way by the mere reiteration of his own assertions' (p. 177). Edward's absorption in advertising renders him an uncritical phonograph like the provincial bourgeoisie. Wells emphasizes this return to the dogma of old when, on his deathbed, Edward clasps at the idea of an afterlife. The scene echoes George's early life in Bladesover when, at a funeral, he heard 'the talk about souls, the strange battered old phrases that were coined ages ago' (p. 47). Language limits thought not simply when it appeals to instinct, but when it conceals its instinctive roots, presenting itself as transparent truth.

Wells explored the creative possibilities of instinct invading speech most fully in the hero of his *History of Mr Polly* (1909). Dissatisfied with life as a small-town shopkeeper, Polly burns down his shop and begins a new, peripatetic life. His defiance of convention is expressed as much in his speech as in his actions, as he distorts words to suggest new connotations. He delights in 'Sesquippledan verboojuice' and 'Eloquent Rapsodooce', as the narrator explains:

> Words attracted him curiously, words rich in suggestion, and he loved a novel and striking phrase ... New words had terror and fascination for him; he did not acquire them, he could not avoid them, and so he plunged into them. His only rule was not to be misled by the spelling. That was no guide anyhow. He avoided every recognised phrase in the language and mispronounced everything in order that he shouldn't be suspected of ignorance, but whim.[105]

Polly's verbal innovations are not only driven by status anxiety, since he continues to coin them when speaking to himself. He replaces the old, forgotten metaphors behind words with new ones, revitalizing adjectives with vivid, concrete associations. He describes young tailors as 'full of Smart Juniosity. The Shoveacious Cult', while their tired, middle-aged rivals look sadly 'de-juiced' (p. 52). After colliding with a man in the street, he recalls engaging in 'jawbacious argument', evoking the frenzied movement of their vocal apparatuses (p. 107). His habit of reshaping language mirrors his gradual realization that, 'if the world does not please you, *you can change it*' (p. 243). Words are not permanent; they are improvised tools to be experimented upon. The narrator describes Polly 'the uncontrollable phrasemonger' as 'an artless child of Nature, far more untrained, undisciplined and spontaneous than an ordinary savage' (pp. 304–05). Metaphors burst out of him involuntarily, colliding with polite, regulated speech. Amidst debates with his neighbour Rusper he develops the notion

> that Rusper's head was the most egg-shaped head he had ever seen; the similarity weighed upon him; and when he found an argument growing warm with Rusper he would say: 'Boil it some more, O' Man; boil it harder!' or 'Six minutes at least', allusions Rusper could never make head or tail of, and got at last to disregard as a part of Mr. Polly's general eccentricity. (p. 195)

Sylvia Hardy argues that Polly's manglings of English 'create a new reality', challenging traditional dogmas such as the religion embodied in Canterbury Cathedral, which he dismisses as 'metrorious urnfuls' and 'dejected angelosity' (p. 57).[106] Although Polly's metaphoric outbursts are often comedic, he is not simply the butt of Wells's comedy. As in the above passage, much of the laughter derives from the confusion which his language causes unimaginative listeners. As one who 'specialised in slang and the disuse of English' (p. 28), Polly practises the mental-linguistic 'Freedom' that Wells the essayist had preached, reconnecting with the anarchic babble of instinct.

Wells's idea of language as a collision of instinct and convention prefigures later ideas now usually identified with modernism. Pioneers of the Futurist and Dadaist movements such as F. T. Marinetti and Kurt Schwitters developed 'sound poems' composed of raw phonemes, imagined as instinctive outbursts unmediated by social tradition.[107] We might also think of James Joyce's many coinages and dismantlings of Standard English in *Ulysses* (1918–20). It is an interesting question, then, why Wells did not push his linguistic experiments further. His misspellings and coinages remain confined to the reported speech of characters, enclosed by Standard English narration. His essay on spelling blames printers and publishers for restricting such experiments, acting as 'orthodox spelling police'.[108] Nonetheless, Victorian publishers failed to suppress the linguistic experiments of Edward Lear and Lewis Carroll, who influenced Wells's private doggerel verse. While writing supportively of literary experimenters like Joyce, the older Wells withdrew from emulating them. Reviewing *A Portrait of the Artist as a Young Man* (1914–15), he praised its author as 'a bold experimentalist with paragraph and punctuation'.[109] Yet, in 1928 he wrote to Joyce of *Ulysses*: 'You have turned your back on common men – on their elementary needs and their restricted time and intelligence ... Your work is an extraordinary experiment ... To me it is a dead end'.[110] Wells's concern for a universal 'common man' points to his shifting priorities as imaginative fiction gave way to instructions for building a global state. As Chapters 1 and 2 above have demonstrated, Wells's search for rational world government required the curbing of linguistic diversity. This inevitably also meant the curbing of the babbling instincts, which threatened to divide people into private dialects.

Such fragmentation threatened to limit humankind to its primordial instincts. *The Time Machine*'s Eloi illustrate this danger, their sensual cooing cutting them off from ancestral knowledge and thought. Their instinctive, private language of lovers excludes any ambitions beyond amatory union, as the time traveller discovers through his pathetic romance with the Eloi Weena. Wells similarly maintained domestic relations with both his wives, despite his philandering, through what he called 'baby-talk', which 'falsified our relations to the point of making them tolerable and workable'.[111] Couples invent private languages of intimacy to cement their union in spite of conflicting urges. In *Tono-Bungay*, George repeatedly papers over the cracks in his marriage through a similar 'little language' in which 'we were "friends", and I was "Mutney" and she was "Ming"' (pp. 211–12). Such lovers' babble also traps Wells's eponymous protagonist in *Love and Mr Lewisham* (1899) in an unsuitable marriage, forcing him to abandon his ambitions. He wastes hours in the laboratory inventing 'foolish terms of endearment: "Dear Wife", "Dear Little Wife Thing", "Sweetest Dearest Little Wife", "Dillywings". A pretty employment! And these are quite a fair specimen of his originality during those wonderful days ... For Lewisham, like Swift and most other people, had hit upon the Little Language'.[112] As with the Eloi, flowers mediate their relationship as an instinctive sign system. After a seemingly irrevocable row with his wife, Lewisham spots some roses in a shop window, which possess him unawares: 'They caught his eye before they caught his mind ... It was as if they were the very colour of his emotion. He stopped abruptly ... Then he perceived as though it was altogether self-evident what he had to do ... Some weak voice of indiscreet discretion squeaked and vanished' (p. 271). Wells further emphasizes the separateness of these lovers' signs from conscious thought when the ordered flowers fail to arrive and Lewisham is unable to reconcile with his wife verbally: 'He tried to think of something to say that might bridge the distance between them, but he could think of nothing. He must wait until the roses came' (pp. 272–73). Their later reunion comes not through logical discussion but when Lewisham's somnolent wife 'murmured indistinctly a foolish name she had given him', reawakening his passion (p. 294). The novel ends in Lewisham shredding the written 'schema' on which he once planned to become a great intellectual. His ambitions of promoting Darwin and socialism are replaced by the prosaic necessities of maintaining a household. Unlike Wells, who divorced the conventional Isabel to pursue his ambitions, Lewisham fails to break away, entrapped by passionate 'baby-talk'.

Wells did not escape his erratic desires in his second marriage, pursuing affairs and pining for his first wife. In old age he described his sexual urges as his 'lover-shadow': a Jungian unconscious which impelled him towards both promiscuity and jealousy.[113] The power which such instincts continued to hold over Wells's private life seems to have driven him to exclude them all the more from his published work. In his younger years, he had sometimes imagined masculine speech as heroically following instinct and disrupting convention. Conversely, Wells the state builder tended towards the Spencerian model of masculine speech as scientific, God-like detachment from bodily urges. The binary opposite of female speech thus changed from the slavishly conventional to dangerously instinctive, identified with the narrative experiments of New Woman writers and their modernist successors. Wells recalled criticizing his lover Rebecca West in the 1920s for allowing instinctive fancies and impulses into the rational realm of writing:

> She writes like a loom producing her broad rich fabric with hardly a thought of how it will make up into a shape, while I write to cover a frame of ideas ... She prowled in the thickets, and I have always kept close to the trail that leads to the World-State ... [S]he exalted James Joyce and D. H. Lawrence ... and I wrote with an ostentatious disregard of decoration; never used a rare phrase when a common one would serve, and was more of a journalist than ever.[114]

The passage marks Wells's retreat from verbal experimentation, seeking as he does a united, scientific world through a common, engineered speech. 'I am English by origin,' he continues, 'but I am an early World-Man, and I live in exile from the world community of my desires. I salute that finer larger world and its subtler minds across the generations – and maybe ever again someone down the vista, some lingering vestige of my Lover-Shadow, may look back and appreciate an ancestral salutation.'[115] The dialogue between convention and instinct that Wells once imagined enlivening language shrinks to a whisper in his future vision. Experiments with the instinctive bases of speech could only be 'a dead end', obstructing the march towards objective, scientific language. It is significant that, while reproducing examples of his private lovers' languages in his *Autobiography*, the ageing Wells valued them only as psychological specimens. 'There is no need to reproduce any more of them,' he states: 'What matters here is the way in which they wrapped about the facts of life for us and created a quaint and softened atmosphere of intercourse'.[116] The voice that encloses these experiments in misspelling remains standardized and emotionally distant, representing the disembodied 'Brain' of the text's subtitle. It would be left to other writers to answer in earnest his light-hearted rallying call, 'Spell, my brethren, as you will! Awake, arise, O language living in chains'.[117] The imagined interplay between instinct and convention in language would inspire bold literary experiments from which Butler, Hardy and Wells withdrew. Their tales remain sequential narrations in Standard English, privileged as somehow above the instinctive signs and urges they described. As Wells's work shows, such manoeuvres appealed to a dichotomy between instinctive speech and rational writing which their narratives of instinctive signs had undermined.

Conclusion: widening the lens

> Modern science does not know how to cope with meaning ... The real obstacle to biological progress, today, is not lack of data but a pervasive theoretical paradigm that continues to deny the semiotic nature of life.
>
> Marcello Barbieri[1]

> A potato in a dark cellar ... sees the light coming from the cellar window and sends his shoots crawling straight thereto ... we can imagine him saying, 'I will have a tuber here and a tuber there, and I will suck whatsoever advantage I can from all my surroundings' ... The potato says these things by doing them, which is the best of languages.
>
> Samuel Butler[2]

In his classic work on nineteenth-century philology, Hans Aarsleff wrote: 'To the historical understanding, the pseudo-science of an age may be as important as its science'.[3] This study has aimed to extend his point, suggesting that, in the case of philology, what appeared mere pseudo-science to one age may prefigure earnest inquiries in a later one. The lack of clear boundaries in nineteenth-century language studies between what later became distinguished as nature and culture often produced confused, contradictory ideas about language. It sometimes enabled racist, sexist and anti-democratic agendas, in which the supposedly primitive or degraded language of different groups legitimized their disempowerment. However, the lack of dogmatic divisions between nature and culture also allowed writers to ask questions about language which researchers in recent decades have revived. In the recent *Oxford Handbook of Language Evolution* (2012), Maggie Tallerman and Kathleen Gibson observe that '"language" is not a monolithic entity, but rather a complex bundle of traits that must have evolved over a significant time frame, some features doubtless appearing in species that preceded our own'.[4] The lines between human and non-human communication, conventional and instinctive meaning, and agency and automatism are now more blurred than ever. The field of language evolution includes new disciplinary approaches such as genomics and cognitive psychology. However, it remains an inevitably narrative science, creating theoretical stories of where language came from and where it is going. As such, this science both influences and is influenced by wider narratives of human origins and development, and the generic formulas that shape them, such as in literature. Future research might, therefore, pursue the afterlives of the different visions of language evolution discussed here, and their relevance to continuing debates about language.

A recurrent theme of this study has been the search for linguistic authorities to fix meaning and bring signs into perfect correspondence with their referents. Future research could explore the endurance and refashioning of these models of ideal language among later writers. Notions of verbal efficiency and precision continued to influence thinkers and creative writers across diverse areas. Otto Jespersen stressed the idea of progressive verbal efficiency until his death in the 1940s.[5] George Orwell's essay 'Politics and the English Language' (1946) echoed Spencer's arguments for precision and efficiency, instructing writers to 'cut out' superfluous words and 'never use a long word where a short one will do'.[6] Such rhetoric shows the enduring ideal of a neutral style for conveying pre-verbal thought. The efficiency paradigm might also be traced in psychoanalysis. Freud's interpretations of dreams, jokes, and verbal slips relied upon the concept of condensation, in which words or images became freighted with multiple unconscious ideas. Yet, while Spencer had imagined verbal efficiency developing in tandem with mental self-control, Freud placed the two in opposition. The conscious mind only skimmed the surface of language, unaware of its hidden suggestions.[7] This reworking of Spencer's concept is discernible in the 'rhetoric of efficiency' in modernist movements such as imagism, which sought to condense maximum connotations into a minimum of verbal material.[8] The aim became to concentrate efficiently into language not objective knowledge but subjective experience.

Despite these continuities, however, the interwar and postwar periods might also be explored as times of rising suspicion against utopian language schemes. Aldous Huxley's *Brave New World* (1932) depicts a society minutely controlled by scientific elites in which language is part of the

'Neo-Pavlovian conditioning' of all citizens.[9] This centralized control produces docile citizens who parrot official maxims constantly played into their ears as they sleep. While C. K. Ogden promoted a global 'Basic English' in the 1930s (supported by Wells), Orwell would satirize such schemes, linking them with political repression in the Newspeak of *Nineteen Eighty-Four* (1949). The centralized control which utopians had imagined widening verbal resources became, for Orwell, a means of limiting them. One such language controller in the novel states: 'Don't you see that the whole aim of Newspeak is to narrow the range of thought? ... there will *be* no thought, as we understand it now. Orthodoxy means not thinking – not needing to think. Orthodoxy is unconsciousness'.[10] Arguments for linguistic relativism led to the conclusion among many dystopian writers that 'whoever controls language controls the perception of reality as well'.[11]

The progressive ideal of mechanizing language to render it consistent and efficient has been achieved, in a way, through the rise of computer languages. Like Babbage's condensed mathematical notations, such code acts as shorthand for the stream of bytes running through a computer's circuitry. The translation of programming language into electromagnetic impulses realizes, in a limited sense, the utopian dream of language mapping directly on to, and merging with, the physical universe. Bruno Latour observed: 'Now that computers exist, we are able to conceive of a text (a programming language) that is at once words and actions. How to do things with words and then turn words into things is now clear to any programmer.'[12] However, rather than being masters of this code, most computer users are its subjects, engaging only with the programmes which it executes. As twenty-first-century lives become increasingly mediated by unseen, computerized code, so Butler's satirical vision of humans becoming slaves of machines gains a new resonance.[13] Nineteenth-century visions of language mechanization thus offer an interesting historical perspective on contemporary anxieties about the digital world encroaching upon human verbal–mental autonomy.

Visions of language degenerating without prescriptive authorities, although discredited in linguistics, persisted in the twentieth-century imagination as a trope of apocalyptic fiction. Such representations could be explored in relation to the continuing growth of Standard English in the twentieth century. Thus, in George Stewart's novel of scavengers surviving a plague, *Earth Abides* (1949), the new generation resembles Victorian 'savages' who could not distinguish between sex and love: 'the concept of obscenity, you might say, had disappeared, largely because there was only one words for things in their vocabulary ... possibly as a counterpart to the death of romantic love'.[14] Similar reversions characterize Walter Miller's *A Canticle for Leibowitz* (1959) when nuclear war returns the world to medieval language and superstition. With modern science and literature destroyed, Catholic monks in Miller's novel puzzle over surviving scraps of engineering textbooks, regarding them as scholastic mysteries. Outside of the monasteries roam wild cannibals whose speech has disintegrated along with their morality, as is shown when they attack lone travellers with the cry of 'Eat! Eat! Eat!'[15] Civilization remains persistently linked to language in the apocalyptic imagination, both collapsing in tandem.

This study looks forward to current debates over the evolutionary continuity between human and non-human communication. Linguists towards the end of the nineteenth century increasingly spurned discussions of the origins of speech as unempirical. The Parisian *Société de Linguistique* and German Neogrammarians such as Hermann Osthoff and Karl Brugmann dismissed the question as being simply beyond investigation.[16] Yet, by refusing to discuss language origins, linguists fed the equally unproven assumption that language came into existence fully formed.[17] Later, while Saussure's theories emphasized the synchronic nature of signs, Noam Chomsky's universal grammar figured language as a fixed capacity hard-wired in the brain. Instead of developing incrementally, Chomsky argued, speech derived from a uniquely human organ or 'language acquisition device'.[18] Figures such as Derek Bickerton and Steven Pinker have refined this claim, presenting language as a unique 'instinct'.[19] This rhetoric of language marking a genetic break with non-humans avoids discussion of its possible development.[20] Such catastrophism enables the strict division of language into nature (inherited universal grammar) and culture (the speech which this biological programming creates) with no exchange between the two. Yet, no single, consistent grammar has ever been demonstrated to structure all possible utterances, suggesting that language is an activity without an essence.[21] Since the 1960s, numerous psychologists have studied primate communication, identifying as many as sixty-six gesture types among primates, many of them at least partly conventional.[22] Psycho-linguist Philip Lieberman suggests that language 'is distributed over many parts of the human brain ... overlaid on sensorimotor systems that originally evolved to do other things and continue to do them now'. Neural structures in the 'subcortical basal ganglia – our reptilian brain', which once served only emotional and motor functions, seem to adapt under social influences to encode symbols.[23] The more that investigators search for the origin of language, the more it merges with communication systems paralleled in other species.

This problem of language's missing origin has continued to inspire fictional engagements with the potential mental-linguistic life of non-humans. One recent novel which warrants critical study in this area is Colin McAdam's *A Beautiful Truth* (2013), which experiments in representing the possible thoughts or proto-thoughts of animals through free indirect discourse.[24] McAdam depicts the attempts of the psychologist David to teach language to the chimpanzee Ghoul, shifting the narration uncertainly between their different perspectives:

> David was his friend.
>
> ? Machine make Dave tickle Ghoul.
>
> ... When he got things right, the machine gave him pieces of apple.
>
> ... Dave would say put it in a sentence.
>
> Please machine give apple.[25]

McAdam's sparse punctuation and sometimes simplistic syntax suggest that the narration is conveying glimpses of chimpanzee subjectivity. Conversely, this effect could be ironic, reflecting the anthropomorphism of David, who imagines this human-like subjectivity in Ghoul. McAdam's ambiguous, multivoiced narration highlights the difficulty in judging other species' mental lives, since our conceptions of mind are so tied up with our ability to communicate with language. The creationist assumption that thought exists only alongside fully articulate speech continues to obstruct efforts to imagine the evolution of both mind and language.

The missing origin of language can also be seen continuing to complicate prehistoric fiction throughout the last century as it did for pioneers of the genre. William Golding's *The Inheritors* (1955) both seeks and fragments language origins through its narrative of a band of Neanderthals. Their speech oscillates between symbolism and instinctive expression of emotion. Although very sophisticated at reading each other's emotions, they struggle to communicate abstract ideas, as is demonstrated when a log which previously formed a bridge across a river disappears. While expressing that 'the log has gone away', the character Lok cannot imagine or verbalize how this has happened; it is simply 'the log that was not there'.[26] As in London's *Before Adam*, Golding disrupts both narratives of language appearing fully formed and progressing in a linear fashion. Although driven to extinction by Cro-Magnons, the Neanderthals represent an alternative evolutionary path rather than merely an antiquated one. Golding presents their instinctive emotional communication as a kind of telepathy through them sharing mental 'pictures' without words.[27] Björn Kurtén's later *Dance of the Tiger* (1980) engaged with evidence of Cro-Magnons and Neanderthals coexisting for several millennia, imagining communication between them. Such encounters might be compared with those between European and supposedly 'primitive' races in Victorian colonial fiction. While Victorian racial science sought primitive speech in colonized peoples, modern paleontologists continue to seek it in extinct subspecies of *Homo sapiens*. Some have argued that the Neanderthal jaw was only capable of producing two vowels, while their limited social organization and technology suggest some linguistic capacity.[28] Kurtén's Neanderthals marvel at the 'new, full-toned speech, elastic and expressive beyond compare' of Cro-Magnons. In contrast, Neanderthal speech is 'slow-spoken and ritualistic', evoking late-Victorian images of the savage mentally bound by custom.[29] Kurtén's Neanderthals fill the space in the evolutionary story left by old, discredited racist hierarchies. One of them struggles against his physical and neurological deficiencies to produce a pidgin of human speech, declaring: 'Ah spahk Man talk'.[30] Although seeking to challenge catastrophism and teleology in language evolution, Kurtén replicates them through his conventions of representation. Similarly as Standard English often stigmatized dialect as deviant, Kurtén's misspellings characterize Neanderthal speech as a bastardization of the human rather than an alternative. At the same time, paleoanthropological linguistics remains dependent on imaginary narrative due to the paucity of direct material evidence. Some experts in the field have even recently speculated that traces of Neanderthal language might have persisted in human speech following long periods of contact.[31] It will be interesting to see how future prehistoric fiction engages with such visions of language evolution across human subspecies.

Another subject warranting further study is the persistence of concepts of language as a natural growth in anglophone literary culture. While ideas of language contamination and mechanization faded in the academy, they continued to grip the popular imagination. Influential authors, including Hardy, joined the Society for Pure English, which from 1913 to 1946 sought to conserve the literary language of Shakespeare in modern English. Its founder Robert Bridges worried that the global spread of English would cause non-native speakers to 'learn yet enough of ours to mutilate it, and establishing among themselves all kinds of blundering corruptions, through habitual intercourse infect therewith the neighbouring English'.[32]

Morag Shiach notes that such organicist logic informed various 'projects of linguistic "purification" that were part of literary modernism in Britain'.[33] Like the Victorian novelists who desired both the authenticity of dialect and the unity of Standard English, T. S. Eliot experimented with urban dialects in his early works before later seeking 'to purify the dialect of the tribe'.[34] The idea of 'return[ing] to common speech' and its imagined vitality clashed in his aesthetic with the need to 'polish or perfect' language.[35] The aim of reconnecting with the supposed naturalness of speech was possible for Eliot through broadcast performances. Yet, his delivery was not 'natural' but developed in line with elocutionary ideas of the accentless, 'pure' voice.[36] Gertrude Stein worried that words had lost their vitality through centuries of refined use. Like Morris, she yearned for the authentic past of Homer or Chaucer when 'the poet could use the name of the thing and the thing was really there', as opposed to the present when 'they were just worn out literary words'.[37] Yet rather than emulating the old epic styles, she sought to re-energize words by unpicking their associations, such as in her famous line, 'Rose is a rose is a rose is a rose'.[38] However, such experiments also undermined the concept of a golden age when words and things were organically linked, revealing instead endless layers of association.

Morris's efforts to revive the supposedly organic language of the preindustrial past might be compared with J. R. R. Tolkein's later invented tongues drawn from medieval sources. *The Lord of the Rings* (1954–55) treats folk speech as an organic growth entwined with its environment, as is emphasized through the speaking trees or 'Ents'. Their representative Treebeard tells the adventurers: 'my name is growing all the time, and I've lived a very long, long time, so my name is like a story. Real names tell you the story of the things they belong to in my language'.[39] In contrast to such natural language, the evil, industrializing Orcs are portrayed as creatively barren, as the narrator comments: 'it is said that [in past times] they had no language of their own, but took what they could of other tongues and perverted it to their own liking, yet they made only brutal jargons'.[40] Tolkein rejected contemporary theories of an arbitrary relation between sign and referent, stating his belief in 'the fitting of notion to oral symbol' or 'phonetic fitness'.[41] His sentiments echo Müller's idea of sounds originally combining with sense in an organic union. Raymond Williams traced a 'perpetual retrospect to an "organic" or "natural" society' through the history of English literature since the eighteenth century.[42] Equally, perpetual nostalgia for a golden age of natural connections between words and things might be explored as a continuing reaction against the mechanical reproduction of modernity.

Perhaps the most problematic question raised in this study, with which linguists and psychologists are still grappling, is the relationship between instinct and convention in meaning. The influence of Saussure's structural linguists after World War Two encouraged the orthodoxy that meaning was socially constructed with no natural bases.[43] The arbitrary sign rendered phonemes meaningless in themselves and signifying only through systematic combination and contrast with each other. The assumption that signs were arbitrary also became tied to a politics that was suspicious of natural explanations for human behaviour. The Marxist semiotician Roland Barthes framed cultural studies as the exposure of ideological mechanisms that turned 'history into nature'.[44] Only recently have neuro-linguistics seriously challenged the arbitrariness of the sign, with evidence for cross-cultural associations of certain phonemes with specific colours and shapes.[45] Margaret Magnus comments that phonosemantics – the idea of natural relations between sound and meaning – conflicts with Saussurean structuralism and Chomskian generativism because 'its acceptance requires a very different view of language than is generally accepted – a view in which semantics cannot be abstracted away from language itself, and in which language as we know it cannot be abstracted away from man ... It is similar to the observation in quantum electrodynamics that the observer cannot be meaningfully separated from the observed'.[46] To separate meaning from nature is also to separate it from one's self, enabling it to be analyzed and explained objectively. Roman Jakobson similarly traced the institutional turn against phonosemantics further back to the Neogrammarians who 'attempted to discuss sounds in a strictly naturalistic manner and to scrupulously leave aside the problem of the functions they perform in language'.[47] To approach meaning as inextricable from the mechanics of speech and human biology sacrifices the objectivity of the investigator: she becomes inescapably embedded in their processes.

While reacting against structuralism and generativism, phonosemantics might also be understood as a return to old lines of inquiry. Supporters of phonosemantics have persistently argued that neither convention nor instinct wholly determine meaning: the two collide and intersect. Romanes claimed that 'no line of strict demarcation can be drawn between' 'conventional signs' and 'natural signs'.[48] Equally, Magnus states, summing up modern phonosemantic theory, 'sound-meanings' are 'synchronically productive' alongside arbitrary convention, rendering meaning plural and dynamic.[49] Recent research has advanced this idea by comparing non-verbal communication among humans and other primates. Drew Rendall and Michael Owren highlight the interconnectedness of instinct and convention in primate vocal signals. Screams of alarm or aggression appear biologically preprogrammed, yet such signals 'can effectively serve also to highlight or tag salient events in the world, and thereby support additional learning about them'.[50] Infant vervet monkeys are instinctively startled by alarm calls, but only learn to differentiate calls signifying different threats over time. Instinctive vocalizations acquire new associations through the material and social experiences of their users. It is perhaps so difficult to distinguish communicative instinct from convention because they are not conflicting but symbiotic.

These ideas have profound implications for not only understandings of language but also interpretive practices; from literary criticism to 'reading' faces. The psychologist Cynthia Whissell claims to have found instinctive emotional triggers in certain phonemes, irrespective of their conventional combinations. For example, when judging the connotations of made-up words, subjects consistently ascribed 'gentle and positive associations' to *l* sounds and more 'aggressive' ones to *r* sounds. Combining close reading of texts with statistical analysis of the frequencies of certain phonemes, Whissell argues that 'texts of differing emotional effect employ different phonemes at different rates'.[51] Whissell uses such computational tests of 'phonoemotionality' to analyze literature, matching its effects upon readers with frequencies of emotive phonemes.[52] Similarly, Paul Ekman's research has updated Darwin's arguments on expression, claiming to identify cross-cultural emotional signals of the face. Ekman has published widely on this subject and designed courses training people to read emotions through facial cues.[53] A potential danger of such biosemiotics, however, is that they treat emotions and their signs as fixed and universal rather than as variable tendencies that interact with culture. Whissell concedes that emotional-phonetic correspondences can only be understood in the context of their utterance; the frequency of certain phonemes might be conventionally higher in certain forms of discourse, relativizing their effect.[54] She nevertheless assumes an underlying key of natural emotions which map on to phonemes and can therefore be measured computationally, across cultures. She applies such analysis to literary texts, claiming to discover complex shades of emotional connotation. Intriguing as such research is, however, it seems difficult to falsify, since any cluster of supposed phonetic emotion-triggers might be made to 'make sense' in poetic interpretation. While a high frequency of 'rough', 'aggressive' phonemes in an angry harangue might be read as complementing its surface theme, a cluster of 'soft', 'passive', 'pleasant' phonemes in the same passage could be explained as revealing a hidden emotional conflict.[55] Equally, regarding Ekman, it seems ironic that instinctive, universal expressive signals should need to be 'learned' like a foreign language. Ekman's claims to 'unmasking the face' presuppose static, 'natural' emotions which exist separately from culturally conditioned concealments of them. Biosemiotics in the twenty-first century might be used to reinforce reductive nature–culture binaries as well as to challenge them.

This study has explored how fiction can potentially counter such reductive views of communication, presenting speakers as products of both nature and circumstance. Ruth Leys notes that, in opposing the dogma of universal 'basic emotions', stereotyped in stock photographs, 'one finds oneself forced to provide thick descriptions of life experiences of the kind that are familiar to anthropologists and indeed novelists but are widely held to be inimical to science'.[56] I have aimed to illustrate Leys's claim by approaching fiction as a critical testing ground for ideas from the science of language rather than merely a passive reflector of them. Novels can undermine mechanistic theories of language by describing the particulars of daily life, exposing the inadequacy of abstract models of human behaviour. Hence, Grant Allen's *The Great Taboo*, while claiming to illustrate Frazer's universal stages of mythology, also undermines it, revealing parallels between western and 'savage' language. The imaginative worlds of Hardy, Wells and Butler situate every utterance, however apparently instinctive, in a nexus of social relations and conventions. Their characters' emotions are not fixed to mechanistic triggers, but blend with experiential, habitual and imaginative associations. Such fiction is the opposite of Whissell and Ekman's computational abstraction, which attempts to quantify and mechanize emotional signals. By exploring instinct in the context of society, and convention in the context of instinctive bodies, such fiction resists one-dimensional models of communication. Meaning appears plural and dynamic in these tales, with conventional human signs blending into infinite dialogues between organic codes, from sexual attraction to sympathy. Their characters' struggles to express or, rather, unify themselves resonate with William James's observation that instincts 'contradict each other ... *The animal that exhibits them loses the "instinctive" demeanour*, and appears to lead a life of hesitation and choice, an intellectual life; *not, however, because he has no instincts – rather because he has so many that they block each other's path*' (emphases in original).[57] Ekman's psychology claims to crack the code of instinctive signs, revealing humans' 'true' intentions within. The more radical possibility explored by Butler, Hardy and Wells is that there are no true intentions to discover: the speaker dissolves into infinite, interrelated systems of transmission and reception, internal and external, biological and social.

Such visions of humans as the aggregate expressions of organic codes are more relevant than ever in the twenty-first century with the rise of genomics. Equally, the field of biosemiotics has emerged in theoretical biology, approaching life as a complex of sign systems rather than physical quantities. Biosemiotician Marcello Barbieri states: 'the experimental reality is that proteins are manufactured by molecular machines based on the rules of the genetic code . . . the codes are a fundamental reality of life and we simply have to learn how to introduce signs and meanings in science'.[58] This monistic approach to nature and culture has a genealogy leading back to Darwin and Romanes. Mind need not be a divine mystery that separates humans from nature. Instead, it might be reappraised as a meeting of organic processes which 'think', 'feel' and communicate with each other on micro-scales. Wendy Wheeler comments that literature can be understood, through biosemiotics, as expressions of 'the conjuring power' of language 'to *make* (i.e. to model) worlds anew' like the constant mutations of genetic code (emphasis in original).[59] Such thinking would seem inseparable from modern molecular biology, built upon the discovery of DNA. Yet the speculations of Victorians such as Darwin and Butler reveal an older genealogy to biosemiotics. Butler's statement in the epigraph above on the 'language' of a potato reveals the similarity between his ideas of hereditary transmission and adaptation in modern biosemiotics. In the same way in which Butler presented ideas as evolutionary growths over generations instead of individual property, so modern biosemioticians might trace their own intellectual lineage in figures such as Butler.[60] By imagining possible forms of interchange between heredity and environment, language and nature, he and other authors in this study prefigured future paths of exploration.

The prehistory of biosemiotics in Victorian and Edwardian science and philology remains a rich field of potential research, on which this study has only touched. How, for example, did writers and investigators in the period imagine such organic communication systems mediating relations between humans and animals? Amigoni notes that in Butler's *Flesh* a despondent Ernest revives his spirits by visiting the zoo. Watching a family of elephants, 'he seemed to be drinking in large draughts of their lives to the re-creation and regeneration of his own' (p. 361). Amigoni interprets the scene as 'perhaps an enactment of the communicative "information" passed between human and animals', deriving from their common ancestry.[61] Conversely, the domestication of animals might be explored as a base for the formation of new communicative systems with humans. Darwin wrote how 'the dog, since being domesticated, has learned to bark in at least four or five distinct tones'.[62] Canines seemed to have developed a signalling system especially in order to communicate with their human masters, thereby blurring oppositions between nature and artifice. Further, as Butler's potato example shows, a semiotics of life might be extended to organisms radically unlike humans. How, then, did scientists and authors of the period imagine flora and wider ecosystems as sites of communication? Richard Jefferies wrote: 'The plant knows, and sees, and feels', but 'language does not express the dumb feelings of the mind any more than the flower can speak ... the flower has not given us its message yet'.[63] Recent evidence of auditory and gas signals between plants with context-dependent meanings highlights the reconceptualization of the world which biosemiotics demands.[64] Rather than belonging solely to humans and rendering the world an open book to them, signification becomes a natural mechanism of which humans are merely products, not masters.

Mill commented that a fine balance needed to be struck between change and conservation in language, both codifying new knowledge and preserving the old. For language was not only a tool of the present, but a 'conservator' of the mental activity of past ages. This past knowledge might 'fall asleep, as it were', but future investigators could discover new value in the old word meanings hitherto unimagined (see Chapter 3). His comment is an apt reminder of the importance of imagination in scientific inquiry, besides mere adherence to currently recognized 'facts'. Beer has emphasized the 'two-way traffic' between Victorian literature and science, in which each supplied useful metaphors for the other. This study has contended that some of the most radical statements about language in the period were made not in theoretical literature but through the imaginative experiments of fiction. By building narratives upon the ideas of specialists, such fiction was able to test their logic and speculate beyond empirical data. The possible interchange between instinct and custom in language, explored here imaginatively, would be marginalized in the academy before future generations found new value in investigating it. A century and a half after Müller's popular lectures, language is once again under the microscope, not as a single organism but possibly the structuring principle of all life. Spencer accused linguists of his time of turning a tool into an idol. Conversely, the emerging field of biosemiotics suggests that the organic world, which science has long approached as an elaborate machine, might be better imagined as a conversation. The old ideal of humans controlling nature through language is challenged by the possibility that nature is writing us.

Notes

INTRODUCTION: LANGUAGE UNDER A MICROSCOPE

1 Friedrich Max Müller, *Lectures on the Science of Language*, 2 vols. (1861–63) (London: Longmans, 1866), II, p. 354. Further citations are referenced in the text.
2 Herbert Spencer, *The Philosophy of Style* (1852) (New York: D. Appleton, 1884), p. 33.
3 Grant Allen, 'Toft and Croft', *Cornhill Magazine* (May 1894), 521.
4 John Horne Tooke, *The Diversions of Purley; Part One* (1786), 2nd edn (London: J. Johnson, 1798), pp. 531–32.
5 Roy Harris, *The Semantics of Science* (London: Continuum, 2005), p. 86.
6 Hans Aarsleff, *The Study of Language in England, 1760–1860* (1967), 2nd edn (Princeton University Press, 1983), p. 3.
7 E. P. Evans, *Evolutionary Ethics and Animal Psychology* (New York: D. Appleton, 1897), p. 315. See Gregory Radick, 'Primate Language and the Playback Experiment, in 1890 and 1980', *Journal of the History of Biology*, 38:3 (2005), 462–63.
8 See Linda Dowling, *Language and Decadence in the Victorian Fin-de-Siècle* (Princeton University Press, 1986); Christine Ferguson, *Language, Science and Popular Fiction in the Victorian Fin-de-Siècle: The Brutal Tongue* (Aldershot: Ashgate, 2006). Other relevant studies include Megan Perigoe Stitt, *Metaphors of Change in the Language of Nineteenth-Century Fiction: Scott, Gaskell, and Kingsley* (Oxford University Press, 1998); Dennis Taylor, *Hardy's Literary Language and Victorian Philology* (Oxford University Press, 1993); and Cary Plotkin, *The Tenth Muse: Victorian Philology and the Genesis of the Poetic Language of Gerard Manley Hopkins* (Carbondale, IL: Southern Illinois University Press, 1989).
9 Lorraine Daston, 'Scientific Objectivity with and without Words', *Little Tools of Knowledge: Historical Essays on Academic and Bureaucratic Practices* (Ann Arbor, MI: University of Michigan Press, 2000), p. 259. See also Daston and Peter Galison, *Objectivity* (New York: Zone Books, 2007).
10 Tony Crowley, *The Politics of Discourse: the Standard Language Question in British Cultural Debates* (London: Macmillan, 1989), pp. 37–38.

11 George Levine, *The Realistic Imagination: English Fiction from Frankenstein to Lady Chatterly* (University of Chicago Press, 1981), p. 6.
12 Norman Page, *Speech in the English Novel*, 2nd edn (London: Macmillan, 1988), p. 8.
13 See J. W. Burrow, 'The Uses of Philology in Victorian England', *Ideas and Institutions of Victorian Britain: Essays in Honour of George Kitson Clarke*, ed. Robert Robson (London: G. Bell & Sons, 1967), p. 187; Dowling, *Language and Decadence*, pp. xi–xii; and Stitt, *Metaphors of Change*, p. 19.
14 Grant Allen, 'The Struggle for Life Among Languages', *Westminster Gazette*, 1 (2 February 1893), 3.
15 Scholarly discussions of Standard English have traditionally focused on its sociopolitical uses. See Tony Bex and Richard Watts (eds.), *Standard English: The Widening Debate* (London: Routledge, 1999); Lynda Mugglestone, *Talking Proper: The Rise of Accent as Social Symbol* (1995), 2nd edn (Oxford University Press, 2003).
16 See Harris, *Semantics of Science*; Maurice P. Crosland, *The Language of Science: From the Vernacular to the Technical* (Cambridge: Lutterworth Press, 2006); M. A. K. Halliday, *The Language of Science* (London: Continuum, 2004); and Charles Bazerman, *Shaping Written Knowledge: The Genre and Activity of the Experimental Article in Science* (University of Wisconsin Press, 1988).
17 On the influence of philology upon Darwin, see Stephen G. Alter, *Darwinism and the Linguistic Image: Language, Race, and Natural Theology in the Nineteenth Century* (Baltimore, MD: Johns Hopkins University Press, 1999), pp. 14–21.
18 August Schleicher, 'Eine Fabel in Indogermanischer Ursprache', *Beiträge zur vergleichenden Sprachforschung*, 5 (1868), 206–08.
19 Émile Zola, *The Experimental Novel and Other Essays* (New York: Cassell, 1893), p. 8. See Charlotte Sleigh, *Literature and Science* (New York: Palgrave Macmillan, 2011), p. 115.
20 See Ann Ardis, *New Women, New Novels: Feminism and Early Modernism* (New Brunswick: Rutgers University Press, 1990), pp. 6–8; and Angelique Richardson, 'New Women and the New Fiction', *The Oxford History of the Novel in English*, ed. Patrick Parrinder and Andrzej Gasiorek (Oxford University Press, 2010), p. 144.
21 Conversely, Friedrich Kittler argues for a romantic view of the organic origins of speech as female. However, despite being the source of language, the woman remains passive in this formulation, acting as a muse 'getting (other) people – that is, men – to speak'; *Discourse Networks, 1800/1900* (1985), trans. Michael Metteer and Chris Cullens (Stanford University Press, 1990), p. 25. Thus Kittler's account agrees with mine insofar as both describe romantic philology ceding verbal creativity to men.
22 James Clifford, 'On Ethnographic Allegory', *Writing Culture: The Poetics and Politics of Ethnography*, ed. James Clifford and George E. Marcus (Berkeley, CA: University of California Press, 1986), pp. 98–121.

23 These opposing tendencies are comparable to the 'imperial grammar' and 'cultural nationalist' views that Janet Sorensen observes in eighteenth-century language debates. She argues that ideas in this period of 'universal grammar', allied with universal logic, drove early efforts to standardize English; while nationalist concerns for the immediate, particular and intuitive ran against standardization. See *The Grammar of Empire in Eighteenth-Century British Writing* (Cambridge University Press, 2000), pp. 9–16.
24 Jürgen Habermas, 'Towards a Theory of Communicative Competence', *Inquiry*, 13 (winter 1970/71), 372.
25 Peter J. Bowler, *The Invention of Progress: Victorians and the Past* (Oxford: Blackwell, 1989), pp. 10–11.
26 William James, 'Humanism and Truth', *Mind*, 13:52 (1904), 459.
27 See Brigitte Nerlich, *Semantic Theories in Europe, 1830–1930: From Etymology to Contextuality* (Amsterdam: John Benjamins, 1992), p. 209.
28 For previous scholarship on Victorian poetry and philology, see Plotkin, *Tenth Muse*; Taylor, *Hardy's Literary Language*; Dowling, *Language and Decadence*.
29 Sleigh, *Literature and Science*, pp. 11, 51.
30 Patrick Brantlinger, *The Reading Lesson: The Threat of Mass Literacy in Nineteenth-Century British Fiction* (Bloomington, IN: Indiana University Press, 1998), p. 5.
31 Wilhelm von Humboldt, *On Language: On the Diversity of Human Language Construction and its Influence on the Mental Development of the Human Species* (1836), ed. Michael Losonsky, trans. Peter Heath (Cambridge University Press, 1988), p. 21.
32 Burrow, 'Uses of Philology', p. 188.
33 For an introduction to Spencer, see Mark Francis's biography *Herbert Spencer and the Invention of Modern Life* (Stocksfield: Acumen, 2007) and James Kennedy's older but still useful *Herbert Spencer* (Boston, MA: Twayne, 1978).
34 Herbert Spencer, *An Autobiography*, 2 vols. (London: Williams & Norgate, 1904), I, p. 528.
35 Spencer, *Philosophy of Style*, p. 11.
36 See Marina Yaguello, *Lunatic Lovers of Language: Imaginary Languages and their Inventors*, trans. C. Slater (London: Althone Press, 1991), pp. 25–36.
37 Halliday, *Language of Science*, p. 205.
38 William Whewell, *The Philosophy of the Inductive Sciences, Founded upon their History*, 2 vols. (London: John W. Parker, 1840), II, pp. 229–30.
39 See John Locke, *An Essay Concerning Human Understanding* (1689), ed. Kenneth P. Winkler, 2 vols. (Indianapolis, IN: Hackett, 1996), II, p. 178.
40 G. P. Marsh, *Lectures on the English Language* (London: Sampson Low, 1860), p. 647.
41 Michel Foucault, *The Order of Things: An Archaeology of the Human Sciences* (1966) (London: Routledge, 2001), p. 323.
42 George Boole, *Studies in Logic and Probability* (La Salle, IL: Open Court, 1952).

43 On materialist psychology and Victorian epistemology, see Rick Rylance, *Victorian Psychology and British Culture: 1850–80* (Oxford University Press, 2000); Christopher Herbert, *Victorian Relativity: Radical Thought and Scientific Discovery* (University of Chicago Press, 2001); and Anne Stiles, *Popular Fiction and Brain Science in the Late Nineteenth Century* (Cambridge University Press, 2012).
44 Herbert Spencer, *The Principles of Psychology* (London: Longmans, 1855), p. 503.
45 Matthew Arnold, 'The Literary Influence of Academies' (1864), *Essays in Criticism* (London: Macmillan, 1865), pp. 56, 47.
46 See Thomas Dixon, *The Invention of Altruism: Making Moral Meanings in Victorian Britain* (Oxford University Press, 2008), p. 4.
47 Herbert Spencer, 'On the Origin and Function of Music' (1857), *Essays: Scientific, Political and Speculative, 3 vols. (London: Williams & Norgate, 1891)*, II, p. 426.
48 See Herbert, *Victorian Relativity*, p. 44.
49 Robert Chambers, *Vestiges of the Natural History of Creation and Other Evolutionary Writings*, ed. James Secord (University of Chicago Press, 1994), pp. 311, 266. See Ferguson, *Brutal Tongue*, pp. 34–39.
50 Spencer, 'The Genesis of Science' (1854), *Essays*, II, pp. 31–32.
51 Herbert, *Culture and Anomie: Ethnographic Imagination in the Nineteenth Century* (University of Chicago Press, 1991), pp. 65–66.
52 Herbert Spencer, *The Principles of Sociology*, 2 vols. (1875), enlarged edn (New York: D. Appleton, 1895), II, pp. 4, 322; quoted Herbert, *Culture and Anomie*, p. 67.
53 A. H. Sayce, *The Principles of Comparative Philology* (London: Trübner, 1874), p. 80.
54 See *On the Origin of Language: Two Essays by Jean-Jacques Rousseau and Johan Gottfried Herder*, trans. John H. Moran and Alexander Gode (New York: Frederick Ungar, 1966). This romantic tradition would be reworked in Walter Ong's concept of writing restructuring speakers' mental worlds, alienating discourse from the bodily and temporal immediacy of oral society; see *Orality and Literacy: The Technologizing of the Word* (1982), ed. John Hartley, 3rd edn (New York: Routledge, 2012). Jacques Derrida famously critiqued this tradition as a form of 'phonocentrism', which treated writing as a 'supplement' to speech and ignored the equal slipperiness of meaning in oral communication; see *Of Grammatology*, trans. Gayatri Chakravorty Spivak (1967) (Baltimore, MD: Johns Hopkins University Press, 1998), p. 7.
55 Dowling, *Language and Decadence*, p. 160.
56 See Chevalier Bunsen, *Outlines of the Philosophy of Universal History, Applied to Language and Religion* (London: Longmans, 1854).
57 Crowley, *Politics of Discourse*, p. 26.
58 Richard Chenevix Trench, *English Past and Present*, (New York: Red Field, 1855), pp. 13–14.
59 See Simon Winchester, *The Meaning of Everything: The Story of the Oxford English Dictionary* (Oxford University Press, 2004), pp. 62–68.

60 Richard Chenevix Trench, *On the Study of Words* (1851), ed. Roy Harris (London: Routledge, 1994), p. 23.
61 Joss Marsh, *Word Crimes: Blasphemy, Culture, and Literature in Nineteenth-Century England* (University of Chicago Press, 1998), p. 362.
62 William Dwight Whitney, *The Life and Growth of Language* (New York: D. Appleton, 1875), p. 48. See Stephen Alter, *William Dwight Whitney and the Science of Language* (Baltimore, MD: Johns Hopkins University Press, 2005), p. 46.
63 See Nerlich, *Semantic Theories*, pp. 213–14; Geoffrey Sampson, *Schools of Linguistics: Competition and Evolution* (Stanford University Press, 1980), p. 26.
64 Whitney, *Life and Growth*, p. 112.
65 See Moritz Lazarus and Heymann Steinthal, 'Einleitende Gedanken über Völkerpsychologie', *Zeitschrift für Völkerpsychologie und Sprachwissenschaft, I* (Berlin: Dümmler, 1860), pp. 1–73. See Laura Otis, *Organic Memory: History and the Body in the Late Nineteenth and Early Twentieth Centuries* (University of Nebraska Press, 1994), pp. 9–11.
66 G. H. Lewes, *Problems of Life and Mind*, 2 vols. (London: Trübner, 1879), I, pp. 80, 167.
67 Charles Darwin, *The Descent of Man*, 2 vols. (London: John Murray, 1871), II, p. 336.
68 Ibid., I, p. 106.
69 Ibid., I, p. 54.
70 William Scott, *The Deaf and Dumb: Their Position in Society, and the Principles of their Education Considered* (London: Joseph Graham, 1844), pp. 34–36. See also Charles Bell, *Essays on the Anatomy and Philosophy of Expression* (1824), 3rd edn (London: John Murray, 1844).
71 See Charles Darwin, *The Expression of the Emotions in Man and Animals* (London: John Murray, 1872), pp. 1–4, 61–62.
72 Ibid., pp. 356–57.
73 Darwin, *Descent of Man*, II, p. 337.
74 In 1945 the American linguist George S. Lane hailed 'mechanistic' linguistics for removing 'the heritage of speculation' that had 'burdened' earlier investigations; 'Changes in Emphasis in Linguistics with Particular Reference to Paul and Bloomfield', *Studies in Philology*, 42:3 (1945), 476. On the hardening of nature–culture binaries, see George W. Stocking, *Race, Culture, and Evolution: Essays in the History of Anthropology* (1968), 2nd edn (University of Chicago Press, 1982), pp. 196–233; Gregory Radick, *The Simian Tongue: The Long Debate about Animal Language* (University of Chicago Press, 2007), pp. 189–96.
75 Bruno Latour, 'An Attempt at a "Compositionist Manifesto"', *New Literary History*, 41 (2010), 483.

CHAPTER 1   THE FUTURE OF LANGUAGE
IN PROPHETIC FICTION

1 L. L. Zamenhof, 'The Making of an International Language' (1887), *Esperanto (The Universal Language): The Student's Complete Text Book*, ed. John Charles O'Connor (London: Fleming H. Revell, 1903), p. 7.

2 Yaguello, *Lunatic Lovers*, p. 45.
3 Matthew Beaumont, *Utopia Ltd: Ideologies of Social Dreaming in England 1870–1900* (Chicago, IL: Haymarket, 2009), p. 15.
4 E. B. Tylor, *Anthropology: An Introduction to the Study of Man and Civilization* (London: Macmillan, 1881), p. 439. On Victorian prophecy and progress, see Patrick Parrinder, *Shadows of the Future: H. G. Wells, Science Fiction and Prophecy* (Syracuse University Press, 1995), p. 6.
5 Rylance, *Victorian Psychology*, p. 80.
6 James Cowles Prichard, *Researches into the Physical History of Man* (London: John & Arthur Arch, 1813), p. 245.
7 Henry Buckle, *A History of Civilization in England* (1857), 2nd edn, 3 vols. (London: Longmans, 1867), I, p. 20.
8 G. W. F. Hegel, *The Phenomenology of Spirit* (1807), trans. A. V. Miller (Oxford University Press, 1977), pp. 117–18. See Morag Shiach, *Modernism, Labour, and Selfhood in British Literature and Culture, 1890–1930* (Cambridge University Press, 2004), pp. 24–25.
9 Otto Jespersen, *Progress in Language: With Special Reference to English* (London: Swan Sonnenschein, 1894), p. 365.
10 Richard Bailey, *Nineteenth-Century English* (University of Michigan Press, 1996), p. 68.
11 Whewell, *Philosophy of the Inductive Sciences*, I, pp. 51–52.
12 Horne Tooke, *Diversions of Purley*, p. 27. See James H. Stam, *Inquiries into the Origin of Language: The Fate of a Question* (London: Harper & Row, 1976), p. 29.
13 Charles Babbage and John Herschel, *Memoirs of the Analytical Society* (Cambridge: Deighton & Sons, 1813), pp. i–ii.
14 In 1889, Henry Reeve observed, regarding the *OED*: 'there is [now] an amount of industry and scholarship employed in storing and reproducing the knowledge of the world which has never been surpassed'. 'The Literature and Language of the Age', *Edinburgh Review*, 169 (April 1889), 330.
15 Trench, *Study of Words*, p. 5; A. H. Sayce, *An Introduction to the Science of Language* (1879), 4th edn, 2 vols. (London: Kegan Paul, 1900), I, p. 115.
16 On commercial writing styles and phonography, see Bailey, *Nineteenth-Century English*, p. 59; and Lisa Gitelman, *Scripts, Grooves and Writing Machines: Representing Technology in the Edison Era* (Stanford University Press, 1999), pp. 24–30. On the language of telegraphy, see James Carey, 'Technology and Ideology: The Case of the Telegraph', *Prospects*, 8 (October 1983), 303–25; Richard Menke, *Telegraphic Realism: Victorian Fiction and Other Information Systems* (Stanford University Press, 2008), p. 73.
17 Herbert Spencer, *First Principles* (1862), 3rd edn (London: Williams & Norgate, 1870), p. 321.
18 Ibid., p. 374.
19 Mugglestone, *Talking Proper*, p. 21.
20 Spencer, *First Principles*, p. 375.
21 On styles of news writing, see Alan Rauch, *Useful Knowledge: The Victorians, Morality, and the March of Intellect* (Durham, NC: Duke University Press,

2001), pp. 1–3; Toni Weller, *The Victorians and Information: A Social and Cultural History* (Saarbrücken: VDM, 2009), p. 45; Carey, 'Telegraph and Ideology', pp. 4–8; and Bailey, *Nineteenth-Century English*, p. 238. On scientific styles, see Bazerman, *Shaping Written Knowledge*; Halliday, *Language of Science*; and Daston, 'Scientific Objectivity', p. 264.
22 Sayce, *Introduction*, I, pp. 214, 218. On shorthand, see Isaac Pitman, *A Manual of Phonography; or, Writing by Sound* (London: Samuel Bagster & Sons, 1845), p. 9.
23 Spencer, *First Principles*, p. 421.
24 Ibid., 135. See Herbert, *Victorian Relativity*, pp. 44, 53.
25 David Amigoni, *Colonies, Cults and Evolution: Literature, Science and Culture in Nineteenth-Century Writing* (Cambridge University Press: 2007), p. 131.
26 Spencer, *First Principles*, p. 28.
27 Herbert Spencer, *The Principles of Psychology*, 2nd edn, 2 vols. (London: Williams & Norgate, 1870), I, p. 209. See Herbert, *Victorian Relativity*, pp. 55–56.
28 Edward Bulwer-Lytton, *The Coming Race* (London: Blackwood, 1871), pp. 185, 57. Further quotations are referenced in the text.
29 Matthew Arnold, 'The Bishop and the Philosopher' (1863), *The Complete Prose Works*, ed. R. H. Super, 11 vols. (Ann Arbor, MI: University of Michigan Press, 1960–77), III, p. 44.
30 Matthew Arnold, *Culture and Anarchy* (1869), ed. J. Dover Wilson (Cambridge University Press, 1960), p. 6.
31 John Stuart Mill, *A System of Logic* (1843), 8th edn (New York: Harper & Bros., 1882), p. 483.
32 Spencer, *First Principles*, p. 188. See Barri J. Gold, *ThermoPoetics: Energy in Victorian Literature and Science* (Cambridge, MA: MIT Press, 2010), pp. 71–73.
33 Whitney, *Life and Growth*, p. 149.
34 Arthur Lipow, *Authoritarian Socialism in America: Edward Bellamy and the Nationalist Movement* (Berkeley, CA: University of California Press, 1982), pp. 13–14.
35 John Macnie, *The Diothas, or A Far Look Ahead* (1883) (London: Putnam, 1890), p. 109–10. Further quotations are referenced in the text.
36 Boole, *Studies in Logic*, p. 195.
37 George Levine, *Dying to Know: Scientific Epistemology and Narrative in Victorian England* (University of Chicago Press, 2002), p. 68. On the links between spiritualism and objectivity, see Cathy Gutierrez, *Plato's Ghost: Spiritualism in the American Renaissance* (Oxford University Press, 2009), pp. 56–66. Conversely, Ferguson has stressed the role of the racialized body in some spiritualist thought; see *Determined Spirits: Eugenics, Heredity and Racial Regeneration in Anglo-American Spiritualist Writing, 1848–1930* (Edinburgh University Press, 2012).
38 See John Durham Peters, *Speaking into the Air: A History of the Idea of Communication* (University of Chicago Press, 1999), p. 89. Leading Victorian

spiritualists such as Charles Beecher, Robert Owen and Victoria Woodhull were involved in projects for a universal language: see Helen Sword, *Ghostwriting Modernism* (Ithaca, NY: Cornell University Press, 2002), pp. 19–20.

39 See E. B. Tylor, *Primitive Culture*, 2 vols. (London: John Murray, 1871), I, p. 148–50; L. H. Morgan, *Ancient Society* (New York: Henry Holt, 1877), pp. 36–37; George Romanes, *Mental Evolution in Man: Origin of Human Faculty* (London: Kegan Paul, 1888), pp. 116–19. See also Jennifer Esmail, *Reading Victorian Deafness: Signs and Sounds in Victorian Literature and Culture* (Athens, OH: Ohio University Press, 2013); Douglas C. Baynton, *Forbidden Signs: American Culture and the Campaign against Sign Language* (University of Chicago Press, 1996); and Lucy Hartley, *Physiognomy and the Meaning of Expression in Nineteenth-Century Culture* (Cambridge University Press, 2001).
40 Romanes, *Mental Evolution*, p. 147.
41 Tylor, *Primitive Culture*, I, p. 152.
42 Ibid., II, p. 446.
43 Ferguson, *Brutal Tongue*, p. 39.
44 Roger Luckhurst, *The Invention of Telepathy, 1870–1901* (Oxford University Press, 2002), p. 82.
45 See Laura Otis, *Networking: Communicating with Bodies and Machines in the Nineteenth Century* (Ann Arbor, MI: University of Michigan Press, 2001), p. 26.
46 Charles Bray, *On Force, its Mental and Moral Correlates* (London: Longmans, 1866), p. 80, quoted Luckhurst, *Telepathy*, p. 86.
47 Henry Drummond, *The Ascent of Man* (1894) (New York: Cosimo, 2007), p. 185.
48 Edward Bellamy, *The Religion of Solidarity* (1874) (Santa Barbara, CA: Concord Grove Press, 1984), p. 12.
49 Ibid., p. 18.
50 Edward Bellamy, 'To Whom this May Come' (1889), *The Blindman's World and Other Stories* (New York: Houghton, 1898), pp. 401–02. Further quotations are referenced in the text.
51 T. H. Huxley, 'On the Hypothesis that Animals are Automata and its History' (1874), *Method and Results: Essays* (London: Macmillan, 1894), p. 221.
52 Spencer, *Principles of Psychology* (1855), p. 10.
53 See William Hirstein, *Mindmelding: Consciousness, Neuroscience, and the Mind's Privacy* (Oxford University Press, 2012), p. 12.
54 Charles Babbage, *The Ninth Bridgewater Treatise: A Fragment* (1837), ed. Martin Campbell-Kelly (London: Pickering & Chatto, 1989), p. 36.
55 Samuel Weil, *The Religion of the Future; or Outlines of Spiritual Philosophy* (Boston, MA: Arena, 1893), p. 11.
56 See Steven Connor, *Dumbstruck: A Cultural History of Ventriloquism* (Oxford University Press, 2000), pp. 362–63.
57 Byron A. Brooks, *Earth Revisited* (Boston, MA: Arena, 1893), pp. 199–200, 202. Further quotations are referenced in the text.

58 Michael J. Crowe, *The Extraterrestrial Life Debate 1750–1900* (New York: Dover, 1999), pp. 395–97.
59 Francis Galton, 'Sun Signals to Mars', *Times* (6 August 1892), 7.
60 Ferguson, *Brutal Tongue*, pp. 21–25.
61 Axel Madsen, *John Jacob Astor: America's First Multimillionaire* (Hoboken, NJ: John Wiley, 2001), p. 281.
62 John Jacob Astor, *A Journey in Other Worlds* (1896) (University of Nebraska Press, 2003), p. 126. Further quotations are referenced in the text. See James A. Herrick, *Scientific Mythologies: How Science and Science Fiction Forge New Religious Beliefs* (Downers Grove, IL: Intervarsity Press, 2008), p. 203.
63 Spencer, *First Principles*, p. 123.
64 Parrinder argues that these 'future histories' are not simply prophecies but parodies of the prophetic genre; see *Shadows of the Future*, pp. 11–17.
65 Edwin Ray Lankester, *Degeneration: A Chapter in Darwinism* (London: Macmillan, 1880), p. 75.
66 Darwin, *Descent of Man*, 1, p. 60.
67 Darwin, *On the Origin of Species by Means of Natural Selection* (London: John Murray, 1859), p. 455.
68 Darwin did not, however, view all symbols as arbitrary. Gillian Beer notes his interest in natural sound symbolism as a possible basis of speech; see *Open Fields: Science in Cultural Encounter* (Oxford University Press, 1996), pp. 104–05.
69 George Frederick Stout, 'Thought and Language', *Mind*, 16:62 (1891), 194.
70 William James, *Pragmatism* (London: Longmans, Green, 1907), p. 53. On the influence of James on Wells's linguistic ideas, see Sylvia Hardy, 'H. G. Wells and Language', PhD thesis, University of Leicester, 1991, 26.
71 H. G. Wells, 'The Rediscovery of the Unique', *Fortnightly Review*, 50 (July 1891), 106.
72 Ibid., p. 111. See S. Hardy, *Wells and Language*, p. 23.
73 Karl Pearson, *The Grammar of Science* (1892), 2nd edn (London: Black, 1900), p. vii.
74 Ibid., pp. x–xi.
75 H. G. Wells, 'Peculiarities of Psychical Research', *Nature*, 51 (January 1895), 274.
76 H. G. Wells, 'Science, in School and after School', *Nature*, 50 (September 1894), 525–26.
77 H. G. Wells, 'A Story of the Days to Come' (1897), *Tales of Space and Time* (London: Harper, 1900), p. 196. Further quotations are referenced in the text.
78 Edmund Gurney, 'The Problems of Hypnotism', *Mind*, 9:36 (1884), 481.
79 See Chapter 4 for discussion of Wells's interest in the private languages of lovers and families.
80 H. G. Wells, *When the Sleeper Wakes* (London: Harper & Bros., 1899), p. 236. Further quotations are referenced in the text.

81 H. G. Wells, 'The New Optimism', *Pall Mall Gazette*, 58 (21 May 1894), 4.
82 Benjamin Kidd, *Social Evolution* (1894) (London: Macmillan, 1895), p. 309.
83 Wells cites Le Bon in *Mankind in the Making* (London: Chapman & Hall, 1903), pp. 266–67. Steven Mclean argues for the influence of Le Bon on Wells in *The Early Fiction of H. G. Wells: Fantasies of Science* (Basingstoke: Palgrave Macmillan, 2009), p. 86.
84 Gustave Le Bon, *The Crowd: A Study of the Popular Mind* (London: E. Benn, 1896), p. 117.
85 H. G. Wells, 'Intelligence on Mars' (1896), in *H. G. Wells: Early Writings in Science and Science Fiction*, ed. Robert M. Philmus and David Y. Hughes (Berkeley, CA: University of California Press, 1975), p. 178.
86 H. G. Wells, *The War of the Worlds* (London: Heinemann, 1898), p. 6. Further quotations are referenced in the text.
87 Ferguson links the Martians' 'purity' of communication with their ultimate defeat by bacteria. Their closed system of signs and concepts 'prevents the invader from comprehending and thus conquering the seething, sullied space of nation'; *Brutal Tongue*, p. 134.
88 H. G. Wells, *The First Men in the Moon* (London: G. Newnes, 1901), pp. 145–46. Further quotations are referenced in the text.
89 Francis Galton, 'Intelligible Signals between Neighbouring Stars', *Fortnightly Review*, 60 (1896), 661.
90 Edward Sapir, 'The Status of Linguistics as a Science', *Language*, 5:4 (1929), 209.
91 Michael Foster, 'An Address on the Organisation of Science', *British Medical Journal* (7 April 1894), 728.
92 Daston, 'Scientific Objectivity', pp. 262–63.
93 See Peter G. Forster, *The Esperanto Movement* (The Hague: Mouton, 1982), p. 50; and Yaguello, *Lunatic Lovers*, p. 31.
94 Richard Lorenz, 'The Relationship of the International Language to Science', *International Language and Science*, ed. L. Couturat *et al.*, trans. F. G. Donnan (London: Constable, 1910), p. 57.
95 The philologist C. R. Haines observed that 'there is scarcely an important language, classical or modern, which has not furnished its quota to the structure [of English]'; 'The Universal Language', *Macmillan's Magazine*, 65 (March 1892), 375. On the history of arguments for English as a world language, see Crowley, *Politics of Discourse*, pp. 71–73; and Janina Brutt-Griffler, *World English: A Study of its Development* (Clevedon: Multilingual Matters Press, 2002), pp. 107–25.
96 Zamenhof, 'International Language', p. 7.
97 See Forster, *Esperanto Movement*, p. 58; Pierre Janton, *Esperanto: Language, Literature and Community*, ed. and trans. Humphrey Tonkin *et al.* (Albany, NY: State University of New York Press, 1993), pp. 14, 42–43.
98 Zamenhof, 'International Language', p. 8.
99 See Haines, 'Universal Language', p. 376; and Henry Sweet, *A Handbook of Phonetics* (Oxford: Clarendon Press, 1877), p. 196.

100 See John S. Partington, *Building Cosmopolis: The Political Thought of H. G. Wells* (Aldershot: Ashgate, 2003), pp. 21–48; Simon J. James, *Maps of Utopia: H. G. Wells, Modernity and the End of Culture* (Oxford University Press, 2012), pp. 129–31.
101 See Victoria, Lady Welby, *The Witness of Science to Linguistic Anarchy* (Grantham: W. Clarke, 1898). Welby's letters to Wells are held at the Wells Archive, University of Illinois, MSS00071, W-146.
102 H. G. Wells, *Anticipations of the Reaction of Mechanical and Scientific Progress upon Human Life and Thought* (1901) (London: Harper & Bros., 1902), p. 250.
103 Ibid., p. 262.
104 H. G. Wells, *A Modern Utopia* (London: Chapman & Hall, 1905), p. 262. Further quotations are referenced in the text. See Partington, *Building Cosmopolis*, p. 49.
105 His *Modern Utopia* includes 'the actual population of the world with only such moral and mental and physical improvements as lie within their inherent possibilities ... the breed of failure must not increase, lest they suffer and perish, and the race with them' (pp. 136–37). On Wells's inconsistent statements about eugenics, see Partington, *Building Cosmopolis*, pp. 51–56.
106 H. G. Wells, *The World Set Free* (London: Macmillan, 1914), pp. 217–18. Further quotations are referenced in the text.
107 Wells, *Mankind in the Making*, p. 123. This contrasts with Wells's sometimes positive view of the 'babble' instinct (see Chapter 4).
108 Ibid., p. 129.
109 Ibid., p. 391.
110 H. G. Wells, *The Shape of Things to Come*, 2 vols. (1932) (London: Macmillan, 1933), I, p. 418. See S. Hardy, *Wells and Language*, p. 57.
111 H. G. Wells, *World Brain* (London: Meuthuen, 1938), pp. 34–35.
112 H. G. Wells, *The War in the Air* (1908) (Harmondsworth: Penguin, 2005), p. 75. Further quotations are referenced in the text.
113 H. G. Wells, *God the Invisible King* (New York: Macmillan, 1917), p. v.
114 H. G. Wells, 'Popularizing Science', *Nature*, 50 (July 1894), 300.

CHAPTER 2 PRIMITIVE LANGUAGE IN IMPERIAL, PREHISTORIC AND SCIENTIFIC ROMANCES

1 For an overview of the archaeological finds that effected this change, see A. Bowdoin Van Riper's *Men among the Mammoths* (University of Chicago Press, 1993).
2 Sayce, *Principles*, p. 115.
3 See Brian V. Street, *The Savage in Literature: Representations of 'Primitive' Society in English Fiction 1858–1920* (London: Routledge, 1975); Patrick Brantlinger, *Dark Vanishings: Discourse on the Extinction of Primitive Races 1830–1930* (Ithaca, NY: Cornell University Press, 2003) and *Taming Cannibals: Race and the Victorians* (Ithaca, NY: Cornell University Press, 2011); and Bradley Deane,

'Imperial Barbarians: Primitive Masculinity in Lost World Fiction', *Victorian Literature and Culture*, 36:1 (2008), 205–25.
4 William Winwood Reade, *Savage Africa* (New York: Harper & Bros., 1864), p. 443, 450.
5 Romanes, *Mental Evolution*, pp. 192, 175.
6 T. H. Huxley, 'The Evolution of Theology: An Anthropological Study, II', *Nineteenth Century*, 19:101 (April 1886), 485–506, 506.
7 See Auguste Comte, *The Positive Philosophy of Auguste Comte*, trans. and ed. Harriet Martineau, 2 vols. (London: G. Bell & Sons, 1875), II, pp. 155–61; Peter Melville Logan, *Victorian Fetishism: Intellectuals and Primitives* (Albany, NY: State University of New York Press, 2009), p. 10.
8 Spencer, *First Principles*, p. 347.
9 E. B. Tylor, 'On the Origin of Language', *Fortnightly Review*, 4 (April 1866), 547.
10 Ibid., pp. 552–54; F. W. Farrar, *An Essay on the Origin of Language* (London: John Murray, 1860), pp. 62–73; Hensleigh Wedgwood, *On The Origin of Language* (London: Trübner, 1866), p. 19.
11 Tylor, *Primitive Culture*, I, pp. 208, 215.
12 John Lubbock, *Prehistoric Times, as Illustrated by Ancient Remains, and the Manners and Customs of Modern Savages* (1865), 5th edn (London: Williams & Norgate, 1890), p. 572.
13 See Hilary Henson, *British Social Anthropologists and Language: A History of Separate Development* (Oxford University Press, 1974), pp. 11–12; and Joseph Errington, *Linguistics in a Colonial World: A Story of Language, Meaning, and Power* (Oxford: Blackwell, 2008), pp. 3–5.
14 Sayce, *Principles*, pp. 78–79.
15 Sayce, *Introduction*, I, p. 101.
16 Tylor, *Primitive Culture*, I, p. 142.
17 Ibid., I, pp. 16, 276.
18 Walter Bagehot, *Physics and Politics* (1872) (New York: D. Appleton, 1873), p. 53.
19 Tylor, *Primitive Culture*, I, p. 269.
20 Spencer, *Principles of Sociology*, II, pp. 150–51.
21 Street, *Savage in Literature*, pp. 4–5; Ferguson, *Brutal Tongue*, pp. 83–87.
22 Deane, 'Imperial Barbarians', p. 206.
23 Andrew Lang, *Custom and Myth* (London: Longmans, 1884), pp. 290–91, 199.
24 Wendy R. Katz, *Rider Haggard and the Fiction of Empire* (Cambridge University Press, 1987), pp. 145–47.
25 Henry Rider Haggard, *Allan Quatermain* (Chicago, IL: W. B. Conkey, 1887), p. 22. Further citations are referenced in the text.
26 Henry Rider Haggard, *Nada the Lily* (1892) (London: Longmans, 1895), p. 4.
27 Ferdinand de Saussure, *Course in General Linguistics*, trans. W. Baskin (1916) (London: Peter Owen, 1960), pp. 39–40.
28 Andrew Lang, 'Primitive Belief and Savage Metaphysics', *Fraser's Magazine*, 630 (June 1882), 734.

29 Henry Rider Haggard, *King Solomon's Mines* (1885) (London: Cassell, 1907), p. 101. Further citations are referenced in the text.
30 Ferguson notes that Haggard's *She* (1887) pits multilingual Europeans against 'purity of speech' in the ancient Arabic of the supernatural Ayesha; *Brutal Tongue*, p. 133. Errington claims that colonial linguistics revolved around ideas of primevalness and purity; *Linguistics*, pp. 48–69.
31 'Primitive Language', *Cornhill Magazine*, 8:44 (1863), 198.
32 Haggard, *Nada*, p. xi.
33 Brantlinger, *Dark Vanishings*, p. 4.
34 J. G. Frazer, *The Scope of Social Anthropology* (London: Macmillan, 1908), p. 18.
35 R. G. Latham, *Elements of Comparative Philology* (London: Walter & Maberly, 1862), p. 738.
36 Tylor, *Primitive Culture*, I, p. 277.
37 Joss Marsh, *Word Crimes*, pp. 207–18.
38 Brantlinger, *Taming Cannibals*, p. 35.
39 See Ferguson, *Brutal Tongue*, pp. 70–79. For an overview of scholarship on Allen, see William Greenslade and Terrence Rodgers (eds.), *Grant Allen: Literature and Cultural Politics at the Fin de Siècle* (Aldershot: Ashgate, 2005).
40 See, for example, 'Toft and Croft'; 'The Welsh in the West Country', *Gentleman's Magazine*, 253 (August 1882); 'Unsuspected Englishmen', *Longman's Magazine*, 21 (February 1893). Allen thanks A. H. Sayce for his assistance in *The Colour Sense: Its Origin and Development* (London: Trübner, 1879), pp. viii–ix.
41 Grant Allen, 'The Beginnings of Speech', *Longman's Magazine*, 24 (May 1894), 62. Brantlinger notes similar representations of Australian Aborigines as inferior through their supposed inability to master English; see 'Eating Tongues: Australian Colonial Literature and "the Great Silence"', *Yearbook of English Studies*, 41:2 (2011), 125–39.
42 Grant Allen, *The Great Taboo* (London: Chatto & Windus, 1890), p. 57. Further citations are referenced in the text.
43 Allen, 'Beginnings of Speech', p. 63; quoted Ferguson, *Brutal Tongue*, p. 78.
44 Tylor, *Primitive Culture*, I, p. 142.
45 Allen, 'Beginnings of Speech', p. 65.
46 See Henry Thomas Buckle, *History of Civilisation*, I, p. 178; Tylor, *Primitive Culture*, I, pp. 5–6.
47 Grant Allen, 'The Romance of Race', *Cornhill Magazine*, 3 (October 1897), 461.
48 Grant Allen, 'The Reverend John Creedy' (1883), *Twelve Tales* (London: Grant Richards, 1899), p. 13.
49 James Hunt, *The Negro's Place in Nature* (New York: Van Evrie, 1864), p. 16.
50 Herbert Spencer, 'What Knowledge is of Most Worth?' (1859), *Essays on Education and Kindred Subjects* (London: J. M. Dent, 1911), p. 40.
51 Spencer, *Autobiography*, I, pp. 108–09.
52 Ferguson, *Brutal Tongue*, p. 82.
53 Sayce, *Introduction*, I, p. 347.
54 Preface to *Strange Stories* (London: Chatto & Windus, 1884), p. iv.

55 Élie Berthet, *The Pre-Historic World* (1876), trans. Mary J. Safford (Philadelphia: Porter & Coates, 1879), p. 4.
56 Radick, *Simian Tongue*, pp. 18–19.
57 August Schleicher, 'Darwinism Tested by the Science of Language', trans. Alex V. W. Bikkers (1865), *Linguistics and Evolutionary Theory: Three Essays by August Schleicher, Ernst Haeckel and Wilhelm Bleek*, ed. Konrad Koerner (Amsterdam: John Benjamins, 1983), pp. 53–54.
58 Romanes, *Mental Evolution*, p. 313.
59 Sally Shuttleworth, *The Mind of the Child* (Oxford University Press, 2010), p. 246.
60 Charles Darwin, 'A Biographical Sketch of an Infant', *Mind*, 2:7 (1877), 293.
61 Hippolyte Taine, 'On the Acquisition of Language by Children', *Mind*, 2:6 (1877), 252–59.
62 H. G. Wells, 'Morals and Civilisation' (1897), *Early Writings*, p. 223.
63 H. G. Wells, 'A Story of the Stone Age' (1897), *Space and Time*, p. 63. Further citations are referenced in the text.
64 Edward Clodd, *The Story of 'Primitive' Man* (1895) (London: Newnes, 1909), p. 66; quoted Richard Pearson, 'Primitive Modernity: H. G. Wells and the Prehistoric Man of the 1890s', *Yearbook of English Studies*, 37:1 (2007), 63.
65 Patrick Parrinder, 'From Eden to Oedipus: Darwin, Freud, and the Romance of the *Stone Age*', *Anglistik*, 15 (2004), 86.
66 T. H. Huxley, *Evidence as to Man's Place in Nature* (New York: D. Appleton, 1863), p. 122.
67 Darwin, *Descent of Man*, 1, pp. 57, 46.
68 John Lubbock, 'Teaching Animals to Converse', *Nature*, 29 (10 April 1884), 547.
69 Romanes, *Mental Evolution*, p. 103.
70 C. Lloyd Morgan, *Habit and Instinct* (New York: Arno Press, 1896), pp. 325–26.
71 Mclean suggests that Wells may have read Garner's articles in the *New Review*, which later published *The Time Machine*; 'Animals, Language and Degeneration in H. G. Wells's *The Island of Doctor Moreau*', *H.G. Wells: Interdisciplinary Essays*, ed. Steven Mclean (Newcastle: Cambridge Scholars, 2008), p. 26. For an overview of Garner's work, see Radick, *Simian Tongue*, pp. 84–158.
72 H. G. Wells, *A Text-Book of Biology*, 2 vols. (London: Clive, 1893), 1, p. 131.
73 Stanley Waterloo, *The Story of Ab: A Tale of the Time of the Caveman* (Chicago, IL: Way & Williams, 1897), pp. ix–x. Further citations are referenced in the text.
74 Lawrence I. Berkove, 'Jack London and Evolution: From Spencer to Huxley', *American Literary Realism*, 36:3 (2004), 245–47.
75 Jack London, *Before Adam* (1907) (New York: McKinlay, 1917), p. 21. Further citations are referenced in the text.
76 See London's 'The Leopard Man's Story', *Windsor Magazine*, 19:4 (March 1904), 489–91; and Garner's 'Monkey Prosperity', *Windsor Magazine*, 20:3 (August 1904), 341–45.

77 R. L. Garner, 'The Simian Tongue' (1891–2), *The Origin of Language*, ed. Roy Harris (Bristol: Thoemmes Press, 1996), pp. 325–26.
78 Schleicher, 'Darwinism Tested', p. 82.
79 See Daniel Pick, *Faces of Degeneration: A European Disorder, c. 1848–c. 1918* (Cambridge University Press, 1993), pp. 11–15; and William Greenslade, *Degeneration, Culture and the Novel* (Cambridge University Press, 1994), p. 16.
80 T. H. Huxley, *Evolution and Ethics* (London: Macmillan, 1893), pp. 31–36.
81 Cesare Lombroso, *The Man of Genius* (1889) (London: Walter Scott, 1891), pp. 359–60; quoted Pick, *Faces of Degeneration*, p. 117.
82 Daston, 'Scientific Objectivity', pp. 264–76.
83 Pick, *Faces of Degeneration*, pp. 116–17.
84 Quoted Maria Elisabeth Kronegger, *Literary Impressionism* (Lanham, MD: Rowman & Littlefield, 1973), p. 77.
85 Max Nordau, *Degeneration* (1895) (London: Heinemann, 1898), p. 90.
86 Regenia Gagnier, *Individualism, Decadence and Globalization: On the Relationship of Part to Whole, 1859–1920* (Basingstoke: Palgrave Macmillan, 2010), pp. 2–3.
87 Havelock Ellis, 'A Note on Paul Bourget' (1889), *Views and Reviews: A Selection of Uncollected Articles, 1884–1932* (North Stratford, NH: Ayer, 1932), p. 52. See Gagnier, *Individualism, Decadence*, p. 2.
88 Charles Mackay, 'English Slang and French Argot: Fashionable and Unfashionable', *Blackwood's*, 143 (May 1888), 692.
89 Wells, 'Morals and Civilisation', p. 221.
90 Ibid., p. 217.
91 Wells, *The Time Machine* (New York: Henry Holt, 1895), p. 92. Further citations are referenced in the text.
92 H. G. Wells, *The Island of Dr Moreau* (New York: Stone & Kimball, 1896), p. 107. Further citations are referenced in the text.
93 H. G. Wells, *First and Last Things* (London: G. P. Putnam, 1908), p. 46.
94 Mclean argues for a similar anxiety about specialist language alienating scientists from the populace in Wells's *The Invisible Man* (1897); *Fantasies of Science*, pp. 66–71.
95 John Perry, *Jack London: An American Myth* (Chicago, IL: Nelson-Hall, 1981), p. 50.
96 Jack London, *Martin Eden* (New York: Macmillan, 1908), p. 66.
97 Barbara Lundquist, 'Jack London, Aesthetic Theory and Nineteenth-Century Science', *Western American Literature*, 32 (1997), 99–104.
98 London, *Martin Eden*, pp. 89–90, 108.
99 Jack London, *The Scarlet Plague* (1912) (New York: Macmillan, 1915), p. 40. Further citations are referenced in the text.
100 Jack London, *The Iron Heel* (London: Everett, 1908), p. 245. Further citations are referenced in the text.
101 Jack London, *The Letters of Jack London*, 3 vols. ed. Earle Labor, Robert C. Leitz III and I. Milo Shepard (Stanford University Press, 1988), III, p. 1485.

Notes to pages 88–93   191

102 Jonathan Berliner, 'Jack London's Socialistic Social Darwinism', *American Literary Realism*, 41:1 (2008), 66.
103 Friedrich Nietzsche, 'On Truth and Falsity in their Extramoral Sense' (1873), *Philosophical Writings*, ed. Reinhold Grimm and Caroline Molina y Vedia (New York: Continuum, 1997), pp. 98–99.
104 Jack London, 'When the World was Young' (1910), *The Night-born* (New York: Grosset & Dunlap, 1913), p. 83. Further citations are referenced in the text.

CHAPTER 3   ORGANIC ORALITY AND THE HISTORICAL ROMANCE

1 J. W. Donaldson, *The New Cratylus* (1839), 2nd edn (London: John W. Parker, 1850), pp. 70–71.
2 See Alice Chandler, *A Dream of Order: The Medieval Ideal in Nineteenth-Century Literature* (Lincoln, NE: University of Nebraska Press, 1971); Charles Dellheim, *The Face of the Past: The Preservation of the Medieval Inheritance in Victorian England* (Cambridge University Press, 1982); and Stephanie Barczewski, *Myth and National Identity in Nineteenth-Century Britain* (Oxford University Press, 2000).
3 On the nationalist context of comparative philology, see Stephanie Hackert, *The Emergence of the English Native Speaker: A Chapter in Nineteenth-Century Linguistic Thought* (Berlin: De Gruyter Mouton, 2012); Maurice Olender, *The Languages of Paradise: Race, Religion and Philology in the Nineteenth Century*, trans. Arthur Goldhammer (Cambridge, MA: Harvard University Press, 1992), pp. 6–8; Umberto Eco, *The Search for the Perfect Language*, trans. James Fentress (London: Fontana, 1995), pp. 31–44.
4 Farrar, *Origin of Language*, pp. 67–8.
5 William Barnes, 'A Dissertation on the Dorsetshire Dialect', *Poems of Rural Life in the Dorsetshire Dialect* (London: John Russell Smith, 1844), p. 3.
6 Katie Trumpener, *Bardic Nationalism: The Romantic Novel and the British Empire* (Princeton University Press, 1997), p. 33.
7 Eric Griffiths explores this issue in relation to poetry in *The Printed Voice of Victorian Poetry* (Oxford University Press, 1989). See also Penny Fielding, *Writing and Orality: Nationality, Culture and Nineteenth-Century Scottish Fiction* (Oxford: Clarendon Press, 1996).
8 Brantlinger, *Reading Lesson*, p. 16.
9 Charles Kingsley, *Hereward the Wake* (1865) (London: Macmillan, 1910), p. 2. Further citations are referenced in the text.
10 Eric Hobsbawm, *Nations and Nationalism since 1780: Programme, Myth, Reality* (Cambridge University Press, 1992), p. 61. See also Benedict Anderson, *Imagined Communities: Reflections on the Origin and Spread of Nationalism* (1983), 2nd edn (London: Verso, 2006).
11 A. B. Strettell, 'On the English Language and Grammar', *Introductory Lectures Delivered at Queens College, London* (London: Parker, 1849), p. 162.
12 Ibid., pp. 161, 177.

13 Charles Kingsley, *Alton Locke*, 2 vols. (1850) (New York: Co-operative Publication Society, 1898), II, p. 191.
14 Charles Kingsley, 'On English Composition', in Strettell, *Introductory Lectures*, p. 57.
15 Charles Kingsley, *Westward Ho!* (1855) (London: Nisbet, 1890), pp. 7–9. Further citations are referenced in the text.
16 Stitt, *Metaphors of Change*, p. 173.
17 As Fielding comments: 'The idealization of orality turns out to be a strategy in which its assumed "death" is a means for ignoring its survival in marginalized forms'; *Writing and Orality*, p. 5.
18 George Saintsbury, *A History of English Prosody from the Twelfth Century to the Present Day*, 3 vols. (London: Macmillan, 1910), III, p. 247. See Meredith Martin, *The Rise and Fall of Meter: Poetry and English National Culture, 1860–1930* (Princeton University Press, 2012), p. 101; Yopie Prins, 'Victorian Meters', *The Cambridge Companion to Victorian Poetry*, ed. Joseph Bristow (Cambridge University Press, 2000), pp. 92–97.
19 This strategy is comparable to Thomas Carlyle's imagining of the written version of his lectures *On Heroes and Hero-Worship* (1844) as elevated speech, discussed in Ivan Kreilkamp, *Voice and the Victorian Storyteller* (Cambridge University Press, 2005), pp. 18–21.
20 Kingsley, 'English Composition', p. 28.
21 Ibid., pp. 34–35.
22 Freidrich Max Müller, 'Preface', in Charles Kingsley, *The Roman and the Teuton* (1864) (London: Macmillan, 1913), pp. viii–ix.
23 Quoted A. A. Reade, *Study and Stimulants* (Manchester: Heywood, 1883), p. 160.
24 See Louise Lee, 'Voicing, De-voicing and Self-Silencing: Charles Kingsley's Stuttering Christian Manliness', *Journal of Victorian Culture*, 13:1 (2008), 12.
25 Stitt, *Metaphors of Change*, pp. 38–39.
26 R. M. Ballantyne, *Erling the Bold* (London: Nisbet, 1869), p. 236. Further citations are referenced in the text.
27 R. M. Ballantyne, *Norsemen in the West* (London: Nisbet, 1872), p. 73. Further citations are referenced in the text.
28 Allen J. Frantzen, *Desire for Origins: New Language, Old English and Teaching the Tradition* (New Brunswick, NJ: Rutgers University Press, 1990), p. 64.
29 John Richard Green, *A Short History of the English People* (London: Macmillan, 1874), p. 1.
30 See Nancy Stepan, *The Idea of Race in Science: Great Britain 1800–1960* (London: Macmillan, 1982), p. 4; and Ivan Hannaford, *Race: The History of an Idea in the West* (Baltimore, MD: Johns Hopkins University Press, 1996), pp. 277–90.
31 Joseph Bosworth, *A Compendius Anglo-Saxon and English Dictionary* (London: J. R. Smith, 1848), pp. iii–iv.
32 Thomas Carlyle, *Past and Present* (1843) (London: Chapman & Hall, 1897), p. 183.

33 Andrew Wawn, *The Vikings and the Victorians: Inventing the Old North in 19th-Century Britain* (Cambridge: D. S. Brewer, 2000), p. 6.
34 Barczewski, *Myth and National Identity*, p. 137.
35 Edward Freeman, *The History of the Norman Conquest of England*, 6 vols. (New York: Macmillan, 1873), v, pp. 546–47. On the complex relations between race, nation and language in Freeman's thought, see Hackert, *Native Speaker*, pp. 198–99.
36 James Frederick Hodgetts, *The Champion of Odin* (London: Cassell, 1885), p. 279. Further citations are referenced in the text.
37 George Dasent, *Grammar of the Icelandic or Old-Norse Tongue* (London: Pickering, 1843), pp. iv–v.
38 See Wawn, *Vikings and Victorians*, p. 8.
39 quoted Paul du Chailu, *Ivar the Viking* (London: John Murray, 1893), p. xx. Further citations are referenced in the text.
40 Freeman, *Norman Conquest*, v, p. 568.
41 See Jakob Grimm, *Über den Ursprung der Sprache* (Berlin: Ferdinand, 1852), p. 50.
42 Trench, *English Past and Present*, pp. 32–39.
43 J. F. Hodgetts, *The English in the Middle Ages* (London: Whiting, 1885), p. ix.
44 Matthew Arnold, *On the Study of Celtic Literature* (London: Smith, Elder, 1867), p. 134. See Laura O'Connor, *Haunted English: The Celtic Fringe, the British Empire, and De-Anglicization* (Baltimore, MD: Johns Hopkins University Press, 2006), pp. 27–32.
45 On images of Irish primitiveness, see L. P. Curtis, *Anglo-Saxons and Celts: A Study of Anti-Irish Prejudice in Victorian England* (University of New York Press, 1968); and Michael de Nie, *The Eternal Paddy: Irish Identity and the British Press, 1798–1882* (Madison, WI: University of Wisconsin Press, 2004).
46 Freeman, *Norman Conquest*, v, p. 547.
47 On the emergence of the genre, see I. F. Clarke, 'The Battle of Dorking, 1871–1914', *Victorian Studies*, 8:4 (1965), 308–28; and I. F. Clarke, *The Great War with Germany, 1890–1914: Fictions and Fantasies of the War to Come* (Liverpool University Press, 1997).
48 Wawn, *Vikings and Victorians*, p. 223.
49 George Stephens, '"English" or "Anglo-Saxon"', *Gentleman's Magazine*, 36 (1852), 472–76.
50 Henry Sutherland Edwards, *The Germans in France: Notes on the Method and Conduct of the Invasion, the Relations between Invaders and Invaded, and the Modern Usages of War* (London: Stanford, 1874), p. 246.
51 Ibid., p. 247.
52 Quoted in Mary Blackwood Porter, *Annals of a Publishing House: William Blackwood and his Sons*, 3 vols. (Edinburgh: Blackwood & Sons, 1898), III, p. 299.
53 George Chesney, *The Battle of Dorking* (1871) (London: Grant Richards, 1914), p. 86. Further citations are referenced in the text.
54 'Saki' (H. H. Munro), *When William Came: A Story of London under the Hohenzollerns* (1913) (London: John Lane, 1914), p. 31. Further citations are referenced in the text.

55 Lynn Abrams, *Bismarck and the German Empire* (London: Routledge, 1995), p. 24.
56 Edwards, *Germans in France*, p. 59.
57 Walter Wood, *The Enemy in Our Midst* (London: John Long, 1906), pp. 41–42.
58 Ferguson traces this idea in Bram Stoker's *Dracula* (1897). The Count's mastery of English prefigures his attempted invasion, which is opposed by dialects and codes, *Brutal Tongue*, pp. 131–54.
59 Erskine Childers, *The Riddle of the Sands* (1903) (New York: Dodd Mead, 1915), p. 81. Further citations are referenced in the text.
60 Clarke, 'Battle of Dorking', p. 308.
61 P. G. Wodehouse, *The Swoop! or, How Clarence Saved England* (1909) (Rockville, MD: Arc Manor, 2008), p. 21. Further citations are referenced in the text.
62 See Dellheim, *Face of the Past*, p. 16; Jan Marsh, *Back to the Land: The Pastoral Impulse in Victorian England 1880 to 1914* (London: Quartet, 1982), p. 7.
63 William Morris, *Collected Letters*, ed. Norman Kelvin, 4 vols. (Princeton University Press, 1987), II part B, p. 483.
64 See Ibid., I, pp. 13, 258, 576.
65 Farrar, *Origin of Language*, pp. 20, 55–56.
66 William Morris, *A Dream of John Ball* (1886–87) (London: Reeves & Turner, 1888), p. 74.
67 John Plotz, 'Nowhere and Everywhere: The End of Portability in William Morris's Romances', *ELH*, 74:4 (2007), 945.
68 William Morris, *News from Nowhere* (Boston, MA: Roberts Bros., 1890), p. 116. Further citations are referenced in the text.
69 William Morris, 'The Manifesto of the Socialist League', *Commonweal* (February 1885), 1–2.
70 Gagnier, *Individualism, Decadence*, p. 155.
71 Herder, *Origin of Language*, p. 150.
72 Arnold, *Celtic Literature*, p. 175. Arnold's ideas about race were not systematically expressed, and scholars have debated the extent of biological essentialism in his thought; see Frederic E. Faverty, *Matthew Arnold, The Ethnologist* (Evanston, IL: Northwestern University Press, 1951); Robert J. C. Young, *Colonial Desire: Hybridity in Theory, Culture and Race* (1994), 2nd edn (London: Routledge, 2006), pp. 53–84; James Walter Caufield, *Overcoming Matthew Arnold: Ethics in Culture and Criticism* (Aldershot: Ashgate, 2012), pp. 115–23.
73 Morris, *Letters*, II part A, p. 101.
74 Despite this comparison, Arnold and Morris also differed in their views of how much translation should preserve or erase the linguistic otherness of its sources. See Simon Dentith, '*Sigurd the Volsung*: Heroic Poetry in an Unheroic Age', *William Morris: Centenary Essays*, ed. Peter Faulkner and Peter Preston (Exeter University Press, 1999), pp. 63–66.
75 Anna Vaninskaya, *William Morris and the Idea of Community* (Edinburgh University Press, 2010), p. 39.

76 Friedrich Max Müller, *Three Lectures on the Science of Language* (Chicago, IL: Open Court, 1889), p. 49.
77 Morris, *Letters*, II part B, p. 601.
78 Ibid., pp. 769–70.
79 See Vaninskaya, *Idea of Community*, p. 140.
80 J. W. Mackail, *The Life of William Morris*, 2 vols. (London: Longmans, 1899), II, pp. 230–31.
81 See Marcus Waithe, *William Morris's Utopia of Strangers: Victorian Medievalism and the Ideal of Hospitality* (London: D. S. Brewer, 2006), p. xi.
82 Beaumont, *Utopia Ltd.*, p. 181.
83 Plotz, 'Nowhere and Everywhere', p. 946.
84 William Morris, 'The Present Outlook in Politics', *The Unpublished Lectures of William Morris*, ed. Eugene LeMire (Detroit, MI: Wayne State University Press 1969), p. 216.
85 See 'Comrade', *Oxford English Dictionary*, 2nd edn (Oxford University Press, 1989).
86 William Morris, *The Water of the Wondrous Isles* (London: Longmans, 1896), pp. 1, 4, 104.
87 Waithe, *Utopia of Strangers*, pp. 93–94.
88 Morris, *Water*, p. 5.
89 William Morris, *The Well at the World's End* (London: Longmans, 1896), p. 169; see Plotz, 'Everywhere and Nowhere', p. 946.
90 See Norman Kelvin's preface to Morris, *Letters*, II part A, pp. xxvii–xxviii.
91 William Morris, 'The Society of the Future' (1887), *News from Nowhere and Selected Writings and Designs*, ed. Asa Briggs (Harmondsworth: Penguin, 1962), p. 191; see Plotz, 'Everywhere and Nowhere', p. 944.
92 R. Jayne Hildebrand, '*News from Nowhere* and William Morris's Aesthetics of Unreflectiveness: Pleasurable Habits', *English Literature in Transition, 1880–1920*, 54:1 (2011), 4.
93 Linda Dowling, *The Vulgarization of Art: The Victorians and Aesthetic Democracy* (Athens, GA: University Press of Virginia, 1996), p. xiii.
94 William Morris, 'At a Picture Show' (1884), *William Morris: Artist, Writer, Socialist*, ed. May Morris, 2 vols. (Oxford: Basil Blackwell, 1936), II, p. 410.
95 Morris, *Letters*, II part A, p. 770.
96 Quoted in William Archer, *Real Conversations, with Twelve Portraits* (London: Heinemann, 1904), p. 49.
97 Thomas Hardy, *Thomas Hardy's Personal Writings* (Basingstoke: Palgrave Macmillan 1981), pp. 92–93.
98 Barnes, 'Dorsetshire Dialect, p. 12.
99 Thomas Hardy, *Under the Greenwood Tree*, 2 vols. (London: Tinsley Bros., 1872), II, p. 204.
100 Thomas Hardy, *Under the Greenwood Tree*, revised edn (London: Harper & Bros., 1898), p. 266. Further references are to the 1872 edition.
101 Thomas Hardy, *Tess of the d'Urbervilles* (London: Harper & Bros., 1893), p. 404. Further citations are referenced in the text.

102 Thomas Hardy, *The Trumpet-Major* (1884) (New York: Harper & Bros., 1894), p. 314. Further quotations are referenced in the text.
103 Thomas Hardy, 'The Melancholy Hussar of the German Legion' (1890), *Wessex Tales*, ed. Kathryn. R. King (Oxford University Press, 1991), p. 50.
104 Hardy, *Wessex Tales*, pp. 193–94.
105 Ibid., pp. 222–23.
106 Hardy, *Personal Writings*, pp. 92–93.
107 Thomas Hardy, 'A Tradition of Eighteen Hundred and Four', *Wessex Tales*, p. 34.
108 Thomas Hardy, 'A Changed Man', *A Changed Man, The Waiting Supper and Other Tales* (New York: Harper & Bros., 1913), pp. 14–15.
109 Thomas Hardy, 'The Fiddler of the Reels', *Life's Little Ironies* (New York: Harper & Bros., 1894), p. 157.
110 See J. B. Smith, 'Dialect in Hardy's Short Stories', *Thomas Hardy Annual No. 5*, ed. Norman Page (London: Macmillan, 1985), p. 84.
111 Thomas Hardy, 'Interlopers at the Knap', *Wessex Tales*, p. 127. Further citations are referenced in the text.
112 Quoted Mill, *System of Logic*, p. 464. On Hardy and Mill, see Angelique Richardson, 'Hardy and the Place of Culture', *A Companion to Thomas Hardy*, ed. Keith Wilson (London: Blackwell, 2009), pp. 55–58.
113 William Archer, 'Review: *Wessex Poems*', *Daily Chronicle* (21 December 1898). Thomas Hardy, *Collected Letters*, 7 vols., ed. Richard Little Purdy and Michael Millgate (Oxford University Press 1988), II, p. 207. See Taylor, *Hardy's Literary Language*, p. 42.
114 John Stuart Mill, *On Liberty* (1859), 2nd edn (London: Longmans, 1864), p. 13.
115 Mill, *System of Logic*, pp. 476–77.
116 Thomas Hardy, 'Preface' to William Barnes, *Select Poems of William Barnes* (London: H. Frowde, 1908), p. iii.
117 Thomas Hardy, *The Woodlanders* (1887) (London: Macmillan, 1906), p. 415.
118 See Jonathan Bate, 'Culture and Environment from Austen to Hardy', *New Literary History*, 30:3 (1999), 552.
119 Norman Page, *Thomas Hardy: The Writer and his Background* (Southampton: Camelot Press, 1980), p. 164.
120 Thomas Hardy, 'The Withered Arm' (1888), *Wessex Tales*, pp. 58–59.
121 Ibid., p. 72.
122 Page, *Thomas Hardy*, p. 164.
123 Taylor, *Hardy's Literary Language*, p. 251.
124 Bailey, *Nineteenth-Century English*, p. 71.
125 Hardy, 'Preface', p. iii.

CHAPTER 4 INSTINCTIVE SIGNS: NATURE AND CULTURE IN DIALOGUE

1 See Henri F. Ellenberger, *The Discovery of the Unconscious: The History and Evolution of Dynamic Psychiatry* (London: Fontana, 1994), pp. 228–37; Hartley, *Physiognomy*, pp. 176–77.

2 Jean Moréas, 'A Literary Manifesto – Symbolism' (1886), *Symbolist Art Theories: A Critical Anthology*, ed. Henry Dorra (Berkeley, CA: University of California Press, 1995), p. 151.
3 Samuel Butler, 'How to Make the Best of Life' (1895), *Essays on Life, Art and Science* (London: Fifield, 1908), p. 74. For a more detailed study of Butler's idea of speech as a function of heredity, see Will Abberley, '"His Father's Voice": Phonographs and Heredity in the Fiction of Samuel Butler', *19: Interdisciplinary Studies in the Long Nineteenth Century*, 18 (2014), www.19.bbk.ac.uk/index.php/19/article/viewFile/680/964.
4 See Otis, *Organic Memory*, pp. 19–23.
5 See Samuel Butler, *The Way of all Flesh* (1903) (London: Fifield, 1908). Further citations are referenced in the text. After years of engagement, Theobald 'had got into a groove, and the prospect of change [marriage] was disconcerting' (p. 56); Overton dislikes Theobald the more he visits, 'but one gets into grooves sometimes' (p. 93); 'so deep was the groove' into which the graduate Ernest falls that 'he spent several hours a day in continuing his classical and mathematical studies as though he had not yet taken his degree' (p. 207).
6 Gillian Beer, 'Butler, Memory and the Future', *Samuel Butler, Victorian against the Grain: A Critical Overview*, ed. James G. Paradis (University of Toronto Press, 2007), p. 48.
7 George Drysdale, *The Elements of Social Science*, 3rd edn (London: E. Truelove, 1886), p. 73. See Sally Shuttleworth, 'Evolutionary Psychology and *The Way of All Flesh*', in *Samuel Butler*, pp. 143–69, p. 157.
8 Quoted Henry Festing Jones, *The Notebooks of Samuel Butler* (1912) (New York: Dutton, 1917), p. 94.
9 Ibid., p. 93.
10 Samuel Butler, 'Thought and Language' (1890), *Essays*, p. 179.
11 Ibid., p. 227.
12 Ibid., p. 196.
13 Festing Jones, *Notebooks*, p. 109.
14 Butler, 'Thought and Language', p. 196.
15 Samuel Butler, *Life and Habit* (1878) revised edn (New York: Dutton, 1911), p. 156.
16 See Samuel Butler, *Evolution Old and New* (London: Hardwicke & Bogue, 1879), pp. 25–26, 346, 350, 368.
17 G. H. Lewes, *The Physiology of Common Life*, 2 vols. (Blackwood: London, 1860), II, p. 57.
18 Samuel Butler, *Erewhon: or, Over the Range* (1872) (New York: Dutton, 1917), p. 219.
19 Ibid., p. 221.
20 Festing Jones, *Notebooks*, p. 94.
21 Butler, *Life and Habit*, p. 83.
22 Butler, 'Thought and Language', p. 205.
23 See John Trumbull, 'The Prophecy of Balaam', *The Poetical Works of John Trumbull*, 2 vols. (Hartford, CT: Goodrich, 1820), II, pp. 141–46.

24 Gitelman, *Scripts, Grooves*, p. 32.
25 Samuel Butler, *Unconscious Memory* (1880) (London: Fifield, 1910), p. 53.
26 Butler, 'Thought and Language', pp. 226–27.
27 Lewes, *Problems of Life and Mind*, I, p. 160.
28 Samuel Butler, *The Family Letters of Samuel Butler: 1841–1886*, ed. Arnold Silver (London: Jonathan Cape, 1962), p. 146.
29 Ibid., p. 29.
30 Festing Jones, *Samuel Butler, Author of Erewhon (1835–1902): A Memoir*, 2 vols. (London: Macmillan, 1919), II, p. 4.
31 Butler, 'Thought and Language', p. 208.
32 Gillian Beer, *Darwin's Plots: Evolutionary Narrative in Darwin, George Eliot and Nineteenth-Century Fiction* (1983), 3rd edn (Cambridge University Press, 2009), p. 49; Otis, *Organic Memory*, pp. 28–33.
33 Charles Darwin, *The Variation of Animals and Plants under Domestication*, 2 vols. (London: John Murray, 1868), II, p. 404.
34 Butler, *Life and Habit*, pp. 52–53.
35 Lewes, *Problems of Life and Mind*, I, p. 167.
36 Butler's *Evolution Old and New* traced the theory back to Lamarck, Erasmus Darwin, and even Buffon in the eighteenth century. See David Amigoni, '"The written symbol extends infinitely": Samuel Butler and the Writing of Evolutionary Theory', in Paradis, *Samuel Butler*, pp. 142–60.
37 Samuel Butler, *Luck or Cunning?* (1886) (London: Jonathan Cape, 1922), p. 136.
38 Ibid., p. 85.
39 Samuel Butler, 'How to Make the Best of Life' (1895), *Essays*, p. 83.
40 Rosemary Morgan, *Women and Sexuality in the Novels of Thomas Hardy* (London: Routledge, 1988), p. xv.
41 Ralph Pite, *Thomas Hardy: The Guarded Life* (London: Picador, 2007), pp. 328–29.
42 Quoted in 'A Chat with the Author of *Tess*', *Black and White*, 4 (1892), 240.
43 Roger Ebbatson, *The Evolutionary Self: Hardy, Forster, Lawrence* (Brighton: Harvester Wheatsheaf, 1982), pp. 33–34.
44 Richardson, 'Place of Culture', p. 54.
45 Ibid., p. 61.
46 Thomas Hardy, *Desperate Remedies* (1871) (New York: Harper & Bros., 1905), p. 32. Further citations are referenced in the text.
47 Thomas Hardy, *Far from the Madding Crowd* (1874) (New York: Harper & Bros., 1895), p. 234. Further citations are referenced in the text.
48 On music linking humans to nature in Hardy, see Mark Asquith, *Thomas Hardy, Metaphysics and Music* (Basingstoke: Palgrave, 2005); and John Hughes, *Ecstatic Sounds: Music and Individuality in the Work of Thomas Hardy* (Aldershot: Ashgate, 2002).
49 Thomas Hardy, *The Return of the Native* (1878) (New York: Charles Scribner's Sons, 1917), p. 54. Further citations are referenced in the text.
50 Asquith notes the recurrence of this motif throughout Hardy's fiction; *Metaphysics and Music*, pp. 97–99.

51 Thomas Hardy, *The Well-Beloved* (London: Osgood, 1897), p. 150.
52 Colin Brown, *Music in Speech and Speech in Music: Two Lectures* (Glasgow: Bryce & Sons, 1870), p. 4.
53 Hardy, *Well-Beloved*, p. 141.
54 Thomas Hardy, *The Hand of Ethelberta* (1876) (New York: Harper & Bros., 1896), p. 56. Further citations are referenced in the text.
55 Thomas Hardy, *A Laodicean* (1881) (London: Macmillan, 1912), p. 327.
56 Ibid., p. 272.
57 Ibid., p. 161.
58 Quoted in Florence Emily Hardy, *The Later Years of Thomas Hardy 1892–1928* (New York: Macmillan, 1930), pp. 141–42.
59 Hardy, *Letters*, II, p. 97.
60 On the role of this idea in the anti-vivisection movement, see Ferguson, *Brutal Tongue*, p. 115.
61 Caroline Sumpter, 'On Suffering and Sympathy: *Jude the Obscure*, Evolution, and Ethics', *Victorian Studies*, 53:4 (2011), 668.
62 Thomas Hardy, *Jude the Obscure* (New York: Harper & Bros., 1895), p. 68.
63 Ibid., p. 71.
64 Ibid., pp. 252–53.
65 Asquith, *Metaphysics and Music*, p. 99.
66 Phillip Mallett (ed.), '"The Immortal Puzzle": Hardy and Sexuality', *Palgrave Advances in Thomas Hardy Studies* (Basingstoke: Palgrave, 2004), p. 134.
67 Thomas Hardy, *The Life and Work of Thomas Hardy*, ed. Michael Millgate (London: Macmillan, 1984), p. 368. See Tim Armstrong, 'Hardy, History and Recorded Music', *Thomas Hardy and Contemporary Literary Studies*, ed. Tim Dolin and Peter Widdowson (Basingstoke: Palgrave 2004), p. 161.
68 Darwin, *Expression of the Emotions*, p. 356.
69 Hardy, *Life*, p. 230.
70 Thomas Hardy, 'On the Western Circuit', *Ironies*, p. 89.
71 Ibid., p. 91.
72 Ibid., p. 104.
73 Thomas Hardy, 'An Imaginative Woman' (1894), *Wessex Tales* (London: Macmillan, 1917), p. 18. Further citations are referenced in the text.
74 H. G. Wells, 'The Limits of Individual Plasticity' (1895), *Early Writings*, p. 36.
75 Sylvia Hardy, *Wells and Language*, abstract.
76 H. G. Wells, *The Correspondence of H. G. Wells*, ed. David C. Smith, 4 vols. (London: Pickering & Chatto, 1998), I, p. 117.
77 H. G. Wells, 'Of Conversation', *Certain Personal Matters* (London: Lawrence Bullen, 1898), pp. 36, 39.
78 H. G. Wells, *An Englishman Looks at the World* (London: Cassell, 1914), p. 240.
79 Jonathan Sterne, *The Audible Past: Cultural Origins of Sound Reproduction* (Durham, NC: Duke University Press, 2003), p. 255.
80 H. G. Wells, *The Food of the Gods* (1904) (London: Nelson, 1909), pp. 151–52.
81 Ibid., p. 160.

82 Ibid., p. 238.
83 Mugglestone, *Talking Proper*, pp. 2–5.
84 H. G. Wells, *Kipps* (New York: Charles Scribner's Sons, 1905), pp. 170, 204, 71, 236.
85 H. G. Wells, *Tono-Bungay* (London: Macmillan, 1909), pp. 21–22. Further citations are referenced in the text.
86 In Wells's defence, not all of his phonographic speakers are female, and his 'New Woman' novel *Ann Veronica* (1909) depicts its heroine rebelling against patriarchal authority and convention (albeit with a Wells-like male teacher).
87 Sylvia Hardy, *Wells and Language*, p. 26.
88 H. G. Wells, 'Scepticism of the Instrument' (1903), in *A Modern Utopia*, p. 382.
89 H. G. Wells, 'The Pleasure of Quarrelling', *Personal Matters*, p. 247.
90 H. G. Wells, 'The Book of Curses', *Personal Matters*, pp. 128, 132.
91 Taine, 'Acquisition of Language', pp. 257–58.
92 Ibid., p. 255.
93 Wells, *Correspondence*, 1, p. 8.
94 H. G. Wells, *An Experiment in Autobiography: Discoveries and Conclusions of a Very Ordinary Brain (Since 1866)* (London: Cresset Press, 1934), p. 462.
95 See, for example, an early letter to his brother Frank, mocking spelling reform: Wells, *Correspondence*, 1, pp. 36–37.
96 Wells, *Autobiography*, p. 446.
97 H. G. Wells, 'For Freedom in Spelling', *Personal Matters*, pp. 149–50.
98 Ibid., pp. 151–52.
99 See Henry Sweet, *A Handbook of Phonetics* (Oxford: Clarendon Press, 1877).
100 Sayce, *Introduction*, 1, p. 348.
101 Karl Otto Erdmann, *Die Bedeutung des Wortes* (Leipzig: Avenarius, 1900), p. 120.
102 E. W. Scripture, *Elements of Experimental Phonetics* (New York: Scribner, 1902), pp. 390–91.
103 Sigmund Freud, *The Psychopathology of Everyday Life* (1901), trans. A. A. Brill (New York: Macmillan, 1914), p. 80.
104 Gerard Curtis, *Visual Words: Art and the Material Book in Victorian England* (Aldershot: Ashgate, 2002), p. 35.
105 H. G. Wells, *The History of Mr Polly* (New York: Grosset & Dunlap, 1909), pp. 28–29. Further citations are referenced in the text.
106 Sylvia Hardy, *Wells and Language*, p. 139.
107 See Clara Elizabeth Orban, *The Culture of Fragments: Words and Images in Futurism and Surrealism* (Amsterdam: Rodopi, 1997), pp. 36–38. Wells's games with language were not unique, as Valentine Cunningham notes, Victorian 'nonsense' poets like Lear 'anticipate and even rival the extremes of modernist verbal experiment … language on the compelling edge of gibberish'. *The Victorians: An Anthology of Poetry and Poetics* (Oxford: Blackwell, 2002), p. xliii.
108 Wells, 'Freedom in Spelling', p. 152.

109 H. G. Wells, 'James Joyce', *Nation* (24 February 1917), 710.
110 Quoted in James Joyce, *Letters of James Joyce*, ed. Stuart Gilbert, 3 vols. (New York: Viking Press, 1957), I, p. 275.
111 Wells, *Autobiography*, p. 461.
112 H. G. Wells, *Love and Mr Lewisham* (New York: Frederick A. Stokes, 1899), p. 185. Further citations are referenced in the text.
113 H. G. Wells, *H. G. Wells in Love: Postscript to an Experiment in Autobiography*, ed. G. P. Wells (London: Little, Brown, 1984), p. 54. See also Norman and Jeanne Mackenzie, *The Life of H. G. Wells: The Time Traveller* (London: Hogarth, 1987), pp. 250–59.
114 Wells, *Wells in Love*, p. 102.
115 Ibid., p. 235.
116 Wells, *Autobiography*, p. 461. Scholars have been similarly uninterested, with David Smith's edition of Wells's letters including only a few of his experiments in misspelling; the Wells Archive (University of Illinois) holds many more. An exception is Gene and Margaret Rinkel's *The Picshuas of H. G. Wells: a Burlesque Diary* (2006), although this is more concerned with drawings than writing.
117 H. G. Wells, 'Freedom in Spelling', *Personal Matters*, p. 153.

CONCLUSION: WIDENING THE LENS

1 Marcello Barbieri, 'The Challenge of Biosemiotics', *Introduction to Biosemiotics: The New Biological Synthesis* (Dordrecht: Springer, 2008), p. xi.
2 Butler, *Erewhon*, p. 236.
3 Aarsleff, *Study of Language*, p. 3.
4 Maggie Tallerman and Kathleen Gibson, 'Introduction: The Evolution of Language', *Oxford Handbook of Language Evolution* (Oxford University Press, 2012), p. 2.
5 See, for example, Otto Jesperson, *Efficiency in Linguistic Change* (Copenhagen: Munksgaard, 1941).
6 George Orwell, 'Politics and the English Language' (1946), *The English Language*, volume II, *Essays by Linguists and Men of Letters*, ed. W. F. Bolton and D. Crystal (Cambridge University Press, 1969), p. 228.
7 Bernard Burgoyne, *Drawing the Soul: Schemas and Models in Psychoanalysis* (London: Rebus, 2000), p. 127.
8 See Suzanne Raitt, 'The Rhetoric of Efficiency in Early Modernism', *Modernism/modernity*, 13:1 (2006), 836.
9 Aldous Huxley, *Brave New World* (1932) (New York: HarperCollins, 1998), p. 19.
10 George Orwell, *Nineteen Eighty-Four* (1949) (New York: Knopf, 1992), p. 53.
11 Walter E. Meyers, *Aliens and Linguists: Language Study and Science Fiction* (Athens, GA: University of Georgia Press, 1982), p. 163.
12 Bruno Latour, 'Where are the Missing Masses? The Sociology of a Few Mundane Artifacts', *Shaping Technology/Building Society. Studies in*

Sociotechnological Change, ed. Wiebe Bijker and John Law (Cambridge, MA: MIT Press, 1992), p. 255.
13 G. B. Dyson, *Darwin Among the Machines: The Evolution of Global Intelligence* (Reading, MA: Perseus, 1997), pp. 121–23. At the same time, the enduring popularity of the Turing Test as a measure of artificial intelligence reflects the widespread belief that language is the key to consciousness. See James Moor (ed.), *The Turing Test: The Elusive Standard of Artificial Intelligence* (Dordrecht: Kluwer, 2003).
14 George Stewart, *Earth Abides* (1949) (Boston, MA: Houghton Mifflin Harcourt, 1976), p. 219.
15 Walter Miller Jr, *A Canticle for Leibowitz* (1959) (New York: Bantam Dell, 2007), p. 116.
16 Stam, *Inquiries*, pp. ix–xii.
17 Radick, *Simian Tongue*, pp. 190–210.
18 Noam Chomsky, *Aspects of the Theory of Syntax* (MIT Press, 1965), pp. 32–33.
19 Derek Bickerton, *Language and Species* (University of Chicago Press, 1990), p. 190; Steven Pinker, *The Language Instinct: How the Mind Creates Language* (Harmondsworth: Penguin, 1994), p. 334.
20 Patricia Casey Sutcliffe, 'Ideology and the Impossibility of Animal Language', *LACAS Forum*, 34 (2009), 248–49.
21 Geoffrey Sampson, *The 'Language Instinct' Debate* (New York: Continuum, 2005), p. 69.
22 See Catherine Hobaiter and Richard W. Byrne, 'The Gestural Repertoire of the Wild Chimpanzee', *Animal Cognition*, 14 (January 2011), 745–67. For an overview of recent research see Radick, *Simian Tongue*, pp. 360–80.
23 Philip Lieberman, *Human Language and our Reptilian Brain: The Subcortical Bases of Speech, Syntax, and Thought* (Cambridge, MA: Harvard University Press, 2002), pp. 1–3.
24 Similar recent novels include Sara Gruen, *Ape House* (New York: Spiegel & Grau, 2010); Benjamin Hale, *The Evolution of Bruno Littlemore* (New York: Twelve, 2011); and Dennis Meredith, *Solomon's Freedom* (Purlear, NC: Glyphus, 2014).
25 Colin McAdam, *A Beautiful Truth* (New York: Soho Press, 2013), p. 18. See Virginia Richter, 'Ape meets Primatologist: Post-Darwinian Interspecies Romances', *America's Darwin: Darwinian Theory and U.S. Literary Culture*, ed. Tina Gianquitto and Lydia Fisher (Athens, GA: University of Georgia Press, 2014), pp. 360–88.
26 William Golding, *The Inheritors* (1955) (London: Faber & Faber, 1997), pp. 12–13.
27 Ibid., p. 34; Charles De Paolo, 'Wells, Golding, and Auel: Representing the Neanderthal', *Science Fiction Studies*, 27:3 (2000), 72–73.
28 Lieberman, *Reptilian Brain*, pp. 140–49.
29 Björn Kurtén, *Dance of the Tiger: A Novel of the Ice Age* (1980) (Berkeley, CA: University of California Press, 1995), pp. 28, 141. See also Jean Auel's

representation of Neanderthal language in *The Clan of the Cave Bear* (New York: Crown, 1980).
30 Kurtén, *Dance of the Tiger*, p. 41.
31 Dan Dediu and Stephen C. Levinson, 'On the Antiquity of Language: The Reinterpretation of Neanderthal Linguistic Capacities and its Consequences', *Frontiers in Psychology*, 4:397 (July 2013), http://journal.frontiersin.org/Journal/10.3389/fpsyg.2013.00397/
32 Quoted in Bailey, *Images of English* (Cambridge University Press, 1991), p. 206.
33 Morag Shiach, '"To Purify the Dialect of the Tribe": Modernism and Language Reform', *Modernism/modernity*, 14:1 (2007), 21.
34 T. S. Eliot, 'Little Gidding' (1942), *Four Quartets, Collected Poems, 1909–1962* (New York: Harcourt Brace Jovanovich, 1970), p. 204.
35 T. S. Eliot, 'The Music of Poetry' (1942), *On Poetry and Poets* (London: Faber, 1957), p. 31.
36 Mark Morrisson, 'Performing the Pure Voice: Elocution, Verse Recitation, and Modernist Poetry in Prewar London', *Modernism/modernity*, 3:3 (1996), 26–29.
37 Quoted in Thornton Wilder, 'Introduction to *Four in America*', *Gertrude Stein Remembered*, ed. Linda Simon (Lincoln, NE: University of Nebraska Press, 1994), p. 132.
38 Gertrude Stein, 'Sacred Emily', *Geography and Plays* (Boston, MA: Four Seas, 1922), p. 187.
39 J. R. R. Tolkein, *The Lord of the Rings*, 3 vols. (1954–55) (London: Allen & Unwin, 1960), II, p. 68.
40 Ibid., III, appendix F, p. 409.
41 J. R. R. Tolkien, *The Monsters and the Critics and Other Essays*, ed. Christopher Tolkien (London: Allen & Unwin, 1983), pp. 206, 211; see Ross Smith, 'Fitting Sense to Sound: Linguistic Aesthetics and Phonosemantics in the Works of J. R. R. Tolkien', *Tolkien Studies*, 3 (2006), 4.
42 Raymond Williams, *The Country and the City* (London: Chatto & Windus, 1973), p. 96.
43 Margaret Magnus, 'What's in a Word? Studies in Phonosemantics', unpublished PhD thesis, Norwegian University of Science and Technology, 2001, 24–25.
44 Roland Barthes, *Mythologies* (1957), trans. Brian Trench (London: Paladin, 1973), pp. 146–47.
45 See Ramachandran and Hubbard's experiment in which adults consistently linked the nonsense words 'bouba' and 'kiki' with rounded and spiked shapes, respectively, V. S. Ramachandran and E. M. Hubbard, 'Synaesthesia – a Window into Perception, Thought and Language', *Journal of Consciousness Studies*, 8:12 (2001), 3–34. See also Drew Rendall and Alan Nielsen, 'The Sound of Round: Evaluating the Sound-Symbolic Role of Consonants in the Classic Takete-Maluma Phenomenon', *Canadian Journal of Experimental Psychology*, 65:2 (2011), 115–24.
46 Magnus, *Studies in Phonosemantics*, p. 28.

47 Roman Jakobson, *Six Lectures on Sound and Meaning*, trans. John Mepham (Brighton: Harvester Wheatsheaf, 1978), p. 7.
48 Romanes, *Mental Evolution*, pp. 102–03.
49 Magnus, *Studies in Phonosemantics*, p. 29.
50 Drew Rendall and Michael J. Owren, 'Vocalizations as Tools for Influencing the Affect and Behavior of Others', *Handbook of Mammalian Vocalization: An Integrative Neuroscience Approach*, ed. Stefan M. Brudzynski (Amsterdam: Academic Press, 2010), p. 180.
51 Cynthia Whissell, 'Phonosymbolism and the Emotional Nature of Sounds: Evidence of the Preferential Use of Particular Phonemes in the texts of Differing Emotional Tone', *Perceptual and Motor Skills*, 89 (1999), 21.
52 See, for example, Whissell, 'Emotion Conveyed by Sound in the Poetry of Alfred, Lord Tennyson', *Empirical Studies of the Arts*, 20:2 (2002), 137–55.
53 See Paul Ekman, *Unmasking the Face: A Guide to Recognizing Emotions from Facial Cues* (Cambridge, MA: Malor, 2003), and his F.A.C.E. training programme, http://www.paulekman.com. Conversely, recent computational studies have stressed the cultural contingencies of emotional expression; see Rachel E. Jack et al., 'Facial Expressions of Emotion are not Culturally Universal', *Proceedings of the National Academy of Sciences*, 109:19 (2012), 7241–44.
54 Whissell, 'Phonosymbolism', p. 21.
55 Hence, in an analysis of Tennyson's *In Memoriam* (1849), Whissell explains the rise in 'sad and passive' sounds at the end, despite the cheerful event of a marriage, as an unconscious conflict in the poet's feelings: 'Contrary to Tennyson's own interpretation of increasing cheer, the sound shading of the close to *In Memoriam* echoes the grief evident in the saddest parts of the poem'; 'Emotion Conveyed by Sound', p. 146.
56 Ruth Leys, 'How Did Fear Become a Scientific Object and What Kind of Object is It?', *Representations*, 110:1 (2010), 88–89.
57 William James, *The Principles of Psychology*, 2 vols. (New York: Holt, 1890), II, pp. 392–93.
58 Barbieri, 'Introduction', p. xi.
59 Wendy Wheeler, 'The Book of Nature: Biosemiotics and the Evolution of Literature', *The Evolution of Literature: Legacies of Darwin in European Cultures*, ed. Nicholas Saul and Simon J. James (Amsterdam: Rodopi, 2011), p. 183.
60 Donald Forsdyke, 'Samuel Butler and Human Long Term Memory: Is the Cupboard Bare?', *Journal of Theoretical Biology*, 258:1 (2009), 159–63.
61 David Amigoni, 'Charles Darwin's Centenary and the Politics and Poetics of Parenting: Inheritance, Variation, and the Aesthetic Legacy of Samuel Butler', Saul and James, *Evolution of Literature*, p. 84.
62 Darwin, *Descent*, I, p. 54.
63 Richard Jefferies, 'Nature and Books' (1887), *A Century of Early Ecocriticism*, ed. David Mazel (Athens, GA: University of Georgia, 2001), p. 77.
64 Günther Witzany, 'Key Levels of Biocommunication in Plants', *Biocommunication of Plants*, ed. František Baluška and Günther Witzany (New York: Springer, 2012), pp. 1–10.

Bibliography

PRIMARY TEXTS

Allen, Grant. 'The Beginnings of Speech', *Longman's Magazine*, 24 (May 1894), 58–67.
  The British Barbarians (London: G. P. Putnam, 1895).
  The Colour Sense: Its Origin and Development (London: Trübner, 1879).
  The Great Taboo (London: Chatto & Windus, 1890).
  'Preface', *Strange Stories* (London: Chatto & Windus, 1884), pp. iii–vi.
  'The Reverend John Creedy' (1883), *Twelve Tales* (London: Grant Richards, 1899), pp. 11–32.
  'The Romance of Race', *Cornhill Magazine*, 3 (October 1897), 461–71.
  'The Struggle for Life Among Languages', *Westminster Gazette*, 1 (2 February 1893), 3.
  'Toft and Croft', *Cornhill Magazine* (May 1894), 521–31.
  'Unsuspected Englishmen', *Longman's Magazine*, 21 (February 1893), 360–73.
  'The Welsh in the West Country', *Gentleman's Magazine*, 253 (August 1882), 179–97.
Archer, William. *Real Conversations, with Twelve Portraits* (London: Heinemann, 1904).
  'Review: *Wessex Poems*', *Daily Chronicle* (21 December 1898).
Arnold, Matthew. 'The Bishop and the Philosopher' (1863), *The Complete Prose Works*, ed. R. H. Super, 11 vols. (Ann Arbor, MI: University of Michigan Press, 1960–77), III, pp. 40–55.
  Culture and Anarchy (1869), ed. J. Dover Wilson (Cambridge University Press, 1960).
  'The Literary Influence of Academies' (1864), *Essays in Criticism* (London: Macmillan, 1865), pp. 42–78.
  On the Study of Celtic Literature (London: Smith, Elder, 1867).
Astor, John Jacob. *A Journey in Other Worlds* (1896) (Lincoln, NE: University of Nebraska Press, 2003).
Auel, Jean. *The Clan of the Cave Bear* (New York: Crown, 1980).
Babbage, Charles, with John Herschel. *Memoirs of the Analytical Society* (Cambridge: Deighton & Sons, 1813).

The Ninth Bridgewater Treatise: A Fragment, ed. Martin Campbell-Kelly (1837) (London: Pickering & Chatto, 1989).
Bagehot, Walter. *Physics and Politics* (1872) (New York: D. Appleton, 1873).
Ballantyne, R. M. *Erling the Bold* (London: Nisbet, 1869).
Norsemen in the West (London: Nisbet, 1872).
Barnes, William. 'A Dissertation on the Dorsetshire Dialect', *Poems of Rural Life in the Dorsetshire Dialect* (London: John Russell Smith, 1844), pp. 3–37.
Bell, Charles. *Anatomy and Philosophy of Expression* (1824), 3rd edn (London: John Murray, 1844).
Bellamy, Edward. *The Religion of Solidarity* (1874) (Santa Barbara, CA: Concord Grove Press, 1984).
'To Whom this May Come' (1889), *The Blindman's World and Other Stories* (New York: Houghton, 1898), pp. 389–414.
Berthet, Élie. *The Pre-Historic World* (1876), trans. Mary J. Safford (Philadelphia: Porter & Coates, 1879).
Boole, George. *Studies in Logic and Probability* (La Salle, IL: Open Court, 1952).
Bosworth, Joseph. *A Compendius Anglo-Saxon and English Dictionary* (London: J. R. Smith, 1848).
Bray, Charles. *On Force, its Mental and Moral Correlates* (London: Longmans, 1866).
Brooks, Byron A. *Earth Revisited* (Boston, MA: Arena, 1893).
Brown, Colin. *Music in Speech and Speech in Music: Two Lectures* (Glasgow: Bryce & Sons, 1870).
Buckle, Henry Thomas. *A History of Civilisation in England* (1857), 3 vols. (London: Longmans, 1867).
Bulwer-Lytton, Edward. *The Coming Race* (London: Blackwood, 1871).
Bunsen, Chevalier. *Outlines of the Philosophy of Universal History, Applied to Language and Religion* (London: Longmans, 1854).
Butler, Samuel. *Erewhon: or, Over the Range* (1872) (New York: Dutton, 1917).
Evolution, Old and New (London: Hardwicke & Bogue, 1879).
The Family Letters of Samuel Butler: 1841–1886, ed. Arnold Silver (London: Jonathan Cape, 1962).
'How to Make the Best of Life' (1895), *Essays on Life, Art and Science* (London: Fifield, 1908), pp. 69–86.
Life and Habit (1878), revised edn (New York: Dutton, 1911).
Luck or Cunning? (1886) (London: Jonathan Cape, 1922).
'Thought and Language' (1890), *Essays on Life, Art and Science* (London: Fifield, 1908), pp. 176–233.
Unconscious Memory (1880) (London: Fifield, 1910).
The Way of all Flesh (1903) (London: Fifield, 1908).
Carlyle, Thomas. *Past and Present* (1843) (London: Chapman & Hall, 1897).
Chambers, Robert. *Vestiges of the Natural History of Creation and Other Evolutionary Writings* (1844), ed. James Secord (University of Chicago Press, 1994).

'A Chat with the Author of Tess', *Black and White*, 4 (1892), 238–40.
Chesney, George. *The Battle of Dorking* (1871) (London: Grant Richards, 1914).
Childers, Erskine. *The Riddle of the Sands* (1903) (New York: Dodd, Mead, 1915).
Clodd, Edward. *The Story of 'Primitive' Man* (1895) (London: Newnes, 1909).
Comte, Auguste. *The Positive Philosophy of Auguste Comte*, trans. and ed. Harriet Martineau, 2 vols. (London: G. Bell & Sons, 1875).
Darwin, Charles. 'A Biographical Sketch of an Infant', *Mind*, 2:7 (1877), 285–94.
  The Descent of Man, 2 vols. (London: John Murray, 1871).
  The Expression of the Emotions in Man and Animals (London: John Murray, 1872).
  On the Origin of Species by Means of Natural Selection (London: John Murray, 1859).
  The Variation of Animals and Plants under Domestication, 2 vols. (London: John Murray, 1868).
Donaldson, J. W. *The New Cratylus* (1837), 2nd edn (London: John W. Parker, 1850).
Drummond, Henry. *The Ascent of Man* (1894) (New York: Cosimo, 2007).
Drysdale, George. *The Elements of Social Science* (1855), 3rd edn (London: E. Truelove, 1886).
Du Chaillu, Paul. *Ivar the Viking* (London: John Murray, 1893).
Edwards, Henry Sutherland. *The Germans in France: Notes on the Method and Conduct of the Invasion, the Relations between Invaders and Invaded, and the Modern Usages of War* (London: Stanford, 1874).
Eliot, T. S. 'Little Gidding' (1942), *Four Quartets, Collected Poems, 1909–1962* (New York: Harcourt Brace Jovanovich, 1970), p. 203.
  'The Music of Poetry' (1942), *On Poetry and Poets* (London: Faber, 1957), pp. 17–32.
Ellis, Havelock. 'A Note on Paul Bourget' (1889), *Views and Reviews: A Selection of Uncollected Articles 1884–1932* (North Stratford, NH: Ayer, 1932), pp. 48–60.
Erdmann, Karl Otto. *Die Bedeutung des Wortes* (Leipzig: Avenarius, 1900).
Evans, E. P. *Evolutional Ethics and Animal Psychology* (New York: D. Appleton, 1897).
Farrar, F. W. *An Essay on the Origin of Language* (London: John Murray, 1860).
Festing Jones, Henry. *The Notebooks of Samuel Butler* (1912) (New York: Dutton, 1917).
  Samuel Butler, Author of Erewhon (1835–1902): A Memoir, 2 vols. (London: Macmillan, 1919).
Foster, Michael. 'An Address on the Organisation of Science', *British Medical Journal* (7 April 1894), 727–28.
Fourier, Charles. *The Passions of the Human Soul*, trans. Hugh Doherty, 2 vols. (London: Hugh Doherty, 1851).
Frazer, J. G. *The Scope of Social Anthropology* (London: Macmillan, 1908).
Freeman, E. A. *The History of the Norman Conquest of England*, 6 vols. (New York: Macmillan, 1873).
Freud, Sigmund. *The Psychopathology of Everyday Life* (1901), trans. A. A. Brill (New York: Macmillan, 1914).

Galton, Francis. 'Intelligible Signals between Neighbouring Stars', *Fortnightly Review*, 60 (1896), 657–64.
'Sun Signals to Mars', *The Times* (6 August 1892), 7.
Garner, R. L. 'Monkey Prosperity', *Windsor Magazine*, 20:3 (August 1904), 341–45.
'The Simian Tongue' (1891–2), *The Origin of Language*, ed. Roy Harris (Bristol: Thoemmes Press, 1996), pp. 314–35.
Golding, William. *The Inheritors* (1955) (London: Faber & Faber, 1997).
Green, John Richard. *A Short History of the English People* (London: Macmillan, 1874).
Grimm, Jakob. *Über den Ursprung der Sprache* (Berlin: Ferdinand, 1852).
Gruen, Sara. *Ape House* (New York: Spiegel & Grau, 2010).
Gurney, Edmund. 'The Problems of Hypnotism', *Mind*, 9:36 (1884), 477–508.
Haggard, Henry Rider. *Allan Quatermain* (Chicago, IL: W. B. Conkey, 1887).
The Days of my Life: An Autobiography (1926) (Fairford, Gloucester: Echo Library, 2006).
King Solomon's Mines (1885) (London: Cassell, 1907).
Nada the Lily (1892) (London: Longmans, 1895).
Haines, C. R. 'The Universal Language', *Macmillan's Magazine*, 65 (March 1892), 372–75.
Hale, Benjamin. *The Evolution of Bruno Littlemore* (New York: Twelve, 2011).
Hardy, Florence Emily. *The Later Years of Thomas Hardy 1892–1928* (New York: Macmillan, 1930).
Hardy, Thomas. 'A Changed Man' (1900), *A Changed Man, The Waiting Supper and Other Tales* (New York: Harper & Bros., 1913), pp. 1–24.
The Collected Letters of Thomas Hardy, 7 vols., ed. Richard Little Purdy and Michael Millgate (Oxford University Press 1988).
Desperate Remedies (1871) (New York: Harper & Bros., 1905).
'The Distracted Preacher' (1879), *Wessex Tales*, ed. Kathryn. R. King (Oxford University Press, 1991), pp. 167–223.
Far from the Madding Crowd (1874) (New York: Harper & Bros., 1895).
'The Fiddler of the Reels' (1893), *Life's Little Ironies* (New York: Harper & Bros., 1894), pp. 152–74.
The Hand of Ethelberta (1876) (New York: Harper & Bros., 1896).
'An Imaginative Woman' (1894), *Wessex Tales* (London: Macmillan, 1917), pp. 1–32.
Jude the Obscure (New York: Harper & Bros., 1895).
A Laodicean (1881) (London: Macmillan, 1912).
The Life and Work of Thomas Hardy, ed. Michael Millgate (London: Macmillan, 1984).
'The Melancholy Hussar of the German Legion' (1890), *Wessex Tales*, ed. Kathryn. R. King (Oxford University Press, 1991), pp. 39–56.
Preface to William Barnes, *Select Poems of William Barnes* (London: H. Frowde, 1908), pp. iii–xii.
The Return of the Native (1878) (New York: Charles Scribner's Sons, 1917).

Tess of the d'Urbervilles (London: Harper & Bros., 1893).
Thomas Hardy's Personal Writings (London: Palgrave Macmillan, 1981).
'A Tradition of Eighteen Hundred and Four' (1882), *Wessex Tales*, ed. Kathryn. R. King (Oxford University Press, 1991), pp. 32–38.
The Trumpet-Major (1884) (New York: Harper & Bros., 1894).
Under the Greenwood Tree, 2 vols. (London: Tinsley Bros., 1872), revised edn (London: Harper & Bros., 1898).
The Well-Beloved (London: Osgood, 1897).
'On the Western Circuit' (1891), *Life's Little Ironies* (London: Osgood, 1894), pp. 76–106.
'The Withered Arm' (1888), *Wessex Tales*, ed. Kathryn R. King (Oxford University Press, 1991), pp. 57–85.
Hartmann, Eduard von. *The Philosophy of the Unconscious* (1868), trans. William Chatterton Coupland (London: Kegan Paul, 1931).
Hegel, G. W. F. *The Phenomenology of Spirit* (1807), trans. A. V. Miller (Oxford University Press, 1977).
Herder, Johan Gottfried. *On the Origin of Language* (1772), *On the Origin of Language: Two Essays by Jean-Jacques Rousseau and Johan Gottfried Herder*, trans. John H. Moran, Alexander Gode (New York: Frederick Ungar, 1966), pp. 89–177.
Hodgetts, J. F. *The Champion of Odin* (London: Cassell, 1885).
The English in the Middle Ages (London: Whiting, 1885).
Horne Tooke, John. *The Diversions of Purley; Part One* (1786), 2nd edn (London: J. Johnson, 1798).
Humboldt, Wilhelm von. *On Language: On the Diversity of Human Language Construction and its Influence on the Mental Development of the Human Species* (1836), ed. Michael Losonsky, trans. Peter Heath (Cambridge University Press, 1988).
Hunt, James. *The Negro's Place in Nature* (New York: Van Evrie, 1864).
Huxley, Aldous. *Brave New World* (1932) (New York: HarperCollins, 1998).
Huxley, Thomas Henry. *Evolution and Ethics* (London: Macmillan, 1893).
'The Evolution of Theology: An Anthropological Study, II', *Nineteenth Century*, 19:101 (April 1886), 485–506.
'On the Hypothesis that Animals are Automata and its History' (1874), *Method and Results: Essays* (London: Macmillan, 1894), pp. 199–250.
Man's Place in Nature (New York: D. Appleton, 1863).
James, William. 'Humanism and Truth', *Mind*, 13:52 (1904), 457–75.
Pragmatism (London: Longmans, Green, 1907).
The Principles of Psychology, 2 vols. (New York: Henry Holt, 1890).
Jefferies, Richard. 'Nature and Books' (1887), *A Century of Early Ecocriticism*, ed. David Mazel (Athens, GA: University of Georgia Press, 2001), pp. 70–77.
Jesperson, Otto. *Efficiency in Linguistic Change* (Copenhagen: Munksgaard, 1941).
Progress in Language: With Special Reference to English (London: Swan Sonnenschein, 1894).
Joyce, James. *Letters of James Joyce*, ed. Stuart Gilbert, 3 vols. (New York: Viking Press, 1957).

Kidd, Benjamin. *Social Evolution* (1894) (London: Macmillan, 1895).
Kingsley, Charles. *Alton Locke* (1850) (New York: Co-operative Publication Society, 1898).
'On English Composition', *Introductory Lectures Delivered at Queens College, London* (London: Parker, 1849), pp. 28–42.
Hereward the Wake (1865) (London: Macmillan, 1910).
Westward Ho! (1855) (London: Nisbet, 1890).
Kurtén, Björn. *Dance of the Tiger: A Novel of the Ice Age* (1980) (Berkeley, CA: University of California Press, 1995).
Lang, Andrew. *Custom and Myth* (London: Longmans, 1884).
'Primitive Belief and Savage Metaphysics, *Fraser's Magazine*, 630 (June 1882), 734–44.
Lankester, Edwin Ray. *Degeneration: A Chapter in Darwinism* (London: Macmillan, 1880).
Latham, R. G. *Elements of Comparative Philology* (London: Walter & Maberly, 1862).
Lazarus, Moritz, and Heymann Steinthal. 'Einleitende Gedanken über Völkerpsychologie', *Zeitschrift für Völkerpsychologie und Sprachwissenschaft, I* (Berlin: Dümmler, 1860), 1–73.
Le Bon, Gustave. *The Crowd: A Study of the Popular Mind* (London: E. Benn, 1896).
Lewes, G. H. *The Physiology of Common Life*, 2 vols. (London: Blackwood, 1860).
Problems of Life and Mind, 2 vols. (London: Trübner, 1879).
Locke, John. *An Essay Concerning Human Understanding* (1689), ed. Kenneth P. Winkler, 2 vols. (Indianapolis, IN: Hackett, 1996).
Lombroso, Cesare. *The Man of Genius* (1889) (London: Walter Scott, 1891).
London, Jack. *Before Adam* (1907) (New York: McKinlay, 1917).
The Iron Heel (London: Everett, 1908).
'The Leopard Man's Story', *Windsor Magazine*, 19:4 (March 1904), 489–91.
The Letters of Jack London, ed. Earle Labor, Robert C. Leitz III and I. Milo Shepard (Palo Alto, CA: Stanford University Press, 1988).
Martin Eden (New York: Macmillan, 1908).
The Scarlet Plague (1912) (New York: Macmillan, 1915).
'When the World was Young' (1910), *The Night-born* (New York: Grosset & Dunlap, 1913), pp. 65–98.
Lorenz, Richard, 'The Relationship of the International Language to Science', *International Language and Science*, ed. L. Couturat *et al.*, trans. F. G. Donnan (London: Constable, 1910), pp. 53–60.
Lubbock, John. *Prehistoric Times, As Illustrated by Ancient Remains, and the Manners and Customs of Modern Savages* (1865) 5th edn (London: Williams & Norgate, 1890).
'Teaching Animals to Converse', *Nature*, 29 (10 April 1884), 547–48.
Mackay, Charles, 'English Slang and French Argot: Fashionable and Unfashionable', *Blackwood's*, 143 (May 1888), 690–704.
Macnie, John. *The Diothas, or A Far Look Ahead* (1883) (London: Putnam, 1890).

Marsh, G. P. *Lectures on the English Language* (London: Sampson Low, 1860).
McAdam, Colin. *A Beautiful Truth* (New York: Soho Press, 2013).
McLennan, J. M. *Primitive Marriage* (Edinburgh: Black, 1865).
Meredith, Dennis. *Solomon's Freedom* (Purlear, NC: Glyphus, 2014).
Mill, John Stuart. *On Liberty* (1859), 2nd edn (London: Longmans, 1864).
  A System of Logic (1843), 8th edn (New York: Harper & Bros., 1882).
Miller, Walter Jr. *A Canticle for Leibowitz* (1959) (New York: Bantam Dell, 2007).
Moreas, Jean. 'A Literary Manifesto – Symbolism' (1886), ed. Henry Dorra, *Symbolist Art Theories: A Critical Anthology* (Berkeley, CA: University of California Press, 1995), pp. 150–52.
Morgan, C. Lloyd. *Habit and Instinct* (New York: Arno Press, 1896).
Morgan, L. H. *Ancient Society* (New York: Henry Holt, 1877).
Morris, William. *Collected Letters*, ed. Norman Kelvin, 4 vols. (Princeton University Press, 1987).
  A Dream of John Ball (1886–87) (London: Reeves & Turner, 1888).
  'The Manifesto of the Socialist League', *The Commonweal* (February 1885), 1–2.
  News from Nowhere (Boston, MA: Roberts Bros., 1890).
  'At a Picture Show' (1884), *William Morris: Artist, Writer, Socialist*, ed. May Morris, 2 vols. (Oxford: Basil Blackwell, 1936), pp. 382–409.
  'The Present Outlook in Politics' (1887), *The Unpublished Lectures of William Morris*, ed. Eugene LeMire (Detroit, MI: Wayne State University Press 1969), pp. 199–216.
  'The Society of the Future' (1887), *News from Nowhere and Selected Writings and Designs*, ed. Asa Briggs (Harmondsworth: Penguin, 1962), pp. 188–203.
  The Water of the Wondrous Isles (London: Longmans, 1896).
  The Well at the World's End (London: Longmans, 1896).
Müller, Friedrich Max. *Lectures on the Science of Language*, 2 vols. (1861–63) (London: Longmans, 1866).
  'Preface', in Charles Kingsley, *The Roman and the Teuton* (1864) (London: Macmillan, 1913), pp. v–xxix.
  Three Lectures on the Science of Language (Chicago, IL: Open Court, 1889).
Nietzsche, Friedrich. 'On Truth and Falsity in their Extramoral Sense' (1873), *Philosophical Writings*, ed. Reinhold Grimm and Caroline Molina y Vedia (New York: Continuum, 1997), pp. 87–102.
Nordau, Max. *Degeneration* (1895) (London: Heinemann, 1898).
Orwell, George. *Nineteen Eighty-four* (1949) (New York: Knopf, 1992).
  'Politics and the English Language' (1946), *The English Language*, 2 vols., vol. II, *Essays by Linguists and Men of Letters*, ed. W. F. Bolton and D. Crystal (Cambridge University Press, 1969), pp. 217–28.
Pearson, Karl. *The Grammar of Science* (1892), 2nd edn (London: Black, 1900).
Pitman, Isaac. *A Manual of Phonography; or, Writing by Sound* (London: Samuel Bagster & Sons, 1845).
Porter, Mary Blackwood. *Annals of a Publishing House: William Blackwood and his Sons*, 3 vols. (Edinburgh: Blackwood & Sons, 1898).

Prichard, James Cowles. *Researches into the Physical History of Man* (London: John & Arthur Arch, 1813).
'Primitive Language', *Cornhill Magazine*, 8:44 (1863), 197–202.
Reade, A. A. *Study and Stimulants* (Manchester: Heywood, 1883).
Reeve, Henry. 'The Literature and Language of the Age', *Edinburgh Review* (April 1889), 328–50.
Richards, Grant. 'Mr. Grant Allen and his Work', *Novel Review* (1 June 1892), 261–68.
Romanes, George. *Mental Evolution in Man: Origin of a Human Faculty* (London: Kegan Paul, 1888).
Rousseau, Jean-Jacques. *Essay on the Origin of Language* (1781), *On the Origin of Language: Two Essays by Jean-Jacques Rousseau and Johan Gottfried Herder*, trans. John H. Moran, Alexander Gode (New York: Frederick Ungar, 1966), pp. 5–88.
Saintsbury, George. *A History of English Prosody from the Twelfth Century to the Present Day*, 3 vols. (London: Macmillan, 1910).
'Saki' (H. H. Munro). *When William Came: A Story of London under the Hohenzollerns* (1913) (London: John Lane, 1914).
Sapir, Edward. 'The Status of Linguistics as a Science', *Language*, 5:4 (1929), 207–14.
Sayce, A. H. *An Introduction to the Science of Language*, 2 vols. (1879), 4th edn (London: Kegan Paul, 1900).
The Principles of Comparative Philology (London: Trübner, 1874).
Schleicher, August. 'Darwinism Tested by the Science of Language' (1865), trans. Alex V. W. Bikkers, *Linguistics and Evolutionary Theory: Three Essays by August Schleicher, Ernst Haeckel and Wilhelm Bleek*, ed. Konrad Koerner (Amsterdam: John Benjamins, 1983), pp. 1–75.
'Eine Fabel in Indogermanischer Ursprache', *Beiträge zur vergleichenden Sprachforschung*, 5 (1868), 206–08.
Schopenhauer, Arthur. *The World as Will and Idea* (1819), trans. Eric F. J. Payne (London: Phoenix, 1995).
Scott, William. *The Deaf and Dumb: Their Position in Society, and the Principles of their Education Considered* (London: Joseph Graham, 1844).
Scripture, E. W. *Elements of Experimental Phonetics* (New York: Scribner, 1902).
Spencer, Herbert. *An Autobiography*, 2 vols. (London: Williams & Norgate, 1904).
'The Genesis of Science' (1854), *Essays: Scientific, Political and Speculative*, 3 vols. (London: Williams & Norgate, 1891), II, pp. 1–73.
First Principles (1862), 3rd edn (London: Williams & Norgate, 1870).
'On the Origin and Function of Music' (1857), *Essays: Scientific, Political and Speculative*, 3 vols. (London: Williams & Norgate, 1891), II, pp. 400–51.
The Philosophy of Style (1852) (New York: D. Appleton, 1884).
The Principles of Psychology (London: Longmans, 1855), 2nd edn, 2 vols. (London: Williams & Norgate, 1870).
The Principles of Sociology, 2 vols. (1875), enlarged edn (New York: D. Appleton, 1895).

'What Knowledge is of Most Worth?' (1859), *Essays on Education and Kindred Subjects* (London: J. M. Dent, 1911).
Stein, Gertrude. *Geography and Plays* (Boston: Four Seas, 1922).
Stephens, George. '"English" or "Anglo-Saxon"', *Gentleman's Magazine*, 36 (1852), 472–76.
Strettell, A. B. 'On the English Language and Grammar', in Charles Kingsley, *Introductory Lectures Delivered at Queens College, London* (London: Parker, 1849), pp. 154–81.
Stewart, George R. *Earth Abides* (1949) (Boston, MA: Houghton Mifflin Harcourt, 1976).
Stout, George Frederick. 'Thought and Language', *Mind*, 16:62 (1891), 181–97.
Sweet, Henry. *A Handbook of Phonetics* (Oxford: Clarendon Press, 1877).
Taine, Hippolyte. 'On the Acquisition of Language by Children', *Mind*, 2:6 (1877), 252–59.
Tolkein, J. R. R. *The Lord of the Rings*, 3 vols. (1954–55) (London: Allen & Unwin, 1960).
— *The Monsters and the Critics and Other Essays*, ed. Christopher Tolkien (London: Allen & Unwin, 1983).
Trench, Richard Chenevix. *English Past and Present* (New York: Red Field, 1855).
Trench, Richard Chenevix. *On the Study of Words* (1851), ed. Roy Harris (London: Routledge, 1994).
Trumbull, John. 'The Prophecy of Balaam' (1773), *The Poetical Works of John Trumbull*, 2 vols. (Hartford, CT: Goodrich, 1820), II, pp. 141–46.
Tylor, E. B. *Anthropology* (London: Macmillan, 1881).
— 'On the Origin of Language', *Fortnightly Review*, 4 (April 1866), 544–59.
— *Primitive Culture*, 2 vols. (London: John Murray, 1871).
Waterloo, Stanley. *The Story of Ab: A Tale of the Time of the Caveman* (Chicago, IL: Way & Williams, 1897).
Wedgwood, Hensleigh. *On The Origin of Language* (London: Trübner, 1866).
Weil, Samuel. *The Religion of the Future; or Outlines of Spiritual Philosophy* (Boston, MA: Arnea, 1893).
Welby, Lady Victoria. *The Witness of Science to Linguistic Anarchy* (Grantham: W. Clarke, 1898).
Wells, H. G. *Ann Veronica* (London: T. Fisher Unwin, 1909).
— *Anticipations of the Reaction of Mechanical and Scientific Progress upon Human Life and Thought* (1901) (London: Harper & Bros., 1902).
— 'The Book of Curses', *Certain Personal Matters* (London: Lawrence Bullen, 1898), pp. 126–32.
— 'Of Conversation', *Certain Personal Matters* (London: Lawrence Bullen, 1898), pp. 34–41.
— *The Correspondence of H. G. Wells*, ed. David C. Smith, 4 vols. (London: Pickering & Chatto, 1998).
— *An Englishman Looks at the World* (London: Cassell, 1914).
— *An Experiment in Autobiography: Discoveries and Conclusions of a Very Ordinary Brain (Since 1866)* (London: Cresset Press, 1934).

First and Last Things (London: G. P. Putnam, 1908).
The First Men in the Moon (London: G. Newnes, 1901).
The Food of the Gods (1904) London: Nelson, 1909).
'For Freedom in Spelling', *Certain Personal Matters* (London: Lawrence Bullen, 1898), pp. 145–54
God the Invisible King (New York: Macmillan, 1917).
H. G. Wells in Love: Postscript to an Experiment in Autobiography, ed. G. P. Wells (London: Little, Brown, 1984).
The History of Mr Polly (New York: Grosset & Dunlap, 1909).
'Human Evolution: An Artificial Process' (1896), *H. G. Wells: Early Writings in Science and Science Fiction*, ed. Robert M. Philmus and David Y. Hughes (Berkeley, CA: University of California Press, 1975),pp. 211–19.
'Intelligence on Mars' (1896), *H. G. Wells: Early Writings in Science and Science Fiction*, ed. Robert M. Philmus and David Y. Hughes (Berkeley, CA: University of California Press, 1975),pp. 175–78.
The Island of Dr Moreau (New York: Stone & Kimball, 1896).
'James Joyce', *Nation* (24 February 1917), 710.
Kipps (New York: Charles Scribner's Sons, 1905).
'The Limits of Individual Plasticity' (1895), *H. G. Wells: Early Writings in Science and Science Fiction*, ed. Robert M. Philmus and David Y. Hughes (Berkeley, CA: University of California Press, 1975), pp. 36–39.
Mankind in the Making (London: Chapman & Hall, 1903).
A Modern Utopia (London: Chapman & Hall,, 1905).
'Morals and Civilisation' (1897), *H. G. Wells: Early Writings in Science and Science Fiction*, ed. Robert M. Philmus and David Y. Hughes (Berkeley, CA: University of California Press, 1975), pp. 220–28.
'The New Optimism', *Pall Mall Gazette*, 58 (21 May, 1894), 4.
'Peculiarities of Psychical Research', *Nature*, 51 (January 1895), 274.
'The Pleasure of Quarrelling', *Certain Personal Matters* (London: Lawrence Bullen, 1898), pp. 246–53.
'Popularizing Science', *Nature*, 50 (July 1894), 300–01.
'The Rediscovery of the Unique', *Fortnightly Review*, 50 (July 1891), 106–11.
'Scepticism of the Instrument' (1903), *A Modern Utopia* (London: C. Scribner & Sons, 1905), pp. 375–93.
'Science, in School and after School', *Nature* 50 (September 1894), 525–56.
The Shape of Things to Come, 2 vols. (1932) (London: Macmillan, 1933).
'A Story of the Days to Come' (1897), *Tales of Space and Time* (London: Harper, 1900), pp. 165–324.
'A Story of the Stone Age' (1897), *Tales of Space and Time* (London: Harper, 1900), pp. 59–164.
A Text-Book of Biology, 2 vols. (London: Clive, 1893).
The Time Machine (New York: Henry Holt, 1895).
The War of the Worlds (London: Heinemann, 1898).
Tono-Bungay (London: Macmillan: 1909).
The War in the Air (1908) (Harmondsworth: Penguin, 2005).

When the Sleeper Wakes (London: Harper & Bros., 1899).
World Brain (London: Meuthuen, 1938).
The World Set Free (London: Macmillan, 1914).
Whewell, William. *The Philosophy of the Inductive Sciences, Founded upon their History*, 2 vols. (London: John W. Parker, 1840).
Whitney, William Dwight. *The Life and Growth of Language* (New York: D. Appleton, 1875).
Winwood Reade, William. *Savage Africa* (New York: Harper & Bros., 1864).
Wodehouse, P. G. *The Swoop! or, How Clarence Saved England* (1909) (Rockville, MD: Arc Manor, 2008).
Zola, Émile. *The Experimental Novel and Other Essays* (New York: Cassell, 1893).
Zamenhof, L. L. 'The Making of an International Language' (1887), *Esperanto (The Universal Language): The Student's Complete Text Book*, ed. John Charles O'Connor (London: Fleming H. Revell, 1903), pp. 7–20.

SECONDARY TEXTS

Aarsleff, Hans. *The Study of Language in England, 1760–1860* (1967), 2nd edn (Princeton University Press, 1983).
Abberley, Will. '"His Father's Voice": Phonographs and Heredity in the Fiction of Samuel Butler', *19: Interdisciplinary Studies in the Long Nineteenth Century*, 18 (2014). www.19.bbk.ac.uk/index.php/19/article/viewFile/680/964
Abrams, Lynn. *Bismarck and the German Empire* (London: Routledge, 1995).
Alter, Stephen G. *Darwinism and the Linguistic Image: Language, Race, and Natural Theology in the Nineteenth Century* (Baltimore, MD: Johns Hopkins University Press, 1999).
William Dwight Whitney and the Science of Language (Baltimore, MD: Johns Hopkins University Press, 2005).
Amigoni, David. 'Charles Darwin's Centenary and the Politics and Poetics of Parenting: Inheritance, Variation, and the Aesthetic Legacy of Samuel Butler', *The Evolution of Literature: Legacies of Darwin in European Cultures*, ed. Nicholas Saul and James J. Simon (Amsterdam: Rodopi, 2011), pp. 73–86.
Colonies, Cults and Evolution: Literature, Science and Culture in Nineteenth-Century Writing (Cambridge University Press, 2007).
'"The written symbol extends infinitely": Samuel Butler and the Writing of Evolutionary Theory', *Samuel Butler, Victorian against the Grain: A Critical Overview*, ed. James G. Paradis (University of Toronto Press, 2007), pp. 91–112.
Anderson, Benedict. *Imagined Communities: Reflections on the Origin and Spread of Nationalism* (1983), 2nd edn (London: Verso, 2006).
Ardis, Ann. *New Women, New Novels: Feminism and Early Modernism* (New Brunswick, NJ: Rutgers University Press, 1990).
Armstrong, Tim. 'Hardy, History and Recorded Music', *Thomas Hardy and Contemporary Literary Studies*, ed. Tim Dolin and Peter Widdowson (Basingstoke: Palgrave 2004), pp. 153–66.

Asquith, Mark. *Thomas Hardy, Metaphysics and Music* (Basingstoke: Palgrave, 2005).
Bailey, Richard W. *Images of English* (Cambridge University Press, 1991).
  Nineteenth-Century English (Ann Arbor, MI: University of Michigan Press, 1996).
Barbieri, Marcello (ed.). 'The Challenge of Biosemiotics', *Introduction to Biosemiotics: the New Biological Synthesis* (Dordrecht: Springer, 2008), pp. ix–xii.
Barczewski, Stephanie L. *Myth and National Identity in Nineteenth-Century Britain* (Oxford University Press, 2000).
Barthes, Roland. *Mythologies* (1957), trans. Brian Trench (London: Paladin, 1973).
Bate, Jonathan. 'Culture and Environment from Austen to Hardy', *New Literary History*, 30:3 (1999), 541–60.
Baynton, Douglas C. *Forbidden Signs: American Culture and the Campaign Against Sign Language* (University of Chicago Press, 1996).
Bazerman, Charles. *Shaping Written Knowledge: The Genre and Activity of the Experimental Article in Science* (Madison, WI: University of Wisconsin Press, 1988).
Beaumont, Matthew. *Utopia Ltd: Ideologies of Social Dreaming in England 1870–1900* (Chicago, IL: Haymarket, 2009).
Beer, Gillian. 'Butler, Memory and the Future', *Samuel Butler, Victorian against the Grain: A Critical Overview*, ed. James G. Paradis (University of Toronto Press, 2007), pp. 45–57.
  Darwin's Plots: Evolutionary Narrative in Darwin, George Eliot and Nineteenth-Century Fiction (1983), 3rd edn (Cambridge University Press, 2009).
  Open Fields: Science in Cultural Encounter (Oxford University Press, 1996).
Berkove, Lawrence I. 'Jack London and Evolution: From Spencer to Huxley', *American Literary Realism*, 36:3 (2004), 243–55.
Berliner, Jonathan. 'Jack London's Socialistic Social Darwinism', *American Literary Realism*, 41:1 (2008), 52–78.
Bex, Tony, and Richard Watts (eds.). *Standard English: The Widening Debate* (London: Routledge, 1999).
Bickerton, Derek. *Language and Species* (University of Chicago Press, 1990).
Bowler, Peter J. *The Invention of Progress: Victorians and the Past* (Oxford University Press, 1989).
Brantlinger, Patrick. *Dark Vanishings: Discourse on the Extinction of Primitive Races 1830–1930* (Ithaca, NY: Cornell University Press, 2003).
  'Eating Tongues: Australian Colonial Literature and "the Great Silence"', *Yearbook of English Studies*, 41:2 (2011), 125–39.
  The Reading Lesson: The Threat of Mass Literacy in Nineteenth-Century British Fiction (Bloomington, IN: Indiana University Press, 1998).
  Taming Cannibals: Race and the Victorians (Ithaca, NY: Cornell University Press, 2011).
Brutt-Griffler, Janina. *World English: A Study of its Development* (Clevedon: Multilingual Matters Press, 2002).

Burgoyne, Bernard. *Drawing the Soul: Schemas and Models in Psychoanalysis* (London: Rebus, 2000).
Burrow, J. W. 'The Uses of Philology in Victorian England', *Ideas and Institutions of Victorian Britain: Essays in Honour of George Kitson Clarke*, ed. Robert Robson (London: G. Bell & Sons, 1967), pp. 180–204.
Carey, James 'Technology and Ideology: The Case of the Telegraph', *Prospects*, 8 (October 1983), 303–25.
Caufield, James Walter. *Overcoming Matthew Arnold: Ethics in Culture and Criticism* (Aldershot: Ashgate, 2012).
Chandler, Alice. *A Dream of Order: The Medieval Ideal in Nineteenth-Century Literature* (Lincoln, NA: University of Nebraska Press, 1971).
Chomsky, Noam. *Aspects of the Theory of Syntax* (Cambridge, MA: MIT Press, 1965).
Clarke, I. F. 'The Battle of Dorking, 1871–1914', *Victorian Studies*, 8:4 (1965), 308–28.
  The Great War with Germany, 1890–1914: Fictions and Fantasies of the War to Come (Liverpool University Press, 1997).
Clifford, James. 'On Ethnographic Allegory', *Writing Culture: The Poetics and Politics of Ethnography*, ed. James Clifford and George E. Marcus (Berkeley, CA: University of California Press, 1986), pp. 98–121.
Connor, Steven. *Dumbstruck: A Cultural History of Ventriloquism* (Oxford University Press, 2000).
Crosland, Maurice P. *The Language of Science: From the Vernacular to the Technical* (Cambridge: Lutterworth Press, 2006).
Crowe, Michael J. *The Extraterrestrial Life Debate 1750–1900* (New York: Dover, 1999).
Crowley, Tony. *The Politics of Discourse: The Standard Language Question in British Cultural Debates* (London: Macmillan, 1989).
Cunningham, Valentine. *The Victorians: An Anthology of Poetry and Poetics* (Oxford: Blackwell, 2002).
Curtis, Gerard. *Visual Words: Art and the Material Book in Victorian England* (Aldershot: Ashgate, 2002).
Curtis, L. P. *Anglo-Saxons and Celts: A Study of Anti-Irish Prejudice in Victorian England* (University of New York Press, 1968).
Daston, Lorraine. 'Scientific Objectivity with and without Words', *Little Tools of Knowledge: Historical Essays on Academic and Bureaucratic Practices* (Ann Arbor, MI: University of Michigan Press, 2000), pp. 259–84.
Daston, Lorraine, with Peter Galison. *Objectivity* (New York: Zone Books, 2007).
Deane, Bradley. 'Imperial Barbarians: Primitive Masculinity in Lost World Fiction', *Victorian Literature and Culture*, 36:1 (2008), 205–25.
Dediu, Dan, with Stephen C. Levinson. 'On the Antiquity of Language: The Reinterpretation of Neanderthal Linguistic Capacities and its Consequences', *Frontiers in Psychology*, 4:397 (July 2013). http://journal.frontiersin.org/Journal/10.3389/fpsyg.2013.00397/

Dellheim, Charles. *The Face of the Past: The Preservation of the Medieval Inheritance in Victorian England* (1982) (Cambridge University Press, 2004).

Dentith, Simon. '*Sigurd the Volsung*: Heroic Poetry in an Unheroic Age', *William Morris: Centenary Essays*, ed. Peter Faulkner and Peter Preston (University of Exeter Press, 1999), pp. 60–70.

De Paolo, Charles. 'Wells, Golding, and Auel: Representing the Neanderthal', *Science Fiction Studies*, 27:3 (2000), 418–38.

Derrida, Jacques. *Of Grammatology*, trans. Gayatri Chakravorty Spivak (1967) (Baltimore, MD: Johns Hopkins University Press, 1998).

Dixon, Thomas. *The Invention of Altruism: Making Moral Meanings in Victorian Britain* (Oxford University Press, 2008).

Dowling, Linda. *Language and Decadence in the Victorian Fin-de-Siècle* (Princeton University Press, 1986).

The Vulgarization of Art: The Victorians and Aesthetic Democracy (Charlottesville, VA: University Press of Virginia, 1996).

Dyson, G. B. *Darwin among the Machines: The Evolution of Global Intelligence* (Reading, MA: Perseus, 1997).

Ebbatson, Roger. *The Evolutionary Self: Hardy, Forster, Lawrence* (Brighton: Harvester, 1982).

Eco, Umberto. *The Search for the Perfect Language*, trans. James Fentress (London: Fontana, 1995).

Ekman, Paul. *Unmasking the Face: A Guide to Recognizing Emotions from Facial Cues* (Cambridge, MA: Malor, 2003).

Ellenberger, Henri F. *The Discovery of the Unconscious: The History and Evolution of Dynamic Psychiatry* (London: Fontana, 1994).

Errington, Joseph. *Linguistics in a Colonial World: A Story of Language, Meaning, and Power* (Oxford: Blackwell, 2008).

Esmail, Jennifer. *Reading Victorian Deafness: Signs and Sounds in Victorian Literature and Culture* (Athens, OH: Ohio University Press, 2013).

Faverty, Frederic E. *Matthew Arnold, the Ethnologist* (Evanston, IL: Northwestern University Press, 1951).

Ferguson, Christine. *Determined Spirits: Eugenics, Heredity and Racial Regeneration in Anglo-American Spiritualist Writing, 1848–1930* (Edinburgh University Press, 2012).

Language, Science and Popular Fiction in the Victorian Fin-de-Siècle: The Brutal Tongue (Aldershot: Ashgate, 2006).

Fielding, Penny. *Writing and Orality: Nationality, Culture and Nineteenth-Century Scottish Fiction* (Oxford: Clarendon Press, 1996).

Forsdyke, Donald. 'Samuel Butler and Human Long Term Memory: Is the Cupboard Bare?', *Journal of Theoretical Biology*, 258:1 (2009), 156–64.

Forster, Peter G. *The Esperanto Movement* (The Hague: Mouton, 1982).

Foucault, Michel. *The Order of Things: An Archaeology of the Human Sciences* (1966) (London: Routledge, 2001).

Francis, Mark. *Herbert Spencer and the Invention of Modern Life* (Stocksfield: Acumen, 2007).

Frantzen, Allen J. *Desire for Origins: New Language, Old English and Teaching the Tradition* (New Brunswick, NJ: Rutgers University Press, 1990).
Gagnier, Regenia. *Individualism, Decadence and Globalization: On the Relationship of Part to Whole, 1859–1920* (Basingstoke: Palgrave Macmillan, 2010).
Gitelman, Lisa. *Scripts, Grooves and Writing Machines: Representing Technology in the Edison Era* (Stanford University Press, 1999).
Gold, Barri J. *ThermoPoetics: Energy in Victorian Literature and Science* (Cambridge, MA: MIT Press, 2010).
Greenslade, William. *Degeneration, Culture and the Novel* (Cambridge University Press, 1994).
Greenslade, William, and Terrence Rodgers (eds.). *Grant Allen: Literature and Cultural Politics at the Fin de Siècle* (Aldershot: Ashgate, 2005).
Griffiths, Eric. *The Printed Voice of Victorian Poetry* (Oxford University Press, 1989).
Gutierrez, Cathy. *Plato's Ghost: Spiritualism in the American Renaissance* (Oxford University Press, 2009).
Habermas, Jürgen. 'Towards a Theory of Communicative Competence', *Inquiry*, 13 (winter 1970), 360–75.
Hackert, Stephanie. *The Emergence of the English Native Speaker: A Chapter in Nineteenth-Century Linguistic Thought* (Berlin: De Gruyter Mouton, 2012).
Halliday, M. A. K. *The Language of Science* (London: Continuum, 2004).
Hannaford, Ivan. *Race: The History of an Idea in the West* (Baltimore, MD: Johns Hopkins University Press, 1996).
Hardy, Sylvia. 'H. G. Wells and Language', PhD thesis, University of Leicester, 1991.
Harris, Roy. *The Semantics of Science* (London: Continuum, 2005).
Hartley, Lucy. *Physiognomy and the Meaning of Expression in Nineteenth-Century Culture* (Cambridge University Press, 2001).
Henson, Hilary. *British Social Anthropologists and Language: A History of Separate Development* (Oxford University Press, 1974).
Herbert, Christopher. *Culture and Anomie: Ethnographic Imagination in the Nineteenth Century* (University of Chicago Press, 1991).
  Victorian Relativity: Radical Thought and Scientific Discovery (University of Chicago Press, 2001).
Herrick, James A. *Scientific Mythologies: How Science and Science Fiction Forge New Religious Beliefs* (Downers Grove, IL: Intervarsity Press, 2008).
Hildebrand, R. Jayne. '*News from Nowhere* and William Morris's Aesthetics of Unreflectiveness: Pleasurable Habits', *English Literature in Transition, 1880–1920*, 54:1 (2011), 3–27.
Hirstein, William. *Mindmelding: Consciousness, Neuroscience, and the Mind's Privacy* (Oxford University Press, 2012).
Hobaiter, Catherine, and Richard W. Byrne. 'The Gestural Repertoire of the Wild Chimpanzee', *Animal Cognition*, 14 (January 2011), 745–67.
Hobsbawm, Eric. *Nations and Nationalism since 1780: Programme, Myth, Reality* (Cambridge University Press, 1992).

Hughes, John. *Ecstatic Sounds: Music and Individuality in the Work of Thomas Hardy* (Aldershot: Ashgate, 2002).
Jack, Rachel E., with Oliver G. B. Garrod, Hui Yub, Roberto Caldarac and Philippe G. Schyns. 'Facial Expressions of Emotion are not Culturally Universal', *Proceedings of the National Academy of Sciences*, 109:19 (2012), 7241–44.
Jakobson, Roman. *Six Lectures on Sound and Meaning*, trans. John Mepham (Brighton: Harvester, 1978).
James, Simon J. *Maps of Utopia: H. G. Wells, Modernity and the End of Culture* (Oxford University Press, 2012).
Janton, Pierre. *Esperanto: Language, Literature and Community*, ed. and trans. Humphrey Tonkin, Jane Edwards and Karen Johnson-Weiner (Albany, NY: State University of New York Press, 1993).
Katz, Wendy R. *Rider Haggard and the Fiction of Empire* (Cambridge University Press, 1987).
Kennedy, James. *Herbert Spencer* (Boston, MA: Twayne, 1978).
Kittler, Friedrich. *Discourse Networks, 1800/1900* (1985), trans. Michael Metteer and Chris Cullens (Stanford University Press, 1990).
Kreilkamp, Ivan. *Voice and the Victorian Storyteller* (Cambridge University Press, 2005).
Kronegger, Maria Elisabeth. *Literary Impressionism* (Lanham, MD: Rowman & Littlefield, 1973).
Lane, George S. 'Changes of Emphasis in Linguistics with Particular Reference to Paul and Bloomfield', *Studies in Philology*, 42:3 (1945), 465–83.
Latour, Bruno. 'An Attempt at a "Compositionist Manifesto"', *New Literary History*, 41 (2010), 471–90.
  'Where Are the Missing Masses? The Sociology of a Few Mundane Artifacts', *Shaping Technology/Building Society. Studies in Sociotechnological Change*, ed. Wiebe Bijker and John Law (Cambridge, MA: MIT Press, 1992), pp. 225–58.
Lee, Louise. 'Voicing, De-voicing and Self-Silencing: Charles Kingsley's Stuttering Christian Manliness', *Journal of Victorian Culture*, 13:1 (2008), 1–17.
Levine, George. *Dying to Know: Scientific Epistemology and Narrative in Victorian England* (University of Chicago Press, 2002).
  The Realistic Imagination: English Fiction from Frankenstein to Lady Chatterly (University of Chicago Press, 1981).
Leys, Ruth. 'How Did Fear Become a Scientific Object and What Kind of Object is It?', *Representations*, 110:1 (2010), 66–104.
Lieberman, Philip. *Human Language and our Reptilian Brain: The Subcortical Bases of Speech, Syntax, and Thought* (Cambridge, MA: Harvard University Press, 2002).
Lipow, Arthur. *Authoritarian Socialism in America: Edward Bellamy and the Nationalist Movement* (Berkeley, CA: University of California Press, 1982).
Logan, Peter Melville. *Victorian Fetishism: Intellectuals and Primitives* (Albany, NY: State University of New York Press, 2009).

Luckhurst, Roger. *The Invention of Telepathy, 1870–1901* (Oxford University Press, 2002).
Lundquist, Barbara. 'Jack London, Aesthetic Theory and Nineteenth-Century Science', *Western American Literature*, 32 (1997), 99–114.
Mackail, J. W. *The Life of William Morris*, 2 vols. (London: Longmans, 1899).
Mackenzie, Norman and Jeanne. *The Life of H. G. Wells: The Time Traveller* (London: Hogarth, 1987).
Mclean, Steven. 'Animals, Language and Degeneration in H. G. Wells's *The Island of Doctor Moreau*', *H. G. Wells Interdisciplinary Essays*, ed. Steven Mclean (Newcastle: Cambridge Scholars, 2008), pp. 25–48.
Madsen, Axel. *John Jacob Astor: America's First Multimillionaire* (Hoboken, NJ: John Wiley, 2001).
Magnus, Margaret. 'What's in a Word? Studies in Phonosemantics', PhD thesis, Norwegian University of Science and Technology, 2001.
Mallett, Phillip. '"The Immortal Puzzle": Hardy and Sexuality', *Palgrave Advances in Thomas Hardy Studies*, ed. Phillip Mallett (Basingstoke: Palgrave, 2004), pp. 181–202.
Marsh, Jan. *Back to the Land: The Pastoral Impulse in Victorian England, 1880 to 1914* (London: Quartet, 1982).
Marsh, Joss. *Word Crimes: Blasphemy, Culture, and Literature in Nineteenth-Century England* (University of Chicago Press, 1998).
Martin, Meredith. *The Rise and Fall of Meter: Poetry and English National Culture, 1860–1930* (Princeton University Press, 2012)
  The Early Fiction of H. G. Wells: Fantasies of Science (Basingstoke: Palgrave Macmillan, 2009).
Menke, Richard. *Telegraphic Realism: Victorian Fiction and Other Information Systems* (Stanford University Press, 2008).
Meyers, Walter E. *Aliens and Linguists: Language Study and Science Fiction* (Athens, GA: University of Georgia Press, 1982).
Michael, Robert, and Karin Doerr. *Nazi-Deutsch/Nazi-German: An English Lexicon of the Language of the Third Reich* (London: Greenwood Press, 2002).
Moor, James (ed.). *The Turing Test: The Elusive Standard of Artificial Intelligence* (Dordrecht: Kluwer, 2003).
Morgan, Rosemary. *Women and Sexuality in the Novels of Thomas Hardy* (London: Routledge, 1988).
Morrisson, Mark. 'Performing the Pure Voice: Elocution, Verse Recitation, and Modernist Poetry in Prewar London', *Modernism/Modernity*, 3:3 (1996), 25–50.
Mugglestone, Lynda. *Talking Proper: The Rise of Accent as Social Symbol* (1995), 2nd edn (Oxford University Press, 2003).
Nie, Michael de. *The Eternal Paddy: Irish Identity and the British Press, 1798–1882* (Madison, WI: University of Wisconsin Press, 2004).
Nerlich, Brigitte. *Semantic Theories in Europe, 1830–1930: From Etymology to Contextuality* (Amsterdam: John Benjamins, 1992).
O'Connor, Laura. *Haunted English: The Celtic Fringe, the British Empire, and De-Anglicization* (Baltimore, MD: Johns Hopkins University Press, 2006).

Olender, Maurice. *The Languages of Paradise: Race, Religion and Philology in the Nineteenth Century* (1992), trans. Arthur Goldhammer (Cambridge, MA: Harvard University Press, 2008).
Ong, Walter. *Orality and Literacy: The Technologizing of the Word* (1982), ed. John Hartley (New York: Routledge, 2012).
Orban, Clara Elizabeth. *The Culture of Fragments: Words and Images in Futurism and Surrealism* (Amsterdam: Rodopi, 1997).
Otis, Laura. *Networking: Communicating with Bodies and Machines in the Nineteenth Century* (Ann Arbor, MI: University of Michigan Press, 2001).
  Organic Memory: History and the Body in the Late Nineteenth and Early Twentieth Centuries (Lincoln, NE: University of Nebraska Press, 1994).
Page, Norman. *Speech in the English Novel* (London: Macmillan, 1988).
  Thomas Hardy: The Writer and his Background (Southampton: Camelot Press, 1980).
Paradis, James G. (ed.). *Samuel Butler, Victorian against the Grain: A Critical Overview* (University of Toronto Press, 2007).
Parrinder, Patrick. 'From Eden to Oedipus: Darwin, Freud, and the Romance of the Stone Age', *Anglistik*, 15 (2004), 83–91.
  Shadows of the Future: H. G. Wells, Science Fiction and Prophecy (Syracuse University Press, 1995).
Partington, John S. *Building Cosmopolis: The Political Thought of H. G. Wells* (Aldershot: Ashgate, 2003).
Pearson, Richard. 'Primitive Modernity: H. G. Wells and the Prehistoric Man of the 1890s', *The Yearbook of English Studies*, 37:1 (2007), 58–74.
Perry, John. *Jack London: An American Myth* (Chicago, IL: Nelson-Hall, 1981).
Peters, John Durham. *Speaking into the Air: A History of the Idea of Communication* (University of Chicago Press, 1999).
Pick, Daniel. *Faces of Degeneration: A European Disorder, c. 1848–c. 1918* (Cambridge University Press, 1993).
Pinker, Steven. *The Language Instinct: How the Mind Creates Language* (Harmondsworth: Penguin, 1994).
Pite, Ralph. *Thomas Hardy: The Guarded Life* (London: Picador, 2007).
Plotkin, Cary H. *The Tenth Muse: Victorian Philology and the Genesis of the Poetic Language of Gerard Manley Hopkins* (Carbondale, IL: Southern Illinois University Press, 1989).
Plotz, John. 'Nowhere and Everywhere: The End of Portability in William Morris's Romances', *ELH*, 74:4 (2007), 931–56.
Prins, Yopie. 'Victorian Meters', *The Cambridge Companion to Victorian Poetry*, ed. Joseph Bristow (Cambridge University Press, 2000).
Radick, Gregory. 'Primate Language and the Playback Experiment, in 1890 and 1980', *Journal of the History of Biology*, 38:3 (2005), 461–93.
  The Simian Tongue: The Long Debate about Animal Language (University of Chicago Press, 2007).
Raitt, Suzanne. 'The Rhetoric of Efficiency in Early Modernism', *Modernism/modernity*, 13:1 (2006), 835–51.

Ramachandran, V. S., and E. M. Hubbard. 'Synaesthesia – a Window into Perception, Thought and Language', *Journal of Consciousness Studies*, 8:12 (2001), 3–34.
Rauch, Alan. *Useful Knowledge: The Victorians, Morality, and the March of Intellect* (Durham, NC: Duke University Press, 2002).
Rendall, Drew, with Alan Nielsen. 'The Sound of Round: Evaluating the Sound-Symbolic Role of Consonants in the Classic Takete-Maluma Phenomenon', *Canadian Journal of Experimental Psychology*, 65:2 (2011), 115–24.
Rendall, Drew, and Michael J. Owren. 'Vocalizations as Tools for Influencing the Affect and Behavior of Others', *Handbook of Mammalian Vocalization: An Integrative Neuroscience Approach*, ed. Stefan M. Brudzynski (Amsterdam: Academic Press, 2010), pp. 177–85.
Richardson, Angelique. 'Hardy and the Place of Culture', *A Companion to Thomas Hardy*, ed. Keith Wilson (Oxford: Blackwell, 2009), pp. 54–70.
  'New Women and the New Fiction', *The Oxford History of the Novel in English*, ed. Patrick Parrinder and Andrzej Gasiorek (Oxford University Press, 2010), pp. 133–48.
Richter, Virginia. 'Ape meets Primatologist: Post-Darwinian Interspecies Romances', *America's Darwin: Darwinian Theory and U.S. Literary Culture*, ed. Tina Gianquitto and Lydia Fisher (Athens, GA: University of Georgia Press, 2014), pp. 360–88.
Rinkel, Gene and Margaret. *The Picshuas of H. G. Wells: A Burlesque Diary* (Urbana, IL: University of Illinois Press, 2006).
Riper, A. Bowdoin van. *Men among the Mammoths* (University of Chicago Press, 1993).
Rylance, Rick. *Victorian Psychology and British Culture: 1850–80* (Oxford University Press, 2000).
Sampson, Geoffrey. *The 'Language Instinct' Debate* (New York: Continuum, 2005).
  Schools of Linguistics: Competition and Evolution (Stanford University Press, 1980).
Saul, Nicholas, and Simon J. James (eds.). *The Evolution of Literature: Legacies of Darwin in European Cultures* (Amsterdam: Rodopi, 2011).
Saussure, Ferdinand de. *Course in General Linguistics* (1916), trans. W. Baskin (London: Peter Owen, 1960).
Shiach, Morag. *Modernism, Labour, and Selfhood in British Literature and Culture, 1890–1930* (Cambridge University Press, 2004).
  '"To Purify the Dialect of the Tribe": Modernism and Language Reform', *Modernism/modernity*, 14:1 (2007), 21–34.
Shuttleworth, Sally. 'Evolutionary Psychology and *The Way of All Flesh*', *Samuel Butler, Victorian against the Grain: A Critical Overview*, ed. James G. Paradis (University of Toronto Press, 2007), pp. 143–69.
  The Mind of the Child: Child Development in Literature, Science, and Medicine, 1840–1900 (Oxford University Press, 2010).
Smith, J. B. 'Dialect in Hardy's Short Stories', *Thomas Hardy Annual No. 5*, ed. Norman Page (London: Macmillan, 1985), pp. 79–92.

Smith, Ross. 'Fitting Sense to Sound: Linguistic Aesthetics and Phonosemantics in the Works of J. R. R. Tolkien', *Tolkien Studies*, 3 (2006), 1–20.

Sorensen, Janet. *The Grammar of Empire in Eighteenth-Century British Writing* (Cambridge University Press, 2000).

Stam, James H. *Inquiries into the Origin of Language: The Fate of a Question* (London: Harper & Row, 1976).

Stepan, Nancy. *The Idea of Race in Science: Great Britain 1800–1960* (London: Macmillan, 1982).

Sterne, Jonathan. *The Audible Past: Cultural Origins of Sound Reproduction* (Durham, NC: Duke University Press, 2003).

Stiles, Anne. *Popular Fiction and Brain Science in the Late Nineteenth Century* (Cambridge University Press, 2012).

Stitt, Megan Perigoe. *Metaphors of Change in the Language of Nineteenth-Century Fiction: Scott, Gaskell, and Kingsley* (Oxford University Press, 1998).

Stocking, George W. *Race, Culture, and Evolution: Essays in the History of Anthropology* (1968), 2nd edn (University of Chicago Press, 1982).

Street, Brian V. *The Savage in Literature: Representations of 'Primitive' Society in English Fiction, 1858–1920* (London: Routledge, 1975).

Sumpter, Caroline. 'On Suffering and Sympathy: *Jude the Obscure*, Evolution, and Ethics', *Victorian Studies*, 53:4 (2011), 665–87.

Sutcliffe, Patricia Casey. 'Ideology and the Impossibility of Animal Language', *Linguistic Association of Canada and the United States (LACAS) Forum*, 34 (2009), 247–58.

Sword, Helen. *Ghostwriting Modernism* (Ithaca, NY: Cornell University Press, 2002).

Talbot, Norman. '"Whilom, as tells the tale": The Language of the Prose Romances', *Journal of the William Morris Society*, 3:2 (spring 1989), 16–26.

Tallerman, Maggie, and Kathleen Gibson (eds.). 'Introduction: The Evolution of Language', *Oxford Handbook of Language Evolution* (Oxford University Press, 2012), pp. 1–38.

Taylor, Dennis. *Hardy's Literary Language and Victorian Philology* (Oxford University Press, 1993).

Trumpener, Katie. *Bardic Nationalism: The Romantic Novel and the British Empire* (Princeton University Press, 1997).

Vaninskaya, Anna. *William Morris and the Idea of Community* (Edinburgh University Press, 2010).

Waithe, Marcus. *William Morris's Utopia of Strangers: Victorian Medievalism and the Ideal of Hospitality* (London: D. S. Brewer, 2006).

Wawn, Andrew. *The Vikings and the Victorians: Inventing the Old North in 19th-Century Britain* (Cambridge: D. S. Brewer, 2000).

Weller, Toni. *The Victorians and Information: A Social and Cultural History* (Saarbrücken: VDM, 2009).

Wheeler, Wendy. 'The Book of Nature: Biosemiotics and the Evolution of Literature', *The Evolution of Literature: Legacies of Darwin in European Cultures*, ed. Nicholas Saul and Simon J. James (Amsterdam: Rodopi, 2011), pp. 171–84.

Whissell, Cynthia. 'Emotion Conveyed by Sound in the Poetry of Alfred, Lord Tennyson', *Empirical Studies of the Arts*, 20:2 (2002), 137–55.

—— 'Phonosymbolism and the Emotional Nature of Sounds: Evidence of the Preferential Use of Particular Phonemes in Texts of Differing Emotional Tone', *Perceptual and Motor Skills*, 89 (1999), 19–48.

Wilder, Thornton. 'Introduction to *Four in America*', ed. Linda Simon, *Gertrude Stein Remembered* (Lincoln, NE: University of Nebraska Press, 1994), pp. 129–36.

Williams, Raymond. *The Country and the City* (London: Chatto & Windus, 1973).

Winchester, Simon. *The Meaning of Everything: The Story of the Oxford English Dictionary* (Oxford University Press, 2004).

Witzany, Günther. 'Key Levels of Biocommunication in Plants', *Biocommunication of Plants*, ed. Günther Witzany and František Baluška (New York: Springer, 2012), pp. 1–10.

Yaguello, Marina. *Lunatic Lovers of Language: Imaginary Languages and their Inventors*, trans. C. Slater (London: Althone Press, 1991).

Young, Robert J. C. *Colonial Desire: Hybridity in Theory, Culture and Race* (1994), 2nd edn (London: Routledge, 2006).

ARCHIVES

H. G. Wells Papers. Rare Books and Manuscripts Library, University of Illinois, Urbana-Champaign, IL.

ONLINE

F.A.C.E. training programme. www.paulekman.com

Index

abbreviation. *See* efficiency
advertising, language of, 42, 157–9
algebra, 10
   as a perfect language, 32
Allen, Grant, 1, 8, 65–72
   on the autonomy of language change, 4
   The British Barbarians, 67
   The Great Taboo, 13, 65–70, 173
   on origins of speech, 67
   on primitive survivals in the West, 67–8
   'The Reverend John Creedy', 13, 68, 70–2
altruism, 8, 11
ambiguity, 24
   communication without it, 6, 46
   as a disease of modernity, 105
   as a necessity of modern language, 137
   as a symptom of primitiveness, 32, 55
Anglocentrism, 51–3
Anglo-Saxonism, 89–90, 99–101, 104. *See* race
   in literary style, 114
   versus Germanic imperialism, 106
   versus Nordicism, 102
animal communication
   anthropomorphized, 38, 75–6
   recent research, 167–8, 172
animality, of language, 3, 8, 12, 14, 21, 167–8. *See* primitiveness
anthropocentrism, 36–9, 46
   criticism of, 45–8
anthropology
   as 'thick description', 173
   compared with imaginative fiction, 8, 56
   on language evolution, 13, 32
   its overlap with philology, 3
   racialized, 68, 100
apocalyptic fiction, 82–3, 86–8, 166–7
arbitrariness, of signs, 18, 21. *See* convention
Arnold, Matthew
   on Celtic language and literature, 17, 104, 115
   cultural elitism, 27
   on standardized language, 11

artifice, language as, 1, 6, 9–10, 17, 23. *See* nature
Astor, John Jacob
   A Journey in Other Worlds, 38–9
atavism. *See* primitiveness, degeneration
authoritarian linguistics, 12
   criticism of, 43–5
   danger of dogmatism, 84
   through technocracy, 10, 30, 53
   through the twentieth century, 165–7
   and utopianism, 40
automatism, 20, 57
   bodily, 35, 72–3
   as a figure of satire, 134–5, 152–5
   verbal conditioning, 42, 44
autonomy, of language
   efforts to control it, 10
   evolving independently of human will, 2, 4, 6
   imagined as weakening with society's progress, 23

Babbage, Charles, 36, 166
   on abbreviation, 25
babbling
   as instinctive creativity, 151–61
   as language breakdown, 83–4, 163
   as primitive activity to be stamped out, 53
baby-talk. *See* invented languages
Bagehot, Walter, 59
Bain, Alexander, 11, 124
Ballantyne, R. M., 8, 17, 92–3
   Erling the Bold, 98–100
   Norsemen in the West, 17, 98–100, 104–5
Barnes, William
   dialect translation, 126
   influence on Hardy, 121, 125
   links with Kingsley, 93
   on purifying English, 91
   on the purity of dialect, 121
Barthes, Roland, 171
basic English, 166
Baudelaire, Charles, 81

Bell, Charles, 19
Bellamy, Edward, 37
   'To Whom this May Come', 34–6
   Looking Backward, 34
Beowulf, 99, 101
Berthet, Élie, 72
Bible, 100, 132, 137
Bickerton, Derek, 167
biosemiotics, 141, 172, 175
Boole, George, 10, 31
Bosworth, Joseph, 100
Bourget, Paul, 82
Bray, Charles, 33
Bridges, Robert, 169
Brooks, Byron A.
   Earth Revisited, 36–8
Brown, Colin, 142
Brugmann, Karl, 18, 167
Buckle, Henry, 24, 68
Bulwer-Lytton, Edward
   The Coming Race, 27–9, 34, 90
Bunsen, Chevalier, 15
Burnt Njal, 101
Butler, Samuel, 7–8
   afterlife of his ideas, 166
   children echoing parents, 132
   on the difference between thought and language, 133
   Erewhon, 133, 201
   on the instability of word meanings, 137
   instinct versus convention in, 18
   Lamarckian ideas, 129
   on language evolution undermining speaker agency, 129
   Life and Habit, 137
   Luck or Cunning?, 139
   row with Darwin, 138, 140
   The Way of all Flesh, 20, 129–40, 174

Candolle, Alphonse de, 49
capitalism, 15, 17
   imagined as the source of language decay, 113
   its distortion of language, 157–9
   opposing its language, 88–9, 117–20
   supposed inability of colonial subjects to adapt to it, 64
   vitalism a rejection of, 91
Carlyle, Thomas, 15
   on 'hero-poets', 100, 103
catastrophism, 5, 72, 75–6, 167, 169
Catholicism, 94, 167
cavemen. *See* Prehistory
Celtism, 17, 104
censorship, 64–7
Chambers, Robert
   Vestiges of the Natural History of Creation, 12, 138
Chartism, 119
Chesney, George
   The Battle of Dorking, 17, 106–7
Childers, Erskine
   The Riddle of the Sands, 110–11
Chomsky, Noam, 167
Christian Socialists, 93
civilization. *See* primitiveness, progressivism
class
   consciousness, 119
   languages of, 43–4, 88, 154–5
   seeking a common language, 93
classification, danger of becoming dogmatic, 84–6, 88–9
Clodd, Edward
   on confusion of primitive language, 74
code switching, 125–6
colonialism. *See* imperialism
computer programming language, 166
Comte, Auguste, 34, 58
consciousness
   collective, 34–6, 45–8. *See* telepathy, spiritualism, individualism, internationalism
   evolution of, 3, 8, 24, 26–39
   primordial, 57–8
contamination, 80, 169. *See* purism
   through linguistic invasion, 101, 106
contextuality, of meaning, 2, 7, 18, 40–1
control, over language, 3–5, 11, 14, 23–4. *See* autonomy, of language change; authoritarian linguistics
convention, language a product of, 18–19, 26, 121. *See* instinct
   imagined as a symptom of decay, 105, 113
cosmopolitanism, 114–15, 122
   through a monoglot world, 118
Crimean War, 16, 97
culture
   blended with nature, 171–4
   separate from nature, 21, 167, 171
   versus heredity, 14

Dadaism, 160
Darwin, Charles
   animalizing humans, 75, 131
   on communication of domesticated animals, 175
   The Descent of Man, 40
   his expansion of humanity's past, 56
   The Expression of the Emotions in Man and Animals, 145, 180
   inferring prehistory of language, 72

Darwin, Charles (cont.)
  influence on Allen, 65
  on the instability of nature, 123
  on instinct in language, 19–20, 128
  on language acquisition, 73
  on language as adaptation, 38, 41
  natural selection, 14, 74
  On the Origin of Species, 138
  and philology, 5
  sexual selection and language, 18
  on song, 76
  on sympathy, 46
  on variation, 137
Darwin, Erasmus, 9
Dasent, George, 102
decadence, 81–2
degeneration, 14, 80–90. *See* primitiveness
  as breakdown of linguistic authorities, 82–3
  in the later twentieth century, 166–7
  as wordplay and epigrams, 81–2
democracy, 27, 30
  language as a, 30, 125
  threat of mass culture to, 43
Descartes, René, 9, 35
dialect. *See* orality
  dialects of science, 7, 40, 55
  as defence against foreign invaders, 112
  as the life of language, 118
  racialized, 44
  versus Standard English, 94, 121–7, 143–4
dictionaries, 100, 125
  of colonial subjects' languages, 58
  for describing usage historically, 16
  as graveyards of language, 119
  imagined as increasing words' semantic density, 25
  for prescribing usage, 25
disembodiment (of language), 163
  destroying sympathy, 46
  enhancing sympathy, 19
  idealized, 32–4
  as progress, 12, 32–9, 57
  removing agency, 32
  through writing, 93, 95
Donaldson, J. W., 91
Drummond, Henry, 33–4
Drysdale, George, 129–30
Du Chaillu, Paul, 8, 17, 92, 105
  Ivar the Viking, 102–4

Early English Text Society, 16
Eden
  loss of literal belief in, 91
  modern language as a fall from, 15
  as origin of language, 7, 86

education
  in ancient languages, 102, 158
  its different potential meanings, 116
  promoting Standard English, 122, 127
  as rote learning, 152
  scientific, 41
Edwards, Henry, 106, 109
Efficiency, 24–7, 31, 165. *See* mechanization
Egerton, George, 6
Ekman, Paul, 172–3
Eliot, T. S., 170
Ellis, Havelock, 82
elocution, 154–5, 170
Emerson, R. W., 34
energy, language a form of, 29–34, 37
English Dialect Dictionary, 127
English Dialect Society, 127
English studies, 102
Erdmann, Karl Otto, 157
Esperanto. *See* invented languages
etymology, 65, 101–2
  as a microscope, 1
  as a source of meaning, 116
eugenics, 51
euphemism, 65
Evans, E. P., 3
evolutionary theory. *See* Darwin, Spencer
  its challenge to language, 137
experiment, fiction as, 5–6, 152
  among modernists, 170
  anthropological, 56
  associated with degeneration, 81
  its enduring value, 173
  on the improvisational nature of language, 159
  its limits for Victorian authors, 160–3
  playing with word meanings, 81
  prefiguring modernism, 20
  stimulating primordial instincts, 128
  testing philological theories, 2, 7
  as a way of interrogating science's narratives, 175
expression of emotion, 19–20, 60, 132, 141–5, 172–3. *See* Darwin, Charles
extinction, of languages, 6, 56–7
  its supposed inevitability, 64, 79, 127
extraterrestrials, 12
  communication with, 37–9, 45–8

Faraday, Michael, 29
Farrar, F. W.
  on degradation of language, 91, 113
  on onomatopoeiac origins of words, 58
Festing Jones, Henry, 136
fetishism, 58
  of words, 139
Foster, Michael, 49

Fourier, Charles, 140
Franco-Prussian War, 106, 109
Frazer, J. G., 64–5
    The Golden Bough, 66
Freeman, E. A., 101, 105
    on English names, 103
Freud, Sigmund
    on verbal condensation, 165
    on verbal slips, 157
Furnivall, Frederick, 16
futurism, 160
futurology, linguistic, 22–55

Galton, Francis
    on communicating with extraterrestrials, 37, 45, 47
Garner, R. L., 72, 76, 78
gendering
    grammatical, 61
    of primitive speech, 57, 61, 154, 162
    of scientific discourse, 6, 162
generativism. *See* Chomsky
genomics, 165, 174
geology
    as metaphor for language, 1, 5, 120
Germanophobia, 107–11
gesture, 60
    among apes, 167
    as parallel language, 128, 132, 147
    as primordial expression, 20, 32–3, 57–61, 85–6
gibberish. *See* babbling
global English, 49, 103
Golding, William
    The Inheritors, 168–9
Green, J. R., 99
Grimm, Jacob, 3, 103, 114
Gruen, Sara
    Ape House, 202
Gurney, Edmund, 42

Habermas, Jürgen
    ideal speech situation, 6
Haggard, Henry Rider, 56–64
    Allan Quatermain, 13, 60–4
    King Solomon's Mines, 62–3
    Nada the Lily, 60, 63
Hale, Benjamin
    The Evolution of Bruno Littlemore, 202
Hardy, Thomas, 5, 7–8, 20, 92, 121–7, 140–51
    'A Changed Man', 124
    defence of 'pure' English, 169
    Desperate Remedies, 141, 145–7
    on dialect, 18, 121–6
    'The Distracted Preacher', 122–3
    Far from the Madding Crowd, 141–2, 148–9

'The Fiddler of the Reels', 124
The Hand of Ethelberta, 20, 148
'An Imaginative Woman', 150–1
instinct versus convention in, 18
'Interlopers at the Knap', 124
Jude the Obscure, 144–5
The Melancholy Hussar of the German Legion, 122
his methods of representing dialect, 126–7
Return of the Native, 71, 142–3
Tess of the d'Urbervilles, 18, 122, 126, 147–8
'A Tradition of Eighteen-Hundred-and-Four', 123, 126
The Trumpet-Major, 122, 149
Under the Greenwood Tree, 18, 122
The Well-Beloved, 142–3
'On the Western Circuit', 150
'The Withered Arm', 127
The Woodlanders, 125–6
Hegel, Georg, 22, 24
Heimskringla, 101
Helmholtz, Hermann von, 33, 81, 141
Herder, Johann Gottfried, 14, 16
    on semantic relativism, 114–15
heredity, and language, 34, 70, 78, 89–90, 130
historical romance, 2, 6, 8, 14, 17, 92–105
    influenced by documentary history, 98
Hodgetts, J. F., 8, 17, 92
    The Champion of Odin, 102–5
Horne Tooke, John, 1
    on abbreviation, 24
Humboldt, Wilhelm von, 8
Hunt, James, 68
Huxley, Aldous
    Brave New World, 165
Huxley, T. H., 139
    on automatism, 35
    on science and symbols, 58
    on speech dividing humans from animals, 74
hybridity, national-linguistic, 103–5, 115
hypnotism, 42–4

Icelandic, 102, 114, 118
imagism, 165
imitation, 105
    of accent, 154
    among animals, 75
    associated with the body, 12
    an enforcer of social conformity, 73, 135
    of foreign identity, 110
    literary, 95, 99
    as origin of language, 58, 60
    as primitive speech, 6, 13, 61, 69–70
immigration, 101, 109
imperial romance, 2, 6, 8, 56–64

imperialism
  dependent on writing, 93
  as an ideology, 64
  influence on comparative philology, 15
  in Ireland, 117
  linguistics of, 57–9, 64
  as Teutonic heritage, 103–4
  threat to national-linguistic purity, 101, 103–5
individualism
  compromised by heredity, 132–3, 137–8
  versus collectivism, 23, 32, 35–6, 42–7, 50
instinct
  blurred with convention, 75, 128, 164–5
  concept of a 'language instinct', 167
  in language, 18–20, 156–7. *See* babbling, gesture, expression of emotion
  as origin of sympathy, 46, 85–6, 89, 141–5
  racial, 71–2
  religious, 132
  as a threat to civilized language, 80–3, 86–8
  versus convention, 18–19, 128–63
internationalism, 48–55
  and socialism, 114–15
invasion fiction, 8, 17, 106–12
invented languages, 9. *See* internationalism
  and utopianism, 22–3
  of lovers and families, 42–3, 161–2

Jakobson, Roman, 171
James, William, 7, 155
  on instincts contradicting each other, 173
  on nomenclature and pragmatism, 41
Jefferies, Richard, 175
Jespersen, Otto, 24, 165
Joyce, James, 160
Jung, Karl, 162

Kegan Paul, Charles, 96
Kidd, Benjamin, 43
Kingsley, Charles, 7–8, 17, 92–8
  Alton Locke, 93
  Hereward the Wake, 93, 95–8
  influences on his philosophy of language, 93
  on moral superiority of oral past, 96
  Westward Ho!, 17, 93–7
  his writing as transcribed speech, 97
Kurtén, Björn
  Dance of the Tiger, 169
Kymograph, 26

Lamarck, Jean-Baptiste, 9, 140
Lamarckism, 20, 30, 72, 129–30
Lang, Andrew, 60
  on the inaccessibility of truly 'primitive' language, 62

Lankester, E. R.
  on arbitrariness of language 'progress', 40
Latham, R. G., 64
Lawrence, D. H., 162
Lazarus, Moritz. *See* Steinthal
Le Bon, Gustave, 44
Leibniz, Gottfried Wilhelm, 9
Lewes, G. H., 11
  on language as mental tradition, 138
  on originality, 133
  on the 'social organism', 19, 133
lingua franca, 6–7, 12, 53–5
  scientific, 23
Locke, John, 10, 23, 26, 35, 68
logos, 93–4
Lombroso, Cesare, 81
London, Jack, 8
  Before Adam, 77–80, 168
  belief in need for authorities to prescribe language usage, 86–8
  evolutionary fiction, 57
  influence of Darwin and Spencer, 77–8
  The Iron Heel, 88–9
  Martin Eden, 86
  racial memory of proto-language, 77–80, 89–90
  The Scarlet Plague, 14, 86–8
  'When the World was Young', 89–90
Lorenz, Richard, 49
Lubbock, John
  on animal use of signs, 75
  on 'savage' vocabulary, 58
Lyell, Charles, 5

Mackay, Charles, 82
Macnie, John
  The Diothas, 10, 30–2
Mallarmé, Stéphane, 81
Marinetti, F. T., 160
Marsh, G. P., 10
Marx, Karl, 116, 119
materialism, 11, 35, 89
McAdam, Colin
  A Beautiful Truth, 168
McLennan, J. M., 140
mechanization, 7, 9–11, 23–32. *See* efficiency, precision
  anxieties about, 166. *See* automatism
Meredith, Dennis
  Solomon's Freedom, 202
mesmerism, 28
metaphor, 1
  misleading nature of, 59, 88, 134
  as primitive thought, 33, 61
  as 'roots' of language, 3, 101, 116

versus literalism, 137, 139
Mill, J. S.
  on conventionality of language, 124
  on language change, 175
  worried about popular print controlling language, 27, 125
Miller, Walter
  A Canticle for Leibowitz, 167
modernism, 165, 170
morality. *See* censorship, altruism
  anxieties about 'the scientific attitude', 84–5
  breakdown of, 84, 167
  evolution of, 11, 78, 80, 82
  of extraterrestrials, 47
  mechanized, 42
  as repression of the body, 65, 149
  as social power, 126
Morgan, C. L., 75
Morgan, L. H., 32
Morris, William, 8, 17–18, 113–20
  afterlife of his linguistic ideas, 170
  belief in universal values underlying all language, 115–16
  on capitalism causing language decay, 113
  A Dream of John Ball, 113–14
  interest in philology, 113
  News from Nowhere, 5, 114, 116–20
  socialism, 92
  The Water of the Wondrous Isles, 118
  The Well at the World's End, 118
Müller, Friedrich Max, 28, 91, 170, 175
  concept of 'roots', 15–17, 29
  on equality of races, 115–16
  links with Kingsley, 93, 96
  on literature as dead language, 118
  on orality, 93–4
  on philology as a microscope, 1
music, speech as, 11, 19, 36, 132, 142–3

narrative, its role in language evolution, 2–3, 6–7, 165
nationalism, 7, 14–18
  based on imaginary speech community, 4, 93, 106
  Celtic, 117
  and linguistic purity, 16–17, 91–2, 106–12, 127, 185, 188
  and oral culture, 92
  rejection of, 17–18
  as substitute for creation story, 91
  and suppression of speech varieties, 95
  versus localism, 93, 116–17
nature
  language as a natural growth, 91, 169
  language in a state of, 14–16, 94. *See* artifice

Neanderthals. *See* prehistory
Neogrammarians, 18, 167, 171
New Woman, 6, 162
nicknames. *See* wordplay
Nietzsche, Friedrich, 86, 88–9
Nordau, Max, 82, 153. *See* degeneration
Norman Conquest, 95
  as contamination of English heritage, 101, 105
Norse, 17
  efforts to revive its vocabulary in English, 103
  literature, 100–1, 114

objectivity, 2, 8, 14
  as disembodied knowledge, 32
  links with global language movement, 48–50
  of literary language, 5, 7. *See* realism
  rejection of. *See* vitalism
  as self-conscious use of symbols, 57–8
  of scientific language, 3–4, 9, 23–4
  and utopianism, 22
Ogden, C. K., 166
onomatopoeia, 12, 58, 155, 158
orality
  dialect, 16–17
  idealized, 14–16, 95
  imitated by literature, 96–7, 99–100
  and literacy, 15–17, 92–100
  and the primitive mind, 64
  problems with representing it in texts, 92
  and salvage ethnography, 6, 17
organic memory, 70, 130
origin of language, 14, 58–9, 77
  refusals to discuss it, 167
Orwell, George, 165
  Nineteen Eighty-Four, 166
Osthoff, Hermann, 18, 167
Oxford English Dictionary, 16, 25

palaeoanthropology, 13–14, 56–7
pastoralism, 7, 15–16, 109, 127
  as stasis, 92, 119, 123–4
Pearson, Karl, 41
philology, 8, 92
  ideological adaptability of, 106
  its potential to undermine national divisions, 16, 115–17
  through deep time, 3
phonograph, 3, 20, 26, 76
  as metaphor for heredity, 129
  as metaphor for verbal habit, 133, 152–5
  and mortality, 43, 129
phonosemantics, 171–3
physiognomy, 19–20. *See* expression of emotion
pidgins, 44, 104, 169
Pinker, Steven, 167

Pitman, Isaac, 25
plain English, 94
plant communication, 164, 175
poetry, 7
  as natural language, 59, 91
  prose as the highest form of, 96
popularization, 2, 9, 82, 153–4, 186. *See* Mill
pragmatism. *See* James
precision, 25–7, 165. *See* mechanization
prehistory
  its expansion in nineteenth century, 56–7
  in fiction, 8, 72–80, 168–9
  human subspecies, 79–80, 168–9
  hypothetical, 57–8, 72
  non-European languages used as surrogates for, 56–7
Prichard, James Cowles, 24
primitiveness, 8, 12–14. *See* imitation
  as ahistorical, 12–13
  as an antidote to dogma, 84–6, 155
  as cultural isolation, 63–4
  dangerously creative, 14
  enslaved to custom, 13, 62–4
  as masculine individualism, 89–90
  teleology of the concept, 72–4
  tied to the body, 13, 57–62
  translated as archaic English, 62
  unspeakable, 13, 64–72
  versus civilization, 13–14, 56–7, 71–2, 78–9, 86–8
progressivism, 8–14, 22–3
  criticism of, 12, 40–8
  different models of, 6–7
  its reification of language, 18
  symbiotic with prophetic fiction, 22
  and utopianism, 8
Proto-Indo-European, 5
psychology, 11–12, 18–20, 165
  of associationism, 26–7
  eroding the sovereign ego, 35
  of pre-verbal infancy, 73
purism, 17, 91, 169–70
  criticism of, 121, 127
  impossibility of, 104
  as literary style, 102

race, 16–18
  conflated with language, 64–5, 92, 100–5
  instincts, 71–2
  language an unreliable test of, 68–71, 104
  memory, 80, 89, 91, 103
  and romance genre, 56
  and spoken English, 44, 68–9
realism, 2, 4–5, 8
reconstruction, linguistic, 5, 13–14, 101, 113–14

reductionism, the role of the humanities in resisting it, 173–4
reification, of language, 18, 128
  challenging the, 20, 164
relativism, semantic, 4, 11–12, 18, 26–7, 30, 48, 55
religion, comparative, 15
Rig Veda, 15
Romanes, George
  on mental abstraction through language, 57
  on overlap of convention with instinct, 75, 171
  on progressive disembodiment of language, 32–3
romanticism, 14–16, 86
  and organic view of language, 8
Rousseau, Jean-Jacques, 14
Ruskin, John, 113

Saintsbury, George, 95
Saki
  When William Came, 17, 107–9
salvage ethnography. *See* orality
Sapir, Edward, 48
Saussure, Ferdinand de, 26, 167, 171
  on motivation of iconic signs, 61
savagery. *See* primitiveness
Sayce, A. H., 14, 26, 80
  on abbreviation, 25
  on language and race, 69
  links with Allen, 65
  on the multitude of extinct languages, 56
  on primordial speech, 157
  on 'savage' vocabulary, 58
Schleicher, August
  on language extinction, 79
  on primordial speech, 72
  reconstructing Proto-Indo-European, 5
Schleyer, Johann, 49–50
Schopenhauer, Arthur, 140
Schwitters, Kurt, 160
Scott, Walter, 92, 98
Scott, William, 19
Scripture, E. W., 157
sexuality, as a language, 140–1, 145–51
Shaw, G. B., 50
shorthand, 25. *See* Pitman
slang, 14, 82, 112, 157, 160
socialism, 88–9, 162
  and delocalized language, 92, 113
  and language history, 116–18
Société de Linguistique, 167
Society for Psychical Research, 33
Society for Pure English, 169
sociology
  concept of the 'social organism', 128

crowds and mass manipulation, 43–5
reducing agency of individual speakers, 128
sound poetry, 160
Spanish Armada, 93
spelling
  misspelling, 156, 160
  reform, 25, 200
Spencer, Herbert, 80
  afterlife of his philosophy of language, 165
  on evolution of writing, 157
  on the future perfect language, 29
  individualism, 40
  influence on Allen, 65
  influence on London, 86
  on language mechanization, 1, 6–7, 24–7, 175
  on language progress, 9
  on mechanics of perception, 35
  on monolingualism, 68
  on music of emotions, 11, 31, 143
  on the origin of language, 58
  on the 'persistence of force', 29
  on power of verbal custom over primitive mind, 12–13, 59
  on progressive disembodiment of language, 11
  on sympathy, 19
  on the 'unknown cause', 39
Spenser, Edmund, 95, 97
spiritualism, 10, 32–9
standardization, 4–5, 11, 16, 18, 24, 86
  as cultural destruction, 125–6
  destructive of sympathetic instincts, 143–4
  endurance as an ideology, 166
  and internationalism, 51
  and progress, 25
  rendering speech community vulnerable to infiltration, 109–10
Stead, W. T., 38
Stein, Gertrude, 170
Steinthal, Heymann, 19
Stephens, George, 106
Stewart, George
  Earth Abides, 166
Stout, G. F., 41
Strettell, A. B., 93
structuralism, 21, 171
Sweet, Henry, 156
symbolism, 81

Taine, Hippolyte, 73, 155
  inferring prehistoric language, 72
telegraphy, 24–5, 36
  foreshadowing telepathy, 33
  Morse code, 38
telepathy, 11–12, 32–9, 45, 143
telephone, 32–3

Tennyson, Alfred, 15
  In Memoriam, 204
thought
  co-evolving with language, 75
  symbiotic with language, 94, 101, 130, 133
Tolkein, J. R. R.
  The Lord of the Rings, 171
transcendentalism, 34
translation, 17
  failure of, 29
  of 'primitive' languages, 13, 58–9, 74
  of past language for modern readers, 98, 115
Trench, R. C., 7
  on composite structure of English, 103
  influence on Morris, 113
  on language and nation, 16
  on verbal condensation, 25
Trumbull, John, 135
truthfulness
  imagined as stronger in speech than writing, 95–6
  of instinctive signs, 141
  of oral past, 94
  oral authenticity versus textual evidence, 97–9
Tylor, E. B., 143
  on beginnings of speech in gesture, 58
  influence on Lang, 60
  on irrelevance of race to culture, 14, 68
  on primitive survivals in language, 32–3, 67
  on primitive thought, 64
  on progressive control of language, 22
  on rigidity of savage convention, 13, 59
Tyndall, John, 29
typewriters, 36

uniformitarianism. *See* catastrophism
utopia, 2, 6, 8, 10
  historical context of, 22
  and linguistic stasis, 118–20

Verlaine, Paul, 81
Viking fiction, 17, 98–105
vitalism, 6–8, 18
  criticism of, 18
  as criticism of urban, industrial modernity, 108–9
  merged with progressivism, 28
  as nostalgia for past language, 86
vivisection, 84–5, 199
Volapük. *See* invented languages
Völksgeist. See sociology

war, as communication breakdown, 45–6, 53–5
Waterloo, Stanley
  The Story of Ab, 13, 76–7

Webb, Sidney & Beatrice, 50
Wedgwood, Hensleigh, 58
Weil, Samuel, 36
Welby, Victoria, Lady, 50, 186
Wells, H. G., 5, 7–8
  Anticipations, 50
  babbling instincts, 128
  on contextuality of meaning, 23
  The First Men in the Moon, 5, 12, 40, 46–8
  The Food of the Gods, 153–4
  God the Invisible King, 55
  The History of Mr. Polly, 124, 159–60
  influenced by Darwin, 40
  instinct versus automatism in, 20
  instinct versus convention in, 18
  interest in a world language, 49–55
  interest in a world state, 12, 50–1
  The Island of Dr. Moreau, 14, 83–5, 151
  Kipps, 20, 154
  on the language of science, 55
  Love and Mr Lewisham, 161–2
  Mankind in the Making, 53
  A Modern Utopia, 50–1
  'Morals and Civilisation', 82–3
  'The Rediscovery of the Unique', 41
  scepticism of language progress, 23, 40–8
  scepticism of spiritualism, 41
  on science education, 41
  The Shape of Things to Come, 53
  as social planner, 40, 151, 162
  'A Story of the Days to Come', 42–4
  'A Story of the Stone Age', 13, 73–6
  A Text-Book of Biology, 76
  The Time Machine, 83, 85–6, 161
  Tono-Bungay, 20, 154–5, 157–9, 161
  The War in the Air, 53–5
  The War of the Worlds, 12, 45–6
  When the Sleeper Wakes, 12, 43–5
  withdrawal from verbal experimentation, 151–63
  The World Set Free, 51–5
West, Rebecca, 162
Whewell, William, 26
  on the ideal scientific language, 9, 24
  on verbal compression, 24
Whissell, Cynthia, 172–3, 204
Whitney, William Dwight, 40
  on language as a democracy, 30, 125
  versus Müller, 18, 121
Wilkins, John, 9
Winwood Reade, William, 57
Wodehouse, P. G.
  The Swoop!, or How Clarence Saved England, 111–12
Wood, Walter
  The Enemy in Our Midst, 109
wordplay, 81–2, 156

xenophobia, 113. *See* race, nationalism, Germanophobia

Zamenhof, L. L., 22–3, 50
Zola, Émile, 5

CAMBRIDGE STUDIES IN NINETEENTH-CENTURY
LITERATURE AND CULTURE

GENERAL EDITOR: Gillian Beer, *University of Cambridge*

Titles published

1. *The Sickroom in Victorian Fiction: The Art of Being Ill*
   MIRIAM BAILIN, Washington University
2. *Muscular Christianity: Embodying the Victorian Age*
   edited by DONALD E. HALL, California State University, Northridge
3. *Victorian Masculinities: Manhood and Masculine Poetics in Early Victorian Literature and Art*
   HERBERT SUSSMAN, Northeastern University, Boston
4. *Byron and the Victorians*
   ANDREW ELFENBEIN, University of Minnesota
5. *Literature in the Marketplace: Nineteenth-Century British Publishing and the Circulation of Books*
   edited by JOHN O. JORDAN, University of California, Santa Cruz
   and ROBERT L. PATTEN, Rice University, Houston
6. *Victorian Photography, Painting and Poetry*
   LINDSAY SMITH, University of Sussex
7. *Charlotte Brontë and Victorian Psychology*
   SALLY SHUTTLEWORTH, University of Sheffield
8. *The Gothic Body: Sexuality, Materialism and Degeneration at the* Fin de Siècle
   KELLY HURLEY, University of Colorado at Boulder
9. *Rereading Walter Pater*
   WILLIAM F. SHUTER, Eastern Michigan University
10. *Remaking Queen Victoria*
    edited by MARGARET HOMANS, Yale University
    and ADRIENNE MUNICH, State University of New York, Stony Brook
11. *Disease, Desire, and the Body in Victorian Women's Popular Novels*
    PAMELA K. GILBERT, University of Florida
12. *Realism, Representation, and the Arts in Nineteenth-Century Literature*
    ALISON BYERLY, Middlebury College, Vermont
13. *Literary Culture and the Pacific*
    VANESSA SMITH, University of Sydney
14. *Professional Domesticity in the Victorian Novel Women, Work and Home*
    MONICA F. COHEN
15. *Victorian Renovations of the Novel: Narrative Annexes and the Boundaries of Representation*
    SUZANNE KEEN, Washington and Lee University, Virginia
16. *Actresses on the Victorian Stage: Feminine Performance and the Galatea Myth*
    GAIL MARSHALL, University of Leeds

17. *Death and the Mother from Dickens to Freud: Victorian Fiction and the Anxiety of Origin*
    CAROLYN DEVER, Vanderbilt University, Tennessee
18. *Ancestry and Narrative in Nineteenth-Century British Literature: Blood Relations from Edgeworth to Hardy*
    SOPHIE GILMARTIN, Royal Holloway, University of London
19. *Dickens, Novel Reading, and the Victorian Popular Theatre*
    DEBORAH VLOCK
20. *After Dickens: Reading, Adaptation and Performance*
    JOHN GLAVIN, Georgetown University, Washington D C
21. *Victorian Women Writers and the Woman Question*
    edited by NICOLA DIANE THOMPSON, Kingston University, London
22. *Rhythm and Will in Victorian Poetry*
    MATTHEW CAMPBELL, University of Sheffield
23. *Gender, Race, and the Writing of Empire: Public Discourse and the Boer War*
    PAULA M. KREBS, Wheaton College, Massachusetts
24. *Ruskin's God*
    MICHAEL WHEELER, University of Southampton
25. *Dickens and the Daughter of the House*
    HILARY M. SCHOR, University of Southern California
26. *Detective Fiction and the Rise of Forensic Science*
    RONALD R. THOMAS, Trinity College, Hartford, Connecticut
27. *Testimony and Advocacy in Victorian Law, Literature, and Theology*
    JAN-MELISSA SCHRAMM, Trinity Hall, Cambridge
28. *Victorian Writing about Risk: Imagining a Safe England in a Dangerous World*
    ELAINE FREEDGOOD, University of Pennsylvania
29. *Physiognomy and the Meaning of Expression in Nineteenth-Century Culture*
    LUCY HARTLEY, University of Southampton
30. *The Victorian Parlour: A Cultural Study*
    THAD LOGAN, Rice University, Houston
31. *Aestheticism and Sexual Parody 1840–1940*
    DENNIS DENISOFF, Ryerson University, Toronto
32. *Literature, Technology and Magical Thinking, 1880–1920*
    PAMELA THURSCHWELL, University College London
33. *Fairies in Nineteenth-Century Art and Literature*
    NICOLA BOWN, Birkbeck, University of London
34. *George Eliot and the British Empire*
    NANCY HENRY The State University of New York, Binghamton
35. *Women's Poetry and Religion in Victorian England: Jewish Identity and Christian Culture*
    CYNTHIA SCHEINBERG, Mills College, California
36. *Victorian Literature and the Anorexic Body*
    ANNA KRUGOVOY SILVER, Mercer University, Georgia
37. *Eavesdropping in the Novel from Austen to Proust*
    ANN GAYLIN, Yale University

38. *Missionary Writing and Empire, 1800–1860*
    ANNA JOHNSTON, University of Tasmania
39. *London and the Culture of Homosexuality, 1885–1914*
    MATT COOK, Keele University
40. *Fiction, Famine, and the Rise of Economics in Victorian Britain and Ireland*
    GORDON BIGELOW, Rhodes College, Tennessee
41. *Gender and the Victorian Periodical*
    HILARY FRASER, Birkbeck, University of London
    JUDITH JOHNSTON AND STEPHANIE GREEN, University of Western Australia
42. *The Victorian Supernatural*
    edited by NICOLA BOWN, Birkbeck College, London
    CAROLYN BURDETT, London Metropolitan University
    and PAMELA THURSCHWELL, University College London
43. *The Indian Mutiny and the British Imagination*
    GAUTAM CHAKRAVARTY, University of Delhi
44. *The Revolution in Popular Literature: Print, Politics and the People*
    IAN HAYWOOD, Roehampton University of Surrey
45. *Science in the Nineteenth-Century Periodical: Reading the Magazine of Nature*
    GEOFFREY CANTOR, University of Leeds
    GOWAN DAWSON, University of Leicester
    GRAEME GOODAY, University of Leeds
    RICHARD NOAKES, University of Cambridge
    SALLY SHUTTLEWORTH, University of Sheffield
    and JONATHAN R. TOPHAM, University of Leeds
46. *Literature and Medicine in Nineteenth-Century Britain from Mary Shelley to George Eliot*
    JANIS MCLARREN CALDWELL, Wake Forest University
47. *The Child Writer from Austen to Woolf*
    edited by CHRISTINE ALEXANDER, University of New South Wales
    and JULIET MCMASTER, University of Alberta
48. *From Dickens to Dracula: Gothic, Economics, and Victorian Fiction*
    GAIL TURLEY HOUSTON, University of New Mexico
49. *Voice and the Victorian Storyteller*
    IVAN KREILKAMP, University of Indiana
50. *Charles Darwin and Victorian Visual Culture*
    JONATHAN SMITH, University of Michigan-Dearborn
51. *Catholicism, Sexual Deviance, and Victorian Gothic Culture*
    PATRICK R. O'MALLEY, Georgetown University
52. *Epic and Empire in Nineteenth-Century Britain*
    SIMON DENTITH, University of Gloucestershire
53. *Victorian Honeymoons: Journeys to the Conjugal*
    HELENA MICHIE, Rice University
54. *The Jewess in Nineteenth-Century British Literary Culture*
    NADIA VALMAN, University of Southampton

55. *Ireland, India and Nationalism in Nineteenth-Century Literature*
    JULIA WRIGHT, Dalhousie University
56. *Dickens and the Popular Radical Imagination*
    SALLY LEDGER, Birkbeck, University of London
57. *Darwin, Literature and Victorian Respectability*
    GOWAN DAWSON, University of Leicester
58. *'Michael Field': Poetry, Aestheticism and the Fin de Siècle*
    MARION THAIN, University of Birmingham
59. *Colonies, Cults and Evolution: Literature, Science and Culture in Nineteenth-Century Writing*
    DAVID AMIGONI, Keele University
60. *Realism, Photography and Nineteenth-Century Fiction*
    DANIEL A. NOVAK, Lousiana State University
61. *Caribbean Culture and British Fiction in the Atlantic World, 1780–1870*
    TIM WATSON, University of Miami
62. *The Poetry of Chartism: Aesthetics, Politics, History*
    MICHAEL SANDERS, University of Manchester
63. *Literature and Dance in Nineteenth-Century Britain: Jane Austen to the New Woman*
    CHERYL WILSON, Indiana University
64. *Shakespeare and Victorian Women*
    GAIL MARSHALL, Oxford Brookes University
65. *The Tragi-Comedy of Victorian Fatherhood*
    VALERIE SANDERS, University of Hull
66. *Darwin and the Memory of the Human: Evolution, Savages, and South America*
    CANNON SCHMITT, University of Toronto
67. *From Sketch to Novel: The Development of Victorian Fiction*
    AMANPAL GARCHA, Ohio State University
68. *The Crimean War and the British Imagination*
    STEFANIE MARKOVITS, Yale University
69. *Shock, Memory and the Unconscious in Victorian Fiction*
    JILL L. MATUS, University of Toronto
70. *Sensation and Modernity in the 1860s*
    NICHOLAS DALY, University College Dublin
71. *Ghost-Seers, Detectives, and Spiritualists: Theories of Vision in Victorian Literature and Science*
    SRDJAN SMAJIĆ, Furman University
72. *Satire in an Age of Realism*
    AARON MATZ, Scripps College, California
73. *Thinking About Other People in Nineteenth-Century British Writing*
    ADELA PINCH, University of Michigan
74. *Tuberculosis and the Victorian Literary Imagination*
    KATHERINE BYRNE, University of Ulster, Coleraine
75. *Urban Realism and the Cosmopolitan Imagination in the Nineteenth Century: Visible City, Invisible World*
    TANYA AGATHOCLEOUS, Hunter College, City University of New York

76. *Women, Literature, and the Domesticated Landscape: England's Disciples of Flora, 1780–1870*
    JUDITH W. PAGE, University of Florida
    ELISE L. SMITH, Millsaps College, Mississippi
77. *Time and the Moment in Victorian Literature and Society*
    SUE ZEMKA, University of Colorado
78. *Popular Fiction and Brain Science in the Late Nineteenth Century*
    ANNE STILES, Washington State University
79. *Picturing Reform in Victorian Britain*
    JANICE CARLISLE, Yale University
80. *Atonement and Self-Sacrifice in Nineteenth-Century Narrative*
    JAN-MELISSA SCHRAMM, University of Cambridge
81. *The Silver Fork Novel: Fashionable Fiction in the Age of Reform*
    EDWARD COPELAND, Pomona College, California
82. *Oscar Wilde and Ancient Greece*
    IAIN ROSS, Colchester Royal Grammar School
83. *The Poetry of Victorian Scientists: Style, Science and Nonsense*
    DANIEL BROWN, University of Southampton
84. *Moral Authority, Men of Science, and the Victorian Novel*
    ANNE DEWITT, Princeton Writing Program
85. *China and the Victorian Imagination: Empires Entwined*
    ROSS G. FORMAN, University of Warwick
86. *Dickens's Style*
    DANIEL TYLER, University of Oxford
87. *The Formation of the Victorian Literary Profession*
    RICHARD SALMON, University of Leeds
88. *Before George Eliot: Marian Evans and the Periodical Press*
    FIONNUALA DILLANE, University College Dublin
89. *The Victorian Novel and the Space of Art: Fictional Form on Display*
    DEHN GILMORE, California Institute of Technology
90. *George Eliot and Money: Economics, Ethics and Literature*
    DERMOT COLEMAN, Independent Scholar
91. *Masculinity and the New Imperialism: Rewriting Manhood in British Popular Literature, 1870–1914*
    BRADLEY DEANE, University of Minnesota
92. *Evolution and Victorian Culture*
    edited by BERNARD LIGHTMAN, York University, Toronto
    and BENNETT ZON, University of Durham
93. *Victorian Literature, Energy, and the Ecological Imagination*
    ALLEN MACDUFFIE, University of Texas, Austin
94. *Popular Literature, Authorship and the Occult in Late Victorian Britain*
    ANDREW MCCANN, Dartmouth College, New Hampshire
95. *Women Writing Art History in the Nineteenth Century: Looking Like a Woman*
    HILARY FRASER Birkbeck College, University of London
96. *Relics of Death in Victorian Literature and Culture*
    DEBORAH LUTZ, Long Island University, C. W. Post Campus

97. *The Demographic Imagination and the Nineteenth-Century City: Paris, London, New York*
    NICOLAS DALY, School of English, Drama and Film, University College Dublin
98. *Dickens and the Business of Death*
    CLAIRE WOOD, University of York
99. *Translation as Transformation in Victorian Poetry*
    ANNMARIE DRURY, Queens College, City University of New York
100. *The Bigamy Plot: Sensation and Convention in the Victorian Novel*
    MAIA MCALEAVEY, Boston College, Massachusetts
101. *English Fiction and the Evolution of Language, 1850–1914*
    WILL ABBERLEY, University of Oxford